GW00992012

Cambridge Studies in Contentious Politics

Editors

Mark Beissinger   *Princeton University*
Jack A. Goldstone   *George Mason University*
Doug McAdam   *Stanford University and Center for Advanced Study in the Behavioral Sciences*
Suzanne Staggenborg   *University of Pittsburgh*
Sidney Tarrow   *Cornell University*
Charles Tilly   *Columbia University*
Elisabeth J. Wood   *Yale University*
Deborah Yashar   *Princeton University*

Challenging Neoliberalism in Latin America

At the turn of the 20th century, a concatenation of diverse social movements arose unexpectedly in Latin America, culminating in massive anti-free-market demonstrations. These events ushered in governments in Argentina, Bolivia, Ecuador, and Venezuela that advocated socialization and planning, challenging the consensus over neoliberal hegemony and the weakness of movements to oppose it. Eduardo Silva offers the first comprehensive comparative account of these extraordinary events, arguing that the shift was influenced by favorable political associational space, a reformist orientation to demands, economic crisis, and mechanisms that facilitated horizontal linkages among a wide variety of social movement organizations. His analysis applies Karl Polanyi's theory of the double movement of market society to these events, predicting the dawning of an era more supportive of government intervention in the economy and society.

Eduardo Silva is Professor of Political Science and a Fellow of the Center for International Studies at the University of Missouri–St. Louis. He is the author of *The State and Capital in Chile* and co-editor of *Organized Business, Economic Change, and Democracy in Latin America* and *Elections and Democratization in Latin America, 1980–85*. His articles have appeared in *World Politics, Comparative Politics, Development and Change, Latin American Research Review, Journal of Latin American Studies, Latin American Politics and Society*, and *European Review of Latin American and Caribbean Studies*, among others.

Challenging Neoliberalism
in Latin America

EDUARDO SILVA

University of Missouri–St. Louis

CAMBRIDGE UNIVERSITY PRESS
Cambridge, New York, Melbourne, Madrid, Cape Town, Singapore,
São Paulo, Delhi, Dubai, Tokyo

Cambridge University Press
32 Avenue of the Americas, New York, NY 10013-2473, USA

www.cambridge.org
Information on this title: www.cambridge.org/9780521705721

First published 2009

Printed in the United States of America

A catalog record for this publication is available from the British Library.

Library of Congress Cataloging in Publication data

Silva, Eduardo.
Challenging neoliberalism in Latin America / Eduardo Silva.
   p.   cm. – (Cambridge studies in contentious politics)
Includes bibliographical references and index.
ISBN 978-0-521-87993-4 (hardback) – ISBN 978-0-521-70572-1 (pbk.)
1. Neoliberalism – Latin America.   2. Latin America – Economic policy.   3. Latin America –
Social policy.   4. Latin America – Economic conditions – 1982–   5. Latin America – Politics and
government – 1980– Latin America – Social movements   I. Title.   II. Series.
HC125.S534   2009
320.51 – dc22   2009011590

ISBN 978-0-521-87993-4 Hardback
ISBN 978-0-521-70572-1 Paperback

For Rebecca, Raphael, and Jillian

Contents

List of Tables

Preface and Acknowledgments

This project began as a stimulating series of graduate seminars on power, social theory, and contentious politics; and so, my first debt of gratitude goes to the students who accompanied me on that adventure. They nurtured and inspired me. We concluded that the dominant literature on transitions to market economies and liberal democracy missed important facts about those processes. It explained away inequality, denied the legitimacy of claimants when demonstrations occurred, or argued (with patent relief) that destabilizing mobilization had been vanquished. Some studies noted that radical neoliberal reformers were courting social explosion, but offered no further explanation. Yet in the midst of all that theorizing, evidence mounted that neoliberal economic, social, and political reforms were clearly contributing to mobilization by labor, the indigenous, peasants, and the popular sector in general who experienced neoliberalism as exclusion and injustice. This fact nurtured a burgeoning literature in subaltern studies that analyzed particular national or local events in contentious politics, as well as individual movements, especially the indigenous, women, shantytown dwellers, the unemployed, and labor. This rich literature celebrated their unique properties and qualities, thus emphasizing fragmentation and particularity. As valuable as these studies were, I thought they missed a bigger picture. It was time to explore what all this collective "shouting" amounted to on a broader canvas. What if the myriad protests also formed streams of contention in which movements, organizations, and individuals forged horizontal linkages out of frustration and rage against political elites who arrogantly and contemptuously dismissed them? Here was fruitful material for an overarching, comparative study of anti-neoliberal contention in South America. Why did such concatenations of new and old social movements occur in some countries with radical neoliberal projects and not in others? To the extent that they ushered in governments more committed to socialization and planning, did they herald the stirrings of a countermovement to neoliberalism as theorized by Karl Polanyi's double movement of capitalist society?

Many institutions and people helped on this project. Joel Glassman and the Center for International Studies at the University of Missouri–St. Louis awarded fellowships for research leaves; Dean Mark Burkholder of the College of Arts and Sciences provided equipment and authorized research leaves from teaching, most critically when I became chair of the department at the heaviest moment of writing. Lana Stein's support as chair of the Department of Political Science was invaluable. Numerous colleagues offered encouragement, advice, and critical feedback. I would especially like to thank Tony Pereira. His invitation to present a paper on the political economy of import substitution industrialization at the Center for Latin American Studies at Tulane University in 2002 started me thinking along new lines. I am also indebted to Henri Goverde for inviting me to a working conference on "Power and Hegemony" sponsored by the International Political Science Association Research Committee on Political Power at City University New York in the fall of 2004. There, Henri, Philip Cerney, Howard Lentner, and Mark Haugaard offered valuable constructive critiques of my early conceptualizations. For their various contributions I also thank Paul Drake (friend, mentor, and colleague); Ken Roberts; Marcus Kurtz; Moises Arce; David Pion-Berlin; Robert Andolina; Liisa North; Jennifer Collins; Dan Hellinger; Steve Ellner; Jorge León Trujillo; Kurt Weyland; Joel Stillerman; Marc Becker; Carmen Silva; Anni Silva; Patricio Rodrigo; Silvia Borzutsky; Pilar Domingo; Cris Kay; Patricio Silva; Michiel Baud; Kees Koonings; Willem Assies; and Marieke Denissen. Special thanks also go to Bob Baumann, UMSL Center for International Studies, who encouraged me at every turn, giving me strength to redouble my labors. I also owe credit to my research assistants Sudarsan Kant, Leesa Althen, and Sterling Recker for their invaluable efforts, especially their ability to collect data and solve practical problems. Leesa and Sterling assisted in the early stages. Sudarsan came on board just after I began writing in the fall of 2006 and therefore worked on the project the longest. His commitment, humor, and camaraderie provided lighthearted moments and a sense of shared accomplishment that sustained the drive to finish. Lana Vierdag and Raphael Hopkins, Department of Political Science staff, fiercely and selflessly protected my time after I became chair. The constructive critiques of anonymous readers for Cambridge University Press through the various stages of this project immeasurably strengthened the manuscript. Elisabeth Wood, on the editorial board of the Cambridge Studies in Contentious Politics series, made excellent editorial suggestions that improved the final manuscript. Peter Katsirubas, project manager with Aptara, Vicky Danahy, copy editor, and Emily Spangler, assistant to Eric Crahan were a pleasure to work with. I extend special thanks to Eric Crahan, New York Editor for History and Political Science at Cambridge University Press. He ably shaped and shepherded the project along with courtesy, professionalism, and humor. Unknowingly, he even planted a seed that contributed to the writing of this book. Around the time I was conducting the graduate seminars mentioned earlier, I bought a large quantity of books on contentious politics from Cambridge at a Latin American Studies Association International Congress. He noticed and cordially asked if I had a project I wanted to discuss with him. Embarrassed that I had only some loose ideas I replied before leaving the exhibition booth, "No . . . but I'm working on it!"

This book is dedicated to my family, *el norte de mi vida*. My partner Jillian, and our children Raphael and Rebecca have accompanied, sustained, molded, and guided me for more than 25 years. A great deal of them is in it; not the least, their sense of justice and fairness. I also dedicate this work to the memory of Ismael Silva Fuenzalida, anthropologist, intellectual adventurer, *y mi querido Viejo*; my father. Our last conversation in Santiago, Chile, in December 2003, contributed significantly to my desire to see this project through. Reflecting on more than 80 years of turbulent experiences, he said that without rational policies to reduce enduring, glaring, and grossly unjust levels of socioeconomic inequality in Latin America political stability would elude the corner of the world he cared for so deeply and for which he sacrificed so much. On this point we agreed totally. This book extends that conversation.

Eduardo Silva
St. Louis, Missouri
July 2009

List of Acronyms

ABP	Alianza Bravo Pueblo (Fierce Peoples' Alliance)
AD	Alianza Democrática (Chile) (Democratic Alliance)
ADN	Alianza Democrática Nacional (National Democratic Alliance)
APRA	Alianza Popular Revolucionaria Americana (Popular American Revolutionary Alliance)
AP	Acuerdo Patriótico (Patriotic Accord)
AR	Acción por la República (Action for the Republic)
ARBOL	Alianza Renovadora Boliviana (Bolivian Alliance for Renewal)
ARI	Alternativa por una República de Iguales (Alternative for a Republic of Equals)
ATE	Asociación de Trabajadores Estatales (Association of State Employees)
ATJE	Alianza para el Trabajo, la Justicia, y la Educación (Alliance for Work, Justice, and Education)
CGT	Confederación General de Trabajadores (General Confederation of Workers)
CGTP	Confederación General de Trabajadores del Perú (General Confederation of Workers of Peru)
CMS	Coordinadora de Movimientos Sociales (Social Movements Coordinator)
COB	Central Obrera Boliviana (Bolivian Workers Central)
COMIBOL	Corporación Minera de Bolivia (Mining Corporation of Bolivia)
CONADI	Corporación Nacional de Desarrollo Indígena (National Corporation for Indigenous Development)
CONAIE	Confederación Nacional de Indígenas Ecuatorianos (National Confederation of Indigenous Ecuadorians)
CONAMA	Comisión Nacional del Medio Ambiente (National Commission for the Environment)

CONDEPA	Conciencia de la Patria (Conscience of the Fatherland)
CONFENIAE	Confederación de Nacionalidades Indígenas de la Amazonía Ecuatoriana (Confederation of Indigenous Nationalities of the Ecuadorian Amazon)
COPEI	Comité de Organización Política Electoral Independiente (Committee for the Organization of Independent Electoral Politics, a Christian Democratic party)
CPD	Concertación de Partidos por la Democracia (Coalition of Parties for Democracy)
CSUTCB	Confederación Sindical Unica de Trabajadores Campesinos Bolivianos (Unitary Syndical Confederation of Peasant Workers of Bolivia)
CTA	Central de Trabajadores Argentinos (Argentine Workers Central)
CTD	Coordinadoras de Trabajadores Desempleados (Unemployed Workers Coordinators)
CTERA	Confederación de Trabajadores Educacionales de la República Argentina (Confederation of Educational Workers of the Argentine Republic)
CTV	Confederación de Trabajadores Venezolunos (Confederation of Venezuelan Workers)
CUT	Confederación Unitaria de Trabajadores (Unitary Workers Confederation)
ECUARUNARI	Ecuador Runacunapac Riccarimui (Awakening of the Ecuadorian Indian)
FEDECOR	Federación Departamental Cochabambina de Organizaciones de Regantes (Cochabamba Federation of Irrigators Organizations)
Fejuve	Federación de Juntas Vecinales (Federation of Neighborhood Committees)
FL	Frente por la Libertad (Liberty Front)
Frenapo	Frente Nacional contra la Pobreza (National Front Against Poverty)
Frepaso	Frente por un País en Solidaridad (Front for a Country in Solidarity)
FTAA	Free Trade Association of the Americas
FTV	Federación Tierra y Vivienda (Land and Housing Federation)
FUN	Frente de Unidad Nacional (Front for National Unity)
FUT	Frente Unitario de Trabajadores (United Workers Front)
FUTRAYEDO	Frente Unico de Trabajadores Desocupados y Ocupados (United Front of Unemployed and Employed Workers)

List of Acronyms

GDP	Gross Domestic Product
ILO	International Labor Organization
IMF	International Monetary Fund
ISI	import-substitution industrialization
IU	Izquierda Unida (United Left)
MAS	Movimiento al Socialismo (Movement Toward Socialism)
MBL	Movimiento Bolivia Libre (Movement for a Free Bolivia)
MBR-200	Movimiento Revolucionario Bolivariano-200 (Bolivarian Revolutionary Movement)
MDP	Movimiento Democrático Popular (Popular Democratic Movement)
MIP	Movimiento Indigenista Pachakuti (Pachakuti Indigenous Movement)
MIR	Movimiento Izquierda Revolucionario (Left Revolutionary Movement)
MNR	Movimiento Nacionalista Revolucionario (National Revolutionary Movement)
MRTA	Movimiento Revolucionario Tupac Amaru (Revolutionary Movement of Tupac Amaru)
MTA	Movimiento de Trabajadores Argentinos (Argentine Workers Movement)
MTD	Movimiento de Trabajadores Desocupados (Unemployed Workers Movement)
MVR	Movimiento Quinta República (Movement of the Fifth Republic)
NGO	Nongovernmental Organization
NFR	Nueva Fuerza Republicana (New Republican Force)
PI	Partido Intransigente (Intransigent Party)
PJ	Partido Justicialista (Justicialist Party)
PNP	Partido Nacionalista del Perú (Nationalist Party of Peru)
PODEMOS	Poder Democrático y Social (Democratic and Social Power)
PRVZL	Proyecto Venezuela (Venezuela Project)
PUAMA	Pueblos Unidos Multiiétnicos de Amazona (United Multiethinc Peoples of Amazonia)
SERNAM	Servicio Nacional de la Mujer (Women's National Service)
SINAMOS	Sistema Nacional de Apoyo a la Movilización Social (National System for the Support of Social Mobilization)
UCD	Unión del Centro Democrático (Union of the Democratic Center)
UCR	Unión Cívica Radical (Radical Civic Union)
UCS	Unidad Cívica Solidaridad (Civic Union in Solidarity)
UNA	Una Nación Avanzada (An Advanced Nation)

URD	Unión Republicana Democrática (Republican Democratic Union)
UTD	Unión de Trabajadores Desocupados (Union of Unemployed Workers)
YPF	Yacimientos Petrolíferos Fiscales (Fiscal Oil Fields)

1

The Inconvenient Fact of Anti-Neoliberal Mass Mobilization

Between 1989 and 2002, a nationwide massive anti-neoliberal mobilization shook Argentina, Bolivia, Ecuador, and Venezuela to the core. All across each country, protestors rioted, blocked highways and roads, disrupted transport and commerce, staged marches from the interior to the capital, laid siege to capital cities, burned effigies, and attacked and occupied government buildings as well as the offices of transnational corporations. Ferocious street battles with riot police and the army rocked the establishment, leaving behind a toll of dead and wounded that spurred outraged protestors to redouble their efforts. At times, the army and the police refused to fulfill their repressive function.[1]

These events were not just anomic outbursts of rage. In most cases, from inauspicious beginnings in the 1980s and early 1990s, participants patiently built organizational and coalitional capacity and used it for political purposes. This process involved the formation of new social movement organizations (composed of indigenous peoples, the unemployed, pensioners, and neighborhood associations, among others), new unions, and new political parties. These existed alongside traditional union and middle-class movements and political parties, sometimes in competition and sometimes in cooperation. Over time, mobilization became increasingly coordinated and powerful as organizations rooted in cultural, identity, and class politics linked together and reached out to new political parties and, on occasion, to dissident military factions.

Protestors pressured government authorities for reforms to free-market economics and to procedural democracy. They focused on redistributive issues (social insurance and services) and land reform, and questioned ideological commitments to private property rights by pressing for more active state involvement in the economy and society. Material demands intersected indigenous claims for autonomy and citizen rights as well as society-wide protests against corruption, and, in

---

[1] For an overview of anti-neoliberal protests, see Petras and Veltmeyer (2005); Prashad and Ballve (2006). For Argentina, see Rock (2002); Auyero (2004, 2007); López-Levy (2004); Svampa and Pereyra (2003). For Bolivia, see Assies and Salman (2003); Crabtree (2005); Olivera and Lewis (2004). For Ecuador, see O'Conner (2003); Yashar (2005); Zamosc (2004) For Venezuela, see Roberts (2003a); López Maya (1999c); Salamanca (1999); Ellner (2003).

some cases, calls for more participatory forms of democracy. In all four countries, mass mobilization brought down governments that steadfastly supported neoliberalism and contributed to their replacement with political leadership committed, at least in principle, to reforming it.[2]

Massive leftist popular mobilization in Latin America posed an inconvenient fact for the prevailing consensus of the time. It held that globalization (defined as an intensification of the integration of the world-market economy) and the demise of the Soviet Union as an alternative development model led to the triumph of free markets and liberal democracy as a rational, normatively desirable end point in human progress. Persuaded by these trends, responsible political leaders supported market liberalization and demobilized popular sectors in the interest of democratic stability. From this perspective, anti-neoliberal leftist popular mobilization seemed highly improbable. Several additional globalization-driven factors strengthened this outlook. Market liberalization had decimated traditional class-based mass movement organizations, principally labor, thus weakening them significantly. The collapse of the communist bloc made it easier to defeat or contain insurrectionary movements, such as the Shining Path in Peru and the Revolutionary Armed Forces in Colombia.[3]

Analysts, however, also recognized that these momentous trends did not mean the end of contentious politics as such. Taking comfort in the decline of leftist class-based mass movements, they identified a new trend in which movements rooted in identity, cultural, ethnic, citizen, livelihood, and environmental concerns appeared ascendant. Given the turn away from socialist demands and the highly fragmented nature of the postmodern world, these new social movements were not expected to mount concerted nationwide leftist mobilization. And yet, flying in the face of these prevailing interpretations of the neoliberal age, it occurred.[4] Not only that, but, on a larger scale, the episodes of contention that wracked these countries can be interpreted as the most dramatic instances of a leftward trend in Latin American politics as resistance to neoliberalism spills over into the electoral arena across the region.[5]

Why did Argentina, Bolivia, Ecuador and Venezuela develop episodes of anti-neoliberal contention that ended in the fall of governments unabashedly

[2] Those presidents were, in Argentina, Néstor Kirchner (2003–07) and Cristina Fernández de Kirchner (2007–); Evo Morales in Bolivia (2005–); Rafael Correa in Ecuador (2006–); and Hugo Chávez in Venezuela (1998–).

[3] For an introduction to these arguments, see Fukuyama (1992); Sklair (2002); Giddens (1994); Castañeda (1993); Cohen and Rai (2000).

[4] For new social movements, see Slater (1985); Foweraker (1995); Escobar and Alvarez (1992).

[5] What these efforts actually accomplish in terms of reforming neoliberalism remains unclear. At minimum, however, popular mobilization has raised significant challenges to neoliberalism and may herald the beginning of a reform process whose contours we cannot yet know. To the extent that it contributes to a new process of reincorporation of the popular sectors into politics and the extension of economic and social rights to them, we may be at the threshold of a new critical juncture in Latin America (Collier and Collier 1991; Mahoney 2001).

committed to free-market economics and the election of political leaders more interested in social equity? This book argues that the construction of a contemporary version of what Karl Polanyi called market society (Polanyi 2001) was the first of several necessary factors.[6] Beginning in the 1980s and gathering force and coherence in the 1990s, a wide array of neoliberal reforms provided the *motive* for mobilization. They sought to build an entire new order that, as in market society, subordinated politics and social welfare to the needs of an economy built on the logic of free-market economics. Because neoliberal reforms simultaneously affected the economic, political, and social sphere, they threatened a wide variety of popular sector and middle-class groups and raised a gamut of grievances radiating from all three areas.[7] It is crucial to underscore that these episodes of anti-neoliberal mobilization in South America protested *a specific kind of capitalism*, not capitalism in general. The dominant protest movements sought to *reform* neoliberal capitalism, demanding a return to the mixed economy and a larger welfare role for the state, rather than to replace it with an alternative "socialist" or other model.[8]

How could formerly disorganized and ineffectual subordinate social forces mount such strong challenges to seemly hegemonic neoliberal forces? To get at the issue of *capacity*, following Rueschemeyer, Stephens, and Stephens (1992) and Mann (1993, 1986) this book analyzes shifts in political, economic, military, transnational, and cognitive power sources. Chapter 2 specifies these factors and how they reveal four additional necessary variables: political associational space, economic crisis, reformist thrust to major protest movements, and two transformative mechanisms, cognitive (mainly issue framing) and brokerage.[9] Issue framing and brokerage mechanisms, in particular, explain the process by which a wide range of once fragmented and isolated movements formed expanding alliances and coalitions that in some cases included support from political parties and dissident factions of the military (McAdam, Tarrow, and Tilly 2001).

Why did countries such as Peru and Chile, which also implemented extensive free-market reforms, not experience mass popular mobilization in the 1990s and early 2000s? Peru differed on two key conditions: It harbored significant armed insurrectionary movements, and an authoritarian turn under Alberto

---

[6] Topik (1999) and Almeida (2007) have also argued that comprehensive neoliberal reforms in Latin America amount to the construction of market society. Silver (2003) and others make the claim on a global scale.

[7] In other words, the threat mechanism identified by McAdam, Tarrow, and Tilly (2001) affected every major source of social organization, turning it into a powerful agent of movement transformation.

[8] This does not, however, preclude the possibility that the process unleashed by mass mobilization may generate such outcomes in particular cases; for example the Venezuelan leadership claims to be building 21st-century socialism.

[9] McAdam, Tarrow, and Tilly's (2001) appropriation mechanism (in which social actors take over an existing organization and turn it to new purposes) also operated in some instances, but not as systematically as framing, brokerage, and, of course, threat.

Fujimori closed associational space (Roberts 1998; Yashar 2005). Chile lacked the most basic condition: sustained imposition of contemporary market society after redemocratization in 1990. Ever since 1990, center-left governments have been reforming a strong version of market society established by a military dictatorship between 1975 and 1989 (Oppenheim 2007).

Following an exposition of the argument in Chapter 3, Chapters 4 through 7 analyze the development of anti-neoliberal episodes of contention in Argentina, Bolivia, Ecuador, and Venezuela. In each case, analysis specifies how efforts to construct contemporary market society created significant economic and political exclusion among urban and rural labor and even middle classes as they dismantled the old national-populist order. To trace the evolution of episodes of contention, the chapters organize protest events into successive waves of contention. Analysis then focuses on how, in the context of democracy and economic crisis, mobilizing groups demanding reforms to contemporary market society applied cognitive and brokerage mechanisms to forge organizational and coalitional power. These developments combined with traditional and innovative disruptive tactics to force political leaders who unconditionally supported neoliberalism out of office. Chapter 8 shows how variation in key necessary conditions accounts for the absence of similar episodes of anti-neoliberal mobilization in Peru and Chile. The concluding chapter addresses what these episodes of anti-neoliberal mobilization accomplished, and explores their implications for new research.

The Puzzle of Leftist Mobilization in the Age of Global Liberalism

Protest, mass mobilization, insurrection, military coup d'états, and tumultuous politics in general are hallmarks of Latin American politics. Consequently, these recent outbreaks, although not predicted by most theories, in and of themselves were not unprecedented, they disappointed analysts hoping for an era of improved governability. However, leftist mobilization at the turn of the 20th century in Argentina, Bolivia, Ecuador, and Venezuela had a special quality and consequence. It was historically unique because it built in reaction to stubbornly persistent efforts to replace a national-populist order with contemporary market society and democracy – the new path to modernity. Anti-neoliberal mobilization was also extraordinary for its perseverance and its scale at the climax despite the decline of organized labor, the traditional leader of the popular sectors. They forced the resignation of presidents committed to neoliberalism and helped to usher in governments that wanted to reform it.

Indeed, the decidedly leftist cast to these mobilizations in the age of global liberalism was quite surprising and posed a puzzle for Latin American social movement theory, as did the degree of coordination across movement organizations and other political actors. Protesters emphatically demanded that the state reclaim a stronger role in economic development and the provision of welfare. They advocated nationalization of natural resources, controls over international companies, industrial policy, land reform, and subsidized social programs. They clamored for the punishment of corrupt politicians who profited from market liberalization and called for constitutional changes to open formal democratic procedures to social sectors excluded and hurt by neoliberal reforms. Equally unexpected, a wide array of new social movement organizations based on identity, citizen rights, livelihood struggles, and neighborhood improvement formed coalitions with established and new urban and rural labor unions, as well as with new and traditional political parties, and even dissident factions of the military.

Leftist mobilization was simply not expected in the age of globalization. The triumph of global economic and political liberalism, reinforced by the fall of communism and bolstered by prevailing intellectual trends, conspired against it. Economic globalization had decisively changed the balance of structural power in favor of capital, especially international capital, over the territorially bound state. Hence, it made little sense to look to the state for protection from markets (Ohmae 2005).

All over the world the sociopolitical forces that relied on state power to protect them from unfettered markets weakened because market liberalization and sharp reductions in barriers to trade since the 1970s intensified the global integration of production.[10] These conditions gave international capital (and its domestic allies) an edge over states. They rewarded governments that liberalized their trade, production, and financial sectors and that held down factor costs, especially labor. Equally, if not more important, they punished governments that attempted to control or restrain the private sector or to compete with it by promoting industrial policy, public enterprise, large welfare states, labor-friendly regulations, or a tight regulatory environment for business. Given the staggering sums that now crossed borders with ease, territorially bounded states had no alternative but to maintain business-friendly climates. They could ill afford the economically and politically destabilizing effects of huge losses in employment and investment; losses the public sector could not make up for.

The fall of communism in the late 1980s sealed the ideological triumph of liberalism in the world and clinched the mainstream intellectual conviction that leftist development models had lost their appeal and no longer exerted any force around the globe. After the collapse of real socialism, expectations soared that

---

[10] International companies, wielding resources in assets, financial capability, and sales rivaling the gross national products of middle income countries, developed global commodity chains to produce their goods. This allowed firms to take advantage of changing costs related to labor, land, regulatory environment, and taxes. Transnational companies became indispensable for economic growth because they alone could afford the costs of technological innovation and large scale projects. International financial capital expanded at a dizzying rate. Institutional portfolio investors and arbitragers looked for favorable changes in foreign exchange rates, interest rates, financial sector liberalization, and stock markets in "emerging markets." Breathtaking sums of money changed destination in the time it took to strike a few keys. Intense innovation in communications, information technology, and transport made these changes possible (Sklair 2002; Soros 1998; Stiglitz 2002).

mobilization around their banners was a thing of the past. In the 1990s, tne conviction that free-market economics had no rivals deepened (Fukuyama 1992). Its efficiency-maximizing characteristics, as opposed to the inefficiencies and failures of state-led development, made it the only path to the accumulation of wealth. Unleashed from its fetters, only the private sector could supply the huge quantities of investment needed for sustained growth with low inflation and the creation of productive employment. The state, by contrast, not only lacked sufficient capital, it had proven to be an inflation-creating sinkhole for unproductive activities and generator of socially and politically corrosive stagnation (Ohmae 2005, 1995).[11]

Liberal democracy ascendant became the political corollary to economic liberalism because the economic failure of socialism also spelled the political failure of the one party mobilizational state and, it was argued, the social democratic welfare state as well. Liberal democracy emphasized procedural conditions for individual freedom regarding political participation and representation, meaning voting and elections. It absolved the state from commitment to substantive economic or social rights. The state, or rather, government, had a duty to focus on public order and macroeconomic stability, and to establish strong, efficient, legal–rational institutions to support private property rights. Liberal democracy legitimized free-market economics by means of the electoral process (Chan and Scarritt 2002).[12]

If these trends weakened first world mixed economies and welfare states, along with the labor parties and strong unions that sustained them, they destroyed the national-populist state and the organized constituencies that supported it in Latin America. Historically, these had been the labor movement and the populist, socialist, and communist parties they allied with. Those combative movements, forged in the crucible of world-market expansion from the 1870s to the 1920s, and rising to political prominence in the 1930s and the post–World War II period, had been the standard bearers of contentious politics in Latin America. They struck in massive numbers, manned barricades, took over haciendas, turned out by the tens and hundreds of thousands in mass demonstrations, rioted, and suffered death, injury, imprisonment, and exile for their cause. The mode of incorporation of the urban and rural labor movements into national politics defined regimes and

---

[11] Free-market (neoliberal) capitalism (the modern variety of 19th-century Manchester capitalism) was also considered the wellspring of individual liberty. Freed from the oppressive, and discriminating, hand of the state (even in the mixed capitalist economies under Keynesian economics), people gained the liberty to make personal choices in the context of universally applicable and impersonal market rules. One stood or fell depending on one's capacity to rationally exploit market conditions. It was expected that the entrepreneurial spirit, once unleashed, would reject the straightjacket of "cradle-to-grave" welfare states. Rational individuals would simply not undertake collective action to limit personal freedom with the energizing emotional, spiritual, and material satisfactions of the daily hustle and bustle of negotiating markets as reward for their labors at the end of the day (Hayek 1994).

[12] For a more optimistic view, see Glatzer and Rueschemeyer (2005).

political conflict, whether institutionalized by means of electoral politics and legal strikes or openly rebellious or by military putsch well into the 20th century (Collier and Collier 1991).

Economic globalization dethroned the labor movement and associated political parties from their prominent historical position and demoted them to irrelevancy in the new international capitalist system. Analysts noted that market liberalization in the form of decreasing protection against imports for domestic industry, the privatization of public enterprises, the flexibilization of labor codes, falling wages, and the growth of the informal sector of labor (not subject to state regulations such as contracts and payment of benefits and taxes) decimated organized labor. Their sheer numbers declined as industries collapsed because of international competition and as privatized state-owned enterprises shed workers. The growth in cheap, underutilized, and difficult-to-organize labor occupied in precarious employment at substandard wages further undermined unions. Because they could not protect their members' job security and benefits, individuals preferred not to join and unions lost the ability to coordinate politically meaningful mass mobilization (Burgess 2004; Cook 2007; Kurtz 2004; Murillo 2001; Oxhorn 1998; Roberts 1998; Roxborough 1994).

Economic globalization, the fall of communism, and the emphasis on procedural democracy after redemocratization, especially between 1979 and 1989, also severed, or severely weakened, linkages between labor parties and the union movement. In the interest of getting elected and of governability, the former recognized the validity of the neoconservative mantra – there is no alternative (to market liberalization and procedural democracy). Reformed socialist, social democratic, and populist political party leaders used their remaining links to labor to demobilize it.[13] If unionists demonstrated, their protests sputtered because they had no impact on government policy. In the absence of a political amplifying chamber, a numerically weak and fragmented labor movement stood little chance of achieving significant political impact.[14]

[13] Success in elite bargaining between military regime softliners and opposition moderates depended on, among other conditions, the opposition's ability to control the more radical, and hence more mobilization-prone, elements among them. Moreover, an emphasis on procedural rules of political competition, while keeping socioeconomic issues off the table, increased the success of democratization. (O'Donnell and Schmitter 1986). They reduced uncertainty and mollified the fears of socioeconomic elites capable of reverting democratization (Przeworski 1991, 1986). Also see Roberts (1998); Garretón (1993).

[14] Theorists observed that leaders of the reformed political left believed that loyalty to democracy required subordinating socioeconomic demands and renouncing mobilization to avoid polarization. These views had deep roots in Latin American experience since the mid-1960s and in the efforts of intellectuals to learn the lessons to be drawn from it. From different theoretical perspectives they came to the same conclusion. Social mobilization based on redistributive or revolutionary demands substantially contributed to the breakdown of democracy in South America because their threats to socioeconomic elites polarized politics. In a polarizing game of political brinksmanship, leftist political parties mobilized organized labor, peasants, and shantytown dwellers who threatened the core interests of capitalists and landowners – property and profits – and scared middle classes, which drove them to join anticommunist military establishments in

New institutional political economists in the neoclassical tradition seized on this about-face. They argued that market liberalization would, in addition to reviving sustained economic growth, have salutary political consequences. From their perspective, strong public sector involvement in the economy under national populism had turned the state into a target for economic demands by social groups that used their political connections, especially political parties, to obtain economic favors, such as subsidies, employment through public enterprise, welfare, rigid labor codes, housing, and so forth. Rent-seeking behavior by social groups under national populism generated fiscal deficits that fed inflation and retarded rapid economic growth. It also fed social mobilization because politicians wanted votes. Thus, providing material benefits in response to protest was a vehicle for retaining and expanding an electoral base (Crisp and Levine 1998; Dornbusch and Edwards 1991; Huntington 1968; Krueger 1974).

Free-market economic reforms, by contrast, took the state out of much of economic policy making, removing it as a political referent for social groups. The market, not politicians and the state, now allocated most goods and services. Hence mobilization and protest aimed at the state could not resolve organized labor's demands. The expectation was that concentrated, coordinated general mobilization by organized labor would decline as it realized the government would not intercede in its favor. Moreover, it was expected that the labor movement would fragment as unions pursued more company- and sector-specific grievances; not to mention it was also expected that union membership would decline as workers realized unions could not help them.[15]

Last, but not least, the collapse of communism had significant impact on the decline of revolutionary socialist insurgencies, if nothing else because of the withdrawal of the material support they had enjoyed during the Cold War while the governments they fought continued to receive U.S. military aid (Castañeda 1993). Bolstered by the United States, the superior resources of the Peruvian government under Alberto Fujimori contributed to the defeat of the Shining Path guerrillas who lost crucial logistical, tactical, and training aid (Palmer 1994). The same dynamic helped the Colombian government to contain the Revolutionary Armed Forces of Colombia, which, moreover, lost the ideological high ground by turning to the drug economy to survive. Similar, but far more complex, circumstances heavily influenced the resolution of insurgencies in Central America in the early 1990s (Walker and Armony 2000). Meanwhile, in Mexico the emergence of the Zapatistas in 1994 suggested that the insurgency of the future would be regionally based, of short duration, and limited in its demands rather than building the "long march" for total social transformation. In short, an outburst

the overthrow of democracy. Hypermobilization overwhelmed institutional capacity to contain conflict. See O'Donnell (1973); Linz (1978); Mainwaring and Pérez-Liñán (2005); Huntington (1968); Crozier, Huntington, and Watganuki (1975).

[15] Marcus Kurtz (2004) and Manuel Antonio Garretón et al. (2003), albeit from different theoretical and normative approaches, agreed on these points.

of violence to draw attention to long-ignored grievances was followed by more conventional efforts at building a social movement organization and program for noninsurrectionary contentious politics. The Mexican case also seemed to prove that the political establishment could keep such movements isolated, impeding their ability to connect with larger, more established political and social forces.

New Social Movements and Resistance

Despite the decline of class-based movements, protest, demonstrations, and resistance still abounded in the form of decentralized, fragmented identity and subsistence-based movements. Building on a largely European conception of power and postmaterialism in late capitalism, scholars critiqued class for understanding protest and resistance in Latin America. Class analysis posited unity of purpose based on material interests and rigidly defined the subjects of mobilization according to their objective location in the structure of production. Therefore it missed the main sources and characteristics of movement effervescence in Latin America after the 1960s and 1970s: identity and subjectivity (Slater 1994).[16] As the politics of material distribution lost force in advanced capitalism, the bureaucratization of society, the commodification of every aspect of life, and massification of social activity politicized culture and identity (Slater 1985). However, a high degree of fragmentation characterizes the resultant movements because mobilization occurs across many diverse and self-contained issues, such as gender, sexuality, environment, ethnicity, race, urban landscapes, subsistence rights (such as urban squatter movements), livelihood, culture, human rights, democracy, and consumer protection, to name but the most prominent. Fragmentation also occurs because new social movements favor loose nonhierarchical forms of association and because they are often relatively apolitical (Escobar and Alvarez 1992; Mainwaring and Viola 1984).

The new social movements literature had a positive impact because it drew attention to a wider gamut of movement. It conceptualized social subjects beyond class, providing detailed accounts of movement origins, organization, and demands and frequently connected protest to larger political processes (such as democratization and citizen rights). Once the overly optimistic, transformational characterization and the "newness" of new social movements waned, it became possible to see them as one more set of movements including traditional class-based ones. For example, they had political orientations, they made material demands, they could be hierarchical, they might succumb to clientelistic pressures, and many were not even so "new."[17]

Yet, for all the attention paid to the role of women in neighborhood associations, the rise of indigenous people's movements, urban squatter movements,

---

[16] For an excellent review of these positions and constructive critique, see Foweraker (1995).
[17] On this point, see Foweraker (1995). A good example would be Eckstein and Wickham-Crowley (2003).

environmental and racial justice movements, the "new" social movements literature could not account for conditions that linked disparate movements to each other and to class-based movements in episodes of leftist mass mobilization. This was a consequence of the focus on subjectivity, discrete identity, and fragmentation and distinctiveness from class-based movements. The new social movement literature overplayed the extent to which identity politics had overtaken material interest. This emphasis also limited the approaches' utility for uncovering the larger political significance of mass mobilization. It could not grasp the forces that catapulted their subjects to national and international political significance. What had turned them into a substantial challenge to neoliberal economic and social policies and purely formal conceptualizations of democracy? In other words, what explains these episodes of decidedly material-based leftist protest in Latin America's neoliberal era? We turn to this question in the next two chapters after a brief review of alternative explanations.

Alternative Explanations

The democratic consolidation literature argued that institutional insufficiencies in two areas caused anomie and fueled civil unrest in the 1990s. First, weak political institutions fed discontent. Patrimonial state organization bred preferential treatment through clientelism, creating popular resentment. When coupled with inadequate rule of law, political corruption flourished, deepening the disgust of the population for the established order. Weak political parties and party systems embroiled in scandal further alienated citizens from orderly participation in politics. Second, weak economic institutions contributed to poor economic performance that, alongside deepening extreme poverty, further stoked the cauldron of democratic distemper. Financial crises, rigidities in factor adjustments during trade and financial sector liberalization, poor execution of privatization policies, labor-market inflexibility, a welfare system skewed toward middle classes and a labor aristocracy, all courted economic instability and exacerbated poverty and income concentration. These political and institutional deficiencies undermined democratic governance, understood as the capacity of institutions to provide orderly, impartial, and just administration based on universal rules of law, contracts, public policy, and opportunity.

Given this diagnosis of the problem, the consolidation of democracy and free-market economic reforms required proper institutional design and strengthening. Market institutions needed fine-tuning (a technical matter) to ensure that market efficiency would, in fact, generate wealth. Democratic consolidation required building institutions for good governance. These included a Weberian legal–rational state to ensure the rule of law: meaning, universal rules, meritocracy, enforcement of contracts, and a functioning justice system. Strong political parties free of corruption and not beholden to mass organizations (labor and other "populist" social movements) must be encouraged. Equality of opportunity

10

demanded adjusting social assistance, education, and health policies to serve the neediest social groups.[18] Staying the course with improved implementation would eliminate conditions that bred mass mobilization.

This literature was certainly on the right track when it pointed to weaknesses in the state and deep-seated economic problems as important causes of mass protest in Latin America. However, its faith that proper institutional design in support of free-market economics could contain mounting social tension and conflict against neoliberal reforms overlooked an important problem. Institutions are social constructs that crystallize relations of domination and subordination in society (Mann 1993, 1986; Weber 1978). Therefore, analysts steeped in this perspective missed the point that the very institutions they advocated caused inequalities that generated the grievances that drive popular mobilization.

The literature on democratic consolidation and free-market economics suffers from another problem that limits its utility for explaining the anti-neoliberal episodes of contention that swept Argentina, Bolivia, Ecuador, and Venezuela. It conceived of protest only as a matter of public disorder. Civil unrest bred mobs that unscrupulous populist leaders with questionable loyalty to democracy could whip into support for personal political ambitions. By the 1990s, populism had developed into a term that demonized the industrial policies and welfare states from the 1950s to 1980s. It was associated with a bloated state bureaucracy that stunted economic growth. Its fiscal irresponsibility fanned the fires of hyperinflation, unseemly preferential treatment for comfortable middle classes, abandonment of wretches living in extreme poverty, and agricultural decline. And, of course, it caused politically destabilizing mass mobilization that ended in brutal coup d'états by the military in support of fearful socioeconomic elites.

This framing of the problem blinded analysts to the political significance of popular mobilization. They could not recognize protesters as social subjects. Demonstrators only constituted a mob that threatened democratic stability and prudent economic policy. Thus they could not accept that mass mobilization in these cases constituted organized, politically meaningful pressure to reform both neoliberal capitalism and a system of electoral democracy that excluded their substantive demands.[19] Moreover, demonizing "populism" blinded analysts from recognizing the legitimacy of both popular sector demands and the leaders of those movements. Staying the course amounted to an arrogant will to power by dominant sociopolitical forces that contemptuously dismissed popular sector claims. Outraged subaltern social groups interpreted this posture as exclusion and injustice, and resisted if they could.

---

[18] For a useful summary of these views, see Kuczynski and Williamson (2003).

[19] This reaction is analogous to the global expansion of capital in the long 19th century (to 1914). Deborah Yashar (1999) recognized potential conflict in relation to the replacement of corporatism with individual citizen rights and indigenous mobilization.

11

A more sociological and historical perspective echoes the democratic consolidation literature's concern with the consequences of weak states and ineffective economic policy processes (Centeno 2002; Migdal 1998). It contends that 19th-century wars and the type of liberal reforms of the period shaped Latin American state and class formations in ways that have profound implications for contemporary political instability. Miguel Angel Centeno argued that the relative absence of external wars in Latin America and the funding of bellicose conflict through debt rather than taxation created weak states. They failed to establish sufficient autonomy from dominant classes to enforce development models, especially ones that emphasize greater socioeconomic equality. This left an enduring legacy of states with insufficient autonomy and infrastructural power to penetrate society; hence their inability to maintain order and to integrate the societies over which they nominally preside. Under these conditions, current cycles of contentious politics are just another manifestation of political disorder that weak Latin American states are prone to, along with rebellions, military putsches, insurrections, riots, and other forms of popular protest.

James Mahoney (2001) suggested that the imposition of neoliberalism in the late 20th century constituted a critical juncture for Latin America. Mahoney wrote about the consequences of 19th-century liberalism for political liberty and social equality in 20th-century Central America. He argued that the manner in which states imposed liberalism affected distinctive trajectories of state and class formations with profound effects on sociopolitical conflict. Radical policy implementation in El Salvador and Guatemala produced authoritarian regimes confronted by democratization movements. State repression of those movements eventually generated insurrectionary movements. Aborted (radical) policy processes in Nicaragua and Honduras led to foreign domination of the economy and weak national elites who used the state for personal gain and to retain power by controlling patron–client networks, including fractions of labor. Consequently, popular mobilization and insurrection were directed against foreign business and democratization movements did not emerge until the second half of the 20th century. Again, state repression contributed to insurrection (at least in Nicaragua). By contrast, reformist, or mild, liberal policies in Costa Rica contributed to the emergence of democracy and, in relative terms, greater social equality. Mahoney voices concerns that radical or aborted radical efforts in the late 20th century might have similar long-term effects in other parts of Latin America and exhorts policy makers to follow a reformist liberal path.

Centeno's and Mahoney's arguments are explicitly historical. Their appeal here lies in their strong implications for the present. Because the maintenance of order is one of the state's primary functions, arguments that link disorder to state weakness in the form of insufficient administrative control over it and autonomy seem compelling. However, this view assumes that the state is the primary, if not the sole, power network in society. But state strength also hinges on the state's relationship to other organized power networks nationally and internationally,

12

such as the economy, class relations, the military, and ideological production. In other words, state power is relational. It depends, at least in part, on its relationship to these other sources of power in society. A strong state at one time may be weaker at another.[20] A move away from state-centered explanations to frameworks that examine the state in relation to other power networks in society offers a more flexible analytic tool for understanding upsurges in contemporary popular resistance to neoliberalism. It shows that state formation, in and of itself, is not sufficient to explain leftist mobilization. My own argument is that the efforts of domestic and international political and economic forces to impose contemporary market society in the latter part of the 20th century, in conjunction with specific power relations, generated anti-neoliberal counter mobilization in some cases and not in others. I come back to these issues in the concluding chapter.

---

[20] As suggestive as their work is for the present, there are problems with extending their arguments to explain late 20th-century and early 21st-century challenges to neoliberalism. Centeno's framing considers the problem of order (or disorder) only in general and seems unconcerned with understanding the characteristics of particular types of "disorder" and what distinguishes them from others. Mahoney is more concerned with these specifics than Centeno. However, they do not work out because he developed an historical argument for Central America, a region with distinctive characteristics. For example, the connection between two types of drastic liberal reforms (radical and aborted) and movement type (democratization or client–patron network-manipulated quiescence) does not hold. In Argentina and Bolivia, the equivalent of radical liberalism generated popular mobilization, but so did less "pure" liberal reform efforts in Ecuador and Venezuela. Moreover, popular mobilization had economic, political, and cultural motivations. Part of the reason for this difference in movement outcome across time periods, of course, may be that more fully democratic regimes attempted the liberal reforms. Still, by overly focusing on the state, Mahoney also misses that popular mobilization in Central America mixed demands for protection from markets with demands for democratization. People wanted democracy in order to obtain more economic and social justice.

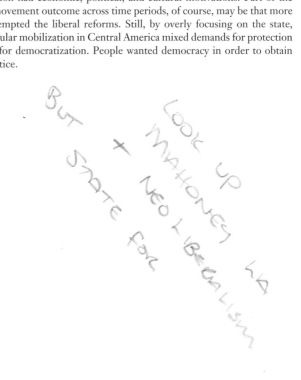

2

Contentious Politics, Contemporary Market Society, and Power

As seen in the previous chapter, a rich literature on new social movements, subaltern groups, and labor and peasant studies shows that movement and protest had not disappeared during Latin America's neoliberal era. These included new social movements (indigenous, environmental, and gender); breakaway, traditional, and new labor movements; and self-help and civic associations (urban services, human rights, democratization). Although they frequently directed action against free-market reforms, this literature emphasized the distinctiveness, fragmentation, and decentralization of movement. What, then, transformed protest by individual movements – frequently localized– into a nationwide concatenation of diverse social actors demanding change on a wide variety of connected issues? What gave them the capacity to force presidents who supported neoliberalism to resign and catapult into office presidents promising to reform neoliberalism?

Part I: Episodes of Contention and Motivation for Anti-Neoliberal Protest

Answering the first question requires, in the first instance, flexible concepts capable of reducing the diversity of protest groups to common denominators. A key common denominator was the fact that the myriad social actors engaged in *contentious politics*. Their actions were episodic (discontinuous) public challenges to government by politically constituted social actors, who, when successful, affected the interests of opposing social groups and established authority (McAdam, Tarrow, and Tilly 2001; Tarrow 1998; Tilly 2004). Equally important, in addition to studying movement formation, this approach draws attention to the grievances and demands of protest groups. It is a small step from here to investigate what those grievances and demands might have in common and how they contribute to building horizontal linkages among diverse popular sector organizations.

Protest events also need to be bundled for descriptive purposes in order to follow changing relationships among diverse participants over time and to establish their political significance. To this end, the boundaries of related protest events can be conceptualized as episodes of contention. Episodes of contention

14

organize protest events over time into meaningful streams with a focus on the transformation of relatively isolated or self-contained early streams of protest into ever-stronger rivers of mobilization as organizations coordinate action on the basis of related collective claims. Episodes of contention may contain distinctive waves (or cycles) of contention. These are surges and ebbs of mobilization around similar grievances (McAdam, Tarrow, and Tilly 2001; Tarrow 1998; Tilly 2004).[1]

Based on these concepts, popular mobilization in Argentina, Bolivia, Ecuador, and Venezuela between 1984 and 2002 can be conceptualized as episodes of resistance to neoliberalism. These involved sustained, albeit rising and ebbing, streams of contention built on collective claims opposing neoliberal economic, political, and social reforms perceived to benefit upper and middle classes allied to transnational economic and political interests. The anti-neoliberal character of contentious action from the mid-1980s to 2002 (and beyond) distinguishes these episodes of mobilization from previous ones.[2] The period spans the initiation of neoliberal reforms to the fall of avowedly pro-neoliberal governments and the at least partial defeat of the political forces that backed them more or less unconditionally, the latter generally marked by the victory in presidential elections of candidates who, once in office, stuck to their mandate to reform neoliberalism (even if only slightly).

The process was not linear. It usually involved several waves of contention. In the earlier waves, declining established labor movements tended to spearhead mobilization against specific economic reforms. Over time, newer social movements took over leadership roles as the traditional labor movement waned. Earlier challenges to neoliberalism usually consisted of parallel streams of contention over wages, prices, employment, land, ethnic rights, democratization (with special emphasis on popular sector participation), quality of life, and corruption in public office. In later waves of contention, these parallel streams began to connect and new political parties frequently made common cause with them. Claim making eventually evolved to demands for higher levels of state involvement in the economy, more welfare, and deepening citizen participation in democratic processes, thus taking on decidedly leftist characteristics, given the emphasis on socialization and planning. Yet, although the rhetoric might have been inflammatory, even revolutionary, at their more pragmatic core demands were calls for the

---

[1] For the related, but less flexible, concept of cycles of contention, see Tarrow (1998).

[2] Movements in the late 1970s and early 1980s focused principally on political change from authoritarianism to democracy. Mobilization under national populism sought to expand decommodification on specific issues, such as labor code, housing, land reform, and social insurance; or protested sporadic IMF-sponsored stabilization programs. Last, but not least, anti-neoliberal episodes of contention differ from the waves of contention that follow them. Once governments and political forces more committed to decommodification in the form of planning and socialization gained political power, contentious politics reflected the backlash of social sectors and political forces that support less state intervention in markets, as evidenced in Venezuela and Bolivia (Starr 2007).

15

reform of neoliberal capitalism, not the replacement of capitalism as such. Nor, as sympathizers lamented, did those demands constitute fully formed coherent national projects.

In summary, the concept of contentious politics offers a flexible tool that permits a shift in focus to the common denominators of diverse movements, protest groups, actions, and objectives. Episodes of contention, and waves within them, organize protest events, conceived as contentious action, for descriptive purposes over time. They map what happened, identify significant social actors and grievances, track when they appear, clarify their relationships to each other, and establish the political significance of protest.

Having laid this foundation, we turn to the first of several factors that explain these episodes of anti-neoliberal mobilization. It addresses the issue of *motive*, the conditions that generated grievances. What was it about neoliberalism that drove people to mobilize and that facilitated the linkage of different streams of contention into escalating cycles?[3] Those streams included socioeconomic grievances against free-market economic reforms; ethnic and cultural rights crystallizing into demands for plurinational societies and some degree of ethnic autonomy; and political claims for greater participation in democratic decision making and less corruption in politics.

Contemporary Market Society and Popular Mobilization in Latin America

A quarter century of wide-ranging neoliberal economic, social, and political reforms added up to a sweeping, ambitious project for a new order; a neoliberal order in which free-market principles provided the maxims to which economic *and* political social action must conform.[4] The attempt to construct this order was a necessary condition for the eruption of episodes of leftist anti-neoliberal popular mobilization that shook Argentina, Bolivia, Ecuador, and Venezuela. Its all-encompassing nature generated the myriad economic, sociocultural, and political grievances that drove separate streams of mobilization. Thus many different types of protest movements were, each in their own way, anti-neoliberal. The fact that grievances and demands could be traced back to a common point – the neoliberal reform project – facilitated the articulation of horizontal linkages among initially decentralized protest movements and thus the merger of parallel streams of contention. What then was the logic of the order neoliberal reforms

---

[3] Although studies exist that examine the relationship between neoliberalism and popular mobilization, they have not theorized what it is about neoliberalism that brings so many different streams of protest together. They tend to be case studies (in edited volumes, journals, and monographs), descriptive, or more concerned about their potential as a revolutionary vanguard: see Bretón (2003); Zamosc (2003); Albó (2004); López Maya (1999c); Lind (2004); Petras and Veltmeyer (2005).

[4] Weber (1978: 31–32) defined order as uniformity of social action in conformity with a set of prescriptions or maxims.

attempted to build? How did it provide a common point of origin for the myriad grievances that animated and connected distinctive protest movements?

The drive to subordinate economic, political, and social organization to market principles since the mid-1980s revived interest in Karl Polanyi's concept of market society and the double movement of capitalist society (Almeida 2007; Block 2003; Munck 2002; Polanyi 2001; Stiglitz 2001; Topik 2001). His analysis of the world's initial experiment with free-market capitalism in the "long" 19th century, and his legitimation of resistance to it, resonates deeply with our time. Polanyi argued that the construction of market society – a *specific* type of capitalism – generated its own opposition. Market society was a form of utopian capitalism that attempted to submit *all* social relations expressed in capital, land, and labor to market principles of exchange and efficiency in the interest of production and profit.[5] It also organized political and social institutions to support the free-market self-regulating economy. Liberal political regimes structured state institutions and oriented policy to enforce private property rights, free trade, and stable money and foreign exchange rates to the virtual exclusion of other values clustered around concepts of welfare and socioeconomic egalitarianism. Thus the state also ensured that labor markets and social insurance schemes remained free of distortions that impeded flexibility and economy efficiency.

Polanyi (2001) claimed that market society could not be the foundation for a stable and just social order. It created social tensions that inevitably led individuals and society to seek protection from the market's destructive power because market society sought to reduce humans to one dimension: that of commodities. The commodification of labor and land, however, was fictitious. Because they involve social relations, labor and land are more than things to be bought and sold: People by definition are not things and land structures an entire way of life. The attempt to reduce them solely to (fictitious) commodities disrupts the ability of people to fulfill vital needs, such as personal and family economic stability, maintenance of status in the community, fulfillment of a sense of justice, not to mention physical survival. Hence people inevitably seek to protect themselves from the impersonal, unpredictable, ever-changing, and frequently destructive powers of the market.

From the logic of these relationships, Polanyi theorized the double movement of capitalist society in which the construction of market society necessarily generated a protectionist countermovement within society. All manner of social

---

[5] A lively debate exists over Polanyi's stress on exchange instead of production to analyze the dynamics of capitalism (Block and Somers 1984). I am less concerned with which circuits of capital have primacy and more interested in their implications for the rise of contentious politics capable of reforming neoliberalism. As industrial labor declines, conditions of exchange and their consequences for peoples' lives loom large not only as sources that nurture new collective identities (and therefore popular sector actors), grievances, and demand greater relevancy. Exchange, to a significant extent, has also replaced the industrial workplace as the primary node of transgressive and disruptive action. One example is the roadblock to breakdown commerce and to starve major cities, thereby forcing the powers that be to pay attention.

groups seek state support to insulate them from market forces, including industrialists, landowners, middle classes, workers, and, of course farmers and peasants. Some do so within established institutions and structures of power. Others mobilize and more or less violently protest against commodification. From the perspective of the mid-1940s, he argued that the historical result of protectionist countermovements to market society during the 1800s and 1900s were fascism, communism, or social democracy, passing through worldwide economic collapse and war.

It bears repeating that "market society" refers to a *specific* form of capitalism. Society was an all-encompassing concept for Polanyi composed of the sum of economic, political, and cultural relations among human beings that order life, provide livelihood and physical well-being, and give it meaning. Thus, for Polanyi, the enormity, and ultimately unworkable utopia, of the liberal project lay in its attempt to reduce social relations in all of these spheres – that is, the totality of human interaction – to the logic of the self-regulating free-market economy (Block and Somers 1984). Polanyi (2001) leaves little doubt that other forms of capitalism, such as social democracy and its variants might be more stable. Masses and socioeconomic elites alike would be less inclined to politically destabilizing mobilization because decommodifying "distortions" to the market would be considered legitimate and necessary policy instruments for a healthy, viable, society – understood as the web of social relations in which people must live. In this sense, Polanyi's framework fits well with the contemporary debate over "varieties" of capitalism and the differences in how they structure relations among the state, capital, and labor – some decommodify more than others (Esping-Andersen 1990; Huber 2002).

Twenty-five years of free-market oriented economic, social, and political reforms in Latin America attempted to construct an order sufficiently similar to Polanyi's market society to hypothesize that the effort generated the dynamics he theorized.[6] Neoliberal reforms sought to subordinate political and social structures to the principles of the self-regulating free-market economy. Thus the attempt to build a contemporary version of market society generated the waves of contentious politics that swept Argentina, Bolivia, Ecuador, and Venezuela and that brought down governments that supported neoliberal order. Those waves of contention were Polanyian defensive reactions to the imposition of market society or the threat of doing so. Because the construction of market society involved reforming economic, political, and social relationships, neoliberal reforms bred

---

[6] Topick (1999) and Almeida (2007) also argued that neoliberalism in Latin America amounted to the construction of market society. Topik argued that it was not a "natural" phenomenon; the state played an important role in creating it. Almeida argued the threat of its imposition generated defensive mobilization, but did not test the proposition. Latin American studies have also shown an interest in applying Polanyi's double movement to uncovering transnational countermovements; see Munck (2007, 2002); Almeida and Johnston (2006). For transnational movements and globalization in general, see Tarrow (2005).

grievances radiating from all three sources. This gave diverse types of protest groups, grievances, and demands their anti-neoliberal character; their origins all lay in the consequences of the neoliberal project. Moreover, although they may have started out as separate streams of contentious politics, depending on additional conditions examined in the next chapter, their common origin provided a mechanism for linking them.

Efforts to construct contemporary market society required dismantling institutions that decommodified social relations. In Latin America, that meant restructuring the national-populist order of the mid 20th century, which itself was a reaction to the original experiment with market society in the region during the long 19th century. For the popular sectors (and for some middle classes too, especially lower-middle classes), this shift affected their degree of *inclusion* or *exclusion* from more equitable and just distribution of life chances than their situation in the market alone permitted.[7] Their opportunities for improved livelihood and access to a more equitable share of the nation's wealth depended on those institutions (Cardoso and Faletto 1979; Yashar 2005). Hence mobilization almost always rallied around defense of those institutions, such as worker-friendly labor policy, subsidies to basic goods and services, efforts to promote social welfare (health, education, housing, urban services, pensions), peasant-friendly (in principle) land reform, and state industrial, employment, and credit policies.

The national-populist period also set benchmarks for the political inclusion of popular sectors that therefore defended their interpretation of those rights and the promise of their expansion. These structured the intermediation between state and society, often in corporatist forms, such as the creation of special bureaus and agencies in ministries and state enterprises to which popular sector and middle-class organizations had rights to representation. These rights were also sources of organizational and political power and existed alongside formal inclusion in strong labor parties or semiformal linkages to labor-friendly parties (Murillo 2001; Roberts 1998; Yashar 2005).

In sum, the defense of the principles and promises of economic, social, and political inclusion is central to understanding contemporary episodes of anti-neoliberal contention. Hence a brief examination of national populism's central characteristics follows. Part I concludes with a specification of how the gamut of neoliberal reforms amounted to the construction of a contemporary version of market society.

National Populism, the State, and Decommodification

Neoliberal reforms transformed the national-populist development model based on import substitution, labor rights, and the welfare state. National populism

---

[7] For the role of inclusion and exclusion in mobilization, see Goodwin (2001); Huber (2005); Silver (2003).

had been Latin America's response to the calamitous failure of free-market capitalism during the great crisis of the 1930s; it was Latin America's version of the Keynesian welfare state and social democracy in the developed world (Cardoso and Faletto 1979). Among other things, then, it sought to partially decommodify labor and land through socialization.

The economic and social policies of the national-populist period broke with the free-market economic orthodoxy of the long 19th century, and the state took on a central role in national development. Suspicious of the bounties of the market, national populists used the state to regulate it, direct it, and partly substitute for it. Import substitution industrialization (ISI) replaced commodity exports as the engine of economic growth.[8] ISI relied on state-led efforts to construct basic industries, develop infrastructure, and build domestic manufacturing behind high protective barriers to trade, subsidies, and restrictions on capital mobility. Distrustful of the foreign sector and domestic elites that prospered along with them ("oligarchs"), they focused on national development and social integration of the popular sector [el pueblo or sector popular].[9] Under national populism public enterprise created employment for blue- and white-collar employees and political leaders recast labor relations more in organized labor's favor (Thorp 1998). These measures expanded the formal sector of employment – that which received contracts and benefits, including protection under the labor code and paid taxes. National populists also constructed a Latin American version of first world welfare states (social security and health), which involved redistributive economic policies (Mesa-Lago 1978). Significant subsidies to basic food items (including cooking oil), energy costs (gasoline), utilities (water and electricity), housing, and transportation (bus fares) complemented that "welfare

---

[8] The degree to which countries adopted various components of this "model" varied (Bulmer-Thomas 2003). The Latin American Six (LA-6) – Argentina, Brazil, Chile, Colombia, Mexico, and Uruguay – began in the 1930s and implemented the full range of policies previously described earlier than other nations, especially industrialization. Already possessing significant industry, ISI replaced commodity exports as the primary "engine of economic growth" by the 1950s. The central Andean countries – Bolivia, Ecuador, Peru – and Venezuela (along with Paraguay and Central America) continued with a commodity export-led growth model until the 1950s and 1960s. After that, they switched to ISI but never achieved the depth of industrialization of the LA-6. By the 1960s and 1970s, all of the South American countries covered in this book had embraced ISI, expanded labor rights, introduced basic welfare institutions, and managed a system of subsidies to basic consumer items.

[9] The popular sectors refer mainly to urban subaltern social groups – many the product of rural–urban migration – many of whom do not fit easily into the developed world's ideals of civilized order. They are the urban squatters, the masses laboring in the informal sector. However, they also encompass formal sector blue-collar workers and low-level clerks who people working-class neighborhoods. The popular sectors' cultural values draw heavily on folkways and "primitive" art forms in music, dancing, painting, weaving, storytelling, and crafts. Their relationship to authority is frequently deferential and permeated by an acceptance of patron–client relationships. The concept deliberately emphasizes a nonclass approach to identity and solidarity, one more amorphous, malleable, and inclusive; see Conniff (1982: 20–21) and Drake (1978: 10–11).

state."[10] It must be stressed, however, that national populism was quintessentially reformist, not revolutionary Marxist (Conniff 1982). Latin American economies and societies remained capitalist, although not laissez faire.

ISI notoriously discriminated against agriculture. The bulk of credit went to industry, and governments supported low food prices for urban constituencies. Not only that, but resources in the agricultural sector disproportionately benefited large-scale domestic or internationally owned capitalist enterprises (Long and Roberts 1994). Still, peasants and indigenous communities did not go completely begging. Land reform from the 1950s to the 1970s offered economic and social rights to significant swaths of indigenous and mestizo peasant communities producing traditional foods for domestic markets (Yashar 2005). Economic rights included more secure land tenure either for individuals or for communities (especially for indigenous), access to subsidized credit and technical help, and state support for infrastructure development (roads, electrification, and irrigation). Social rights centered on the right to organize and, occasionally, on efforts to improve health and education. Although state support for agrarian reform programs dwindled after their inception, they nevertheless created political and legal rights to struggle for improvement (de Janvry 1981; Kay 1999; Kay and Silva 1992).[11]

In short, the national-populist period applied a wide array of mechanisms to protect individuals and communities from the full force of the market. In urban areas, employment in the formal sector (much of it in the public sector) with labor rights and benefits, expanded public health, education, housing, and subsidies for basic consumption constituted elements of decommodification for the popular sector and middle classes (Cook 2007; Drake 1996). In the countryside, although land reform fell far short of its promise for the peasant sector, it created legally protected organizational capacity, a legal framework to struggle for rural labor and land tenure rights, and subsidized credit to partially insulate that sector from markets. Land security as the centerpiece for subsistence and for organizing community life was a key decommodifying instrument for peasants and indigenous communities. Moreover, state subsidies for transportation and energy costs helped the rural as well as the urban population (Kay and Silva 1992). All of these mechanisms were integral parts of the social compacts on which people depended to maintain their livelihood.

---

[10] Additional sources for these aspects of national populism include Cardoso and Faletto (1979); Thorp (1998); Bulmer-Thomas (2003); Conniff (1982); Prebisch (1970); Hirschman (1971); Furtado (1976); and Weaver (2000).

[11] To be sure, the development and expansion of capitalist agriculture, and thus the reduction of inefficient, undercapitalized traditional hacienda-based agriculture, expanded the proletarianization of peasants and rural–urban migration. Nevertheless, throughout this period, peasant forms of production and livelihood strategies remained widespread. Whether they owned or rented, land remained *central* to their survival and identity. Households and communities clung to land for subsistence agriculture, sale of surplus, and complemented these activities with wage income or small-scale commerce (Long and Roberts 1994).

National populism was promiscuous with respect to regime type. It flourished under democratic and military regimes alike, although the former outnumbered the latter.[12] Regardless of regime type, however, national populists emphasized state planning to develop mixed economies and socialization to include the popular sectors in the fruits of development. Given the greater role of the government in development, national populism also stimulated state expansion and centralization. State development corporations planned and financed industrial development (Haber 2006; Furtado 1976). The state also owned and managed complex economic enterprises in mining, communications, infrastructure, basic industry, and large-scale manufacturing firms and agribusiness. The development corporations and specialized state credit agencies also planned and stimulated agricultural development. This affected rural employment, much of it in the public sector, at the local, regional, and national levels (Long and Roberts 1994). State pension and unemployment insurance funds, along with a myriad of subsidy-dispensing agencies also flourished.

For all of its efforts to spearhead industrialization with inclusion of the popular sectors, the national-populist development model suffered from serious problems. Social inclusion, in the main, reached no further than an expanding middle class and the labor "aristocracy" protected by unions in the formal sector (with great numbers employed by the state) and connected to labor parties or otherwise mobilized by the state. A heavy bias toward urban areas existed (Prebisch 1970). Thus a swelling mass of city and rural marginalized poor labored under much more exploitative ("decommodified") conditions. Moreover, states by and large lacked the capacity to coordinate and implement ambitious development plans, although there were "pockets of efficiency" (Kingstone 1999; Montero 2001). ISI did not produce vibrant, internationally competitive domestic manufacturing industries. It did contribute to recurring balance of trade and foreign exchange crises and a host of other market distortions. These, along with social spending and state employment, caused fiscal crises that required International Monetary Fund (IMF)-sponsored stabilization programs (Stallings 1978; Thorp 1998; Weaver 2000).

Nevertheless, and without wishing to minimize the problems of national populism or their scale, the period remains the benchmark by which to measure contemporary achievements. For all of the difficulties, sustained gross domestic product (GDP) growth rates were higher, as were levels of industrialization, development of state institutions, formal employment (with benefits and tax paying), urban and rural labor rights, welfare, government spending on health and education, and concern for peasants and rural workers (Huber 2005; Kay and Silva 1992; Thorp 1998). The problem turned on *extending* social rights and *reforming*

---

[12] "Progressive" military governments implemented national populism in Ecuador and Peru during the late 1960s and 1970s right down to the socioeconomic inclusion of popular sectors (notably land reform and support for labor rights).

inward-looking development to stimulate export-led growth; for it was widely recognized that import suppression was not tenable and that formal employment and social safety nets needed to reach more of the popular sectors (Prebisch 1970).[13]

The decline and ultimate collapse of the national-populist development model spanned two decades from the 1960s to the early 1980s. Leftist and conservative polarization over the extension of state planning and socialization in Argentina, Brazil, Chile, and Uruguay during the 1960s and 1970s caused severe political and economic dislocations that ushered in brutal military dictatorships. These regimes sought to *eliminate* social rights and to *replace* state-led development with the market. In most countries, reform of ISI, welfare policies, and human capital development systems came slowly or not at all. Many tried to borrow their way out of trouble during the second half of the 1970s and early 1980s, a period of high international financial liquidity. International economic and financial crisis in the early 1980s – which precipitated the Latin American debt crisis – forced economic adjustment that paved the way for a concerted program of free-market economic reforms that dismantled national-populist institutions.[14]

Recommodification: Contemporary Market Society

The crisis of national populism and authoritarianism unleashed twin processes of free-market economic reforms and democratization that were attempts to construct a contemporary version of market society. They sought to reorganize economic relations on neoclassical economic principles and to restructure political and social institutions to support free-market capitalism. They attempted to *recommodify* capital, labor, and land (which necessitated drawing the teeth from organized urban and rural social groups). State restructuring ("modernization") and a turn to private social insurance structures reinforced commodification. The market, through the price system, would determine the allocation of capital, labor, and land. Politics (the state and representative systems) and social insurance schemes, ideally, should be restructured so as not to interfere with the market or, at worst, interfere only minimally. Needless to say, the construction of contemporary market society by means of neoliberal economic, social, and political reforms necessitated the rollback of the nonmarket principles that underpinned the national-populist order.[15]

Although the timing, sequencing, and intensity of application varied across cases, in general neoliberal economic restructuring involved stabilization policies and "first stage" structural reforms (Edwards 1995; Haggard and Kaufman

---

[13] For the politics of reforming ISI to stimulate export growth, see Haggard (1990).

[14] For the political economy of the fall of ISI and the Latin American debt crisis, see O'Donnell (1973); Collier (1979); Foxley (1983); Frieden (1991); Stallings and Kaufman (1989).

[15] Overviews of Latin America's "Great Transformation" include Haggard and Kaufman (1995) and Williamson (1993, 1990).

1995). Stabilization policies addressed deep fiscal crises, severe problems in the balance of payments, and hyperinflation. Following monetarist neoclassical economic theory, policy prescriptions emphasized balanced budgets, restrictive monetary (high interest rates) and fiscal policies (slashing government expenditures by shedding workers and programs), and stable unitary foreign exchange rates. This forced immediate retrenchment of state commitments to economic development (industrial policy, public works, and credit for rural development and the cooperative movement), ended attempts to create the Latin American equivalent to full employment policies and the welfare state, generated sharp reductions in government spending for health, education, and pension plans, and eliminated or deeply cut the myriad subsidies that supplemented income for middle and popular sectors (Solimano, Aninat, and Birdsall 2000).

These measures aimed to reestablish monetary stability, that is, to control inflation and to generate savings to pay back international creditors. They sought to eliminate politically generated market distortions such as state industrial policy, price controls, negotiated wages, and subsidies to all manner of social groups including labor and peasants. They were also a first step toward the recommodification of labor and land because they dismantled or weakened institutions and bargaining mechanisms that protected people, especially the popular sectors and the middle classes, from the market (Bates and Krueger 1993; Foxley 1983).

First stage structural reforms in Latin America concentrated on economic liberalization in finance and investment, trade, and agriculture, with an emphasis on foreign private investment and privatization of public enterprise. These reforms got the state out of the business of directing and regulating banking, credit, and other financial transactions and turned them over to a deregulated private sector. This freed the price system to allocate resources more efficiently. Privatization reduced fiscal pressure on the state and returned assets to the private sector, which, it was assumed, would manage them more effectively. Trade liberalization removed many of the distortions that had discriminated against more dynamic and less fiscally taxing export-led economic growth, while foreign investors replaced the state as the major and more reliable sources of development finance (Edwards 1995; Taylor 1999; Williamson and Kuczynski 2003). These policies eliminated the national populist state's capacity to plan and direct economic development and to influence formal sector employment (Tokman and O'Donnell 1998). The market, actually domestic and international conglomerates, took over those functions (Silva 2002). Meanwhile, labor code reforms emphasizing flex labor and privatization of state companies weakened unions, further commodifying workers (Cook 2007; Drake 1996).

Second stage neoliberal reforms restructured social sector institutions along market principles in health care, education, pensions, and social assistance programs. Policy emphasized privatization of services, decentralization, and means-tested as opposed to universal coverage, all of which shifted risk management on individuals. Downsized, restructured public systems, at best, focused on delivery of basic social services to the poor by targeting pockets of poverty, and with special poverty alleviation (safety net) programs (Abel and Lewis 2002; Gerstenfeld 2002; Graham 2000; Grindle 2000; Huber and Solt 2004; Madrid 2003; Raczynski 1998; Tokman and O'Donnell 1998). This redressed national populism's bias toward middle classes and a labor "aristocracy."

Latin American countries varied greatly with respect to their timing in undertaking these policies, which ones they pursued, and the degree to which they implemented them. Early reformers included Chile, Argentina, and Uruguay in the second half of the 1970s. For most countries, the debt crisis of the 1980s serves as a common starting point, beginning with fiscal stabilization policies. Moreover, not all countries adopted neoliberal economic reforms with equal zeal. Chile proved a radical neoliberal reformer from the beginning, followed by Mexico and Bolivia in the mid-1980s, and joined by Argentina and Peru in the early 1990s. By contrast, Ecuador, Venezuela, Uruguay, Colombia, and Brazil followed more cautious, stop–start routes in the 1990s. In all cases, however, the push was on to replace the state with the private sector on investment, employment, and welfare decisions (Haggard and Kaufman 1995; Weyland 2002).

The consolidation of liberal democracy and reform of state institutions were the political corollary to neoliberal economic reforms. Liberal democracy in Latin America entailed small government structured to support the neoliberal economic and social agenda, especially the protection of private property rights. Consensus among political elites of the necessity for neoliberal reforms meant that redistributive issues and a larger role for the state in economic and social development were simply off the policy agenda (Diamond and Plattner 1995; O'Donnell and Schmitter 1986; O'Donnell, Schmitter, and Whitehead 1986; Pereira, Maravall, and Przeworski 1993). In contrast, security for private property rights – especially against nationalization – and monetary stability received first priority. Thus the institutional capacity of finance ministries and central banks expanded, and, with few exceptions, most other economic line ministries and government agencies became subordinate to them. Meanwhile, most state institutions lost funding, fired personnel, bled remaining qualified professionals because of uncompetitive public sector salaries, and had their missions drastically redefined (usually through deregulation, privatization, or both) so as to interfere as little as possible with private sector activity. As a result, they often lacked the resources to carry out their responsibilities. Regulatory procedures were frequently redesigned on business model customer service lines that emphasized voluntary compliance to relieve pressure on the agency and the user alike (Schneider and Heredia 2003).

Having abdicated a positive role of the state for advancing substantive rights and for directing development, liberal democracy emphasized procedural processes and rights for free and fair elections. These covered competition for elected office, participation in elections, civil liberties to guarantee effective competition and participation, and universal citizen rights.[16] Who was elected to office, however, should not affect neoliberal economic and social policy. It was expected that responsible political leaders recognized these as the only path to sustained economic development.[17]

Exclusion, Grievances, and Demands

If episodes of anti-neoliberal contention in Argentina, Bolivia, Ecuador, and Venezuela were protective reactions to the construction of contemporary market society, grievances and demands should be linked to the commodification inherent in the dismantlement of national populism. Beverley Silver (2003) offers a useful entry point to uncover those linkages. If the expansion of self-regulating market capitalism destroyed the social institutions that sustained livelihoods, and if people affected by this process, which they experience as *exclusion* and *injustice*, naturally seek defenses against it, then Polanyi-type mobilization should involve "backlash resistances to the spread of a global self-regulating market" either because livelihoods disappear through underemployment and unemployment or because governments abandoned the established social compacts on which people depended to maintain their livelihood or both.[18]

Thus efforts to construct contemporary market society contributed to defensive mass mobilization because the commodification inherent in the process created significant economic, social, and political exclusion, which people perceive as an injustice. Because neoliberal reforms affect all major forms of social organization, a great variety of subordinate social groups mobilized to defend against threats from one or more neoliberal policies. Their demands flowed directly from their grievances.

A growing literature on the effects of neoliberalism shows that economic reforms created significant economic and social exclusion, causing negative changes in class situation for urban and rural labor and the middle classes (Huber and Solt 2004; Wood and Roberts 2005).[19] The literature established strong positive correlations between high levels of socioeconomic exclusion (as compared

---

[16] For citizen rights, see Yashar (2005); Foweraker (2005); and Roberts (2005).

[17] For introductions to the vast literature on democracy and democratization, see O'Donnell, Schmitter, and Whitehead (1986); Przeworski (1995, 1991); Dóminguez and Lowenthal (1996); Mainwaring, O'Donnell, and Valenzuela (1992); Linz and Stepan (1996); Diamond (1999); Di Palma (1990); Hagopian and Mainwaring (2005).

[18] This brings Silver (2003) close to the moral economy arguments of Scott (1976). Almeida (2007) made similar arguments for Latin America.

[19] As nations reintegrated into the world economy based on a primary product export-led development strategy, and in the midst of rapid deindustrialization, economic concentration led by conglomerates stunted formal sector employment. In a deregulated business environment economic volatility – rapid climbs and falls of GDP – flourished. Privatized services (health, education, pensions) became more expensive and their markets segmented in favor of upper-income levels. Land markets thrived for capitalized agriculture turning peasants into workers at a faster pace than before as they lost the little land they had at higher rates than before. Mestizo and indigenous peasant communities faced disintegration.

with the national-populist period) and mobilization. A dramatic transformation in the labor market was a key indicator of exclusion under neoliberalism. The informal sector of labor exploded because of privatization, deindustrialization, the downsizing of state agencies and services in the interest of fiscal restraint, an emphasis on agricultural commodities, and, very significantly, an antiunion and strong pro-flexible labor posture (Fernández-Kelly and Shefner 2006; Pérez Sáins 2005). Precarious working conditions, self-employment in low level service jobs and commerce, poor and unstable earnings, no benefits, and no tax contributions characterize this sector. Moreover, open unemployment rates in many cases remained persistently high compared with those of the national-populist period, while income concentration increased, as, in most cases, did poverty. Improvements in average real wages in some cases, such as Bolivia, did not diminish the sense of exclusion, because a shrinking proportion of the economically active population earned them. Wages in the expanding informal sector were usually well below that average. The cost of everything rose with devaluation and deregulation of price controls. Land tenure for small holders became more insecure, as did farming conditions. Last, rising concentrations of income and land were corollaries of the neoliberal development model (Abel and Lewis 2002; Stallings and Peres 2000; Tokman and O'Donnell 1998).

The grievances and demands of popular sector and some middle-class movements in Argentina, Bolivia, Ecuador, and Venezuela support the argument that they were Polanyi-like defensive reactions to contemporary attempts to recreate market society. They exhibit strong links to the indicators of exclusion previously discussed and they seek to decommodify economic and social life. Demonstrators protested privatization of public enterprises and flex-labor policies that pushed formal sector workers into the ranks of informal labor. They demanded state support for full employment, including public sector employment. They sought to stem the collapse of state support for social insurance, health, education, and employment. Claims for just wage and salary adjustments, usually by public sector employees (including teachers and health care providers, often doctors) abounded. Demonstrators and movement organizations repudiated ideological commitments to strict private property rights, demanding more active involvement of the state in the economy either through (re)nationalization, implementing some semblance of industrial policy, or a greater commitment to welfare. Peasants insisted on state support for land reform. Land hunger, as always, was an issue. But so was the provision of adequate credit, infrastructure, and price protection. In the Andean countries these postures intersected with indigenous peoples' claims for ethnic rights and forms of autonomy, all the while sharing, supporting, and pushing for the same economic demands of nonindigenous popular sectors. Cuts in the myriad subsidies to popular sector consumption were frequent and significant sources of grievances, leading to demands for their restitution. Hence many protests called for the reinstatement of food, fuel, transportation, and housing subsidies in addition to price controls.

In other words, protest movements and organizations demanded greater state involvement in planning and socialization, albeit within the context of a capitalist economy, which also gave them their reformist rather than revolutionary socialist character. Claimants focused on reestablishing economic nationalism and the mixed economy. State intervention in the domestic economy would help protect popular sector and middle-class livelihoods that depended on labor and land. Economic nationalism, state intervention, and planning would also buffer against the rapacious appetite of international capital, ensuring that more of the nation's savings would be available for domestic needs. Those needs included greater policy emphasis on social equity, on protecting people from the market when they cannot work (social insurance including health), protecting workers with more labor-friendly labor codes, supplementing incomes for low socioeconomic strata, and investment in education and health services to support social mobility.

The construction of contemporary market society in Latin America also involved attempts to subordinate politics (the state) and most other forms of social interaction (society) to market principles. Consequently, subaltern social groups in Argentina, Bolivia, Ecuador, and Venezuela also suffered from political exclusion as liberal democracies consolidated. The literature on democratization offers substantial evidence that, to varying degrees, liberal democracy stripped them of institutional channels to press their demands in both the executive and the legislative branches of the state, thus effectively cutting them out of the policy-making process. Mechanisms involved extensive use of executive decrees, legislative abdication by granting extraordinary powers to the executive, and consensus among major political parties (including those purportedly representing popular sectors) on the need for neoliberal economic reforms (Carey and Shugart 1998; O'Donnell 1996). Not only that, but presidential administrations and their party supporters consistently, arrogantly dismissed the legitimacy of popular sector (and some middle-class) grievances, claims, and demands. These mechanisms replicated themselves at lower levels of government, such as provinces and municipalities.

Given the widespread political exclusion of popular sector and some middle-class social groups, Polanyi-like demands for protection need not focus on economic claims exclusively (Silver 2003: 18–20; Wolf 1999: 282). In their attempt to maintain or restore livelihoods, status, and meaning to life, Polanyi-like anti-neoliberal contentious politics also included demands to protect, reinstate, or even suggest new political and sociocultural institutions for the inclusion of their interests in policy formulation. These focused on abrogating rule by decree, insisting on legislative debates, building new political parties to undermine pro-neoliberal party consensus, curbing rampant political corruption that enriched office holders while popular sectors suffered worsening conditions,[20] and

---

[20] Corruption became a symbol of public sector betrayal of the popular sectors who were asked to sacrifice so much in the interest of the country's "modernization."

proposing constituent assemblies to install more participative democracy for popular sectors. Streams of anti-neoliberal contention also included protests demanding the resignation of presidents, ministers, governors, and mayors.

In the final analysis, political exclusion, understood at its most basic as the capacity of pro-neoliberal reform forces to ignore popular sector demands, was a powerful force behind the unification of streams of anti-neoliberal mobilization. As public officials denied them, delayed them, and betrayed them by negotiating and then reneging on concessions, movement leaders recognized they needed to band together to generate more power behind their protests.

Of course, grievances do not lead unproblematically to participation. To strengthen the connection, wherever sources permit, this book focuses on the link between grievances articulated by movement organizations and the perspectives of those participating in the mobilization. Given space and data limitations, I limit this aspect of the explanation (from grievances to protest) to key moments and countries.

There was, however, an area in which subaltern social groups, especially the indigenous, gender, and environmental movements, found more favorable grounds for claim making. Liberal democracy also emphasized procedural political and individual citizen rights. As long as they kept property issues off of their agendas, these groups found the liberal democratic state to be more inclusive toward their interests.[21] Favorable legislation, supportive state agencies, and accommodation to territorial and cultural claims by the indigenous resulted. New social movements used these opportunities to build and strengthen their organizations (Van Cott 2005; Yashar 2005). The same was true of neoliberal state deconcentration policies. These were efforts to devolve greater administration responsibility to units of local government; sometimes even accompanied by decentralization, which entailed the transfer of resources to local governments invested with greater decision-making power over how to allocate them.

Part II: Power in Episodes of Anti-Neoliberal Contention

Part I argued that attempts to construct a contemporary market society were a necessary condition for episodes of leftist anti-neoliberal contention in Argentina, Bolivia, Ecuador, and Venezuela; meaning the emergence of mass mobilization capable of toppling pro-neoliberal governments and, eventually, contributing to their replacement with administrations seeking to reform it. But that does not account for the *capacity* of mobilized popular sectors and their middle-class allies

---

[21] Although social policy may have had some positive redistributive effects, these were too modest to offset the high levels of inequality in the region; see Stallings and Peres (2000:150). Hence I assume that possible improvements in social sector delivery and expenditures were too slight to offset the exclusionary characteristics of neoliberal economic and labor policies. Because this cancels their potential effect, I focus on economic and political exclusion and their consequences for Polanyi-like defensive reactions.

to achieve that outcome. A relational approach to power offers a useful first cut into this problem. The "power of movement" in these cases depended a great deal on (1) the power of the forces constructing contemporary market society and (2) the creation of horizontal linkages among many different movements and protest organizations. Thus it was not just that popular sectors mobilized resources.[22] It was also that, over time, a shift in power relations between pro-neoliberal forces and subordinate social groups diminished the capability of the former to control or isolate the latter.

This perspective requires an account of the power resources pro-neoliberal forces relied on to implement neoliberal reforms. These power resources enforced the exclusion of popular sector concerns from the policy agenda, which contributed to the disarticulation of popular sector and some middle-class movements (especially among state employees), and thus neutralized the political impact of protest. Analysis can then turn to changes that weakened pro-neoliberal forces and created conditions that channeled the exclusion of popular sectors into new forms of organization and coordination, the main source of strength for subordinate social groups.

The relational approach to power draws attention to the fact that actors' capabilities depend, in part, on those of others and that actors are enmeshed in distinctive and overlapping-power networks. What might those power sources and networks be? This book examines society-wide events in the context of globalization. Thus it focuses on the shifting political, economic, transnational, ideological, and military power sources of contending actors (Gourevitch 1986; Mann 1993, 1986; Rueschemeyer, Stephens, and Stephens 1992).

These categories facilitate the construction of historically specific power arrangements. Four features of those power sources emerge as additional necessary conditions for episodes of anti-neoliberal contention in Argentina, Bolivia, Ecuador, and Venezuela at the turn of the 20th century and their absence in Peru and Chile. First, the presence or absence of adequate associational space for citizens to congregate publicly significantly affected political power.[23] On a continuum of political associational space, democratic regimes offer the greatest legally sanctioned opportunities for citizens to organize in pursuit of their interests. However, as the literature on democratization established, the political liberalization of authoritarian regimes also creates opportunities for mobilization (O'Donnell and Schmitter 1986).[24] Both regime forms, but especially liberal democracy, restrained the state's capacity for repression. Relative freedom to associate provided political space necessary for aggrieved social groups to build associational power (organizational capacity) and collective power (coalitional capacity). Thus democracy and, to a lesser degree, political liberalization

---

[22] For the original formulation of resource mobilization theory, see Tilly (1978).

[23] I borrow the concept of political associational space from Yashar (2005).

[24] Inclusionary or "populist" authoritarian regimes also offer associational space (Stepan 1978).

in authoritarian regimes complicated the exercise of political power for neoliberal forces and provided resources for mobilizing popular sectors. By contrast, the collapse of democratic regimes and imposition of conservative authoritarianism, the period of greatest repression, made it easier for neoliberal forces to impose their policies with impunity. Second, lackluster economic performance and outright economic crisis, compounded by international economic recessions, adversely affected the economic and political power of neoliberals and spurred popular sectors (and middle classes) to mobilize. Third, mobilizing forces applied ideological power by using cognitive and brokerage mechanisms to organize and to form alliances. A fourth additional necessary condition overlaps political, ideological, and economic power sources of mobilizing forces. It mattered a great deal whether they were reformist and resorted to a repertoire of contention that stopped short of armed violence or whether they sought to overturn capitalism and supported armed insurrection (Parsa 2000; Yashar 2005).

These considerations address two problems in Polanyi's (2001) work. First, he undertheorized power relations. Polanyi (2001) forcefully argued for the centrality of state power in the construction of market society, and his analysis indirectly drew on additional economic causes. Intra-dominant class squabbles among financial, manufacturing, and landowning elites over protection from market forces produced policy incoherence that adversely affected economic performance at the domestic and international system levels. Extreme hardship caused by international economic crisis that followed caused countermovements to market society that were either terrifying, such as fascism, or more benign, such as social democracy. Nevertheless, although his work alluded to these factors, it lacked a framework that articulated how state, economic, and transnational power sources affect structures of domination and generate mobilization. Second, Polanyi was not interested in specifying either the subordinate social groups that participated in the countermovement or the combination of factors that affected the dynamics of mobilization. They were simply masses that he assumed would rise up.

A relational approach to power built on overlapping power networks also contributes to solving problems in the contentious politics literature. It takes the focus off of movements exclusively and situates them in relation to other sociopolitical actors. Thus factors that appeared external to the movements, such as "political opportunity structures" (political institutions) or "environmental factors" (frequently economic and international variables) become integral components of an explanatory framework, instead of, in the worst cases, *deus ex machina* invoked to explain shifts in movement development. As the literature on contentious politics recognizes, it was difficult to specify what was included or excluded in those concepts (Campbell 2005; Goodwin 2001; McAdam, Tarrow, and Tilly 2001; Tarrow 1998). By contrast, a relational approach to power permits more systematic specification of those factors, their causal relationships, and their effects on protest movements and their opponents.

To take just one example, democracy is more than a political opportunity or an environmental factor strictly external to mobilizing groups and that provides favorable conditions for collective and contentious action. It conditions both the capabilities of dominant social forces and of excluded subordinate social forces engaging in contentious politics. It is integral to the fate of both. What mobilizing forces do and what they can accomplish is not independent of the action and resources of those that dominate them. Moreover, how democratic institutions condition capabilities and impact episodes of anti-neoliberal contention can be specified in ways that should hold across cases.

More recent studies in contentious politics, especially of rebellion and revolution, have focused on interactive relationships. They examine the impact of state actions on subordinate social groups with special attention to how state policy articulates the connection between political power and excluded subordinate social groups. States that respond to mobilization with actions (even small ones) and assurances of inclusion pull the teeth from mobilizing forces. States that respond with harsh repression and continued exclusion leave popular sector groups no way out but to escalate mobilization and, eventually, to turn to insurrection (Goldstone and Tilly 2001; Goodwin 2001; McAdam, Tarrow, and Tilly 2001; Parsa 2000).

This state-centric approach to contentious politics explains a great deal about the dynamic that drove challenges to neoliberalism in South America at the turn of the 20th century. However, it underplays the fact that the state is but one of several overlapping (or interconnected) power networks in society. What the state does or does not do, what it can or cannot accomplish, is also conditioned by what occurs in the economy, ideological trends, transnational forces, and, last but not least, its relationship to military power. Moreover, these same power sources also affect the relative capabilities of mobilizing forces. Thus, when state-centric approaches to contentious politics consider those factors (and they often do), they too are treated as externalities (or residual variables) to the main explanatory framework, for example as "environmental" factors that condition the direction of the main causal variables (state action). My approach builds on these insights, but it seeks to incorporate these different power sources solidly into the framework for explaining contemporary challenges to neoliberalism in Argentina, Bolivia, Ecuador, and Venezuela and their absence in Peru and Chile.[25]

To develop that framework, Part II of this chapter examines the concepts of political, economic, transnational, ideological, and military power sources. The discussion, necessarily static, specifies terms and relationships. The heart of explanation, of course, lies in the *mixture* of those factors in concrete cases and

---

[25] Foran (2005) has developed an explanation for third-world revolutions that includes diverse power sources and their interaction in the theoretical framework, and thus comes closer to the theoretical concerns of this book. However, the outcome he explains, social revolution, is significantly different from mine, reformist episodes of anti-neoliberal contention whose political goals stop significantly short of rebellion and social revolution. Thus we differ somewhat on key factors.

how their shifting relationships affected contentious politics that posed reformist challenges to neoliberalism in South America. Chapter 3, a full exposition of the argument, addresses these issues as a lead-in to the empirical chapters.

Power in Relations of Domination and Subordination

Political, economic, transnational, ideological, and military clusters of power engender the structural bases and resource capabilities upon which social order and domination rest (Gourevitch 1986; Haggard and Kaufman 1995; Mann 1993, 1986; Rueschemeyer, Stephens, and Stephens 1992).[26] As used here, order means uniformity of social action in conformity with a set of prescriptions or maxims. Domination refers to the probability that commands will be obeyed (Weber 1978: 31–32).[27] Reinforcing linkages between power clusters strengthen established order. Conflicting linkages loosen the bonds of social control, permitting mobilization in defiance of commands by authorities (Mann 1993, 1986). The concrete structures and institutions of these power clusters affect the *relative* capabilities of dominant and subordinate social forces.

Power most commonly refers to the capacity to make others do what they otherwise would not, to keep issues off the policy agenda, or ensure that people remain unaware that resistance is even an option (Bachrach and Baratz 1962; Dahl 1968; Lukes 1986). This definition emphasizes the distributional nature of power. It is a zero-sum game of head-to-head confrontations between opponents in which increases in the power of one side entails the diminution of the power of the other.

But power also has a *relational* dimension. A social actor may transcend his or her limitations in a head-to-head conflict with a more powerful opponent by collaborating with others who have similar grievances and goals. *Collective power* is a particularly relevant instance of this dimension for the development of social protest. It refers to the ability of power actors to form horizontal linkages, to coordinate action, and to establish coalitions and alliances. Collective power is at its height when those collaborations include actors from two or more power clusters; for example, when social movements or protest organizations coordinate with political actors, draw international support, span social classes, and include the military (Mann 1993, 1986; Parsons 1960; Silver 2003). Analysis, however, does not consist of linear tallying up of power resources for one side or another. It must disentangle structural and institutional linkages and how they affect the relative power of dominant and subordinate social forces that stand in reciprocal relationships to each other.

---

[26] Structural power refers to relations of domination and subordination rooted in one's position in political and economic institutions. More instrumental forms of power depend on control of specific resources to obtain one's objectives. Concrete situations involve a mixture of both.

[27] Weber (1978: 212) added that genuine domination requires a minimum of voluntary compliance, an interest in obedience.

Political Power

Political power primarily refers to the power of the state understood in organizational and administrative terms as the territorial centralization of regulation, backed ultimately by the coercive capabilities of the police, judiciary, and the military (Mann 1993: 26; Weber 1978). State strength, then, depends in part on its infrastructural power, the degree to which its institutions effectively penetrate the territory it claims as its jurisdiction. It also rests on the state's capacity to control the forces of coercion (despotic power), especially the military, which, in Latin America, may exhibit some independence.[28] Because this Weberian perspective conceptualizes the state as administrative organization for rule, it argues that state managers can, in theory, have autonomy from social groups in decision making. This makes state managers power actors in their own right, pitting them against social groups. How much autonomy, if any, they exercise is an empirical issue (Evans 1995; Evans, Rueschemeyer, and Skocpol 1985; Lustig 1998; Skocpol 1979).[29]

However, the state is also an arena in which contending social forces vie for control or support of its institutions to further their interests (Mann 1993, 1986; Miliband 1983). This has two critical consequences. First, elite cohesion may affect state power. This applies to cohesion among top ministerial posts, as well as to elites in control of organizations that link society to the state, such as political parties, employer associations, and, perhaps, organized labor. A lack of cohesion debilitates state managers (Evans, Rueschemeyer, and Skocpol 1985; Goldstein 1986; Krasner 1978; Skocpol 1979). Second, the form of interest articulation between state and society is a critical dimension of political power that affects the relative power of state managers and social forces (Berger 1981; Cardoso and Faletto 1979; Katzenstein 1985). It matters a great deal if regimes are democratic, liberalizing or democratizing authoritarian, or authoritarian governments, busy closing down previously existing associational space.

---

[28] Mann (1986) argued that the military, in principle, constituted an independent source of social power, although he recognized that successful modern states controlled it. Because Latin American militaries have a tradition of independent action, Mann's original formulation is more relevant and is discussed later.

[29] Weberians also argue that state power depends on the type of authority structures that link different administrative and territorial units. The two most commonly referred to types are legal–rational bureaucracy and patrimonialism. The former is considered modern. Its universal process-oriented rules coupled with authority based in and limited to the jurisdiction of specific administrative units (bureaus), it is argued, are best suited for orderly, efficient management of highly complex industrial societies. By contrast, outmoded personalistic politically or economically motivated granting of authority to subordinates, who frequently control independent power sources, cause corruption (the use of public office for private gain), contradictions, and conflicts that have negative consequences for governance. These problems, especially corruption and political infighting among power holders that ruin efficient and effective policy making, thus inflame feelings of injustice among the citizenry that may spur mobilization (Collier 1999; Skocpol 1979).

Democracy complicates the exercise of state power, not the least because it ensures the existence of multiple power centers and it offers opposition forces legal rights to political organization and participation (Campbell 2005; Dahl 1968; Tarrow 1996). Elections, political parties, and the party system are significant instruments of political power.[30] Thus democratic stability (the ability to contain conflict within established institutional channels) depends on the strength and stability of political parties and the party system. Low electoral turnout and voter rejection of established political parties in favor of new ones may debilitate state managers. They may be at odds with the new electoral trends or unable to forge legislative coalitions. Conversely political parties may be unstable personal electoral vehicles for political elites; thus elite splits may cause constant shifting of coalitional dynamics (Diamond et al. 1999). By the same token, democracy at times forces state managers and party officials in government to be creative in the management of institutional rules and manipulation of multiple power centers to push ambitious reform agendas, all the while, without violating due process (Carey and Shugart 1998). Stretching constitutional interpretation too far or flat out unconstitutional procedures may also fan feelings of injustice among the citizenry and stoke the fires of protest.

Democracy affects the relative power of state managers and subordinate social forces in other crucial ways. For one, it restricts the capacity of state managers to exercise severe and indiscriminate repression of the citizenry (Goldstone and Tilly 2001; Tarrow 1998). States of siege or of exception – the imposition of martial law – must be called under carefully defined conditions, for a limited time, and formal and informal rules limit the lethality of coercive measures.

Democracy strengthens mobilized groups in another way. In addition to protecting them from state-sponsored violence, it guarantees citizen rights to organize, to assemble, and to peacefully protest for political purposes, meaning to pressure state and political party leadership. Those rights create political associational space for organizing and for the expression of opposition (Tarrow 1998; Yashar 2005). But they are also power resources because social groups, especially popular sectors, use them to expand the substantive content of formal citizen rights (Rueschemeyer, Stephens, and Stephens 1992). Without them, as in highly repressive authoritarian regimes, mass protest of a reformist nature becomes virtually impossible, and with "no other way out" popular sectors (and middle classes) may turn to armed insurrection (Goodwin 2001).

These same restrictions and advantages apply to a lesser extent in liberalizing or democratizing authoritarian regimes, as we shall see in the Chilean case in Chapter 8. Political space opens for the "resurrection of civil society." Political

---

[30] However, whether they are stabilizing or not depends on concrete conditions, not on a priori assumptions based on the number of parties or the presence or absence of labor parties and conservative parties.

parties resurface to contest elections (no matter how rigged). Labor unions and all matter of social, ethnic, and identity-based movements redouble organizational efforts and publicly challenge official policy. Authoritarian governments ease up on repression in the interest of legitimating a transition they are attempting to control. The authorities, however, frequently arbitrarily rescind the limited freedoms they have granted and repress viciously. This is the uncertainty democratizing forces must live with in transitions from authoritarian rule (O'Donnell and Schmitter 1986).

Authoritarian regimes in the process of closing political associational space, especially after the breakdown of democracy, strengthen state managers in relation to citizens. They may repress, and repress severely, without (or with very weak) legal restraints. Thus they can implement neoliberal reforms with greater impunity.

These factors notwithstanding, the state's power also depends on its ability to perform critical economic, welfare, and governance functions (Anglade and Fortín 1985; Lindblom 1977). The state in industrial and postindustrial societies has a responsibility to manage economic instruments to ensure adequate investment for economic growth, employment, and some degree of social equity and support for people who cannot work (Esping-Andersen 1990). Capitalist states use a wide variety of instruments to accomplish these functions, from the mixed economy and social democratic welfare regimes that emphasize socialization and planning to more hands-off arrangements focused on varying degrees of regulation and liberal welfare states. Failure to fulfill these functions may create motivation for social mobilization (Gourevitch 1986). People in desperate circumstances may resort to contentious politics to force the state to recognize their plight and apply policy instruments to address it. In any case, because citizens hold the state liable for the performance of these functions, it is to the state – much more than to employers and corporations – that they lift their voices. Of course, in capitalist societies the state is highly dependent on the market economy for its capacity to fulfill its economic and welfare functions, as well as its organizational integrity, which depends in part on its capacity to extract resources from the private sector (Przeworski and Wallerstein 1988). We turn then to a discussion of economic power.

Economic Power

Economic power depends on effective possession of economic resources (Mann, 1993: 26).[31] In capitalist societies, the dominant classes – the various fractions of capital and landowners – control most economic resources based on the production, distribution and exchange of goods. Of course, states may also control economic resources to the extent that they engage in planning and socialization.

---

[31] Here Mann acknowledges he is following Marx.

The mixed economy, in which the state directs public investment and develops public ownership in key sectors of the economy and manages major social insurance institutions, is the strongest expression of state economic power in capitalism (Gourevitch 1986; Lindblom 1977).

Dominant class-based social groups use their economic power to defend their interests in profits and favorable investment conditions against both labor and the state. Through the market, they control labor by enveloping it in a web of social relations on which it depends for living. The discipline of the marketplace (dependence on employment to purchase goods and services necessary for survival and perhaps to prosper) keeps people focused on working instead of mobilizing to appropriate profits for redistribution and to regulate labor relations (Mann 1993, 1986; Marx and Engels 1992; Polanyi 2001). By the same token, capital exploits the state's dependence on it for critical investment and employment functions (and on which the state's tax base depends) to limit the latter's attempts to control markets. Threats of investment strikes that would reduce employment and taxable resources constitute the bluntest instrument (Lindblom 1977; Przeworsky and Wallerstein 1988).

Effective exercise of this power depends significantly on capital's capacity to generate investment and employment through economic growth (Gourevitch, 1986; Rueschemeyer, Stephens, and Stephens 1992; Silver 2003; Tarrow 1998). Therefore economic crises, prolonged instability, or both, caused by changes in the structure and dynamism of the world economy, the domestic economy, or both, significantly weaken the economic power of dominant class-based social groups. They loosen an employer's hold over labor because the market no longer offers credible prospects for livelihood. Social groups mobilize in support of alternatives; the state may intervene more directly in the economy. Consequently, economic crisis, volatility, and prolonged weakness, as is well known, are major contributing causes for mass mobilization (Foran 2005; Gourevitch 1986; Skocpol 1979).

The economic power of subordinate class-based social groups (urban and rural labor, shantytown dwellers, peasants, and middle classes) rests on their ability – actual or threatened – to withhold labor, the indispensable commodity they possess that capital and landowners need. This depends on two factors. The first one centers on their organizational capacity. Historically, this involved the unionization of urban and rural labor and the formation of labor parties (Rueschemeyer, Stephens, and Stephens 1992). After the unraveling of the Fordist system of production, community organization emerged as an effective organizational tool for semiskilled and unskilled workers, which in Latin America are closely associated with the informal sector (Silver 2003). The second one hinges on their ability to disrupt production and *exchange*.[32] Here the contentious politics literature

---

[32] As will be seen, disruption of exchange is a central feature of our episodes of anti-neoliberal contention.

emphasizes the diversity of instruments used – the repertoire of contention, such as strikes, roadblocks, marches, mass demonstrations, and attacks on government buildings and private property (Tarrow 1998).

Of course, social movements do not always follow class lines, as the literature on new social movements attests. Michael Mann (1993: 28) bridges the gulf between class and identity politics well. He argues that classlike movements are never pure; they mix with noneconomic interests. This fits the situation of indigenous movements in Latin America well. They mix both cultural and class-based forms of organization, and thus their demands focus on long-standing economic grievances as well as cultural and ethnic rights (Collins 2006; Van Cott 2005; Yashar 2005; Zamosc 1994).

In sum, the organizational capacity of subordinate social groups rests on forging *associational power* and *collective power* (Parsons 1960; Silver 2003). Associational power refers to organizing along the lines of class, identity, or other specific interest. Confederations of like organizations are the highest instance, such as urban labor and peasant confederations (Rueschemeyer, Stephens, and Stephens 1992). Collective power involves coordination among two or more organized social sectors, such as urban formal sector labor, peasants, indigenous, the informal sector of labor, neighborhood associations, and so on. Collective power reaches an even higher plane when it involves coordination among popular sector organizations, middle-class groups, and political parties, and, at times, the military and state officials.

Military Power

Military power, according to Mann (1986), is concentrated, despotic, and therefore a coercive power based on the force of arms. It is highly hierarchical in its administrative organization and can bring concentrated violence to bear to enforce its will. Historically, military organization was a source of social power in its own right. It coexisted with political administration for rule but was not entirely subject to it. In the modern epoch, however, as Weber (1978) established, that is no longer the case, and the military is considered to be an integral part of the state. Although it complicates matters, I have chosen to consider the military more as an independent power because in Latin America it is often not under control of the state and frequently acts as an arbiter of political power. With whom the military allies (including the popular sectors on occasion) is of great consequence in Latin American politics.

Transnational and Ideological Power

Domestic sources of state and economic power, nevertheless, are insufficient to explain the eruption of anti-neoliberal episodes of contention in the developing world. Class power – expanded to include the popular sector as opposed to just urban and rural organized labor – and state power possess a strong *transnational dimension* rooted in the structure of the international state system and the international political economy (Arceneaux and Pion-Berlin 2005; Gourevitch 1986; Mann 1993, 1986; Rueschemeyer, Stephens, and Stephens 1992). Dominant states, regional political and economic institutions, and international capital apply political and economic power to control subordinate states and economies of the periphery and semiperiphery of the international system. However powerful they may be, they must largely act in cooperation with local state and socioeconomic elites. Thus international factors heavily condition outcomes in developing countries, although they rarely determine them (Haggard 1990).

In Latin America, the regional hegemon, the United States, actively endorses neoliberal economics. So do key multilateral financial institutions such as the IMF, the World Bank, and the Inter-American Development Bank, as well as transnational corporations. Their support for free-market economics has been constant, and they frequently help developing countries design economic stabilization and structural adjustment policies. But they cannot fine-tune the international economy sufficiently to avert *international economic crises*, and it is these crises that most weaken the economic power resources of dominant classes and political actors who back neoliberal economics.[33] Instead, these institutions, led by the IMF, and in conjunction with developed country states and private banks, exist to manage economic crises when they occur. They insist on orthodox economic stabilization and free-market structural adjustment programs, assuming these are the path to sound economic management and renewed economic growth.

These crises and policy prescriptions contribute strongly to popular sector mobilization. Latin American countries are dependent on the financing these institutions offer to stave off economic collapse and, whether they want to or not, they feel compelled to comply. Movement leaders, and many ordinary people who suffer from the impact of economic crises and neoliberal policies to overcome them, understand the connection between international sources of power that support neoliberalism and the domestic application of those policies. Consequently economic nationalism, an antiglobalization posture, suffuses resistance to stabilization and economic restructuring programs.

However, international forces also indirectly support movements that resist neoliberalism. After the collapse of communism, the United States, the Organization of American States, international financial institutions such as the World Bank and the Inter-American Development Bank, and the European Union all strongly endorsed democratization. This support favors mobilizing social groups

---

[33] They can, however, contribute to deepening economic crisis within countries because their policies in downward movement in the business cycle emphasize deflationary measures. This applies especially to the role of the IMF.

for the reasons previously mentioned. Outright military rule is not an option, and coups d'état that might have been acceptable in the mid-1900s no longer are.[34] Hence political elites may be forced to negotiate more with challengers to neoliberalism than they otherwise would.

Transnational movements also strengthen mobilizing popular sector groups. International nongovernmental organizations (NGOs) may directly fund them. They also organize meetings, conferences, courses, and more formal organizational ties, such as membership in international movement associations that bring people together and help to generate ideas (Tarrow 2005; Yashar 2005). However, research on these processes is just beginning and the data are too incomplete for sustained treatment in this book. Therefore I will come back to these issues in the conclusion with tentative statements rather than analyze them systematically in the country chapters.

Ideological power derives from the capacity of ideas to shape policy options and principles of social organization, that is, to guide our understanding of the world and action. Neoliberals believe that market principles are the best for organizing efficient institutions. Because this is a book about challenges to neoliberalism, I focus more directly on the role of ideas in forging *associational* and especially *collective power*.

McAdam, Tarrow, and Tilly (2001) drew attention to the mechanisms that transform movements and demonstrations from isolated instances of protest into growing streams of mobilization, a process known as scale-shift. In addition to threat, which is implicit in the neoliberal agenda, I use cognitive and brokerage mechanisms. Cognitive mechanisms shift perceptions about problems, especially, in this book, when innovative issue framing resonates with broader audiences and draws them in. Brokerage refers to nodes of contact that link previously unconnected movement organizations. These mechanisms connect the grievances and goals of movements and individual protestors to broader policy and political purposes. Thus they are crucial for strengthening mobilization by expanding associational and collective power. For the sake of simplicity, I have placed brokerage in the ideological power category because the actors performing the brokerage function draw heavily on framing for their success.[35] Thus the framing and brokerage mechanisms become very useful for explaining why class-based and identity-based movements join forces in episodes of popular mobilization.

Other well-established mechanisms include threats to people, competition among and within movement organizations, and social appropriation. In this book, economic, social, and political exclusion created by sweeping neoliberal reforms inherently threaten broad and diverse social groups. Competition among

---

[34] For the authoritarian turn, see O'Donnell (1973); Cardoso and Faletto (1979); Collier (1979).

[35] The brokerage function could also be considered as a factor in building organizational power based on shared interests; hence it could also fall in the economic power category.

movements also influenced mobilization, but it appears more episodically and therefore is not treated systematically. The same is true of the appropriation mechanism in which social actors take over an existing organization and turn it to new purposes.

Conclusion

This chapter argued that the attempt to construct a contemporary version of market society was a necessary condition for the popular mobilizations that gripped Argentina, Bolivia, Ecuador, and Venezuela between the mid-1980s and 2003. Economic, social, and state restructuring threatened the institutions, policies, and practices that under national populism had decommodified labor and land for urban and rural popular sectors and many middle-class social groups (especially those dependent on state employment) (Almeida 2007). The implementation of neoliberal reforms created widespread economic and political exclusion of the popular sectors. In other words, both the threat and the reality of neoliberal economic, political, and social reforms generated the grievances, demands, and sense of injustice that drove defensive mobilization. Thus the myriad claims that animated protest during the neoliberal era usually had a common origin – attempts to construct contemporary market society.

A focus on protest as contentious politics facilitates the identification of multiple strands of politically significant contention that spring forth from those grievances and demands. Their common grounding in economic, political, and social problems created by the construction of contemporary market society – or the threat thereof – permits us to distinguish most protest events during the neoliberal era from mobilization during previous periods. These anticontemporary market society episodes of contention began with separate streams of mobilization that linked up over two or more waves of contention. Over time, the common origin of highly varied grievances and demands facilitated the articulation of horizontal linkages among protest organizations. It also sharpened the political purpose of mobilization: the replacement of pro-neoliberal administrations with administrations committed to reforming neoliberalism to include the economic and political interests of the popular sectors and some middle-class groups. Our episodes of anti-neoliberal contention end when something approximating that goal was accomplished.

Part II specified four additional conditions that accounted for these episodes of anti-neoliberal contention at the turn of the 20th century and their absence in Peru and Chile, which also had far-reaching neoliberal reform projects. These were the presence or absence of political associational space; the presence or absence of economic crisis; the application of framing and brokerage mechanisms to form coalitions among anti-neoliberal movements; and the reformist nature of major mobilizing forces versus armed insurrection. These factors emerged from a relational conception of power that posited that an increase in the capability of movements also depended on corresponding decline of power of forces that supported neoliberalism. Whether this occurred depended on the mixture of economic, political, ideological, military, and transnational power capabilities in the empirical cases.

3

The Argument: Explaining Episodes of Anti-Neoliberal Contention in Latin America

Why, at the turn of the 20th century, did Argentina, Bolivia, Ecuador, and Venezuela have episodes of anti-neoliberal popular mobilization that forced the collapse of pro-neoliberal governments and contributed to their eventual replacement with political forces interested in reforming neoliberalism? As seen in the previous chapter, the dismantlement of protections from the market for popular sectors (and middle classes) threatened significant economic and political exclusion. This was the first, and fundamental, necessary condition. In all of the cases, regardless of the degree to which neoliberal reforms were implemented, this generated the *motivation* – the grievances – for mobilization.

Because the construction of contemporary market society was an attempt to build an entire new social order – touted as modernization – it involved a comprehensive program of economic, political, and social reforms. Therefore, Polanyi-like defensive mobilization to challenge neoliberalism encompassed a wide variety of demands that, moreover, protest organizations consciously linked by tracing them back to neoliberalism's transformative project. Demands for economic and social reforms to neoliberalism focused on policies to protect individuals – or groups – from the full force of the market in the workplace, in education, and health care. Given widespread unemployment and underemployment, claim making extended to full employment policies and greater economic nationalism in the hopes of employment and to gain more control over investment and profits. Hence anti-neoliberal mobilization protested privatization, reduction of subsidies, and the dismantling of state economic development institutions. Political exclusion drove demands for greater citizen participation in policy making (including ethnic group desires for plurinational states), for political parties that better represented subaltern interests, and for cleaning up government corruption. Frequently these demands were bundled into calls for constituent assemblies to remake a country's political institutions.

Power in the Construction of Contemporary Market Society

The transformation of these grievances and demands into the *capacity* to challenge neoliberalism by means of expanding mobilization depended on shifts in power relations between the supporters of neoliberal reforms and the popular sectors, middle classes, and other political actors. This usually took place over several waves of anti-neoliberal contention. Throughout, domestic pro-neoliberal forces (political leaders, political parties, technocrats, socioeconomic elites, and sectors of the middle class) relied on the political power of the state, the economic power of capital, and significant support from transnational political and economic sources to implement and sustain free-market reforms and to control opponents.

Transnational economic and political power sources strongly influenced Latin America's turn to neoliberal economics. In the context of the crisis of national populism, the expansion of international capital markets strengthened the foreign sector's capacity to demand domestic economic reform in return for necessary investment funds for economic growth. Changes in the structure of international production by rapidly growing transnational corporations had the same effect (Gereffi 1994). Multilateral development banks and the U.S. government backed private international capital and pressured Latin American states into adopting neoliberal reforms (Haggard and Kaufman 1995). By the 1990s, transnational political forces, principally the United States, the European Union, and the Organization of American States, also advocated democratization in Latin America (Arceneaux and Pion-Berlin 2005; Lowenthal and Treverton 1994; Whitehead 2002).

Nevertheless, the state – a major source of political power – played a much more direct role in the construction of contemporary market society (Topik 2001). Control over centralized administration and regulation provided pro-neoliberal forces, to varying degrees, with levers to impose and enforce major economic stabilization and structural adjustment programs. The pace, length, and extent of these reforms may have varied, but in one form or another governments announced their intention to impose the full package and then did their best to deliver.[1]

In Argentina, Bolivia, Ecuador, and Venezuela, democratic regimes complicated state managers' exercise of political power by limiting their constitutional authority to circumvent congress to implement neoliberal economic reform. The means political leaders found to push their policy agenda forward were also key instruments of political exclusion for popular sectors and, often, sectors of the middle class and even, occasionally, adversely affected business interests. Presidents relied on closed, cohesive technocratic teams to design policy and implemented them largely by decree. Thus, whenever possible, they bypassed their

---

[1] An extensive literature examines the causes for variation in the adoption of neoliberal economic reforms, in which state capacity looms large. Neoliberal reformers also attempted to shed vestiges of patrimonial rule and to strengthen legal–rational bureaucracy. This took the form of anticorruption, cronyism, and clientelism campaigns and efforts to develop first world-style modern judicial systems.

own political party's (or party coalition) involvement in policy making as well as broader legislative deliberation and controls. Sometimes this occurred with the acquiescence of congress (emergency enabling laws), which required majority party coalitions. Other times, presidents stretched their prerogatives to the limit, risking the eruption of bitter conflicts between the executive and legislative branches of government.

Neoliberals expected that the economic power of international and national business sectors would then take over. Macroeconomic stability, investment, and rapid sustained economic growth would boost employment and real incomes. These improvements would generate broader societal support for contemporary market society, or at least quiescence, making it easier to isolate and control protestors.

It was also hoped that over time citizens would internalize a free-market ideology. They would come to think of markets as the source of individual liberty and the wellspring of plenty. They would come to embrace the justness of the impersonal universal rule of the market to allocate opportunities and wealth over unjust, discriminatory political mechanisms.

Interestingly, neoliberals did not think of identity- and postmaterialist-based movements as threats because they appeared to be compatible with market reforms and democratization. The very nature of their concerns – with, perhaps, the partial exception of the environmental movement – focused attention on noneconomic issues. Demands centered on equality of rights for women, recognition of ethnic and cultural diversity, cleaning up pollution, and inclusion of these groups – largely by means of nongovernmental organizations – in the policy-making process. Governments addressed these issues by expanding citizen rights, creating modest new government agencies, passing legislation supporting bilingual education, or decentralizing state administration in favor of expanding local autonomy at the municipal level (as occurred in Bolivia) to address indigenous demands for more local control. These measures required only modest resources for their implementation, much of which came from multilateral development banks. They did not involve revisions of market reforms.

Anti-Neoliberal Contention

In virtually all of the cases, organized labor (once the most developed and powerful transformational subaltern movement) spearheaded mobilization during the opening wave of anti-neoliberal contention.[2] However, changing political and economic fortunes caused declines in its associational, collective, and disruptive power that made it ineffectual. In part, that decline was due to the severance or

---

[2] In Argentina, the labor party's structure facilitated the co-optation of the major labor confederations. However, dissenting unions protested independently.

isolation of organized labor from its sources of political power, that is, to its connection to political parties and state agencies, and how incumbents manipulated those institutions to control organized labor. Moreover, as previously discussed, economic stabilization policies of the 1980s, deindustrialization, labor relations reform, and privatization weakened the economic power of private and public sector labor unions. On those rare occasions when food riots broke out or when citywide or regional mobilization gained traction, the state's coercive power sufficed to reestablish order. To control mobilization, governments used tried and true combinations of riot police and army units with a variety of crowd-control techniques, from clubs, tear gas, water cannons, and rubber bullets to declaring states of exception that imposed some form of martial law for a limited time (frequently between 30 and 90 days). These suspended citizen guarantees of assembly, speech, and unreasonable search and seizure by security forces. All of these measures were compatible with democratic rule, although states of emergency stretched the concept, especially if invoked frequently and when protestors died.

From this low point, the popular sectors in Argentina, Bolivia, Ecuador, and Venezuela reconstructed associational power and, in the first three cases, collective power over several waves of contention. These transformations in popular sector movements were also their sources of political and disruptive power. Political capability hinged on rebuilding associational power (creating new organization and recasting existing ones) and forging collective power (coalition building across new, recast, and traditional movement organizations and across clusters of power). This permitted the mobilization of large numbers of people (masses) to exercise disruptive economic power. These episodes of anti-neoliberal contention ended with the eventual election of governments committed to reforming contemporary market society. The power deflation of political and economic forces supporting neoliberalism contributed to this outcome.

The reconstruction of associational and collective power depended on five necessary conditions (see Table 3.1). The *first two* were (1) persistent economic and political exclusion caused by determined efforts to construct contemporary market society in the context of (2) adequate political associational space for popular sector organizing; in this case, all four countries had democratic regimes. The specific characteristics of protest movements, as well as their relationship to the state and political parties, heavily influenced the process in individual cases. The key, however, was the emergence of protest movements capable of making up for the deflation in popular sector power caused by the decline of a traditional labor movement.

With respect to the development of associational power, dogged efforts by government authorities to promote privatization, deregulation, employer-friendly reform of labor relations, and fiscal retrenchment generated breakaway union confederations when established ones collaborated in reforms or otherwise proved incapable of effective resistance (defined as forcing the government

Table 3.1. *Expanding Episodes of Anti-Neoliberal Contention*

Factors	Argentina 1989–2003[a]	Bolivia 1985–2003[a]	Ecuador 1984–2006[a]	Venezuela 1989–1998[a]	Peru 1990–2000[b]	Chile – 1 1983–1986[a]	Chile – 2 1990–2007
Long-term market society project creating stark political and socioeconomic exclusion	Yes	Yes	Yes However, implementation less consistent than that of Argentina or Bolivia	Yes However, implementation less consistent than that of Argentina or Bolivia	Yes	Yes 1975–89	No Market economy with significant political and socioeconomic inclusion
Associational political space, favorable/not favorable	Favorable, democratic regime	Favorable, democratic regime	Favorable, democratic regime	Favorable, democratic regime	Unfavorable, 1992 Repressive authoritarian turn	Favorable, 1980 liberalizing authoritarian regime	Favorable, democratic regime
Economic volatility and crisis	Yes, particularly 1995 and 2000–4	Yes, but less than other cases, mainly reflected in GDP/capita from 1999 to 2003	Yes, particularly 1988–90 and 1999–2001	Yes, particularly 1990 and 1994–97	Yes, particularly 1989–93 and 1999–2002	Yes, 1983–85	No
Reformist thrust to major protest groups or significant armed conflict	Yes	Yes	Yes	Yes to 1992 In 1992 significant armed violence erupts with two coup d'état attempts and continued coup threat afterwards	No Significant armed conflict with Shining Path and MRTA 1985–1993	Yes Contentious politics erupts against market society between 1983 and 1986	Yes Insofar as protest exists
Issue framing and brokerage mechanisms to link protest groups	Yes	Yes	Yes	Efforts in that direction to 1992 broken off in reaction to coup attempts	No Impeded by armed conflict	Yes	No

(continued)

47

Table 3.1 *(continued)*

Factors	Argentina 1989–2003	Bolivia 1985–2003	Ecuador 1984–2006	Venezuela 1989–1998	Peru 1990–2000	Chile – 1 1983–1986	Chile – 2 1990–2007
Outcome							
Episode of contention develops in which popular sector associational and collective powers build and neoliberal political and economic power deflate	Yes	Yes	Yes	Tentatively yes to 1992. From 1993 to 1998, decentralized contention is the norm. Meanwhile, the established political system suffers a power deflation	No However, Fujimori and his regime suffer a power deflation in 2000 at the hands of congressional opposition supported by international sector	Yes However, military regime does not collapse. It retains cohesion, steps up repression, and economy recovers	No
Outcome							
Episode of contention ends in elected governments committed to reform of market society	Yes Néstor Kirchner 2003	Yes Evo Morales 2005	Yes Rafael Correa 2006	Yes Hugo Chávez 1998	No Alan García elected president in 2006. He maintains a strong market model, although with more attention to social equity	No But mobilization forces military regime to adhere to democratization according to the regime's own 1980 constitution. Military loses to democratic elections in 1989.	Center-left governments committed to political and socioeconomic inclusion in the context of a market economy have ruled since 1990.

[a] Dates correspond to periods with imposition of market society and anti-neoliberal contention.
[b] Dates correspond to periods with imposition of market society without anti-neoliberal contention.

to negotiate). They also stimulated organization among the unemployed, the underemployed in the informal sector, pensioners, territorial organizations (such as neighborhood associations), new political parties, and secret cabals within the military. Meanwhile, insecurity over land as neoliberalism encouraged agribusiness, oil exploration, and other encroachments on small-scale or communal landownership threatened indigenous peoples. So did credit, price, and infrastructure policies. In Ecuador and Bolivia, the aforementioned government policies to promote the cultural and ethnic identities of the indigenous intertwined with neoliberal agricultural policy and, in Bolivia, with U.S. coca eradication efforts. These circumstances pushed indigenous movements into the forefront of anti-neoliberal contention in these two cases.

Collective power built on the proliferation of anti-neoliberal movements. These included organized labor, pensioners, retirees, state employees and public sectors workers (including teachers, university professors, and other professionals), the unemployed, and the myriad urban self-help groups in working-class neighborhoods and shantytowns. Indigenous organizations mixed economic grievances with cultural and ethnic claims because rising prices hit their people hard as did less credit and infrastructure for small-scale farming, and growing land insecurity in the face of agribusiness or, in the case of coca growers, U.S. drug policy.

The unwillingness of pro-neoliberal governments over time to acknowledge the legitimacy of the protestors or their demands, much less to seriously engage them, perpetuated political and economic exclusion and feelings of injustice. The fact that presidents who campaigned on promises to reform neoliberalism reneged on their electoral mandate and supported the neoliberal policy agenda exacerbated those feelings. Faced with this stonewalling, or outright betrayal, as protest movements gained in organizational strength and mobilizing capacity they began to form horizontal linkages. They coordinated national mobilization, significantly increased disruptive capability, and thereby at critical moments dramatically amplified the pressure they brought to bear on the government.

Although the specifics varied in each case, some patterns emerged. For example, new breakaway union confederations, frequently centered on state employees, reached out to newly formed organizations of the unemployed, the underemployed, and pensioners. In some cases they also supported neighborhood organizations. Argentina and Ecuador were the best examples of this pattern, but it was also present in Venezuela through 1992, and in Bolivia with the "Coordinadora del Agua" in Cochabamba. The common threats previously discussed motivated indigenous organizations to collaborate with peasant unions, especially in Bolivia and Ecuador. In some cases the lines between the two blurred significantly. The fact that both urban and rural free-market economic reforms originated in a comprehensive neoliberal program helped bring together rural, indigenous, and urban mobilization. In virtually every case, in the latter stages of anti-neoliberal episodes of mobilization, in the middle of economic crisis, established labor confederations made common cause with breakaway ones, with rural unions, and with indigenous organizations. At the apex of mobilization, varying combinations of middle-class groups and military factions joined the fray.

The capacity to frame issues to facilitate coalition building among separate movements and to broker those alliances constituted a *third necessary condition* for the development of anti-neoliberal episodes of contention. Issue framing was crucial for rebuilding popular sector associational and collective power. Framing connected personal problems, and those of social groups, to the economic and political exclusion generated by the construction of market society. Whatever was going on with the traditional labor movement, framing was critical for the emergence of new organizations interested in resisting neoliberal reforms, that is, for expanding associational power. Issue framing contributed to the collective power of the popular sectors because neoliberal reforms, which had required consistent support from the state, affected a wide swath of economic, political, and social relations. Consequently, over time, disparate popular sector organizations realized that many of their troubles – whether economic, political, or social – had a common origin and that it required significantly more pressure on the state than they could exert individually to force fundamental changes. As these cognitive changes occurred, they began to forge cooperative relations among themselves and with anti-neoliberal organizations from other power clusters, namely political parties and, in some cases, dissident military. Economic crisis generally accelerated this process.

Discourse usually framed popular sector common interests in opposition to neoliberalism's overarching ideological project and its society-wide effects. In this framing, globalization's detrimental impact had its roots in the will of domestic and international political and economic elites to exploit and dominate the popular sectors, which robbed them of the necessary conditions for *life* (meaning the protection of individuals from the market in the interest of improving livelihood). This steamroller affected *all* popular sector groups, and even middle classes. Therefore all had an interest in economic nationalism and instruments of decommodification in order to rebuild the conditions necessary for *life for all*. Given the enormity of the forces arrayed against them, and their will to politically exclude the popular sectors, only a common front stood a chance of changing policy.

In short, neoliberalism's society-wide state-directed reforms – frequently instigated and strongly supported by transnational economic and political power actors – provided independent popular sector movements and organizations with a common point of reference that, with proper framing, brought them together and gave them a common target. From this recognition, the leadership of the various movement organizations brokered alliances and coalitions by linking previously unconnected sites. In the process, they transformed the specific grievances and demands of individuals and organizations to broader political purposes, such as national policy proposals and, ultimately, a comprehensive challenge to neoliberalism.

Although brokerage mechanisms varied, four were the most common. First, major movement leaders seeking to build coalitions arranged "summit" meetings and created encompassing organizations to promote cooperation.[3] Frequently they mounted congresses, conventions, seminars, and discussion groups to stimulate interaction among movement organizations. Second, leaders were often members of dense organizational networks involving labor unions, leftist parties, indigenous movements, and self-help, human rights, and a host of other associations. Overlapping membership, or only one or two degrees of separation among leaders, also facilitated contact and cooperation. Participation in campaigns and events (mobilization) also brought movement heads together. Third, movement leaders encouraged open, general assembly-style deliberation for decision making. Here, leaders from different units within a movement organization and across movement organizations consensually set policy and action.

Wherever it existed, for example among indigenous peoples, communal forms of social organization also served as brokerage mechanisms. Leadership drew on them to mobilize their "people." Community members were angry over high prices, poor and deteriorating working conditions, government abuse, and a host of personal problems aggravated by the upheavals neoliberal reforms caused. Leaders harnessed communal decision-making institutions and norms of reciprocal obligations to mobilize members on behalf of national policy objectives.

Because they were excluded from the political process, either directly or by Machiavellian maneuverings that sidelined their interests, popular sector forces used their associational and collective power to exercise massive disruptive economic power to force the authorities to negotiate. The repertoire of contention varied considerably. Private and public sector organized labor, including middle-class employee associations, focused on strikes, including hunger strikes. However, less and less of the workforce was unionized as deindustrialization and privatization advanced. Because direct confrontation in the workplace, the point of production, no longer carried the same force, other means of exerting disruptive economic power emerged. Struggle shifted to disrupting exchange: the transportation of goods. Demonstrations and protests increasingly focused on the roadblock to disrupt commerce, thus generating economic loss, and as a means to lay siege to cities by cutting agricultural supplies to them. Meanwhile, mass demonstrations in city centers by all manner of movement organizations, including traditional unions, shut down the business of government with demonstrations, marches, and by attacking and occupying government buildings (and sometimes corporate buildings). Middle-class neighborhoods expressed their

---

[3] For the role of leadership, networks, and congresses of activists as brokerage mechanisms, see Mario Diani (2003).

anger and frustration by massive pot-and-pan-banging campaigns and voluntary blackouts.

The discussion of repertoires of contention introduces a *fourth necessary condition* for the emergence and trajectory of episodes of anti-neoliberal contention in Argentina, Bolivia, Ecuador, and Venezuela. In the first three cases, the bulk of mobilizing popular sector groups sought to reform free-market capitalism and to deepen democracy with repertoires of contention that stopped short of armed rebellion and revolution to replace it with socialism or some other transformational order. Whatever violence occurred during demonstrations stopped well short of that. In short, the absence of significant armed insurrection was crucial to the outcome. From this analysis, it follows that the turn to violence in Venezuela with two aborted coups in 1992 explains its divergent path (the absence of collective power building among the movements challenging neoliberalism).

A *fifth necessary condition* for the emergence, trajectory, and "success" of episodes of anti-neoliberal contention was persistent economic weakness and recurring economic crises. It debilitated the economic and political power of neoliberalism. Volatile economic growth was the primary expression of economic weakness in Argentina, Bolivia, Ecuador, and Venezuela. Periods of economic growth were followed by steep downturns. Economic slowdowns, sharp recessions, and, in the late 1990s, economic depressions rivaling that of the 1930s. The state, with the government at its head, appeared incapable of fulfilling its economic and welfare functions. The promise of stable, sustained economic growth with expanding opportunities and income for a large majority, the basic condition for social quiescence (if not ideological acceptance), never materialized. Instead, governments uniformly responded with procyclical, deflationary economic policies that reinforced the logic of the market.

Drastically worsening economic and social conditions dramatically sharpened changes in the class situation of the popular sectors. Increasingly bleak prospects of securing the minimum necessities for livelihood, no matter how humble, over 10 to 25 years motivated ever more desperate, angry, outraged, and betrayed people in cities and the countryside to mobilize. Orthodox stabilization policy in the context of more open and deregulated economies exacerbated poor working conditions and brought on massive unemployment and ubiquitous underemployment in the burgeoning informal sector. Worse, governments pointedly excluded popular sector interests from policy responses to economic crisis while forcing them to pay a greater share of the burden of economic adjustment. In virtually every case, the largest expansions in associational and collective power, and the most significant contentious events, took place during an economic crisis. This is one of the reasons the most spectacular mobilizations occurred at the turn of the 20th century, a period of world recession that contributed to economic depressions in South America.

Over time, persistent economic weakness and crisis also debilitated the political power of neoliberalism and facilitated the construction of new linkages among popular sectors, political parties, and state institutions. This, in conjunction with escalating mass mobilization, hastened the end of pro-neoliberal governments. For example, in most cases, elite cohesion behind the neoliberal project dissolved. This opened opportunities for congresses to challenge administration policy. Political parties linked to popular sectors availed themselves of this power and at times coordinated institutional opposition with mobilization to amplify their points. Moreover, democracy limited the degree of repression states could carry out. Wholesale violations of human rights and use of state terror to subdue demonstrations and their leaders was, as a rule, not possible. However, when presidents significantly escalated violent repression of demonstrators, they exacerbated their problems. When excessive force was used, civilian political leaders tended to lose control over the armed forces and the police. This occurred most clearly in Venezuela, Ecuador, and partially in Bolivia.[4] In Ecuador, dissident factions of the military overtly coordinated with mobilizing popular sector forces, thus augmenting their collective power. In the case of Argentina, repression contributed to elite splits that eventually forced the president's resignation.

Electoral and party system volatility also weakened neoliberals politically. The creation of new parties boosted the collective power of mobilizing popular sectors that had established linkages to them. Faced with the political exclusion of their substantive economic and social demands, and made more desperate by persistent economic hard times, citizens exercised their right to vote. As their hopes for economic recovery with employment and welfare dimmed, and as established political parties betrayed their electoral mandates, voters abandoned them for new ones or supported factions of established parties interested in reforming neoliberalism, more committed to the mixed economy and welfare concerns. These developments in institutional contention in conjunction with escalating contentious politics hastened the demise of administrations committed to neoliberalism. Massive anti-neoliberal mobilization also contributed to the loss of support for neoliberal incumbents of majority political parties in congress and from the military. This forced the ouster of sitting presidents and ushered in governments more inclined to act on mandates to reform it. Of course, the extent to which these new governments depart from neoliberalism varies substantially, with Venezuela and Bolivia at the more extreme end and Ecuador and Argentina at the other.

Divergent Cases: Peru and Chile

Why did Peru and Chile – who both implemented ambitious neoliberal reforms – not experience similar episodes in leftist popular mobilization? They differed on crucial factors. Peru closed political associational space after President Alberto

---

[4] The contentious politics literature emphasizes that once mobilization occurs how the state uses its repressive power influences the course of events; it makes the difference between escalation to revolution or containment of revolutionary impulses.

Fujimori engineered a palace coup d'état in 1992 to implement neoliberal reform. He then presided over a nominally democratic polity and mainly ruled with support from the military. Peru also had to contend with a full-fledged insurgency. These two factors increased the repressive capacity of the state, especially when Fujimori's government stepped up the campaign against the Shining Path guerrillas. Authoritarian government and the guerrilla war also made it difficult for reformist movements to build associational and collective power, as had occurred in the other four cases. Reformist movements did not have the same freedom of assembly and peaceful protest. Alliances with opposition political parties were not possible, and neither were alliances with the Shining Path. Indeed, in the countryside, and later in urban areas, the Shining Path created a wedge between popular sectors.

Chile's situation was more complex. A military government constructed contemporary market society between 1975 and 1989, and subsequent democratic governments retained the basic tenets of the free-market economy it had imposed. For these reasons, Chile is widely regarded as a successful model of marketization that potentially contradicts the evidence that the construction of contemporary market society generates strong countermovements. However, this interpretation misses a crucial point raised in this book. Since redemocratization in 1990, Chile no longer has been constructing a contemporary *market society*, the fundamental necessary condition for massive nationwide challenges to neoliberalism.

Market society is characterized by persistent and extensive economic, political, and social exclusion. However, democratic Chile has been *reforming* market society to make it more inclusionary by offering greater protection for individuals from the market and by enfranchising citizens. Since 1990, Chile has been ruled by a center-left coalition of parties that had been banned and repressed during the military dictatorship. Once in government, they steadily improved welfare, although income remains concentrated at the top. Poverty levels, for example, declined rapidly. Budgets for social expenditure increased significantly. Attempts were also made to reform the labor code inherited from the dictatorship. Equally important, center-left governments steadily amended the constitution passed by the military to rid it of special clauses that protected the interests of conservatives. This improved political inclusion for Chilean citizens. Last, but not least, Chile experienced sustained economic growth and avoided the economic crisis that wracked its neighbors. In other words, Chile has a market economy, but has moved sufficiently away from market society to discourage concentrated contentious politics of the type that racked Argentina, Bolivia, Ecuador, and Venezuela.

However, anti-neoliberal mobilization did occur in Chile between 1983 and 1984, a period in which the five necessary factors aligned. First, economic, social, and political exclusion were very high after years of radical neoliberal reforms and closed authoritarian rule. Second, in an effort at legitimation following approval of the 1980 constitution in a questionable plebiscite, the military government slightly opened political associational space and eased up on indiscriminate repression. During the ensuing tenuous process of political liberalization, as O'Donnell and Schmitter (1986) hypothesized, civil society was resurrected. Opposition political parties were tolerated, although they were still technically illegal. A new labor code began to function, relegitimizing unions, although they were all but emasculated. Third, during 1983–84, Chile suffered its worst economic depression since the 1930s as the international debt crisis of that era took its toll.

The conjuncture of these three factors sparked a revival of contentious politics. After that, as occurred in the previous cases, two additional factors facilitated the further expansion of opposition collective power. First, framing and brokerage permitted resurgent political parties to gain control of the anti-neoliberal movement. Framing linked economic policy reform (decommodification) with democratization. This connected many different types of movement organizations. Extensive overlapping membership between political party and movement leadership permitted political parties to coordinate large-scale monthly demonstrations. International organizations, especially the Ford Foundation, but also European-based associations, supported the rebirth of political parties. Second, the main opposition movements were reformist. They did not seek to overthrow the military regime by means of armed revolt. They wanted to force a negotiated transition to full democracy with the military earlier than that contemplated in the 1980 constitution, reasoning that once in office they could reform neoliberal economics.

Authoritarian regimes, being what they are, can arbitrarily close political associational space. The Chilean military government defeated these movements in 1986 following a significant increase in repression. The protests ended, and the moderate center-left opposition party coalition accepted the political transition process of the 1980 constitution. They eventually succeeded in turning political liberalization into democratization with the intention of reforming neoliberal economic and social policies.

4

Argentina

Mass mobilization rocked Argentina in December 2001, shattering its image as a model transition to free markets and democratic consolidation. All across the land, demonstrators stood at roadblocks spoiling to confront riot police; they staged massive banner-filled marches on government centers, banged pots and pans, and made decisions in impromptu popular assemblies. Everyone participated, working people, poor people, unemployed people, pensioners, aged retirees, young lower-class toughs, respectable middle-class people, and the entire seething mass chanting "*que se vayan todos*," out with the whole rotten political class! The outpouring of rage caused a political crisis that, among other events, forced the president of the nation, Fernando de la Rúa, to resign. And yet, for all its drama, December 2001 was but the crest of sustained anti-neoliberal protest that from humble beginnings in 1990 expanded over three distinct waves.

Building Contemporary Market Society, 1989–95

The accumulation of frustration, anger, and despair at the economic and political exclusion caused by radical free-market reforms of the 1990s must be understood against the backdrop of Argentina's national-populist order. Economic nationalism, planning, and socialization had left a legacy of state enterprises, particularly in energy, telecommunications, transportation, utilities, and infrastructure. The state promoted public education and supported a public pay-as-you-go pension system that in 1980 covered close to 70 percent of the economically active population, one of the most comprehensive in the region (Murillo 2001). High levels of state employment were a corollary of the state's economic activity, bolstering middle classes but also skilled labor. The labor code protected formal sector workers.

Peronism, the legacy of Juan Domingo Perón, became the core of Argentine politics. To support national populism in the 1940s and 1950s, Perón incorporated organized labor into the political process and built a labor party (Collier and Collier 1991; Corradi 1985). This had profound consequences for Argentine politics. Perón constructed state–labor relations along corporatist lines. Peronist dominated unions, concentrated in the Confederación General de Trabajadores (CGT; General Confederation of Workers), gained legal rights of representation, marginalizing other unions, which made the CGT the largest and most powerful Argentine labor confederation. Moreover, the state had the power to intervene in internal union affairs. The CGT, despite internal tensions, was loyal to Perón, his heirs, and national populism, which made it a formidable political foe. It routinely struck to discredit non-Peronist governments by mounting crippling general strikes that defeated legislation and deposed presidents. The CGT was also the backbone of Perón's labor party, the Partido Justicialista (PJ; Justicialist Party). CGT unions shaped party policy; union leaders stood for election in national, provincial, and local contests and were appointed to state posts, such as the Labor Ministry. The CGT and the PJ staunchly supported national-populist principles.

Officially recognized, and, therefore, CGT-affiliated, unions consistently defended two organizational resources. First, worker-friendly labor codes provided job security and rigid job categories boosted union employment; thus unions gained and retained membership because they mediated work rules. Second, Peronist unions traditionally managed state welfare funds [*obras sociales*], particularly in health care.

Economic Stabilization, Restructuring, and State Reform Under Carlos Menem

Carlos Menem, who ran a populist presidential campaign for the Peronist Party, took office in late 1989 in the midst of a deep economic and political crisis. Just five years earlier, Raúl Alfonsín of the Radical Party had presided over Argentina's return to political democracy after a long spell of brutal labor-repressive military rule from 1976 to 1983 (Corradi 1985). Alfonsín's "heterodox" economic policies to overcome the nation's foreign debt crisis and resume economic growth failed. The country sank into economic stagnation with falling wages and rising inflation, which skyrocketed into hyperinflation in 1989.[1] In the midst of the Radical Party's deepening unpopularity, mounting economic problems, and massive CGT-led protests, the Justicialista Party, purged of unsavory leaders and promoting a new image of moderation, decisively won the 1989 presidential election and gained control of Congress.[2]

The economic crisis inherited by Menem, hyperinflation and foreign debt payment in particular, underscored policy failure. Argentine recovery depended on the renegotiation of massive foreign debt, renewal of international capital flows, and repatriation of Argentine flight capital. The international institutions necessary for recovery – the IMF, foreign capital, the World Bank, and

---

[1] This policy combined orthodox stabilization policy measures with unorthodox ones such as controls on wages and foreign exchange along with expansionary fiscal policy.

[2] For the "impossible game," see O'Donnell (1978). For policies in the Alfonsín government, see Vacs (2006); Smith (1989).

the U.S. government – made free-market economic stabilization and restructuring a condition for debt relief and access to international capital markets. This pressure created a willingness to try free-market policies (Teichman 2004, 2001). Thus, although the military government of 1976–83 and Alfonsín's administration had laid the groundwork for free-market adjustment, Carlos Menem's embraced those reforms and implemented them much more rapidly and thoroughly. Menem and his top advisors also devised a political strategy to implement the new policies, one that concentrated power in the presidency.

Between 1989 and 1995, Menem implemented a comprehensive market-oriented economic stabilization and restructuring program to wring inflation out of the economy, turn over responsibility for economic growth to the private sector, and regain credibility in international capital markets. Expanding the market required dismantling the remnants of the national-populist state. By the end of 1995, an aggressive privatization program had divested the Argentine state of most public firms as well as large swaths of the social security system, shifting risk onto individuals by establishing a mixed public–private system (Tedesco and Barton 2004:106; Teichman 2001: 112). Administrative reform rounded out efforts to downsize the federal state by substantially cutting employment in the civil service (Rinne 2003: 34). Radical trade and financial sector liberalization, tax reform (an 18-percent value-added tax), and price deregulation completed the economic reforms. These measures drastically cut trade and financial sector protections, subsidies to business and consumers, price and wage controls, and foreign exchange intervention. Labor code reforms intended to relax protection for workers rounded out the reform program. In 1991, dismissals and rehiring were subject to fewer restrictions and less taxes (Murillo 2001; Tedesco and Barton 2004: 112–13).

Economy Minister Domingo Cavallo's Convertibility Plan, launched in April 1991, was the centerpiece of Menem's price stabilization policy. Initial inflation-fighting measures had failed.[3] The Convertibility Plan whipped inflation quickly. It set the Argentine peso at parity to the U.S. dollar and required the Central Bank to maintain freely convertible reserves of gold and foreign currency at 80 percent of the monetary base (Tedesco and Barton 2004). Thus the Plan prohibited the monetization of the fiscal deficit and ensured that money supply growth followed the private sector's demand for domestic assets. The Central Bank became an independent state agency mandated to enforce the Convertibility Plan (Fanelli and Frenkel 1999).

Stabilization policy and free-market-oriented reforms restructured the Argentine state in the service of laissez faire economics. Administrative and economic reforms shrank the state and eliminated its entrepreneurial functions (Rinne

---

[3] These centered on a preannounced crawling peg floating exchange rate policy coupled with a tight money policy, but they also involved steep raises in the price of public utilities (effectively cutting state subsidies) and massive layoffs of public sector employees (Fanelli and Frenkel 1999: 54).

2003: 38). The Argentine state emerged shorn of institutional levers to conduct an activist industrial policy in support of a mixed economy or to administer an expansive welfare state. Equally important, the patronage sources and policy instruments that sustained the political forces behind national populism (especially in the PJ and sectors of the military) were sharply curtailed.

Power and the Construction of Argentine Market Society

State power was crucial for neoliberal reforms. Menem and his technocrats centralized decision making in the presidency and the Ministry of Economy to neutralize potential opposition. Three key measures passed in the first six months (July–December 1989). First, the Law for the Reform of the State gave the executive decree powers to privatize and cut the civil service. Second, the Omnibus Economic Emergency Act expanded the executive's decree powers to change laws governing subsidies, regulatory statutes of all kinds, and restraints on capital markets. In signing this act, Congress, and especially the Radical Party (Argentina's second largest party at the time), abdicated its deliberative role. Third, judicial reform increased the number of Supreme Court justices, allowing Menem to stack the court and override legal challenges to economic reforms. In 1990, an omnibus decree vastly augmented the powers of the Ministry of Economy to implement those reforms, especially privatization (Teichman 2001).

The concentration of decision making in the executive conferred enormous power on the framers of free-market reforms. These included a cadre of technocrats, appointed for their personal loyalty to Menem (and not necessarily from his own party) as well as free-market ideals, and World Bank officials who drafted and initiated policy (Teichman 2001). Policy implementation, especially privatization, involved selected social actors. International capital bought controlling shares in many companies. Argentine conglomerates received preferential access to blocks of public company shares in a corrupt process that lacked transparency and accountability (Manzetti 1999).

Support from the international sector and state power, however, were not sufficient for the implementation of neoliberal reforms. Argentina was still a democracy; therefore opposition was lawful. Menem's biggest challenge was to neutralize dissention in his own political party and from organized labor. His reforms cut deep against the founding national-populist core of what had been Argentina's majority labor-based party. To control the national-populist factions of his party and in the CGT, Menem used appointments or special recognition of loyalists and rewards to loyal unions.[4] In the Justicialista Party, Menem appointed loyalists in top positions and to stand for elections (even if they were not party members), thus marginalizing dissidents or expelling them from the party

---

[4] For a brief period after redemocratization in 1983, following its first loss in a free and fair election, the party encouraged institutionalization but Menem put an end to that experiment by reviving the party's patrimonial practices to gain control of it (McGuire 1997).

(Acuña 1994: 54; McGuire 1997; Teichman, 2001: 165). He also directed government spending to the poorer regions of Argentina, which helped him to gain control over a majority of governorships and of Congress because these states were overrepresented in the legislature, especially in the Senate (Gibson 1997; Eaton 2005).

Getting control of the CGT was critical to Menem's neoliberal project. A transformation in the linkages of organized labor to the PJ after 1983 facilitated Menem's manipulation of unions to stifle effective opposition. They allowed Menem to use appointments and corporatist controls to split organized labor. Reformist factions within the party replaced traditional Peronist mechanisms of union participation in policy making with clientelist networks. These practices transformed the Justicialista Party from a labor-dominated party to a machine party in which unions played a much smaller role (Levitsky 2003).

To ensure labor quiescence to neoliberal reforms, Menem also manipulated union competition. He granted the loyal majority faction of the CGT – the CGT-San Martín – the right to participate in the policy process. Their willingness to restrain militancy was crucial because many of the unions in this faction represented public sector workers in the government (Kelsey and Levitsky 1994: 8; Murillo 2001). When necessary, Menem used corporative arrangements to repress uncooperative unions. To thwart dissident union opposition to privatization – usually affiliated with the smaller CGT-Azopardo – he issued a decree in 1990 prohibiting strikes in essential services. The state also fired the leaders of striking telephone workers and dissolved their union, and manipulated elections in the gas union to ensure the rise of proreform leadership (Cook 2007; Dinerstein 2003a; Epstein 1992; Erro 1993).

By collaborating with privatization, loyal union leaders hoped to make the best of a difficult situation. They exchanged protection of organizational resources for a loss in numerical strength that was due to employment reductions. Displaced workers received generous severance packages. Individual workers, and, more important, unions themselves (and therefore their leadership), gained the right to buy shares in privatized companies. The state channeled welfare funds to help workers adjust to new economic circumstances through cooperative unions. Loyal union leaders received government appointments, especially in the Labor Ministry. With control over these selective incentives, cooperative unions hoped to significantly weaken competing unions (Kelsey and Levitsky 1994: 8; Murillo 2001).

However, social security and labor code reforms introduced in 1992 threatened the organizational resources of unions much more directly. Peronist unions traditionally managed state social welfare funds (especially health care). These threats to their organizational resources prompted the two competing factions of the CGT to unite and stage a general strike, after which ambitious free-market-oriented pension reform, welfare reform, and labor flexibilization bills were softened. For example, unions gained the right to manage private pension administration firms, retained the right to obras sociales, and flexible labor rules were watered down (Cook 2007; McGuire 1997; Murillo 2001).

Although Argentine neoliberal reformers controlled significant sources of political power, they also received considerable support from international and domestic political–economic sources. The World Bank and the IMF provided technical expertise and crucial loans, and their seal of appoval opened the doors to private international capital. The U.S. government's Brady Plan assisted with limited, but timely, debt relief (Teichman 2001: 107–11). All insisted on orthodox stabilization and free-market economic reforms as a condition for their economic support. Domestic capital also contributed political and economic support. It actively participated in privatization and repatriated large sums of capital sent abroad. Moreover, the influx of investment and revenue from privatization renewed economic growth with low inflation (Manzetti 1999).

Exclusion and the Foundations of Militant Resistance, 1989–95

During Menem's first administration, popular sector organizations – and especially unions – along with center-left nationalist political forces interested in opposing neoliberalism suffered profound political exclusion. The transformations of the old Peronist labor party, the concentration of power in the executive, the omnibus Economic Emergency Laws, and manipulation of the corporatist state–union relationship eliminated the capacity of political parties and organized labor to oppose free-market reforms. Small Justicialista Party factions, leftist political parties, surviving popular sector organizations, and dissident unions were impotent. Never was their isolation and ineffectualness clearer than in 1992, when the two factions of the CGT united in relatively successful defense of their control over welfare funds and then resumed their collaborationist stance (Murillo 2001).

Political exclusion, however, in conjunction with emerging patterns of economic exclusion, caused new forms of popular sector associational and collective power to emerge and reinvigorate anti-neoliberal contentious politics. These first stirrings of associational and collective power – largely ignored at the time – formed the core of what eventually became the major strand of resistance to neoliberalism.

Associational power emerged with the creation of a new independent union confederation, the Central de Trabajadores Argentinos (CTA; Argentine Workers Central). At its core stood two highly militant public sector unions that had participated in the dissident CGT-Azopardo. These were one of the major teachers' unions, the Confederación de Trabajadores Educacionales de la República Argentina (CTERA; Confederation of Educational Workers of the Argentine Republic) and one of the major state employees unions, the Asociación de Trabajadores Estatales (ATE; Association of State Employees). When the CGT-Azopardo made up with the CGT-San Martín in 1992, these unions formed an alternative union central committed to challenging neoliberalism (McGuire 1997; Murillo 1997). The fledgling CTA, however, lacked allies in organized labor (or among political parties) capable of vesting their militancy with national visibility and impact. How, then, could it build a militant mass movement?

Innovative issue framing solved the problem. As economic growth resumed, deepening privatization and fiscal retrenchment drove unemployment far above historical norms, more than doubling between 1991 and 1994. Meanwhile, the informal labor sector and poverty continued to rise beyond historical standards during that period (see Table 4.1). Not captured in these figures were equally important transformations in the livelihoods of workers, and the popular sector in general. The elimination of subsidies to food staples, energy, utilities, and transportation significantly impoverished the lives of individuals and families who already lived on the edge of subsistence. Hunger lurked. This was especially true among the expanding mass of the poor and workers laboring in the informal sector (Svampa and Pereyra 2003). In light of these shifts in class situation, the CTA *reframed* the concept of "work" and the identity of "worker" to include everyone regardless of their relationship to the world of work, not just those in officially recognized unions of the formal sector.

The CTA's founding documents enshrined principles of autonomy from the state and political parties and stressed internal democracy. It opened affiliation to all social organizations that expressed the reality of the five-million Argentines living with the hardships of precarious working conditions. These included the employed workers, the long-term unemployed, retirees and pensioners, and the self-employed without employees (informal sector workers).[5] The CTA rejected the neoliberal concept of hunger as the incentive for individuals to accept any work at any price and denounced popular sector political exclusion caused by the centralization of power in the executive. It stressed a Polanyi-like defense and restoration of workers' rights (decommodification) enshrined in state commitment to full employment with an emphasis on formal sector work with benefits, social insurance (pensions, health, and welfare), and education. It pledged to fight for the inclusion of social and economic rights in the struggle to deepen democracy.

To turn strategy into reality, the CTA relied on a proven repertoire of contention but with an innovative twist. Militants of CTA-affiliated teachers' and state employees' unions combined strikes with demonstrations and marches on government buildings to protest neoliberal policies *and* to build associational power. They calculated that marches and demonstrations would attract people from other excluded and largely unorganized social groups adversely affected by neoliberal reforms, such as the unemployed, retirees, and pensioners. The repertoire of contention included disruptive and frequently transgressive tactics,

[5] Burzaco Declaration, 17 December 1991, and Statutes of the CTA, 14 November 1992.

Table 4.1. *Argentina: Economic and Social Indicators*

	1980	1990	1991	1992	1993	1994	1995	1996	1997	1998	1999	2000	2001	2002	2003	2004	2005	2006	2007[a]
GDP	1.4	−1.4	10.6	9.6	5.9	5.8	−2.9	5.5	8.0	3.8	−3.4	−0.8	−4.4	−10.8	8.6	9.0	9.2	8.5	8.7
GDP/CAP		−2.8	9.2	8.2	4.5	4.9	−4.1	4.1	6.6	2.5	−4.6	−2.0	−5.6	−11.9	4.2	8.0	8.1	7.4	7.6
Income Distribution[b]																			
D1	2.8	2.3				2.1			2.1		1.2			1.8				1.2	
D2	4.0	3.9				2.9			3.3		2.3			3.4				2.4	
Q2	10.6	8.7				8.8			9.5		7.3			9.2				7.9	
Q3	15.7	14.2				14.1			13.4		11.7			12.3				12.5	
Q4	21.7	20.9				21.0			19.9		19.1			18.4				19.6	
D9	14.4	15.2				16.9			16.1		15.6			14.3				15.6	
D10	30.9	34.8				34.2			35.8		42.9			40.7				40.8	
Unemployment	2.6	6.1	5.1	7.0	9.3	12.2	16.4	17.3	14.9	12.9	14.3	15.1	17.4	19.7	17.3	13.6	11.6	10.2	8.8
Informal[c]		47.5	48.6	49.6	50.8	52.5	53.3	53.6	53.8	49.3		47.7	45.7			44.5	43.3		
Poverty																			
Total	10.4																		
Urban	8.5	21.0	25.5				28.4				29.9			45.0		29.4	26.0	21.0	
Rural	19.0																		
Average Wage Index[d]	128.8	99.1	100.4	101.7	100.4	101.1	100.0	99.9	99.3	99.0	101.1	106.2	105.4	90.7	89.1	*92.1*	*97.6*	*106.1*	*118.9*
Minimum Wage Index[e]	132.4	28.4		57.9	74.9	103.4	100.0	99.8	99.3	98.4	99.6	*100.0*	*101.1*	*81.3*	*84.0*	*129.8*	*171.1*	*193.2*	*219.6*

[a] Estimated.

[b] *D9* and *D10* = richest quintile; *D1* and *D2* = poorest quintile. Data not reported for all years.

[c] Informal sector data reported only from 1990 to 2005 in constant format. Data not reported for all years.

[d] Average wage index between 1980 and 2003 based on 1995 = 100; 2004–7 based on 2000 = 100 (in italics).

[e] Minimum wage index between 1980 and 1999 based on 1995 = 100; 2000–7 based on 2000 = 100 (in italics).

Sources: Economic Commission for Latin America and the Caribbean, *Statistical Yearbook* (Santiago: ECLAC, 1980–2007) and *Economic Survey of Latin America* (Santiago: ECLAC, 1980–2007). Labor statistics from International Labor Organization, Labor Overview: *Latin America and the Caribbean* (Lima: ILO, 1994–2007). For comparability of data, I have not filled in missing years with other sources.

especially in public spaces such as in front of government buildings (Svampa and Pereyra 2003).

Two new labor organizations in addition to the CTA rounded out the initial development of popular sector associational power. One was the Movimiento de Trabajadores Argentinos (MTA; Argentine Workers Movement), a new dissident minority faction of the CGT centered on transportation workers (Cook 2007). The other one was the Corriente Combativa Clasista (Combative Class Current), created around 1994, and headed by the leader of the Municipal Employees and Workers Union of Jujuy – Carlos "Perro" Santillán – a militant of the Revolutionary Communist Party. Under his leadership, Jujuy emerged as a particularly combative province (Svampa and Pereyra 2003).

The collective power of challengers to neoliberalism also had their humble beginnings during this period. Largely because of the brokerage of the CTA leadership, the CTA, the Movimiento de Trabajadores Argentinos, and the Combative Class Current formed a Mesa de Enlace (Coordinating Committee) in March 1993. Their common origin as dissident CGT unions created a dense network of connections among their directors. These networks provided nodes of contact that the CTA's president, Víctor de Gennaro, exploited. He organized frequent meetings that forged enduring linkages between them. Often this involved traveling to the provinces or bringing key leaders in from the provinces. The Mesa de Enlace transformed the power of isolated, fledgling, individual labor organizations. It allowed them to coordinate strategy and tactics for anti-neoliberal contentious action, thus increasing their potential to bring pressure on the government (Laufer and Spiguel 1999: 18; Svampa and Pereyra 2003: 38).

The gestation of a new political party further bolstered nascent collective power. In early 1991, a group of eight leftist Justicialista congressmen, spurred on by their profound isolation in the Justicialista Party, joined the Frente Grande (Broad Front), a coalition of leftist parties formed in the 1980s that had renounced armed revolution and embraced classic social democratic postures (Hodges 1993; McGuire 1997). They hoped to build a genuine electoral opposition to Menem's Justicialista Party and neoliberalism, especially given the perception that the Radical Party had abdicated that role when it signed the omnibus economic emergency laws.[6] In late 1994, another party, formed by a defecting Justicialista Party senator, merged with the Frente Grande and gave birth to a larger opposition party, Frepaso (Frente por un País en Solidaridad; Front for a Country in Solidarity). Frepaso was a response to threats of continued political exclusion. Menem had engineered a constitutional amendment that allowed him to run for reelection, which the Radical Party supported. Clearly a more committed opposition party was needed (McGuire 1997: 249–51).

---

[6] The Congress, especially the Radical Party, ceded that power under duress. For details, see Rinne (2003) and Schvarzer (1998: 68–69).

From the very beginning, a conscious strategy to build collective power forged close ties among the CTA, the Frente Grande, and later the Frepaso. Their militant or leftist backgrounds facilitated this approach. Indeed, the CTA actively participated in the founding of Frepaso, and some its leaders later became candidates for provincial and national legislative office. However, the CTA never became the union arm of Frepaso, as the CGT was to the Justicialista Party, and it reserved the right to pursue other political options. The CTA and Frepaso agreed that defeating neoliberalism required a long-term two-pronged strategy of mass mobilization and electoral politics. Mass mobilization would keep issues in the public eye, discredit incumbents, and build an electoral base. Their elected officials would not only represent them, but also participate in organizing contentious action and help negotiate subsequent demands with the authorities.

Relegated to the Provinces

The CTA and Frepaso worked diligently to turn these strategies into reality. However, in the depths of their isolation between 1992 and 1994, these fledgling organizations were hardly powerhouses, and most contentious politics took place in remote provinces of the interior, far from the limelight of national centers of power. Nevertheless, contentious politics in the provinces, frequently led by CTA-affiliated unions and supported by dissident local officials, patiently built the foundations of associational and collective power that became much more significant in Menem's second administration.

CTA-affiliated teachers' and state employee unions were strongest in the provinces, where they mobilized against public administration decentralization. The teachers' union opposed devolution of administrative control of secondary education to provincial governments. Both unions protested provincial government fiscal retrenchment and national government plans to place public health administration under local government control. Federal government efforts to shift fiscal and administrative responsibility on to lower levels of government deeply worried public sector unions. They believed that an insufficient transfer of funds from the central government to the provinces would cripple the ability of provincial and municipal governments to carry out their administrative mandates. They feared that the secular decline in wages and working conditions since Alfonsín's administration would worsen (Murillo 2001; Murillo and Ronconi 2004).

These fears came true. Wages were low, pay arrears frequent, and layoffs increased in the context of local economies with few alternatives to public sector employment (Dinerstein 2001; McGuire 1996; Svampa and Pereyra 2003). Public sector unions in the provinces struck against decentralization, demanding overdue wages (up to three months in arrears), and protested wage reductions, suspensions, layoffs, losses in job security, welfare cuts, and government corruption in the management and implementation of local fiscal retrenchment (Dinerstein 2001). These strikes generally occurred in provincial capital cities or major towns and involved marches and demostrations against provincial and municipal government institutions. As planned by the unions, contentious action involved unemployed formal sector workers, the underemployed, the chronically unemployed, students, and small-scale entrepreneurs and merchants. Their participation significantly magnified the impact of the union's contentious action. At the height of some demonstrations, the repertoire of contention included attacks on government buildings and the residences of politicians who supported neoliberal reforms in which they were sacked and burned.

The most emblematic event occurred in Santiago del Estero on 16 December 1993. It was remarkable for its scale, its level of violence, and national media attention that turned it into an example and a warning. Similar protests occurred in Jujuy (1990–95), Córdoba (June 1995), San Juan (July 1995), and Río Negro (September and October 1995).

Santiago del Estero epitomized the exclusion of the Argentine interior provinces in the early 1990s. Nearly a third of households had unsatisfied basic needs, placing it second only to Jujuy. It also had one of the lowest income and life-expectancy levels. Public services, the most important source of employment, accounted for 46 percent of economic activity in the province (Zurita 1999).

In the midst of generalized poverty, the negative impacts of administrative decentralization and fiscal stabilization on a community dependent on government employment motivated local defensive anti-neoliberal protest. The local application of national neoliberal policies affected the breakdown of everyday routines for people, fueling their grievances. The corruption of state political leaders and their cronies who profited from the implementation of neoliberal reforms was another source of discontent. It symbolized the political exclusion of residents hurt by policy reform. Throughout 1993, public sector unions harnessed those grievances for Polanyi-like defensive mobilization.

An accumulation of citizen rage over the disruption of daily life, the obliteration of frames of reference for meaningful decent living, official corruption, and political impotence burst on 16 December 1993 in Santiago del Estero. Three-month arrears in payment of public sector employees (including police) coupled with the signing of the state's Ominbus Law (local implementatinof national policy) in December were the detonators. One protestor recalled: "We had not been paid for the past three months ... and the social security system was suspended and I couldn't go to the doctor ... We were so angry ... " (Auyero 2003: 125). Another explained:

Before the December 16 thing happened, the public workers, those workers who depend on the province government, hadn't been able to receive their salaries. It had been at least three months without payment of wages. People did not have money for medicines or food. The stores did not let you buy on credit anymore. All the mutual aid societies were closed. It was a terrible chaos. I was an independent worker, but my husband depended on the provincial government. In a certain way, the whole situation affected me too, because sales went down and I went broke. (Auyero 2003: 123)

On 16 December, desperate and betrayed public sector unions called a demonstration in front of the Government House against the Omnibus Law. It threatened unemployment for hundreds of temporary workers, public employee salary reductions, and privatization of most public services (Auyero 2003: 124). The crowd swelled to around 5,000 and, after halfhearted riot control, the police (who also suffered from salary arrears) abandoned the scene. The enraged crowd attacked, looted, and set fire to the Government House, moved on to the Courts a few blocks away and then to the Legislature. Residents understood these were the seats of local political power responsible for their plight and wanted to punish their occupants:

When we were in the Government House, the public employees were clapping at the fire. It seemed natural to move on to the Congress. And while we were going there the feeling was that it had to be the same. It was at the Congress where the most anger had accumulated because legislators had voted in favor of the Ley Omnibus... So it seemed to them that, having already settled their differences with the Government House and the Courthouse, the Congress was next. (Auyero 2004: 132)

Although the media characterized the Santiagazo as a spontaneous social explosion, it was not. In February 1993, public sector unions, especially teachers and retired workers, began a drumbeat of sustained and steadily increasing protest to local implementation of administrative decentralization and fiscal stabilization. There were two strikes and street demonstrations in January, over 10 in February, over 15 by June, then a jump to over 25 by October, and almost 30 between October and the first two weeks of December (Auyero 2003: 128).

The spiral of protest that culminated in the Santiagazo developed in no small measure because the teachers' and pensioners' unions (the most active ones) brokered linkages among a wide range of organizations. The very act of protesting created early connections. First, frequent demonstrations brought the three main teachers' unions together on a regular basis, facilitating the formation of a collective front. Second, those protests also attracted other public sector unions: health care employees, state banking employees, courthouse employees, public administrators, and meat workers. This contact permitted the leadership of the teachers' unions to forge tighter connections with them. A teachers' union leader explained, "We were constantly going to demonstrations, together with all the people of the communities... We would all unite" (Auyero 2003: 127). On 11 November 1993, their efforts bore fruit. They organized a series of meetings that brought all of the aforementioned organizations together in the Frente Gremial de Lucha (Labor Front for Struggle). Their purpose: to mobilize all workers against the Omnibus Law. The Front's founding document blamed "the three branches of the government (executive, legislative, and judiciary) for the plight of both public sector employees and citizens in general and demands the investigation and punishment of those responsible for the economic and social chaos [repression]" (Auyero 2003: 136).

Although CTA-sponsored mobilization failed to win significant concessions, these early challenges in the provinces – and success in attracting national attention in Santiago del Estero – laid the foundations for more organized and sustained efforts in the future.[7] Facilitated by the Mesa de Enlace, the CTA spearheaded the expansion of this wave of mobilization. It organized a nationwide protest march in July 1994, a general strike in August 1994 with the Movimiento de Trabajadores Argentinos and another general strike in April 1995. Meanwhile, the CTA and Frepaso encouraged the organization of unemployed workers in the working-class and peripheral neighborhoods of Buenos Aires, a very important step for the next cycle of contention (Laufer and Spiguel 1999; Svampa and Pereyra 2003).

These new popular sector and middle-class organizations, along with the fledgling Frepaso, formed the core of the major Argentine opposition bloc to neoliberalism. Their strategy for expanding contentious politics relied on mass mobilization driven by strikes, marches, and demonstrations. They supported the electoral politics of Frepaso, and Frepaso elected officials supported union-led mass mobilization. This was a reformist bloc. Member organizations did not mobilize for socialist insurrection. They advocated the restoration of the mixed economy, full employment, labor rights, universal social insurance, and price supports for the popular sector. By the same token, Frepaso was social democratic, not revolutionary Marxist. The movement's immediate goals were to stop implementation of labor rights rollbacks, fiscal retrenchment, and education reform and to defeat Menem's Justicialista Party at the polls (local, provincial, and national).

The Changing Face of Contentious Politics, 1995–99

During Menem's second administration, the associational and collective power of the popular sectors grew rapidly. The second wave of anti-neoliberal contention that gripped Argentina between 1996 and 1998 spiraled upward in contrapuntal fashion between the provinces and greater Buenos Aires until the end of 1997, only to ebb in 1998; a year that, nevertheless, witnessed important advances in the collective power of popular sectors. Innovative additions to the repertoire of contention, with increasing disruptiveness and transgression, accompanied that process. By the end of the period, organizing in the provinces and Buenos Aires, improved coordination within and between emerging blocs, and the electoral success of Frepaso gave the movements challenging neoliberalism national impact. These advances contributed the political decline of Menem and the defeat of

---

[7] I have emphasized general patterns to show that mobilization in the provinces constituted Polanyi-like defense challenges to neoliberalism. However, in each instance, contentious politics had spontaneous and profoundly local characteristics (Auyero 2007, 2005, 2004; Svampa and Pereyra 2003).

Table 4.2. *Argentina: Presidential Elections, 1983–2007*

Candidate	Party	1983	1989	1995	1999	2003	2007
Raul Alfonsin	**UCR**	**51.9%**	–	–	–	–	–
Italo Lüder	PJ	40.2%	–	–	–	–	–
Oscar Allende	PI	2.3%	–	–	–	–	–
Carlos Saúl Menem	**PJ**	–	**48.5%**	–	–	–	–
Eduardo César Angeloz	UCR	–	37.1%	–	–	–	–
Others	UCD	–	14.4%	–	–	–	–
Carlos Saúl Menem	**PJ**	–	–	**49.9%**	–	–	–
Carlos Octavio Bordon	FPS	–	–	29.3%	–	–	–
Horacio Massaccesi	UCR	–	–	17.0%	–	–	–
Fernando de la Rúa	**ATJE**	–	–	–	**48.5%**	–	–
Eduardo Alberto Duhalde	PJ	–	–	–	38.1%	–	–
Domingo Cavallo	AR	–	–	–	10.9%	–	–
Néstor Kirchner	**PJ**	–	–	–	–	**22.0%**[a]	–
Carlos Menem	FL	–	–	–	–	24.4%[a]	–
Cristina Fernández Kirchner	**PJ**	–	–	–	–	–	**44.9%**
Elisa Cario	ARI	–	–	–	–	–	22.9%
Roberto Lavagna	UNA	–	–	–	–	–	16.8%

Boldface indicates winning candidate, party, and percentage of the vote. For the full name of political parties see the acronyms section.

[a] A second round between Menem and Kirchner was scheduled for 18 May, but on 15 May, Menem, who was trailing badly in opinion polls, withdrew from the race, leaving Kirchner elected unopposed.

Sources: The Europa World Yearbook (1982–2007), http://psephos.adam-carr.net/countries/a/argentina/argentina2003, http://www.towsa.com/andy/index.html.

the PJ in the presidential election of 1999 (see Table 4.2). What changed from Menem's first presidency?

Political power to deepen neoliberal reforms eroded during Menem's second presidency. The Radical Party's abdication of meaningful opposition strengthened Frepaso, which gained elected seats at the local, provincial, and federal levels (see Table 4.3). The tussle over the constitutional amendment permitting Menem's reelection unleashed latent leadership conflicts within the PJ. As a result

Table 4.3. *Argentina: Distribution of Seats in the Chamber of Deputies, 1983–2005*

Year	Presidential Party	PJ	UCR	Frepaso	ATJE	AR	UCD	PRO	Peronismo	Others	Total
1983	UCR	111	129	–	–	–	–	–		14	**254**
1987	UCR	105	117	–	–	7	–	–		25	**254**
1991	PJ	119	85	–	–	10	–	–		40	**254**
1995	PJ	137	69	26	–	–	–	–		25	**257**
1999	UCR	101	–	–	127	12	–	–		17	**257**
2005	PJ	118	36	–	–	13	–	12	31	47	**257**

For the full name of political parties see the acronyms section.

Sources: Levitsky and Murillo (2005: 120, 210); The Europa World Yearbook (1982–2006).

of these tensions, the Argentine Congress refused to renew Menem's omnibus emergency powers. Thus he had difficulty expanding privatization, social security, state modernization, and labor-market reforms. There were, however, two measures that profoundly affected mobilization. First, the federal government forced greater retrenchment on provincial governments to reduce national fiscal deficits. Second, under pressure from the World Bank, and with its financial support, the Employment Act of 1995 contained emergency relief employment plans – workfare (Andrenacci, Neufeld, and Raggio 2001; Oviedo 2001; Svampa and Pereyra 2003).

On the surface, it appeared that the political and economic exclusion of political party, popular sector, and middle-class forces opposed to neoliberalism had eased. However, the consolidation of existing reforms meant significant relief in the conditions of unemployment, underemployment, and the struggle for subsistence for the popular sectors – the fundamental conditions that *motivated* anti-neoliberal contentious politics – was not expected.

Regional and international economic crises, beginning with the Mexican peso crisis of 1994, weakened the functional power of the state that supported "Menemism." Because the neoliberal state would not intervene to smooth out business cycles the economic crisis significantly increased socioeconomic exclusion, relief plans notwithstanding. The economy contracted sharply in 1995, and real wages declined. Official unemployment, which had increased steadily during the first Menem presidency, spiked between 1994 and 1997, reaching what was for Argentina a shocking 17.3 percent. This was easily three to four times the historical level of unemployment during a period in which informal sector employment peaked at an equally shocking 53.8 percent in 1997. Record unemployment and informal sector employment statistics persisted, despite a brief recovery in GDP growth rates between 1996 and 1997. Poverty levels, already unaccustomedly high in 1990 because of the ravages of the debt crisis of the 1980s, climbed to an unimaginable 30 percent of the urban population, again three times the historical levels.

These circumstances dramatically increased the pool of people disposed to join movements based on a broadly inclusive identity of "worker" and the pressing need for stable work and livelihood. Moreover, in working-class neighborhoods and shantytowns across the nation, the concentration of unemployed and underemployed was much higher than the national average. Among the popular sectors, economic crises exacerbated the precariousness of their livelihoods and sharpened the struggle for subsistence, as did welfare restructuring and rising prices for services and food that were due to neoliberal reforms. So did the fact that many of the formal sector workers who had lost their jobs because of downsizing after privatization or to fiscal austerity had, for various reasons, exhausted their severance and compensation packages. Hunger and deprivation lurked, fueling the emergence of an unemployed workers' movement that spanned the nation.

Argentina

The associational and collective power of popular sector and middle-class challengers to neoliberalism expanded rapidly during this period. Several specific factors contributed to this trend. First, fiscal retrenchment in the provinces exacerbated socioeconomic exclusion, especially among public sector employees, fueling mobilization at the local and provincial level. Second, there were the unintended consequences of the 1995 Employment Act. Burgeoning need outstripped program budgets, and Peronist patronage networks controlled relief distribution. In many neighborhoods, people outside of those patronage networks mobilized to obtain unemployment subsidies and to expand relief programs. Moreover, in the Argentine union tradition of welfare implementation, the government granted larger movement organizations' control over relief funds. Third, the state stepped up repression. But because Argentina was a democracy, repression could not be at a scale that crushed movement organizations; and, as is well established in the literature, it escalated contentious action (Auyero 2007; Goldstone and Tilly 2001; Oviedo 2001; Svampa and Pereyra 2003; Tarrow 1998).

The expansion of associational and collective power exhibited several important characteristics. First, organizing the unemployed turned from idea to reality; the locus for organization spread from the workplace to the community, where the jobless and underemployed lived in high concentrations and where local networks could be exploited. These developments provided a bridge between union-centered groups and enduring popular sector struggles for urban subsistence and services. Second, the process had distinctive geographic dimensions. It began in the interior (and frequently more impoverished) provinces of Argentina and then expanded to Buenos Aires, especially between 1996 and 1997. Third, popular sector movement organizations engaged state authorities in a more sustained manner, and their protests forced negotiations and concessions, especially with respect to obtaining and managing relief plans (Oviedo 2001; Svampa and Pereyra 2003).

The contentious action and demands of the major mobilizing groups reveal their Polanyi-like defensive character and their reformist and noninsurrectionary orientation. They held meetings, marched, demonstrated, blocked roads, and fought riot police, pressing for public commitment to employment creation, unemployment protection, and the restitution of subsistence, labor rights, local economic development, and dignified living. Outrage at political and union-leader corruption in negotiations over neoliberal reforms (especially privatization and state restructuring), opaque policy processes, and the lack of government accountability raised claims for cleaner government, greater transparency, and improved accountability. These grievances addressed the mechanisms of political exclusion at all levels of government linked to neoliberal reforms. Framing and brokerage mechanisms transformed individual grievances into associational and collective power.

Transformation in Anti-Neoliberal Contentious Politics: The Interior Provinces

A social explosion in the province of Neuquén on 20–25 June 1996, followed by a succession of similar events the following year in Neuquén on 9–19 April, Salta 8–14 May, and Jujuy in the second half of May, transformed contentious politics in Argentina.[8] National media attention made them symbols of resistance worthy of emulation. They triggered an upward spiral in anti-neoliberal contention when similar mobilization spread across impoverished interior provinces.

The towns of Cultral-Co and Plaza Huincul in Neuquén and General Mosconi and Tartagal in Salta were stark examples of neoliberal reform-driven patterns of socioeconomic exclusion and their effect on contentious action. These were oil towns separated by only a few kilometers built during the national populist period and dominated by the state-owned Yacimientos Petrolíferos Fiscales (YPF; Fiscal Oil Fields). The company was the largest employer, paid its full-time workers well, and gave them generous retirement, health, housing benefits, and even recreational benefits (Auyero 2004: 139; Svampa and Pereyra 2003: 103–4).

The privatization of Yacimientos in 1991–92 had profound exclusionary consequences, shattering a way of life that had existed for 40 years. The Peronist oil union abandoned workers in return for organizational resources (Murillo 2001). Unemployment rates were as high as 30 percent of the economically active population, and half the population lived below the poverty line (Auyero 2004: 139).[9] Worse, by 1996, unemployment benefits had run out and most self-employment (small businesses and microenterprises) ventures begun with severance compensation had failed (Svampa and Pereyra 2003: 106–8). Neither regular social assistance nor new employment relief programs could accommodate need (Auyero 2004: 139). The specific trigger for mobilization in these "ghost" towns varied according to local conditions, as did the exact composition of instigators, participants, and grievances. Nevertheless, the main characteristics of the first great town uprising in Neuquén between 20 and 25 June 1996 became generalized in provincial anti-neoliberal contention that followed the next year.

Significant developments in popular sector associational and collective power, and roiling discontent, preceded the 1996 town uprising at Cutral-Co and Plaza Huincul. Beginning in late 1994, unemployed workers, frequently from the privatized oil company and state agencies, formed neighborhood-based unemployed commissions in Neuquén Capital, Cutral-Co, and other towns. Enterprising leaders brokered a transformation in the site of labor-based contentious politics from

---

[8] The popular sector forces that drove it featured multiple decision-making centers and exhibited tremendous spontaneity, vitality, and inventiveness. For analytical purposes, however, I focus on common patterns, contributions, and consequences of the most significant events, first in the provinces and then in the more central urban areas, especially Buenos Aires.

[9] Nationally, YPF had employed 51,000 persons in 1990; by 1997 the privatized company had only 5,600 employees. The Neuquén region lost 4,246 jobs (80–85 percent of the workforce), most within a year. Salta suffered a similar fate, with 3,400 job losses (Svampa and Pereyra 2003).

the factory to the community. They drew on dense social and dissident left-ist political party and union networks to create coordinating commissions that established common goals and action plans (Oviedo 2001: 15). The commissions adopted open assembly-style decision making. In late 1995, they began protesting Peronist-controlled workfare programs and demanding increases in the value of workfare plans (Oviedo, 2001: 15).

Blatant economic and political exclusion by new provincial authorities esca-lated the conflict. Felipe Sapag won the October 1995 elections for governor, campaigning for "real job creation" over relief. But his administration cut work-fare benefits from 200 to 150 pesos and introduced co-payments. In Neuquén Capital, 4,000 teachers, state employees, and members of the city's coordinating commission of the unemployed protested these outrages on 22 February 1996. In April 5,000 workers blocked a road for several hours, protesting cuts in workfare benefits. In Cutral-Co (the second largest city in the province), a 500-strong pop-ular assembly pressured the municipal government to declare "total rejection" of the provincial government's policy (Oviedo 2001: 30).

Discontent in Neuquén had opened an opportunity to build collective power for the CTA scarcely a month before the Cutral-Co/Plaza Huincul town upris-ings. It used its organizing expertise, resources, and leadership to broker linkages among the province's commissions and coordinating associations of the unem-ployed. The specific mechanism, quite common among popular sectors, was the convention. In this case the CTA organized the First Congress of the Unem-ployed of Neuquén on 24 May 1996. The Congress brought the CTA's executive board in contact with some 200 delegates from the provincial capital, Cutral-Co, and other towns (Oviedo 2001: 30).

The First Congress transformed isolated commissions and coordinators of the unemployed into a more unified bloc. It defined a common platform and plan of action. Demands included (1) minimum unemployment insurance of $500 without means testing or co-payments from 16 years of age, and with benefits (social security, holiday bonuses, and vacations); (2) temporary "private contract" state workers should become permanent contracted employees; (3) rescinding decrees that cut the salaries of teachers and state employees; (4) a halt to massive public sector firings; and (5) a reduction in the work week without pay cuts. To support these demands, the First Congress resolved to organize a province-wide march "against hunger and unemployment" for 20 June, the day the Cutralcazo began (Oviedo 2001: 30–31).

In this context of roiling discontent, Governor Sapag's sudden cancellation of a promised agrochemical plant – a source of desperately needed employment – was a final betrayal, a bitter confirmation of economic and political exclusion. In response, the provincial chapters of the CTA-affiliated teachers' and state employees' union, disgruntled local politicians, and local notables formed an impromptu multisectoral commission [*multisectorial*] to pressure the authorities. The "multisectoral" called for a march and a roadblock of national Route 22.

Loosely organized groups of picketers [*piqueteros*] drawn from the unemployed commissions defended the roadblocks. They developed assembly-style decision making that undermined local politicians' mediating role with the local authorities.

Their demands were rooted in problems created by neoliberal reforms. They included genuine (formal sector) jobs, unemployment relief, moratoriums on local taxes, electricity, and gas bills, as well as cheap credit for local businesses and revival of the fertilizer project. After the third day, frustrated by the callous dismissal of their suffering by the authorities, they also demanded the governor negotiate with them personally at the roadblock (Auyero, 2004: 140–41).

At the roadblock picketers developed an assembly style of decision making, which later became generalized as popular assemblies. Popular assemblies were a new brokerage instrument because they were open-air, freewheeling gatherings that brought popular sector (and middle-class) organization leaders and individuals together to develop resistance tactics, logistics, and negotiating strategies. In the process they became cognizant of their distinctive collective identity and interests. Thus the popular assembly transformed the relationship of piqueteros to local politicians and notables on the one hand, and to state authorities on the other. At the beginning of the mobilization, the latter controlled negotiation. The popular assemblies undermined local politicians' mediating role with the local authorities; piqueteros insisted on direct negotiation, thus gaining a measure of independence.

Repression generated a new form of mobilization: the *pueblada* [town uprising]. As negotiations through established institutional channels (local politicians) broke down, the provincial government decided to clear the roadblocks by force. Unexpectedly, a massive outpouring of townsfolk – some 20,000 strong – defended the picketers at the roadblocks against the local and provincial police. Teachers, professors, doctors, lawyers, accountants, salespeople, and housewives stood with unemployed workers and poor people from housing projects (Auyero 2004: 143).

Feelings of anger, betrayal, and desperation rooted in mounting economic and political exclusion clearly motivated the protestors (Auyero 2004: 145). One demonstrator exclaimed, "On Sunday the 23rd, Sapag treated us as if we were criminals . . . it was terrible. Picketers were furious: hunger is not a crime!" (Auyero 2004: 141). A mother explained, "My son asked me why we were on the road. I told him: 'look son, this pueblo needs to be heard. The people in this town need to be aware of the things we are losing, of the things the government is taking away from us.'" Protestors repeatedly stated, "We want work. We give them [the country and its leaders] electricity, gas, and petroleum and this is how they repay us. Let [the governor] come before us! Sapag needs to give us a solution [jobs, relief]. We are 30,000, not 5,000. The whole town is here. There are no politicians here, the people, the town is here" (Auyero 2002: 158).

National media attention and the failure of repression forced Sapag and most of his cabinet to Cutral-Co to negotiate conditions for lifting the blockade. Short-term concessions included workfare plans for the unemployed and the suspension of debt burdens, mainly for merchants and small businesses. Longer-term promises involved public works projects to stimulate employment. These were not fulfilled, however, perhaps because once mobilization ended the popular assemblies dissolved and established institutions absorbed their leadership (Svampa and Pereyra 2003: 112).

A dramatic surge in anti-neoliberal contention occurred a year later with the rapid fire explosion of puebladas in Neuquén, Salta, and Jujuy between April and May 1997. These puebladas involved conscious diffusion – with local adaptations – of the main characteristics of the town uprising at Cutral-Co and Plaza Huincul the year before. Their success at forcing negotiation persuaded others to emulate them. Moreover, the leaders of the Jujuy pueblada deliberately timed it to prolong the cycle of contention in the provinces – and focus national political visibility on their problems (Laufer and Spiguel 1999; Oviedo 2001; Svampa and Pereyra 2003).

In these and subsequent mobilization in the provinces, multisectorals became a common form of collective power. These were loosely coordinated coalitions of union organizations (the CTA, the Movimiento de Trabajadores Argentinos, and the Combative Class Current), local politicians (often Frepaso, but also disgruntled Justicialistas and more radical leftist parties), local notables and businesspeople, and unions of unemployed workers. They drew a cross section of people to demonstrations swelling their numbers.

Their demands were Polanyi-like appeals for protection from the effects of market reforms. In Cutral-Co, citizens insisted that the authorities honor the agreement that ended the previous year's pueblada. In General Mosconi-Tartagal, the slate of demands reflected the diversity of the popular assembly that brought together the unemployed workers' union, the teachers' union, the Workers' Party, local Frepaso council members, unions belonging to the Combative Class Current, and small-business associations (Kohan 2002: 31–32). Two key demands were the establishment of unemployment compensation of 400 pesos or 5,000 permanent jobs (along with an explicit rejection of workfare handouts) and the creation of a development fund for the region with oil sector royalties. Business and middle-class demands centered on debt and mortgage payment issues. In Jujuy, in addition to similar postures, the Frente de Gremios Estatales demanded raising taxes on big-business and agrarian or sugar companies to satisfy local needs (Kohan 2002: 13–14).

All of these cases experienced a prior process of associational and collective power building in which popular sector leaders used social and political networks to forge horizontal linkages among their fledgling organizations. In Cutral-Co/Plaza Huincul, the CTA-affiliated teachers' union worked with Frepaso city council members who had clientelistic relationships to unemployed youths. In General Mosconi in the northern province of Salta, the various commissions of the unemployed and coordinating commissions established a strong Unemployed Workers Union in 1996 (Laufer and Spiguel 1999; Svampa and Pereyra, 2003). The protests in Mosconi-Tartagal were the first in which an unemployed workers' union played a central role, demonstrating the true potential of these organizations. It became a model for the rest of Argentina.

In Jujuy, one of the poorest provinces in Argentina, Carlos "Perro" Santillán, the militant head of the Municipal Workers and Employees Union and a key provincial and national leader of the Corriente Combativa Clasista labor movement (of which these unions were a part), kept up a steady drumbeat of work stoppages, slowdowns, marches, and demonstrations. In the close-knit networks of provincial union politics, he brokered the creation of the Frente de Gremios Estatales. By tirelessly arranging individual and group meetings with local union leaders, he brought together a formidable alliance of 14 local unions that included the CTA teachers' and state employee unions and health employees. They opposed firings, labor flexibilization, unemployment, pay cuts and arrears, pension plan reform, and budget cuts. They staged general strikes and hunger strikes and occupied public buildings. In addition to his role in forming the Frente de Gremios Estatales, Santillán also enlisted the local committees and coordinators of the unemployed for the May 1997 mobilization (Kohan 2002: 13–14).

The Frente de Gremios Estatales was a major development in anti-neoliberal contentious politics. In addition to coordinating contentious action, it gave protestors a stable and experienced organization capable of formulating a platform of demands and of maintaining popular sector cohesion in negotiations with the authorities and other organizations in the "multisectoral," such as the local Catholic Church, opposition political party leaders, and local business leaders (Laufer and Spiguel 1999: 26–28). In another major innovation, the Frente de Gremios Estatales, a non-Peronist popular sector organization, was given control over the administration of workfare and relief programs (Svampa and Pereyra 2003: 33 and 34).

The puebladas of Neuquén, Salta, and Jujuy established the innovative, highly transgressive and disruptive roadblock as a central element in the repertoire of anti-neoliberal contention. The roadblock's transgressive quality lay in its capacity to force confrontations with the police and therefore draw media attention. Because disruption of the workplace had lost effectiveness in severely depressed local economies, the unemployed and their allies disrupted vital transportation arteries (Ferrara 2003: 39; Scribano 1999; Svampa and Pereyra 2003).

The roadblocks, in turn, created a new identity for unemployed protestors – the *piquetero* [picketer] and a new form of decision-making, the popular assembly (Laufer and Spiguel 1999; Oviedo 2001; Svampa and Pereyra 2003). Roadblocks were open-ended events and had to be protected from attempts to dismantle them. Drawing from the militant union tradition of picketing during strikes, the (usually young) unemployed men and women who guarded the roadblocks around the clock appropriated the piquetero identity. They developed a subculture involving camps, work rules, and established *ollas populares* [soup kitchens]. Supporting organizations as well as citizens (who called each other *vecinos*, meaning neighbors) provided money, food, and other forms of aid.[10] Piqueteros developed an assembly style of decision making, as previously discussed in the case of the 1996 Neuquén pueblada. Popular assemblies undermined local politicians' mediating role with the local authorities because piqueteros insisted that negotiations be conducted at the roadblocks, thus inhibiting traditional politics of patronage and co-optation to blunt protest (Svampa and Pereyra 2003; Oviedo 2001).

The roadblocks' transgressive and disruptive characteristics generated repression to clear them and the pueblada to defend them. In the opening phases of negotiation, intransigent or duplicitous postures by provincial and local officials invariably failed to persuade protestors to lift them. When the mere presence of riot police did not cause the piqueteros to disperse, they attacked them with batons, tear gas, and rubber (or occasionally even lead) bullets. Outraged at the arrogant, willful disregard for their felt grievances, of their citizenship rights, and way of life, the whole town would come out to defend them. Middle-class persons – such as teachers, professors, doctors, lawyers, accountants, salespeople, and housewives – mobilized alongside unemployed workers and poor people from housing projects (Auyero 2004: 143).

Simmering local grievances around privatization, jobs, working conditions, and debt relief motivated individuals to participate in the roadblocks and puebladas. In the second pueblada at Cutral-Co/Plaza Huincul in April 1997, protestors turned out in anger and frustration over the provincial government's betrayal: It had reneged on promises of jobs and economic development following the 1996 pueblada. A municipal worker grumbled, "In the barrios [poor neighborhoods] they [the politicians] promised hope for change, that enterprises would come. After that they urged people not to block roads, not to protest in front of the municipality, not to burn tires in the road because if we did businesses would not come. Four years of this and the firms have still not come" (Svampa and Pereyra 2003: 117). A determined piquetero exclaimed, "We want work; we stay on the roadblock until there is stable work" (Oviedo 2001: 36). An unemployed oil worker vented, "I can't go from working in petroleum to planting potatoes (Svampa and Pereyra 2003: 117).

---

[10] For example, at Tartagal-Mosconi they provided transportation and camp material for the 8-day roadblock that cut commerce to Bolivia on Route 34 for 8 days. Businesspeople (merchants) supplied food. A feeling of downward mobility, of being robbed of a good, decent, and dignified quality of life by neoliberal reforms, united them (Barbetta and Lepegna 2001; Svampa and Pereyra 2003: 124–25). Still, social strata did not mix (Barbetta and Lepegna 2001: 244–45).

In General Mosconi and Tartagal, enraged citizens protested neoliberal reform-driven hard times. A militant of the Unemployed Workers Union explained:

"Here the multinationals have taken all the wealth, here the multinationals have left only desolation and death, and we sink into the most humiliating poverty, and we have to live hand to mouth dependent on good for nothing relief plans, [and yet] with all our local resources [oil] we possess everything necessary to live well." (Svampa and Pereyra 2003:123)

The destruction of a way of life built around the state oil company in Salta found expression in other framings as well. These centered on emotional references to the "recovery of the family" and the "recovery of life." This word choice suggested a yearning to reconstruct the social ties neoliberal reforms ripped apart. Protestors in General Mosconi demanded rights to stable, formal sector jobs that allowed them to live with dignity (Giarraca and Wahren 2006).

Without wishing to minimize the extent of violence used to clear roadblocks, because Argentina was democratic, riot control, for the most part, stayed within the upper limits of "permissible" force. Although repression to clear roadblocks occasionally killed protestors and injured many more, suppressing the puebaldas would have required even stronger measures that might lead to massacres. This, of course, was not permissible in a democracy, especially because Argentina was still traumatized by the human rights violations of all-too-recent military governments. Even worse for the local authorities, the scale of mobilization and repression attracted national media attention (Oviedo 2001; Svampa and Pereyra 2003).

Thus puebladas compelled the authorities to negotiate with protestors. Negotiations generally involved high-level provincial officials, including the governor, local authorities, and, not infrequently, representatives of the national government. The concessions that followed fell into a pattern. The most frequently granted were short-term ones centered on the allocation of workfare plans for the unemployed, debt relief (largely for small-business people), and food supplements. Some protests also obtained commitments by the provincial government, with national government support, for longer-term development goals such as public works and public housing programs, as well as immunity from prosecution for the picketers (Laufer and Spiguel 1999: 26–28; Oviedo, 2001; Svampa and Pereyra, 2003: 114–15, 124).[11]

The demonstration effect of the oil town and Jujuy puebladas reverberated throughout the country. Between April and June 1997, protestors, frequently organized in impromptu "multisector" associations, blocked roads in many other Argentine provinces. As a result, by 2000 the roadblock was a "form of protest

---

[11] For a full description of benefits to the region, see Svampa and Pereyra (2003: 118–23).

[that] had been learned and adopted throughout the entire country" (Auyero, 2004: 130).[12]

Transformation in Anti-Neoliberal Contentious Politics: Buenos Aires

Mobilization and the associational and collective power of anti-neoliberal popular sector forces in Buenos Aires, the center of national political power, expanded significantly between 1995 and 1998. Two poles developed. On the one hand, the CTA, the Combative Class Current, and Frepaso built coalitions with nonunion popular sector organizations, many of which had their origins in the rebirth of urban subsistence movements. On the other hand, more radical leftist groups, also drawing mainly from urban subsistence movements, formed new independent organizations of unemployed workers (see Table 4.4).[13]

The CTA spearheaded the movement to boost associational and collective power through *framing* mechanisms. Its slogan, *la nueva fábrica es el barrio* [the new factory is the neighborhood], expressed the shift from workplace to community as the center for organizing and for contentious politics in large urban areas (Svampa and Pereyra 2003). It articulated the previously discussed expanded meaning of worker, the imperative to organize, and the principle of solidarity that united them. This framing facilitated communication with community-based working-class and urban squatter movements demanding urban services and subsistence rights (Eckstein 1989). After all, neoliberal reforms made difficult lives even harder across the popular sectors. Unemployment and underemployment soared in sprawling working-class districts like La Matanza as factories closed, with flex labor and migration from impoverished rural areas. Working hours increased as wages remained stagnant or declined. Bitterness and despair over the CGT-affiliated unions' complicity rankled. As income shrank, hunger and malnutrition, especially among children, grew (Alderete and Gómez 1999: 3–4, 13).

The CTA's framing was an effective organizing tool. It restored the dignity and self-worth of the unemployed, emphasizing they were the victims of neoliberal policy not their personal failing. Fliers of the Unemployed Workers Movement (Movimiento de Trabajadores Desocupados, or MTD) (October 1996) illustrate the point. One read, "The lie that we are responsible for our unemployment, misery, and desperation is over ... *those who govern us and their accomplices are responsible for our desperation.*" Another declared, "We, the unemployed are millions of human beings [of all ages] who have lost everything in economic terms. But we will never lose our dignity. They want to reduce us to statistics ... but we

---

[12] Those provinces included Chubt, Córdoba, Santa Fe, Río Negro, Tucumán, and Neuquén.
[13] These tendencies notwithstanding, as in the provinces, the myriad organizations that flourished in Buenos Aires had diverse origins, objectives, and organizational characteristics that invested their actions, alliances, and efforts to coordinate contentious action with great fluidity and spontaneity.

Table 4.4. *Piquetero Membership and Control of Workfare Benefits*

Piqueteros' Organization Designation	Year Born	Number of Members	Number of Workfare Benefits Controlled by Organization	Workfare/ Members	Month/Year	Sources
Federación Tierra y Vivienda (FTV)	1998	125,000	75,000	0.60	June 2004	*La Nación*
		120,000	75,000	0.63	Dec 2003	*Clarín*
		–	36,000		Nov 2002	*La Nación*
		65,000	45,000	0.69	Sept 2002	*Clarín*
Corriente Classista Combativa	1998	70,000	50,000	0.71	June 2004	*La Nación*
		120,000	42,000	0.35	Dec 2003	*Clarín*
		–	21,000		Nov 2002	*La Nación*
		65,000	45,000	0.69	Sept 2002	*Clarín*
Barrios de Pie	2001	60,000	7,000	0.12	June 2004	*La Nación*
		–	6,000		Nov 2002	*La Nación*
		4,000	–		July 2002	*Lucha Int.*
Movimiento Integrado de Jubilados y Desocupados	2001	60,000	7,000	0.12	June 2004	*La Nación*
		60,000	9,000	0.15	Dec 2003	*Clarín*
		–	7,300		Nov 2002	*La Nación*
		–	9,000		Sept 2002	*Clarín*
		30,000	–		Sept 2002	*Lucha Int.*
		12,500	–		July 2002	
Bloque Piquetero (Polo Obrero, Teresa Rodríguez, FTC, CUBa)	2001	35,000	20,000	0.57	Sept 2002	*Clarín*
Polo Obrero	1999	25,000	20,000	0.80	June 2004	*La Nación*
		29,000	23,000	0.79	Dec 2003	*Clarín*
		–	10,000		Nov 2002	*La Nación*

Organization	Founded				Date	Source
Teresa Rodríguez	1998	–	5,000		Nov 2002	*La Nación*
Frente de Trabajadores Combativos (FTC)		70,000	–		Dec 2004	*Schiappacasse*
		7,000	2,800	0.40	June 2004	*La Nación*
Coordinadora de Unidad Barrial (CUBa)		5,000	–		Feb 2005	*Segundo Enfoque*
		4,680	1,140	0.24	June 2004	*La Nación*
MTD Aníbal Verón	1997	30,000	5,000	0.17	Dec 2003	*Clarín*
		7,000	–		Jan 2005	*Segundo Enfoque*
Coordinadora Aníbal Verón	2001	–	7,000		Nov 2002	*La Nación*
		15,000	9,000	0.60	Sept 2002	*Clarín*
		7,000	–		July 2002	*Lucha Int.*
Movimiento Sin Trabajo Teresa Vive	2001	95,000	–		Dec 2004	*Schiappacasse*
		–	5,000		Nov 2002	*La Nación*
Movimiento Territorial de Liberación	2001	5,000	–		Dec 2004	*Schiappacasse*
		–	4,000		Nov 2002	*La Nación*
FUTRADEYO		650	–		Dec 2004	*Schiappacasse*
UTD Mosconi – Salta	1996	2,000	–		Feb 2004	*La Jiribilla*
		7,000	–		July 2002	*Lucha Int.*
MTD – Neuquén		1,200	800	0.67	Dec 2003	*Darrio Río Negro*
CCC – Neuquén		500	230	0.46	Dec 2003	*Darrio Río Negro*
Barrios de Pie – Neuquén		600	400	0.67	Dec 2003	*Darrio Río Negro*
Polo Obrero – Neuquén		250	230	0.92	Dec 2003	*Darrio Río Negro*
Teresa Vive – Neuquén		500	262	0.52	Dec 2003	*Darrio Río Negro*

For the full name of piquetero organizations see the acronyms section.

are not statistics, we are human beings" (Balladares et al. 2005: 81). The message struck a chord. A member of the Movimiento de Trabajadores Desocupados explained, "At the time I lived in 'Lo Palito, most people were self employed and unemployed, so . . . well, we got busy because we realized the only way to do something was to organize, to begin pressuring somewhere" (Flores 2005: 78).

The associational power of the popular sectors in and around Buenos Aires expanded rapidly with the formation of independent organizations of the unemployed from surviving urban subsistence movements.[14] Emboldened by a modest success in obtaining food relief and the first Neuquén pueblada, leaders of urban subsistence movements organized the "First March against Hunger and Unemployment" on 6 September 1996. The march was the founding event of the Movement of Unemployed Workers (Svampa and Pereyra 2003: 39–41). March leaders formed several MTDs that later merged into the MTD Teresa Rodríguez.[15] In 1997, after the puebladas of Neuquén and Salta, they took on piquetero identity and set up roadblocks in Buenos Aires and La Plata (also in Buenos Aires province) to wrestle workfare and relief assistance plans from the authorities (Garrido 2005). This period also witnessed the development of Unemployed Workers Coordinators (Coordinadoras de Trabajadores Desempleados, or CTD) in many working-class and urban squatter neighborhoods around Buenos Aires such as Lanús, Almirante Brown, Solano, Florencio Varela, and La Plata (Barral 2005).

These developments fanned an upward spiral of mobilization through August 1997 as movement organizations sought immediate relief. They also pressed larger economic claims advocating reflationary policy. Political goals included weakening incumbent politicians who supported neoliberalism with an eye to replacing them in the 1998 presidential and congressional elections. Newly formed unemployed workers organizations staged 33 piquetero-guarded roadblocks in Buenos Aires city and province during this period (Table 4.5). In most cases, mirroring protest in the provinces that included assembly-style decision making and negotiation, authorities gave in to demands for more workfare relief plans and food assistance.

Meanwhile, the CTA, which gained legal recognition as a new labor confederation in May 1997, and its allies organized national strikes, marches, and demonstrations on the capital city. Building on the events in Neuquén and Salta, and to keep pressure on national authorities, the CTA-affiliated teachers union brought educators from the provinces and the capital who camped at the Plaza Dos Congresos in Buenos Aires to protest meager wages and working conditions (Auyero 2004: 130). Following that, the Mesa de Enlace coordinated a second Federal March for Work in which 70,000 marchers from around the country

---

[14] For details, see Svampa and Pereyra (2003: 38).
[15] They usually took the name of the neighborhood that was their organizational base or of fallen comrades.

Table 4.5. *Evolution of Roadblocks per District, 1997–2003*

Province	Population	Percentage over Country's Total	1997	1998	1999	2000	2001	2002	2003[a]	Total	%
Buenos Aires	14,381,806	38	23	9	82	119	452	587	194	1,466	28%
Jujuy	613,983	2	37	13	1	79	136	414	56	736	14%
Capital Federal	3,049,941	8	11	9	58	51	170	299	120	718	14%
Salta	1,090,047	3	4	0	2	41	59	212	42	360	7%
Tucumán	1,308,414	3	7	0	23	48	55	122	20	275	5%
Santa Fe	3,128,696	8	9	4	13	21	39	129	55	270	5%
Córdoba	3,122,302	8	22	1	4	11	34	158	20	250	5%
Neuquén	581,539	2	10	7	10	52	66	42	14	201	4%
Chaco	962,601	3	2	0	4	24	75	60	8	173	3%
Mendoza	1,627,108	4	0	2	2	8	48	69	7	136	3%
Río Negro	630,548	2	1	0	21	2	78	14	7	123	2%
Catamarca	324,086	1	0	0	1	7	40	53	12	113	2%
Misiones	1,018,263	3	1	2	0	3	29	36	7	78	1%
Entre Ríos	1,121,970	3	3	0	4	16	14	30	4	71	1%
San Juan	582,931	2	1	0	0	9	8	41	8	67	1%
Corrientes	934,637	2	1	0	18	4	14	7	3	47	1%
Chubut	457,856	1	5	0	2	6	10	10	2	35	1%
Santa Cruz	212,234	1	2	1	3	3	5	17	1	32	1%
La Rioja	287,045	1	0	3	0	1	20	6	0	30	1%
Formosa	516,017	1	0	0	0	4	13	10	0	27	1%
Santiago	730,977	2	0	0	0	0	6	12	3	21	0%
Tierra del Fuego	121,405	0	1	0	1	3	5	4	8	22	0%
San Luis	371,798	1	0	0	1	1	5	4	0	11	0%
La Pampa	310,725	1	0	0	2	1	2	0	0	5	0%
TOTAL	37,486,929	100	140	51	252	514	1,383	2,336	591	5,267	100%

[a] Until May 31.

Source: Centro de Estudios Nueva Mayoría.

converged on Buenos Aires in mid-July (Laufer and Spiguel 1999: 29). A month later, the CTA and the Combative Class Current called a general strike (Svampa and Pereyra 2003: 29).

Leaders used several brokerage mechanisms to create associational and collective power. These transformed dispirited individuals into motivated protestors. They turned the remnants of urban self-help movements into challengers of neoliberal reforms.

Working-class neighborhoods were not organizational vacuums. One brokerage mechanism involved dense networks of leftist political parties, squatters' movement leaders, neighborhood associations, and local residents. These networks facilitated communication among them, not the least because overlapping membership created nodes of contact. Juan Carlos Alderete, an unemployed textile and metallurgical worker since 1994, was archetypal. He was the respected leader of squatter settlement struggles that created the Santa Elena neighborhood in La Matanza in the 1980s. He was also a militant of the Revolutionary Communist Party and its labor arm, "Perro" Santillán's Combative Class Current. Adhering to their national strategy beginning in 1996, Alderete used his leadership reputation and skills to organize commissions of unemployed workers affiliated with the Combative Class Current that eventually extended to nearly 100 neighborhoods (Kohan 2002, 17–19).

The initial problem was getting people to overcome the shame of unemployment and to recognize that the government's neoliberal policies were the cause of their troubles. In this context, means of struggle became a second brokerage mechanism. In May 1996, Alderete, in his role as president of the María Elena neighborhood association, established an olla popular at the San Justo plaza. The olla popular was a traditional tool in the popular sector's repertoire of contention. Because people were hungry, they came. Because it lasted for weeks, it created a space where people congregated, exchanged experiences, recognized their common plight, and took courage. The unemployed also met leaders of the neighborhood associations, development centers, and cooperatives (Svampa and Pereyra 2003: 41). Organizers, frequently women, focused the anger, frustration, and despair of the pobladores. In Aldrete's words, "Recognition of profound suffering lies at the core of organizing the masses of unemployed; we must respect that pain and transform it into strength and will to struggle, directing hatred to its proper place, against Menemism" (Alderete and Gómez 1999: 7). And so, the olla popular at San Justo transformed urban struggles of the 1980s for land, services, and property titles into challenges to Menem's neoliberal economic and labor policies. The olla popular at San Justo organized 26 neighborhoods.

To engage the authorities, 1,000 unemployed workers and families marched on the municipality. Their leadership embodied the fledgling alliance of the Combative Class Current, Frepsaso, and the CTA. For example, Alderete for the Combative Class Current and Mary Sánchez as head of the CTA-affiliated teachers' union and founding member of Frepaso negotiated food assistance, their nonnegotiable demand, direcly with the mayor. Equally important, implementation bypassed the Justicialista Party's client–patron network (Alderete and Gómez 1999: 13–14; Svampa and Pereyra 2003: 38–39).[16]

Similar experiences occurred all over metropolitan Buenos Aires and nearby provinces. Ollas populares and popular assemblies connected the unemployed and popular sector leaders wishing to organize them. These were the origins of the MID and the CTD. They demonstrated, marched, and blocked roads to force the authorities to engage them. Food distribution and workfare were the most frequent concessions (Flores 2005; Kohan 2002; Oviedo 2001; Svampa and Pereyra 2003).

Conventions and congresses were the principal brokerage mechanisms by which unemployed workers' organizations connected, established common platforms, and coordinated contentious action. This transformed local struggle into broader events that attracted media attention. The authorities' fear of "puebladas" at the center of Argentine politics encouraged concessions, further emboldening coordinated action.

For example, after occupying the municipal building with help from the Combative Class Current-affiliated pensioners' association, Alderete organized a "plenary" of the Combative Class Current's neighborhood unemployed workers commissions in January 1998, which acted relatively independently. The plenary allowed leaders to overcome fears of discord and repression. This facilitated permanent interaction among the various commissions with the establishment of a popular assembly that met every Saturday in a school. The experience transformed collective action by expanding the scale of mobilization and negotiating power of the unemployed commissions of the Combative Class Current (Alderete and Gómez 1999: 18–20). Demands now expressed a more policy-oriented challenge to neoliberalism including those of new allies, such as the pensioners' and Toty Flores' organization in La Juanita:

1. Low-income housing
2. Reopening closed factories and rehiring of fired workers
3. Minimum pension of $450
4. Defense of universal, free, public education and health care
5. Moratorium on foreign debt repayment
6. Defense of the Banco de la Nación (the state bank)
7. Unity of the labor movement and a 36-hour general strike

---

[16] The full slate demands read: (1) food for the families of the unemployed to be distributed weekly by neighborhood associations, development centers, or cooperatives; (2) 100,000 public works jobs, including water service and neighborhood infrastructure; (3) unemployment subsidies to cover everyone; (4) free transportation passes for the unemployed to look for work; (5) exemption from utility and tax payments for the unemployed; (6) implementation of 6-hour shifts in the workplace; (7) rescind legislation permitting the indiscriminate firing of municipal workers; (8) prohibit persecution of popular sector leaders and repression of public demonstrations.

Although the CTA and Frepaso restrained mobilization after 1997 as part of their national and local electoral strategy, they and allied organizations used the surge of unemployed workers movements to build associational and collective power. For example, as previously discussed, the Combative Class Current used its plenary to establish an unemployed workers commissions' branch, which substantially expanded the collective power of the CTA–Frepaso–Combative Class Current alliance. By the same token, in August 1997, the CTA and Frepaso, with the Workers Party and the Revolutionary Communist Party, convened the First National Convention of the Unemployed in La Matanza, Buenos Aires. The convention attracted ample representation from the unemployed workers movement (Dinerstein 2001: 5; Oviedo 2001). As result of this event, the CTA and the Revolutionary Communist Party–Combative Class Current bloc formalized their working relationship. They agreed on a network structure to coordinate mobilization by unemployed workers organizations. The more radical Workers Party remained uninterested (Svampa and Pereyra 2003: 41).

The collective power of the CTA–Combative Class Current web expanded exponentially on 18 July 1998 when the CTA created the Land and Housing Federation (Federación Tierra y Vivienda, or FTV). The FTV transformed an extensive network of urban subsistence movements in Buenos Aires, led by Luis D'Elía, into a more coordinated system. As previously seen, their struggles moved beyond urban subsistence to challenging neoliberal policy. This, in turn, exponentially increased the mobilizing capability of the CTA–Frepaso–Combative Class Current alliance.

The CTA's leader, Víctor de Gennaro, brokered this transformation of collective power over several encounters in which both leaders realized their mutual interest in opposing neoliberal reforms. The form of struggle initially brought them together. In 1997, D'Elía established a protest encampment demanding food aid in front of the National Congress right next to one organized by De Gennaro's CTA-affiliated teachers union – the White Tent. The CTA then organized a conference in El Tambo – D'Elía's La Matanza stronghold – on land, housing, and environmental health. It brought more than 300 delegates together and got them thinking about coordinating activities (Svampa and Pereyra 2003: 45). A larger follow-up conference, the aforementioned First National Convention of the Unemployed in La Matanza, provided the opportunity to forge tighter linkages among them.

D'Elía had much to offer. He was an entrepreneurial popular sector leader who believed in flexible, nonideological coalition building to establish the broadest possible diversified support base. He had led the land takeover and subsequent struggles for legal title and urban services that established El Tambo beginning in 1986. Under neoliberalism D'Elía developed a two-pronged organizing strategy. One approach involved the reproduction of material life in the settlement. Between 1995 and 1998, he organized extensive networks of self-help groups around hunger and food distribution, such as the Food Network and Red de

Barrios. These networks included neighborhood associations, childcare centers, and cooperatives. Their conventions drew upward of 300 such organizations. He also cultivated support from human rights groups and Christian base communities. The other approach pursued external alliances to obtain resources – all outside Peronist Party networks. These involved pragmatic relationships with authorities and political parties (Svampa and Pereyra 2003: 39–44).

The CTA formally created the Federación Tierra y Vivienda in 1998, thereby coordinating more than 200 community organizations in all Argentina. A national convention defined three lines of action: poverty and unemployment; land and housing; rural-peasant problems. The CTA formulated national strategy, D'Elía was president of the national directorate, and regional headquarters were organized. The coalition between Federación Tierra y Vivienda and the CTA worked thanks to the close association between D'Elía and Alderete. In fact Alderete was the brokerage lynchpin. His union background as the national leader of the Combative Class Current cemented his connection to the CTA. His neighborhood-organizing background and close ties to popular sector self-help organizations made a working relationship with D'Elía possible (Svampa and Pereyra 2003: 58–59).

Economic Crisis and the Third Wave of Anti-Neoliberal Contention, 1999–2001

Frepaso's and the CTA's electoral strategy contributed to the victory of Fernando de la Rúa in December 1999, which raised hopes for reforming neoliberalism. The new president headed a coalition of the declining Radical Party and waxing Frepaso, dubbed the Alianza. Although de la Rúa was from the conservative wing of the Radical Party, Frepaso obtained the vice presidency and important ministries. The CTA-led anti-neoliberal protest bloc restrained mobilization in expectation of policy change.

But conditions did not improve. The Asian financial-crisis-induced world economic downturn, followed by the Brazilian currency crisis of 1999, caused a four-year contraction that sapped the economic and political power of de la Rúa's ill-fated government (see Table 4.1). As investment, growth, and employment shrank, steadfast implementation of harsh IMF-sponsored economic stabilization programs to defend the Convertibility Plan dashed expectations of significant shifts from the neoliberal order.[17]

Socioeconomic exclusion soared to new heights, stoking citizen indignation to the breaking point. Unemployment climbed steadily to 19.7 percent in 2002. Jobs were not even available in the informal sector as it shrank from 49.3 percent in 1998 to 45.7 percent in 2001. Meanwhile, official poverty figures, which stood

---

[17] For Argentine economic policy during this period, see Tedesco and Barton (2004).

at 10.4 percent in 1980 and had nearly tripled by 1995, soared to an unimagined 45 percent in 2001.[18] The trend toward income concentration continued unabated, now markedly at the expense of the middle classes (see Table 4.1). Thus, although employment losses and downward mobility affected all socioeconomic groups, this time it especially hit the middle classes.

The pointed political and economic exclusion of popular sector and middle-class interests pushed their frustration, rage, despair, and indignation to new heights. In this third wave of anti-neoliberal contention, the associational and collective power of anti-neoliberal social forces expanded sharply over four distinct phases. All across the nation Argentines mounted a relentless stream of protest to force policy reform, eventually demanding the president's resignation.

Resurgence of Popular Sector Mobilization, 1999–November 2001

The opening phase of the third wave of anti-neoliberal contention began just days after de la Rúa took office on 10 December 1999. Economy Minister José Luis Machinea, of the Radical Party, proposed orthodox stabilization to shore up the peso and cut fiscal spending, even though the fiscal deficit was a manageable 2.4% of GDP (Rock 2002). Bowing to IMF demands, he recommended reducing federal government revenue sharing to the provinces (Eaton 2005).

Although Peronist governors and the Congress eventually blocked revenue-sharing cuts, the immediate effects of fiscal retrenchment and de facto reductions in federal revenue sharing were new puebladas in Corrientes and in Salta (Tartagal and Mosconi). These puebladas displayed new developments in associational power. First, the conflict in Corrientes, which had begun in March and had come to a head in June and July, exploded again on 13 December 1999 (Auyero 2005; Oviedo 2001). In the absence of CTA–Frepaso-initiated mobilization, *"self-convened"* teachers, government employees, students, and the unemployed blocked a major artery at a bridge and were cleared by fierce repression that left two dead and many more injured. Federal mediators defused the situation by paying back wages to teachers but ignored demands from the other groups (Oviedo 2001: 69).

A second development in associational power drove the nearly simultaneous puebladas in Salta. In July 1999 the Workers Party finally formed its own piquetero arm: the Polo Obrero, an unemployed workers association. Led by Polo Obrero, piqueteros of the Mosconi Union of Unemployed Workers blocked roads in Tartagal and Mosconi, demanding reinstatement of fired public employees. They resisted repression and won their demands (Oviedo 2001: 71–73).

The Workers Party's decision to create its own unemployed workers organization grew out of frustration with the lull in organized mobilization and the

---

[18] That statistic captures only urban poverty rates; rural ones were higher still. Moreover, given the defense of the peso's value, wage indexes for those fortunate to have jobs in the formal sector remained steady.

reformist and welfare assistance orientation of the CTA-led bloc. Mobilization by self-convened piqueteros in Buenos Aires and interior provinces finally convinced the Workers Party that, orthodox Marxism notwithstanding, the unemployed movements had revolutionary potential (Oviedo 2002, 2001: 65–66).[19] Although the Polo Obrero's substantive demands were not so different from those of the "reformist" organizations they criticized, it advocated a much more aggressive, confrontational, and sustained strategy of contentious action. It wanted to keep unrelenting pressure on the authorities and to create revolutionary conditions for more far-reaching reforms to neoliberalism.

These protests failed to change policy. In April 2000 Economy Minister Machinea proposed new IMF-sponsored adjustment measures to stabilize an economy sliding deeper into recession (by the end of the year GDP had contracted nearly another percent). These included bills to flexiblize labor, cut public sector wages, and deregulate union-administered health insurance and assistance.

This policy tack, and other political issues, weakened the political power of the government. They aggravated strained relations between the Radical Party and Frepaso and prompted the CTA-led anti-neoliberal movement bloc to break with the Alianza. The resignation of Vice President "Chacho" Alvarez (of Frepsaso) in October 2000 formalized the Alianza's breakdown (Levitsky and Murillo 2005; Tedesco and Barton 2004).

These developments set the stage for the second phase of this wave of contention that spanned from May 2000 to March 2001. Mobilization surged strongly as the anti-neoliberal popular sector blocs simultaneously, although without much formal coordination, staged four massive general strikes, accompanied and interspersed with marches and roadblocks. The surge began when the CTA and the Movimiento de Trabajadores Argentinos (with Corriente Clasista Combativa support) called a general strike for 5 May 2000. Public transportation in Buenos Aires shut down, and roadblocks occurred in Buenos Aires province as well as in San Luis, Tucumán, Jujuy, and Santa Cruz (*Clarín* 3–6 May 2000). Later that month a massive pueblada in Mosconi and Tartagal (Salta province) led by independent unemployed workers organizations demanding implementation of past agreements – especially job creation and renewal of work relief plans – defeated police repression and obtained a commitment (brokered by national authorities) for short-term relief (Oviedo 2001: 74–75).[20]

On 9 June 2000, all three labor confederations, the CGT (defending control over obras sociales), the Movimiento de Trabajadores Argentinos, and the CTA, staged a massive 24-hour general strike that counted with 60–85 percent

---

[19] The usual provinces saw the greatest upsurges, such as Buenos Aires, metropolitan Buenos Aires, Jujuy, Neuquén, Corrientes, and Santa Fe, and newer places like Río Negro and Tucumán; see Table 4.2 and Oviedo (2001: 62–68).

[20] These tactics became a model for obtaining concessions in remote interior provinces outside the national media limelight where police repression tended to be more violent (Svampa and Pereyra 2003).

adherence in metropolitan Buenos Aires (Dinerstein 2001: 5). The strike also succeeded in provinces with large urban concentrations such as Córdoba, Santa Fe, Buenos Aires province, Río Negro, and Catamarca. Teachers and transport workers had a strong showing in Neuquén, San Luis, San Juan, La Rioja, and Ushuaia (*Clarín* 10 June 2000).[21]

Another wave of mobilization hit Argentina in November 2000. The CTA, Federación Tierra y Vivienda, the Combative Class Current piquetero bloc, and independent unemployed workers' organizations, such as the Polo Obrero, blocked roads throughout Buenos Aires working-class suburbs, especially La Matanza. Foregoing repression, the government granted workfare plans and food assistance, sparking even more roadblocks in southern Buenos Aires (Oviedo 2001, 79–80; Svampa and Pereyra 2003).[22] The month culminated with a third general strike, replete with marches on public buildings and roadblocks called by the CTA, the MTA, and the Combative Class Current to protest the death of Aníbal Verón in a recent Mosconi pueblada and to repudiate economic stabilization policies. The CGT joined in the following day. The strike succeeded in metropolitan Buenos Aires and the provinces of Buenos Aires, Córdoba, San Juan, Salta, Jujuy, and Tucumán (*Clarín* 24 and 25 November 2000; Dinerstein 2001: 5–6).

These demonstrations won popular sector protestors emergency relief but failed to change national policy. In March 2001, newly appointed Economy Minister Ricardo López Murphy announced plans for a draconian economic stabilization program. It proposed cutting fiscal spending by nearly two-billion pesos (dollars) to meet IMF demands attached to a 39.7-billion-dollar loan negotiated toward the end of November 2000 (Rock 2002). The new economic measures hit public sector employees, pensioners, and students particularly hard.

All three trade union centrals called a fourth general strike, with marches, demonstrations, and roadblocks on 21 March 2001. The general strike contributed to the prompt resignation of the minister who lasted only three weeks in office (Seoane 2002). Frequent roadblocks organized by the myriad organizations of the unemployed resumed during May in La Matanza demanding, and receiving, renewal of the relief plans (Svampa and Pereyra 2003). Interior provinces, such as Mosconi in Salta on 17 June 2001, had to fight harder for relief. Protestors faced fierce repression that brought in national mediators who negotiated a solution (Svampa and Pereyra 2003).

Still the government refused to budge. To appease the international financial community, de la Rúa appointed Domingo Cavallo, the architect of the

---

[21] The CTA and unemployed workers organizations followed this up with a march (Marcha Grande) from 26 July to 9 August 2000 where columns from several provinces converged with Buenos Aires organizations in front of the National Congress to submit a proposal for unemployment compensation, job retraining, and dependent support (Svampa and Pereyra 2003).

[22] The authorities were less willing to negotiate without first attempting to repress protestors in more remote interior provinces.

convertibility plan, finance minister. Argentina was dependent on the IMF for loans to support peso parity with the dollar, to meet foreign debt obligations, and for its seal of approval in negotiations with international capital. The IMF insisted Argentina implement stringent fiscal stabilization targets, especially a reduction in federal revenue sharing with the provinces, as a condition for an eight-billion-dollar loan. Cavallo obliged, announcing a zero-deficit plan. The program envisioned immediate reduction of the public deficit by cutting fiscal spending – with the exception of foreign debt service – to the level of tax collection (balanced budget); it also proposed a 13 percent cut in the salaries of public employees (30 percent in the case of workers who earned more than $500), firing personnel, slashing spending for universities, and state employees were to receive part of their salaries in new bond issues (Dinerstein 2001). Unemployed workers' movements, public sector employees, university professors, students, and others immediately protested, and the three main labor confederations convened a general strike for 19 July.

Hunger, the need for employment, dignity, and feelings of political exclusion drove people in Buenos Aires and the interior provinces to mobilize. The member of a popular assembly explained: "I discovered that many of my neighbors . . . were hungry . . . It is absolutely clear that hunger is there on the street, people need to eat today while they struggle for meaningful policy change. That's why we also pressure the Buenos Aires government for food baskets" (Caram 2002: 147). Another protestor exclaimed: "[Blocking roads] helps us emotionally; you have a space where you can express your anger, this is necessary because we are not heard. What we need is a job, one that is dignified" (López Levy 2004: 83).

Similar grassroots testament supports the argument that repression, the bluntest expression of political exclusion, contributed to mobilization. A former municipal state employee, now a clerk for the Unión de Trabajadores Desocupados, Mosconi explained:

I used to be against roadblocks, but when repression began I went. How to put it, one goes because it's like an instinct, one doesn't think about it. Somewhere a siren wails or young people pass by shouting and you join them; you don't care that you might be beaten or killed. You go out, and when you get there [to the roadblock] and you run into the police, you ask yourself: Why am I here? And then you see your neighbor, someone you know has nothing to do with this but who is there anyway, that shows people support it. (Svampa and Pereyra 2003: 126–27)

A surge in popular sector collective power made a third round of mobilization qualitatively different from preceding ones. The CTA and the Polo Obrero coordinated contentious action in the capital and provinces independently of general strikes called by labor confederations, but supported by them. Equally important, as will be detailed later, popular sector organizations included policy-oriented reforms to neoliberal economics in their demands. Coordinated popular sector mobilization in August and September 2001 contributed significantly to the deepening political crisis of de la Rúa's government, ratcheting up pressure to abandon orthodox economic stabilization in the interest of governability.

The reformist CTA-led anti-neoliberal protest bloc used the by now-well-established brokerage device of the convention to effect this transformation in popular sector collective and disruptive power. It convened the First National Assembly of Piqueteros, held on 24 July 2001 in La Matanza, Buenos Aires. The convention included independent piquetero organizations such as the Movmiento Teresa Rodríguez, the Movimineto de Trabajadores Desocupados of southern Buenos Aires, pensioner organizations, neighborhood associations, and the Polo Obrero. The CTA–Federación Tierra y Vivienda–Combative Class Current bloc hoped to unite the movement under their leadership. But there were too many differences with the Movimiento Teresa Rodríguez and the Movimiento de Trabajadores of southern Buenos Aires and with the Workers Party's Polo Obrero (Seoane 2002; Svampa and Pereyra 2003: 78).

The rift deepened during the Second National Piquetero Convention on 4 September 2001 convened by the CTA–Federación Tierra y Vivienda–Combative Class Current bloc to rally movements behind their Frenapo (Frente Nacional contra la Pobreza, National Front Against Poverty) initiative. The Polo Obrero and the Movimiento Teresa Rodríguez, who were drawing closer together, felt the time was ripe to gain greater independence from the "reform-" minded CTV-led bloc. Building associational power, they formed a competing, piquetro bloc, the Bloque Piquetero Nacional. It included the Movimiento Teresa Rodríguez and several smaller organizations (see Table 4.4), and it drew several independent unemployed workers organizations into its orbit.

Although an overarching piquetero confederation did not form, the creation of two relatively cohesive blocs of piquetero organizations capable of coordinating mobilization with independent organizations was a significant increase in the collective power of the popular sector. The CTA-led bloc was more closely linked to the dissident union movement, reformist minded, willing to work with parties and authorities in defense of employment, the mixed economy, and social insurance. The Bloque Piquetero Nacional was more militant, ready to use violence to resist repression, and linked to more revolutionary parties. Its ultimate goal was to provoke a political crisis and constituent assembly to build popular power.

The First and Second Piquetro Assemblies also crafted a national platform of demands far beyond immediate emergency relief:

1. Abrogation of the "zero-deficit" stabilization program
2. Cessation of illegitimate foreign debt service
3. Revision of the national budget "which only extends the social massacre of our families and children"
4. Renationalization of banks, the pension system, and former state-owned companies

5. Due process and freedom for jailed protestors
6. Expansion of work relief programs
7. Moratorium on firings, layoffs, and suspensions (Seoane 2002; Svampa and Pereyra 2003: 210).[23]

Returning to the popular sector's capacity to coordinate sustained pressure on the government on behalf of these demands, during the First National Convention the two piquetero blocs *agreed on a program of national mobilization* beginning 31 July 2001. True to their resolution, piqueteros coordinated a campaign of three nationwide roadblocks on consecutive Tuesdays between 31 July and 17 August, lasting 24, 48, and 76 hours, respectively, and that gained national media attention (Oviedo 2001; Svampa and Pereyra 2003: 71).[24] The "nationalization" of the roadblock, hitherto provincial or local in nature, marked a qualitative shift in the politics of resistance; not only because they were national in scope but also because they were independent of labor confederation strike action (although the CTA and the MTA supported them) (*Clarín* 1 August 2001). Moreover, protests extended to interior provinces (Dinerstein 2003b, 2001; Seoane 2002). The Second Assembly agreed to mount a 24-hour nationwide mobilization to begin on 6 September followed by a 36-hour mobilization on the next Thursday, ending with a march on the main government centers (such as the Plaza de Mayo in Buenos Aires) (Seoane 2002; Svampa and Pereyra 2003: 210).

"Que se Vayan Todos," December 2001

As contentious politics expanded sharply, the economic and political power of de la Rúa's government plummeted (Schvarzer 2003). GDP contracted 4.4 percent in 2001 and urban unemployment climbed toward 20 percent, leaving de la Rúa feeling utterly dependent on the IMF and international capital, which insisted on strict stabilization policies. Politically, Frepaso was imploding. The Peronist Party mounted intransigent opposition to a Radical Party presidency; a tactic strengthened by the victory of a more national-populist faction of the Peronist

---

[23] Thus, despite their ideological disapproval of "relief," many of the independent MTD organizations and the Polo Obrero used obtaining emergency work relief programs and food assistance as practical incentives to organize and mobilize their militants in the interest of larger strategic objectives.

[24] In between the second and third nationwide roadblocks, on 8 August 2001 the CTA organized a march to Plaza de Mayo (about 10,000–15,000 people according to official sources), and roadblocks occurred throughout the nation. The epicenter was in La Matanza, but there were about 300 roadblocks in all of Argentina. Five-thousand people participated in Neuquén and Entre Ríos. In La Matanza CCC and MST public hospital workers and teachers turned out (*Clarín* 8 August 2001). *Clarín* stories of 9 August and 9 September 2001 give more details – especially for calls for a third wave of mobilization for 76 hours the following week by the CTA–CCC–FTV. The Polo Obrero and other MTDs clearly participated in these events.

Party in midterm congressional elections, which gave Peronists a majority in the legislature in December (Llanos and Margheritis 2006).[25]

From this weak position, de la Rúa's administration launched a desperate attempt to save the convertibility program. On 3 December 2001, scarcely a week before the newly elected members of Congress were to take office, Finance Minister Cavallo – the architect of the convertibility plan – decreed the "*corralito*" [playpen] to contain a run on dollar deposits in banks because of devaluation rumors. The corralito closed all banks and then severely restricted withdrawals from accounts trapping many people's savings in failing banks (Dinerstein 2003a: 191). This final outrage set off a social explosion that precipitated the political crisis that forced de la Rúa's resignation on 20 December 2001.

The corralito summed up the public's anger with the entire neoliberal project: anger toward a heartless IMF – symbol of international capitalism – that forced unreasonable stabilization targets on the country with callous disregard of its consequences for livelihood; anger at politicians for not standing up to the IMF's demands and, thus, for their complicity in foisting a policy of hunger and deepening misery on Argentines while protecting international finance and domestic capital; anger over the corruption of politicians throughout the whole process (most recently seen in scandals over administration attempts to bribe senators to vote for a labor flexibilization bill); anger over persistent support for fiscal, economic, and social policies that translated into a bleak future of mushrooming unemployment, precarious work, and job insecurity (Armony and Armony 2005; Auyero 2006; Dinerstein 2003a).

That anger was a symptom of deeper causes for the pent-up rage that exploded in December 2001: the political and economic exclusion of ordinary Argentines since 1989. Despite mounting mobilization, clear voter signals for change with their support of the Alianza in 1999, and even clearer electoral messages in returning Peronists to power in midterm congressional elections when the Alianza ignored those signals, despite all this, the government insisted on supporting IMF-sponsored orthodox economic stabilization programs. The freeze on bank deposits and Cavallo's insistence on the zero-deficit program crystallized rage against persistent, willful, arrogant political and economic exclusion (Dinerstein 2003a).

Protestors' demands reflected those exclusions. Punishment for corrupt politicians – the choral chant of *que se vayan todos* [out with all incumbents] – expressed a visceral yearning for political inclusion in defense of their interests; perhaps a new crop of elected officials sidelined by neoliberalism would do a better job of shielding them from predatory markets. Lifting the freeze on bank deposits was a cry for protection from international and domestic finance. The middle class called for the government to stand up to the IMF and end recessionary policies and to protect formal sector jobs. Popular sectors insisted on nationalizing privatized

---

[25] For the crisis of representation, see Torre (2005); Levitsky (2005).

companies, reflationary fiscal policies, and wage protection, and implementation of the full array of the employment-centered union platform they had developed in the past. This included protection from dismissals and pay cuts; annual 6–8 percent pay increases; expansion of the unemployment relief program with a monthly 350-peso floor; and participatory budgeting at the municipal level like the one in Porto Alegre, Brazil.[26] These were all Polanyi-like defensive demands for protection from predatory free markets and their agents.

Events moved quickly after the government announced the corralito on 3 December 2001. On 12 December, two days after the new Congress – with its Peronist majority – convened, the CTA coordinated marches on the Congress and the Plaza de Mayo, respectively. In this event, independent piquetero organizations became violent (*Clarín* 12 December 2001). Unrest spread that evening, with blackouts and roadblocks in Greater Buenos Aires, La Plata, and the provinces of Salta and Jujuy. Notably, middle classes made their first appearance, honking horns and banging pots and pans.

The next day, 13 December, all three major labor confederations (CGT, CTA, and Movimiento de Trabajadores Argentinos) staged a 24-hour general strike, demanding an end to the corralito and repudiating government economic policy (*Clarín* 11 and 13 December 2001). This seventh general strike against the Alianza government paralyzed the productive sectors of the economy and state offices across the country. In a significant expansion of the collective power of anti-neoliberal protest, the commercial sector joined in closing retail stores; even small proprietors participated (*Clarín* 14 December 2001). The adherence of middle-class professionals, skilled technicians, university professors, and other sectors not especially friendly to unions was a significant occurrence during this event (*Clarín* 14 December 2001); they were key actors in the actions of 19–20 December. Another significant change was violent incidents by piquetero groups from all three blocs, including barricades, assaults on government buildings, arson, and attacks on local politicians, in Neuquén, Córdoba, Rosario, San Juan, and the Buenos Aires province cities of Pergamino and Mar del Plata.

Middle-class adherence to the strike and violence caused the CGT (and the Peronist Party) to worry that events were spinning out of control, and so it abandoned sustained mobilization in favor of tripartite negotiation over policy changes with political parties and the manufacturers' peak association. But events took on their own dynamic. A week earlier the IMF had suspended standby loan disbursements because the Argentine government had not met fiscal stabilization targets. Thus, under IMF pressure and amid daily reports of worsening economic conditions, de la Rúa and Cavallo ignored the demands of mobilized Argentines and asserted their unwavering support for convertibility and fiscal austerity. They announced plans to cut between six- and nine-billion pesos from the federal

---

[26] For demands, see "La crisis Argentina," *En Defensa del Marxismo* 29 (January, 2001); Peruzzotti (2005); Auyero (2007, 2006, 2005); Svampa and Pereyra (2003); Dinerstein (2003a); Rock (2002).

budget, threatening pensions and state employee salaries. Desperate attempts by de la Rúa to orchestrate a dialogue with the Radical Party (which had also abandoned him), the Justicialista Party, and the Peronist unions failed.[27]

In this atmosphere of political and economic decomposition, order broke down in the provinces as desperate, hungry people began to loot stores, mainly food markets (Rosario and Mendoza) beginning 14 December 2001. Looting continued over the next few days and spread to Concordia (Entre Ríos) and other cities. Local and federal government authorities sent police and the army to guard major supermarkets and repress looters. Local piquetero associations, who spearheaded some of the looting, also organized food distribution to impoverished neighborhoods to avoid it.[28] Over the next two days, pickets in front of markets, looting, and sacking spread in Buenos Aires and in the provinces. Repression caused wounded and a few deaths.

The desperate need of poor people claiming the right to feed their families and pushed beyond endurance by neoliberal reforms and orthodox economic stabilization were an explosive mixture. Facing television cameras, a looter cried, "There's a lot of hunger ... there're no jobs. I have eight children; my husband is sick, I don't have enough to survive" (Auyero 2007: 5). In Rosario a woman despaired: "We are hungry, we want food; we want to work. We have big families, we all have four or five kids, and we can't feed them" (Auyero 2007: 136).

The popular sectors were keenly aware of their political exclusion. They held absent, unwilling, or deceptive authorities responsible for their suffering: "We are dying of hunger because we are all unemployed. And the politicians are to be blamed for that." There was no way out but to loot. "Four months ago they cut the *Planes Trabajar* [workfare]. Two months ago they stopped giving bags of food. And yesterday they closed the soup kitchen. What are we going to do?" (Auyero 2007: 137–38).

The evidence strongly suggests that (mainly) Peronist political brokers in working-class neighborhoods [*punteros*] promoted the lootings. They distributed flyers and circulated rumors convoking residents to specific locations. They shepherded them to markets, helped them avoid the police, and led attacks on stores. They transformed the desperate need of people into political action: the destabilization of de la Rúa's government (Auyero 2007; Kohan 2002).

Events exploded between 19 and 20 December 2001. On 19 December, as people began to stream into Buenos Aires city center to demand the resignation of Cavallo and all other elected officials, de la Rúa declared a 30-day state of siege to restore order. Not cowed by the threat of force, the populace disobeyed. For the first time, protest included massive participation by middle classes, who began banging pots, honking horns, and turning out into the streets of their

---

[27] These data are culled from *Clarín* news reports, December 2001.

[28] Neighborhood-based piquetero organizations blocked access to major supermarkets (especially those linked to "transnational capital"), threatening to break in to force free disbursement of food (*Clarín* 18 December 2001; Svampa and Pereyra 2003: 82–84).

neighborhoods all over Buenos Aires and cities across the nation. Still banging their pots and organizing caravans, many marched on to public government buildings throughout Argentina. In Buenos Aires they converged on the presidential residence of Los Olivos, the house of Cavallo, the national Congress, and the Plaza de Mayo.[29]

For the middle class, the corralito was the final outrage. They interpreted it as theft by international and domestic banks in cahoots with corrupt politicians. It destroyed daily routines; anger mounted as it dragged on with no end in sight. Waiting in lines for hours to withdraw their meager weekly allotments politicized them. There they shared personal stories of the collective tragedy that had befallen them (Fernández Anderson 2006).

The corralito unleashed deep frustration over the country's direction. A 1999 survey of middle-class Buenos Aires residents found they believed social inequality, the lack of freedom, and injustice undermined Argentine democracy (Sautu 2001). In 2002 they thought Argentina lacked effective social rights because the state did not fulfill its role in the provision of work, health, education, and housing. Banks and big companies were equally untrustworthy (Sautu and Perugorría 2004).

The plight of the downwardly mobile middle class was particularly poignant. This category included professionals, teachers, public employees, skilled labor, and merchants who were acutely aware of their condition: "I was middle class, now I am lower class. I have to cut back on going out, buying clothes, even on food sometimes." Many connected personal problems to the nation's larger socioeconomic drama: "It's an economic problem of the country, it is a problem of the damned convertibility [program], I suppose it must be the lack of work" (Lvovich 2000: 62–63).

The declaration of a state of siege on 19 December broke the dam. It inflamed feelings of political exclusion. Politicians lacked connection to people's anguish over the collapse of the banking system, economic crisis, rampant unemployment, tax increases, and falling income (Pérez, Armelino, and Rossi 2003). Middle classes interpreted the state of siege as a return to the authoritarian and repressive tactics of the military that had to be resisted: "We cannot allow this to happen again in Argentina. It already happened to our parents and grandparents ... I am going out to protest always to defend our democracy, freedom, justice, and free speech (Anderson 2006: 11).

The dam that repressed these feelings burst on 19 December. An 18-year old female participant recalled:

"On the 19th I was at home very depressed over reports of lootings and, especially, repression ... We heard on TV that people were banging pots ... so my brother and I timidly began making noise on the balcony ... we heard more banging ... we went down to the

---

[29] For detailed accounts, see Carrera and Cotarelo (2003); Kohan (2002); Camarasa (2002); Bonasso (2002); Altamira (2002).

street euphoric and saw many neighbors turning out making noise. We blocked the street, lit fires, and went to some high rises to turn people out into the streets... Then I heard people shouting we should go to the Congress... I went with my brother and saw barricades and people at every corner... [There was a great tumult at the Plaza Congreso]... I was very excited... Then the repression came and I was very angry... We had a right to be there. (Di Marco and Palomino 2003: 157–58)

Police repressed the throng of demonstrators viciously, but the multitude grew into a pueblada as piquetero organizations joined the fray, organizing roadblocks and combating riot police (Altamira 2002; Kohan 2002). Repression motivated individuals to spontaneous protest: "I thought it great that our people who have suffered so much repression and death, instead of staying at home crying under their beds after the declaration of state of siege we all took to the street." "On 20 December the trigger for me was the military repression and beatings of the Mothers [of the Plaza de Mayo]. I dropped everything, changed clothes, and came to fight, it was that simple" (Di Marco and Palomino 2003: 67–68). Official figures counted 25 dead and hundreds of wounded. Meanwhile, widespread roadblocks, sacking, and looting of stores broke out in poor neighborhoods. De la Rúa, abandoned by all of the major political forces of Argentina, faced with the repudiation of those who elected him – the middle class – and whom he was forced to repress, resigned on 20 December 2001 (Svampa and Pereyra 2003).

Because the vice presidency remained unfilled, the Peronist-dominated Congress selected Adolfo Rodríquez Saá for the presidency. He immediately defaulted on the foreign debt to force a renegotiation. Meanwhile, mobilization continued. Whereas it had been spontaneous in December, with no single organization or bloc leading it, very soon after de la Rúa's resignation the Bloque Piquetero Nacional coordinated a wave of highway blockages throughout Argentina, working with other groups, such as independent piquetero organizations and even the CTA bloc. Meanwhile, poorer, and even some middle-class, neighborhoods held popular assemblies to organize local services, schools, and food cooperatives (Dinerstein 2003a; Rock, 2002: 56–57; Svampa and Pereyra 2003).

Simmering mobilization and tensions inside the Justicialista Party forced Rodríguez Saá's ouster, and Eduardo Duhalde, the Peronist candidate de la Rúa had defeated in 1999, was appointed on 1 January 2002. He immediately devalued the peso (ended convertibility). Nevertheless, he faced the formidable task of taming a mobilized and highly organized popular sector. On the day he took office, rioting and demonstrations where protestors chanted *que se vayan todos* rocked Buenos Aires and the rest of the country. In Buenos Aires they marched to the buildings representing the three branches of government demanding the resignation of Congress and the Supreme Court. Meanwhile, piqueteros "blocked major roads and highways throughout the country demanding food and jobs... [and] began to physically attack [politicians] on the street in restaurants, and other public places" (Levitsky and Murillo 2005: 38–39).

Aftermath

What did a decade of leftist anti-neoliberal contentious politics achieve? It did not usher in an era of sweeping economic and political antimarket reform. Instead, it propelled to power center-left political forces committed to the mild reform of contemporary Argentine market society based on economic growth with equity. These policies, however, fall far short of being a comprehensive national development project or contemporary version of social democracy. Nevertheless, they sufficed to equilibrate the Argentine economy and polity and to demobilize society.

The debacle of the Alianza government in 2001 paved the way for the presidencies of Néstor Kirchner (2003–7) and his wife Cristina Fernández de Kirchner (2008–present) who represented a faction of the Peronist Party that was philosophically and pragmatically more committed to the party's traditional "populist" principles.[30] Their administrations have defended national socioeconomic interests over the IMF and international capital; they also addressed a number of popular sector and middle-class grievances repeatedly expressed during Argentina's episode of anti-neoliberal contention. Second, they tackled the burning issues of impunity and corruption in government associated with the neoliberal programs of the military government in the late 1970s and Menem in the 1990s.

Economic and political policies that made Néstor Kirchner one of the most popular presidents in contemporary Argentina included the following. First, in a sharp break with Menem and de la Rúa, Néstor Kirchner took a tough nationalist stance in negotiations with the IMF and international creditors (Epinoza and Riley 2004). His economic minister renegotiated Argentina's near $90 billion debt with the IMF at favorable terms that left the government more funds for social policies. Indeed, in 2005, with petrodollar aid from Venezuela's Hugo Chávez, Argentina paid off the whole loan, thus regaining a measure of economic and political autonomy for the nation (Campbell 2006). Second, for the first time in more than a decade, a president supported union collective bargaining and higher minimum wages, a dramatic change from the wage-depressing policies of the recent past. Combined with tight labor markets, these policies propelled a 70-percent increase in real wages. Third, Kirchner passed a social security reform act that extended coverage to more than a million unemployed and informal sector workers. His administration launched a public works program, supported by a fivefold increase in resources for housing and infrastructure, and funding for

[30] Kirchner, who represented the Frente por la Victoria faction of the PJ, obtained 22 percent of the vote to Menem's 24.3 percent. Under investigation for corruption, Menem was sure to lose a run-off election and conceded to Kirchner, who was sworn in on 25 May 2003. The Frente para la Victoria faction of the PJ gained an overwhelming plurality in the chamber of deputies in both elections. Out of 257 seats, it won 127 in 2003 and 118 in 2005. Smaller allied political parties gave it a clear working majority. By contrast, the Radical Party, the next largest, only won 46 in 2003 and 36 in 2005 (Europa World 2007).

education and scientific research increased substantially (Levtisky and Murillo 2008: 17). His government also controlled the rates of privatized utility companies (Campbell 2006).

Following the economic meltdown of 2001, Kirchner's government benefited from sustained rapid GDP growth at an average of nine percent a year between 2003 and 2007. Argentina's export-led economic model, a competitive exchange rate, and surging commodity prices drove that growth. Inflation was under control, and Argentina enjoyed surpluses in both trade and in the current account (Europa World 2007). Although this was essentially a continuation of the free-market model, living standards improved. "Private consumption increased by 52 percent between 2002 and 2007 [and] unemployment rates and poverty rates were halved" (Levitsky and Murillo 2008: 17).

Kirchner also addressed political demands that had fueled popular sector and middle-class mobilization. He opened an investigation into corruption among Supreme Court justices appointed by Menem to stack the court in his favor. Eventually this prompted the resignation of six of the nine justices. New court nomination procedures were established to ensure transparency and accountability, and the size of the court was ultimately reduced to five, thus reversing Menem's court-packing moves. Kirchner also addressed widespread disgust and despair over the impunity with which the forces of order had committed human rights violations while repressing Argentine citizens, especially during the last military government (1976–83). He removed several high-ranking military and police commanders from their posts under the principle that crimes must be punished and those who murdered innocent civilians had to face justice. He pushed through legislation that rescinded laws that limited prosecution for human rights violations. By 2006 more than 500 erstwhile military and police officers were charged. (Campbell 2006; Europa World 2007: 527; Levitsky and Murillo 2008).

In addition to these measures, Kirchner's administration included leaders of more moderate piquetero organizations in the design and implementation of policies that addressed their demands and policy proposals. For example, in 2004 they met with the minister of social development (the president's sister) and the minister of labor to discuss forms of collaboration with the government and to establish channels for future deliberation. Granting piquetero organizations control over the distribution of workfare programs also became more widespread (Espinoza and Riley 2004; Svampa and Pereyra 2003). This more open, inclusive, and less overtly repressive response signaled an important recognition by the government: Popular sector demands were legitimate, just, and worthy of inclusion on the policy agenda.

These mechanisms of political and socioeconomic inclusion sufficed to demobilize the masses who had risen to defend against perceived exclusions and injustices inherent in the construction of contemporary market society. Although the reforms – with the arguable exception of taking on the IMF – were mild, they sufficed because of the fragmentation of the popular sector and middle-class

movements (Wolff 2007). The horizontal linkages (collective power) they had
built were strictly conjunctural and tenuous. Thus the inclusion of moderate
leaders in the policy process and giving them control over resources like workfare plans deepened the rifts between them and the more radical organizations
of the Polo Obrero. The latter continued to organize roadblocks, especially in
2004, but they lacked support from the other groups. Moreover, with economic
recovery and greater effective political representation, middle classes became dis-
interested in protest and concerned over the threat to public order and personal
security that radical young tough piqueteros posed. This facilitated a government
crackdown on these groups and their leadership (Espinoza and Riley 2004; Wolff
2007).

The resurgent economy, improved social indicators, more inclusive social
and labor policy, and measured nationalist stances conferred great popularity
on Néstor Kirchner. He declined to run for a second term, passing the baton
on to his wife, Cristina Fernández de Kirchner, who won handily.[31] Her government made social policy a priority. Her husband's social policies had done
little, if anything, to redistribute wealth and reduce income inequality. They had
not really addressed poverty; economic growth was responsible for declines, but
poverty and income inequality were still higher in 2007 than in the mid-1990s
(Levitsky and Murillo 2008: 28).

Increasing social expenditures required raising revenue to control inflation,
which was becoming worrisome. Given rising commodity prices, in the first
months of her administration, Cristina Fernández tried pushing an export tax
increase through the legislature. Large-scale landowners and agribusiness, backed
by the powerful Argentine Agricultural Federation, strongly opposed the measure, citing high income taxes and rising transportation costs. They enlisted
the support of family farmers. Together, beginning in March 2008, agricultural
exporters launched a "strike" against the government. They withheld their products from both export and domestic markets, causing food shortages and a decline
in export earnings. After tortuous wrangling, the tax hike failed in the Senate in
mid-July, which meant sectors of her own party had rebelled against her. Following this humiliating defeat, the president attempted to restore credibility with
ordinary Argentines. In recognition that inflation rates were eroding incomes,
she increased the minimum wage by 27 percent. She also decreed the renationalization of two airline carriers; a popular move, given widespread support for the
buyback (Airriess 2008; Dunn 2008).

In the final analysis, the episode of anti-neoliberal contention contributed to
the rise of a political faction in the Peronist Party committed to economic growth
with greater equity in the context of a capitalist world economy. With the electoral

[31] She won 45 percent of the national vote; almost double that of her closest competitor. The Peronist
Party also won 23 governorships and pro-Kirchner Peronists won 160 of 257 seats in the House
of Deputies and 47 of 74 Senate seats (Levitsky and Murillo 2008: 16).

success of the Kirchner faction of the party, Argentina no longer automatically aligned with the United States or with the prescriptions of the Washington consensus as preached by the IMF, the World Bank, and transnational corporations. Political forces represented by the Kirchner administrations insist on a measure of national autonomy without retreating to the inward-looking development of national populism. That autonomy is placed at the service of diversifying trading partners (including within Latin America). It also ensures the nation has more resources to invest in the domestic economy, including those for social services, and greater flexibility in what it chooses to invest. The problems Cristina Fernández de Kirchner has faced suggest that moving to a more proactive social policy to reduce poverty and inequality may be difficult; especially if it is to be based on increased revenue. The stirrings of a new world economic downturn may force her to postpone the effort as reduced economic growth impacts debt amortization and revenue even further.

5

Bolivia

Like that of Argentina, Bolivia's episode of anti-neoliberal contention spanned three distinctive waves. In the first one, shocked and desperate traditional unions protested President Víctor Paz Estenssoro's (1985–89) New Economic Policy and its consolidation under Jaime Paz Zamora (1989–93). They were defeated. In the second wave, President Gonzalo Sánchez de Lozada (1993–97) deepened neoliberal reforms, sparking a new wave of mobilization. Although the government contained protest, portentous changes occurred in the development of popular sector associational and collective power. The third wave began during the Hugo Bánzer–Jorge Quiroga (1997–2002) administration and crested in Sánchez de Lozada's second presidency (2002–3). Important declines in the economic and political power that sustained neoliberalism and transformations in the associational and collective power of challengers culminated in massive nationwide demonstrations that forced Sánchez de Lozada to resign. After a brief caretaker government, Bolivians elected center-left President Evo Morales in 2005.

One difference with all cases and several with Argentina shaped anti-neoliberal contention in Bolivia. Bolivia, unique in South America, experienced a major social revolution in 1952. As a result, it had a veteran, highly militant, and – unlike Argentina – independent labor confederation. Bolivia was much poorer than Argentina, with a far less diversified and industrialized economy based on mineral extraction. Thus even modestly successful neoliberal reform could not dampen mobilization. Unlike Argentina, Bolivia possessed a large rural labor force with a relatively traditional peasantry in the highlands and proletarian rural workers in the lowlands, especially in regions of new development such as Santa Cruz and Beni, where agribusiness flourished. Finally, indigenous peoples make up a majority of the population. The Quechua and Aymara are the largest, predominately rural, ethnic groups concentrated in the highlands and lowland valleys. A variety of indigenous nations inhabit more sparsely populated Amazonia. Given the last two differences with Argentina, contentious action involved urban *and* rural social groups; the latter dominated by organized mainly indigenous peasantry.[1] Thus issue framing on ethnic identity was crucial in organizing resistance. Moreover, although there was a higher degree of fragmentation among anti-neoliberal popular sector organizations than in Argentina, they frequently supported each other when they mobilized. In those struggles, reformist demands for economic nationalism, the mixed economy, formal sector employment, and protection from market forces intertwined with claims for indigenous rights.

National Populism and the Initiation of Contemporary Market Society

The analysis of contentious politics during the neoliberal era must be understood against the backdrop of Bolivia's 1952 social revolution and the national-populist era that followed. From it emerged key institutions and leaders, including a democratic regime dominated by the Movimiento Nacionalista Revolucionario (MNR; National Revolutionary Movement) led by Víctor Paz Estenssoro and Hernán Siles Suazo. The MNR was a "big tent" party that embraced radical middle-class intellectuals, the urban working class, peasant organizations, technocrats, and emerging business sectors (Klein 1992). The miners' union, the Federación Sindical de Trabajadores Mineros de Bolivia, which was in the forefront of the fighting, became the militant core of the principal trade union confederation, the Central Obrera Boliviana (COB; Bolivian Workers Central). Railway workers, factory workers, and oil and gas workers were also significant forces in the COB (Healy 1991). The COB had strong leftist tendencies, and radical leftist political parties and factions of the MNR vied for control.[2] Although the COB helped the largely indigenous peasants (Quechua and Aymara) unionize after the 1952 revolution, they quickly established their independence, rose up in the countryside, and took over *latifundia* [large estates] by force. To protect his new reformist national-populist regime at a time of growing Cold War anxieties, during his first presidency Paz Estenssoro implemented an agrarian reform; the peasantry, satisfied with land ownership, became a conservative force that he used against the more radical leftist pressures of the miner-led COB whom he always mistrusted (Klein 1992; Lazarte 1989).

In the 1950s and 1960s, MNR governments built a national-populist state and promoted state-led development. They expropriated foreign-owned mining companies, principally tin, which became state enterprises as did the oil and gas industry, airlines, utilities, railroads, and a host of other enterprises. A powerful state agency, the Corporación Minera de Bolivia (COMIBOL; Mining Corporation of Bolivia), managed the mining enterprises with tin as the nation's principal source of foreign exchange. Import substitution industrialization with its

---

[1] To be fair, there was rural mobilization in the interior provinces of Argentina, and it supported roadblocks and puebladas; the rural population just was not a major actor because of its small size. For rural mobilization in Argentina, see Giarraca (2001).

[2] Those leftist parties included the Partido Obrero Revolucionario, Partido de la Izquierda Revolucionario, and the Partido Comunista Boliviano.

myriad subsidies and price regulations, followed; so did credit and development agencies for the major economic sectors such as the Ministry of Agrarian Reform, the Banco Agrícola, Banco Minero, Fondo de Exploración Minera, and the Banco del Estado. The popular sector (and middle classes too) benefited from subsidies to basic foodstuffs, energy, and other utilities, transportation, and credit for farmers (Klein 2003).

Equally important, the Bolivian revolution developed a corporatist system of state–society interest intermediation. COB-affiliated urban and peasant unions, along with industry associations and government officials, received leadership posts in the ministries that regulated their sector and obtained representation on the official policy-making boards of the various development corporations and economic sector credit agencies (Klein 2003). This, not so much political parties, was the principal mechanism of political representation and participation in policy making for social groups. Indeed, in the more remote rural areas, indigenous peasant unions took on most local government functions and represented the community to higher government authority. Political parties were mainly electoral vehicles to gain access to state institutions as a means for distributing power, patronage, and economic opportunity to middle-class professionals.

Although the MNR helped create the COB, it was not a labor party because the COB chose independence. Nevertheless, close ties existed between the MNR and the COB. In return for political support the COB received patronage positions, favorable policy, and other resources. Despite this cozy relationship, if the COB objected to MNR policy, it mobilized, sometimes calling for devastating general strikes (Lazarte 1989).

These conflicts contributed to the collapse of the MNR government in 1964 and its replacement with a populist military regime, which, ironically, gave birth to the second and third major political parties of the 1980s and 1990s. The Movimiento de Izquierda Revolucionario (MIR; Leftist Revolutionary Movement) formed in the early 1970s, drawing from the left wing of both Christian Democracy and the MNR (Klein 2003: 228). Former dictator Hugo Banzer created a third major political party, the Alianza Democrática Nacional (ADN; National Democratic Alliance), at the end of his rule and expanded it in 1979 to compete in national elections (Klein 2003: 239).

Important changes in the organized peasantry occurred during populist military rule in the 1960s and 1970s. First, a military–peasant pact promised to address peasant grievances and unified peasants in a state-controlled national confederation. However, land tax reforms, repression, and the rise of indigenous ethnocultural identity stimulated the formation of an independent peasant union movement from 1968 to 1979. Katarismo, one of two competing indigenous movements, took control of the peasant unions seeking their autonomy.[3] It

---

[3] Indigenismo was the second strand. It held that there were two Bolivias, one of exploited indigenous peoples and one of dominant whites. It was a separatist movement demanding liberation for the indigenous.

blended class consciousness – defense of a peasant class – with claims for tradi-tional ethnic and cultural rights that translated into demands for a Bolivian state tolerant of ethnic diversity and that integrated indigenous and western forms of government (Healy and Paulson 2000).

The intertwining of class consciousness and ethnic rights allowed Kataristas to form alliances with other social movements and leftist political parties (Van Cott 2005: 53). Thus, during Bolivia's tumultuous transition to democracy, which began in 1978, the COB helped them to form a politically independent uni-fied campesino organization, the Confederación Sindical Unica de Trabajadores Campesinos Bolivianos (CSUTCB; Unitary Syndical Confederation of Peasant Workers of Bolivia), which mainly represented highland peasants including those from the Cochabamba valley, and that affiliated with the COB. Kataristas, led by Genaro Flores, dominated the CSUTCB well into the 1980s (Healy 1991; Healy and Paulson 2000). However, the COB's orthodox Marxist focus dictated the subordination of peasants to the vanguard of the proletariat, in this case the min-ing and manufacturing unions; hence the CSUTCB did not wield much influence in the COB (Ticona 2000: 119–29).

Labor–peasant cooperation flexed its muscles in two formidable waves of con-tention during redemocratization between 1979 and 1985. First, in support of democratization, the tin-miner-led COB and the CSUTCB staged massive strikes and roadblocks that paralyzed the country and drew in other political and social forces at their apex in August 1982 (Rivera-Cusicanqui 1991; Van Cott 2005; Yashar 2005). Second, in October 1982, military rule gave way to democracy when President Hernán Siles took office at the head of the Unidad Democrática Popular, a coalition of leftist political parties.[4] Unfortunately, military rule had left Bolivia in difficult economic straits, compounded by the beginning of the Latin American debt crisis (Grindle 2000: 106–7). Siles began an economic sta-bilization program, although he proposed a gradual, heterodox model similar to Alfonsín's in Argentina. The COB set off a second wave of intense mobilization (with CSUTCB support) that lasted until 1985.[5] Inflation skyrocketed, and, his government in tatters, Siles held presidential elections a year ahead of schedule in June 1985 (Conaghan and Malloy 1994: 121–23; Dunkerley 1993: 131; Ibáñez Rojo 2000).

Building Contemporary Market Society

Amidst a wave of national protests against IMF-sponsored orthodox economic stabilization policies, hyperinflation, and a depressed national economy, Siles passed the presidential sash to Víctor Paz Estenssoro (1985–89). He promptly

---

[4] This coalition included the National Revolutionary Movement of the Left (the president's party), the Communist Party of Bolivia, and the Movement of the Revolutionary Left (Dunkerley 1993).

[5] The COB staged nine general strikes and a staggering 1,799 protest events that included strikes, marches, roadblocks, demonstrations, and hunger strikes (Laserna 1985).

dismantled the political system he had helped to build with the implementation by decree of the New Economic Policy.

The New Economic Policy was an orthodox "shock" economic stabilization program that initiated a sustained effort to construct contemporary market society in Bolivia. It entailed currency devaluation, uniform and free-floating exchange rates, and the liberation of interest rates. Fiscal stabilization measures eliminated price and wage controls and froze public sector wages while prices for fuel, utilities, and other services rose. Public enterprises tightened budgets. Public sector banks cut loans and subsidies, hitting the mining and traditional agricultural sectors especially hard. On the revenue side, the New Economic Policy applied a tax reform focusing on value-added taxes. Economic reforms also opened Bolivia to international trade by slashing customs tariffs (Conaghan and Malloy 1994: 140–45; Edwards 1995: 74 and 220–21; Grindle and Domingo 2003: 319–24; Jenkins 1997).

The New Economic Policy began a process of state reform that reduced its size and functions. Public sector downsizing focused mainly on the COMIBOL. Between 1985 and 1986, 24,600 public employees lost their jobs and another 8,550 followed in 1987 as most mines closed or drastically curtailed production. The COMIBOL workforce alone fell from 30,000 workers to 7,000 in the same period, and even the state hydrocarbon company fired 4,000 employees, reducing its workforce to 5,000. All told, public sector employment fell 17 percent between 1985 and 1987 (Grindle 2003: 323; Klein 2003: 245).

In recognition of the social effects of structural adjustment, the New Economic Policy established an Emergency Social Fund, largely supported by external sources. These included the World Bank, the U.S. Agency for International Development, and the governments of Switzerland, Holland, Sweden, and Canada. The fund created temporary relief jobs for poor people mainly through public works in infrastructure projects (Conaghan and Malloy 1994: 151; Edwards 1995: 288; Grindle 2003: 323).

Jaime Paz Zamora's presidency (1989–93) deepened the New Economic Policy. He closed the Banco Agrícola, Banco Minero, and Fondo de Exploración Minera, sharply curtailed state credit functions, and further reduced workers in the state mining and agricultural sectors (Edwards 1995: 220–21). A 1992 law enabled the privatization of 100 out of 159 firms. Implementation, however, was slow (Grindle 2003: 324).

Power

It took considerable political power to design and implement the New Economic Policy and subsequent neoliberal reforms.[6] Centralization of state power was the

[6] The administration of Hernán Siles made one important contribution to the new democratic state; it brought the military under civilian control.

first key factor. Paz Estenssoro, and subsequent administrations, relied on tight-knit teams of neoliberal technocrats without ties to the old guard of the MNR and with connections to international financial institutions who designed their economic reform programs in secret (Grindle 2003: 327–28).[7] Second, the Bolivian constitution granted the executive broad powers to rule by decree, enabling the president to bypass legislative debates. Paz Estenssoro made full use of this faculty in the initiation and implementation of reform with Decree 21060 on 29 August 1985 and subsequent decrees (Grindle 2003: 329–33).

Third, political party pacts explained the relative absence of legislative debate for many of the major reforms that were enacted by law. Bolivia emerged from its long period of military-dominated rule (and after the implosion of the United Left during Siles Zuaso's government) with a fragmented multiparty system dominated by the MNR, ADN, and the MIR. Bolivian electoral law empowers the Congress to select the president if no candidate receives an outright majority. Thus, beginning with Paz Estenssoro, presidents approached one (or more) parties to form viable governing coalitions (Gamarra 1994; 2003). Paz Estenssoro (MNR) formed the Pacto por la Democracia (Pact for Democracy) with the ADN, in part because the ADN had run on a platform of free-market reforms to confront the country's deep economic crisis (Grindle 2003: 337). Jaime Paz (MIR) constructed the Acuerdo Patriótico (Patriotic Accord) with the ADN. For the most part, ministerial and other government positions, along with the political power flowing from the patronage they made possible, were a driving force behind the strange ideological bedfellows these coalitions generated.

Coercion was the fourth major element of political power behind the implementation of neoliberal economic, political, and social reforms. Faced with a militant COB, Paz Estenssoro distanced himself from the national-populist faction of the MNR – which he had helped to build – and the COB. Not being able to manipulate the COB as Menem had done with the CGT, Paz Estenssoro knew it would mobilize against the New Economic Policy. Therefore he used his constitutional prerogative to declare a 90-day state of siege. This gave him, and subsequent presidents, the right to suspend constitutional guarantees and use the army to repress protests.

Bolivia is one of the poorest countries in Latin America, which magnifies the significance of international support for its neoliberal turn. Next to political power, international support for short- and medium-term economic recovery was probably the secondmost important pillar for neoliberal reforms. The New Economic Policy technocratic team understood this (Conaghan and Malloy 1994: 195–97).

---

[7] U.S. economist Jeffrey Sachs and Minister of Planning and Coordination Gonzalo Sánchez de Lozada were central characters. Ironically, the ADN's presidential campaign had already developed a free-market economic reform program. Paz Estenssoro and his economic team adopted much of it (Grindle 2003: 327).

The renegotiation of Bolivia's external debt on favorable terms was a significant step. Jeffrey Sachs from Harvard University, one of the architects of the New Economic Policy, brokered a favorable agreement with the IMF. It included renewal of standby credits without imposing further restrictive conditions and a much larger loan from its Enhanced Structural Adjustment facility in 1988. The United States agreed that, in the interest of economic recovery, Bolivia should not be forced into drastic debt repayment schemes. In return, Bolivia cooperated with U.S. efforts to militarize drug eradication efforts in lowland jungles, beginning with Operation Blast Furnace – a joint U.S.–Bolivian military operation – in 1986 (Conaghan and Malloy 1994: 194–95). The IMF and the U.S. government's seal of approval paved the way for the renegotiation of Bolivia's three-billion-dollar foreign debt obligations with international creditors (Edwards 1995: 74).

Bilateral aid also supported the New Economic Policy. As previously mentioned, finance for the Social Emergency Fund came from many governments, in addition to the United States and the World Bank (Conaghan and Malloy 1994: 197). International support for Bolivia continued strong into the 1990s. In 1999 foreign aid covered 30 percent of government spending and amounted to 7 percent of GDP. Approximately 500 nongovernmental organizations operated in Bolivia, and the country ranked 12th in per-capita aid in the world (Klein 2003: 250).

Exclusion

The imposition of the New Economic Policy by "shock treatment" caused profound economic and political exclusion of the popular sectors, deeply threatening their livelihood and leaving them without defenses within established political institutions. This was strong motivation to mobilize for militant labor organizations that were unmistakably under attack. The political power sources previously discussed sealed the political exclusion of popular sector and peasant groups most adversely affected by neoliberal reforms. The policy process sidelined traditionalists within the major parties, especially the MNR, thus freezing the urban popular sector groups and peasants who supported them out of policy discussions (Grindle 2003: 333–34). Moreover, as Planning Minister Sánchez de Lozada acknowledged, economic reforms, especially public sector downsizing, had political purposes. They weakened the COB whose militancy and political strength had challenged many a government since its foundation. The restructuring of COMIBOL was the key to the emasculation of the COB because mine workers were historically its militant core. Fiscal retrenchment weakened public sector unions in general; and in Bolivia's corporate system of interest intermediation, the downsizing of sector-specific state credit and development bureaus undermined the political and economic power of urban and rural unions alike.

Economic exclusion had several dimensions. A shift from formal to informal sector employment featured prominently among them. Although official unemployment figures, after an initial spike, improved during Paz Zamora's government, it was clear that job creation was strong only in the informal sector of the economy. Moreover, GDP per capita, which also declined sharply at first, grew only erratically afterwards. Meanwhile, although Bolivia has always been a poor country, poverty levels between 1984 and 1993 remained shockingly high, always above 50 percent in urban areas and never below 77 percent in the countryside. The rise in prices of staple foodstuffs, utilities, fuel, and transportation among other goods and services due to the reduction or elimination of subsidies added to the sense of economic exclusion. For most, they canceled out any improvements in real wages and in the minimum wage, which, in any case, applied only to the declining formal sector of employment (see Table 5.1).

Regional economic conditions and the effect of specific neoliberal policies concentrated urban and rural exclusion in the *altiplano* [high-plains] region. Traditional centers of economic development in the altiplano in the departments of La Paz, Oruro, and Potosí were declining in favor of new economic development poles in the lowland departments of Santa Cruz and Beni. The mountain valley of Cochabamba prospered because it was a hub between the two regions. Much of the change lay in the collapse of the state-owned tin-mining industry of the altiplano in favor of oil and gas in the lowlands. Trade liberalization and the elimination of state credit for industrial policy contributed to the decline of the small domestic manufacturing sector, concentrated in the highland cities. The traditional sector of agriculture centered in the altiplano lost competitiveness while agroexport crops in the lowlands grew, reinforcing the militancy of the highlands. In the altiplano, this shift increased flexibilization of labor; largely indigenous peasants lost land, credit, and markets for their crops. The closure of the state agricultural development bank exacerbated the problem. Peasants became seasonal labor or relied on nonfarm income for their livelihood. These difficulties contributed to the urbanization of rural labor as peasants swelled the ranks of informal employment in local towns and cities when there was no work in the country (Kay 2004).

U.S.-sponsored drug eradication policies threatened coca growers in the lowlands. The coca sector had grown significantly, in part because of internal migration patterns from the declining altiplano. Coca-growing peasants, insofar as they lived close to urban areas, also enlarged the lowland informal sector. Coca eradication was linked to neoliberalism because the United States threatened to withhold foreign aid if the Bolivian government did not accept the program. Those funds were critical for the success of neoliberal stabilization and restructuring programs to overcome Bolivia's debt crisis (Healy 1991, 1988).

Resistance, Defeat, and New Beginnings, 1985–93

When Paz Estenssoro launched the New Economic Policy with Supreme Decree 21060 on 29 August 1985, urban labor in cooperation with the (largely

Table 5.1. *Bolivia: Economic and Social Indicators*

	1980	1990	1991	1992	1993	1994	1995	1996	1997	1998	1999	2000	2001	2002	2003	2004	2005	2006	2007[a]
GDP	0.6	−4.6	5.4	1.7	4.3	4.8	4.7	4.5	4.9	5.2	0.5	2.3	1.6	2.7	2.4	4.2	4.4	4.8	4.6
GDP/CAP		2.3	2.8	−0.8	1.8	2.1	1.3	2.0	2.4	2.8	−1.8	0.1	−0.6	0.4	−0.3	1.9	2.2	2.6	2.4
Income Distribution[b]																			
D1		0.7				2.0			1.6		0.3			0.3					
D2		2.7				3.4			3.1		1.0			1.2					
Q2		8.7				9.8			9.0		5.9			5.5					
Q3		13.1				13.5			13.6		11.5			10.3					
Q4		20.6				19.8			20.5		20.2			18.3					
D9		16.1				15.9			15.3		17.3			15.8					
D10		38.2				35.6			37.0		43.9			48.7					
Unemployment	5.8	7.2	5.9	5.5	5.9	3.1	3.6	4.0	4.3	4.1	7.2	7.5	8.5	8.7	9.2	6.2	8.2	8.0	
Informal[c]		56.9	56.1	56.6	61.2	61.3	63.6	63.1	56.6			62.8		67.1					
Poverty																			
Total		52.6							63.2		62.7				63.9	63.9			
Urban						51.6								52.0	53.8	53.8			
Rural						79.1			77.3		81.7			79.2	80.6	80.6			
Average Wage Index[d]	56.6	87.6	82.1	85.5	91.2	98.5	100.0	100.5	106.6	110.1	117.0	115.9	120.3	124.1	*111.1*	*114.1*	*110.0*	*101.2*	*98.4*
Minimum Wage Index[e]	51.5	84.9			92.7	102.1	100.0	96.7	98.6	114.5	123.2	*100.0*	*110.8*	*116.0*	*116.9*	*112.0*	*106.3*	*111.1*	*109.7*

[a] Estimated.
[b] *D9* and *D10* = richest quintile; *D1* and *D2* = poorest quintile. Data not reported for all years.
[c] Informal sector data reported only from 1990 to 2002 in constant format. Data not reported for all years.
[d] Average wage index between 1980 and 2002 based on 1995 = 100; 2003–2007 based on 2000 = 100 (in italics).
[e] Minimum wage index between 1980 and 1999 based on 1995 = 100; 2000–2007 based on 2000 = 100 (in italics).

Sources: Economic Commission for Latin America and the Caribbean, *Statistical Yearbook* (Santiago: ECLAC, 1980–2007) and *Economic Survey of Latin America* (Santiago: ECLAC, 1980–2007). Labor Statistics from International Labor Organization, Labor Overview: *Latin America and the Caribbean* (Lima: ILO, 1994–2007). For comparability of data, I have not filled in missing years with other sources.

indigenous) peasantry mobilized significant associational and collective power against it in a wave of COB-led anti-neoliberal contestation that continued through the administration of Jaime Paz Zamora (1989–93). Indeed, fully understanding the threat that the New Economic Policy posed, the COB responded almost immediately by calling a massive general strike in early September that gripped the highland departments of La Paz, Oruro, Potosí, as well as Cochabamba. Mine workers, factory workers, railway workers, oil workers, transportation workers (including airlines), telecommunications workers, bank employees, and teachers walked off the job, paralyzing those economic sectors. They marched 25,000 strong on La Paz, staging demonstrations and hunger strikes. In mid-September, the CSUTCB announced peasant roadblocks to support urban strikers.[8]

When the COB declared the general strike indefinite because of the government's refusal to negotiate, Paz Estenssoro rejoined, "If I allow the unions to continue doing this, I will become another Siles Zuazo, and I am not Siles."[9] Making good on his threat, he decreed a 90-day state of siege on 20 September. Troops and tanks took up positions in La Paz and other major cities and highways. They surrounded and raided the COB headquarters, five union halls, a radio station, San Andrés University, and the COMIBOL. Approximately 500–600 union officials and strikers were arrested (thousands around the country); 150, including 18 executive committee members, were sent to internal exile in the northern lowlands. Meanwhile, a clandestine command directed the now-illegal strike, which began to fizzle because of the government's strong repression. On 3 October, tin miners ended the strike in return for the release of 97 detained union members. The state of siege was lifted in December.[10]

During this first wave of anti-neoliberal mobilization, the COB articulated a nonrevolutionary agenda.[11] It railed that neoliberal reforms created unemployment, hunger, and impoverishment and that they surrendered Bolivia to foreign capital. The COB framed resistance in Polanyi-like defense of traditional urban union-centered concerns: the protection of formal sector employment, pay, and working conditions along with nationalist defense of public enterprise and industrial policy to counterbalance international capital and its domestic allies, perennial enemies of the popular sector. To the extent that rising prices because of devaluation and the elimination of subsidies for basic necessities sharply eroded the earnings of sectors least capable of generating income, COB framing reached out to all low-income and low-middle-income groups, unionized or not.

The COB, however, was reduced to a shadow of its former self by the end of this period. The dismembering of COMIBOL, the closing of tin mines, and

---

[8] *New York Times* 1–6 September 1985; *Latin America Weekly Report* 6 and 13 September 1985; Xinhua General Overseas News Service, 10 September 1985.

[9] *Latin America Weekly Report* 13 September 1985.

[10] *New York Times* 20–21 September 1985, 4 October 1985, and 19 December 1985.

[11] See footnote 8 for sources.

the massive firing of tin workers destroyed the historical militant core of organized labor, disarticulated the COB, and exacerbated internal tensions. The COB
never recovered its role as the axis that articulated popular sector demands, organized contentious politics, and forced governments to negotiate (García et al.
2000; Sanabria 2000). By the same token, internal struggles within the CSUTCB
eroded its ability to mobilize highland indigenous peasants. Vigorous repression
in the form of the state siege called at crucial moments compounded COB and
CSUTCB leadership problems.

Thus, although the COB still called general strikes, by the early 1990s its capacity to mobilize large numbers of workers and peasants and to ensure adherence
to the strike call was significantly diminished. Still, as if by reflex, the COB challenged neoliberal policies with traditional forms of contention: work stoppages,
the general strike, the hunger strike, and demonstrations (García et al. 2000). If
they were too successful, the government asserted its authority by declaring a
state of siege.[12]

New Sources of Popular Sector Associational and Collective Power

Even as traditional urban labor-led centers of mobilization and political power
waned, new sources of popular sector associational power emerged in the form of
the coca-grower federations of the Chapare in the department of Cochabamba
and the Yungas region of the department of La Paz. The indigenous highland
peoples, principally Quechuas and Aymaras, consume coca leaves for many purposes, and from ancestral times coca has had deep economic, symbolic, and ritual
meaning. Coca was not only intimately intertwined with Andean highland indigenous culture and identity, its cultivation was also legal. Because coca was legal,
coca growers had organized peasant unions during the 1970s and early 1980s.
These had the same rights to representation as other peasant groups.

In the 1980s many former tin miners migrated to the Chapare and became
coca farmers. U.S.-led efforts to destroy the supply and production of cocaine
and coca motivated them to broker a significant expansion of union organizing.
They shared their organizing expertise with local unions and imbued them with
their militancy (Crabtree 2005: 36).[13] By the late 1980s, 160 coca-grower peasant
unions organized into five federations, with 85 percent in two of them, and one of
those affiliated with the CSUTCB.[14] The Cochabamba federations also created
a Coordinating Committee (Van Cott 2005: 58).

---

[12] See, for example, a COB-supported teacher's strike in the first three months of Paz Zamora's
government (Associated Press 31 October 1989; United Press International 15 November 1989;
Associated Press 15 November 1989; *Latin America Weekly Report* 30 November 1989; Associated
Press 16 November 1989).

[13] The Chapare was a relatively new area of colonization and coca growing that opened up after the
Chaco war with Paraguay in the early 1930s (Patzi Paco 1999: 48–51).

[14] The local coca unions of the Yungas were also organized into five federations (Van Cott
2005: 58).

These leaders relied on unique functions their organizations performed to enlist members and to secure their participation in mobilization. As customary in rural Bolivia, the coca unions also acted as local governments, settling property disputes, establishing transport fares, and even collecting taxes on coca leaf markets and using the revenue to fund public works (Healy 1991); and they interfaced with regional and national political authorities. Under these circumstances, local populations were by definition members of the union and noncompliance with its directives – including decisions to mobilize – could have serious repercussions for individuals and their families.

The coca growers' militancy stiffened significantly during Paz Estenssoro's administration when, at the behest of the United States, who threatened to cut off economic aid, the Bolivian government – in cooperation with U.S. troops – began coca eradication programs.[15] Coca federations responded to this direct threat to their livelihood with roadblocks involving thousands of peasants, forcing the government to negotiate.

The expansion of coca-grower associational power and militancy in opposition to U.S.-sponsored eradication programs gradually produced significant changes in the CSUTCB and the COB. The CSUTCB had been suffering from debilitating internal problems because of the decline of Katarista leaders. Leaders of the coca growers' movement saw an opportunity to broker a revitalization of the CSUTCB. They recognized that their capacity to force governments to negotiate gave them tremendous appeal, which they used to successfully contest CSUTCB internal elections. As a result, the CSUTCB spent considerably more effort on the coca growers' struggle. The remaining more experienced and politically connected CSUTCB national leadership, in the interest of reinvigorating their peasant union confederation, aided coca federations in negotiation with the government over coca laws from 1987 forward (Healy 1991, 1988; Pinto Ocampo 2004: 6–7).

Coca growers' federations also stimulated collective power by bringing peasants and urban labor together. Regional trade unions (the Central Obrera Departamental de Cochabamba) supported the coca federations; as did university students and employees, miners, factory workers, and schoolteachers who between March and July 1987 protested a draft anticoca law (Ley del Régimen de la Coca y Sustancias Controladas) (Healy 1991). Meanwhile, the relative success of the coca growers' struggle convinced COB national leadership to support them in the interest of reviving their own declining fortunes. They provided organizational and negotiating expertise and good offices when the coca federation entered into talks with the government (Healy 1988; Pinto Ocampo 2004: 7–8). Moreover, lobbying against proposed laws connected coca federations to leftist political parties eager to associate with them to rebuild constituencies after

---

[15] During Siles' government they had focused on lobbying for marketing and price regulation.

the debacle of Siles' Unidad Democrática Popular government (Healy 1991: 104–5).[16]

The framing of the coca issue contributed significantly to the revitalization of peasant sector associational power and to the peasant–urban labor node of popular sector collective power. Coca federations used indigenist and cultural images of resistance to the Bolivian state and U.S.-led imperialism to defend an economic goal, saving the livelihood of peasants lacking alternatives (Albó 1999: 476; Patzi-Paco 1999: 49–50). The antistate and anti-U.S. discourse of the Chapare federations was familiar and appealing to the COB and allied leftist parties. It fit well with their criticism of U.S. interventionism and U.S. support for local economic elites and military at the expense of the popular sectors (Healy 1991: 101, 1988; Patzi-Paco 1999: 86).

The intertwining of cultural and identity framings with economic motivations became a key feature of anti-neoliberal mobilization during the 1990s and beyond. Yet the relative success of the coca growers' movement signaled another important change that reverberated beyond the peasant movement. The basis for relatively successful organizing (as measured by capacity to mobilize and to force negotiation) had shifted away from the factory and the mine (and other places with a high density of workers) to territorially based forms (Spronk 2006: 9). The coca growers labored in a remote territory where the state had little penetration and where farmers worked small plots in low population densities with an assured market at high prices. When threatened, farmers could simply move farther into the interior. These characteristics made it nigh impossible for the government to cripple this economic sector and its unions as it had done with tin miners, where shutting down key firms with a concentrated work force did the trick (Sanabria 1999: 53–54).

In the 1980s and early 1990s, coca-grower mobilization was mainly a regional phenomenon (Healy 1991: 102–3). Yet it was an incubator for transformations in popular sector associational and collective power that blossomed in the second and third waves of anti-neoliberal contention. During those waves their stream of contention joined others with unanticipated and surprising consequences.

Second-Generation Neoliberal Reforms

The presidency of Gonzalo Sánchez de Lozada (1993–97) – the architect of the New Economic Policy under Paz Estenssoro – gave new impetus to neoliberal economic, political, and social reforms. Privatization under the Capitalization Law of 1994 was the principal economic measure (Grindle 2000: 115; Grindle 2003: 331). Neoliberal reforms also addressed education, pensions, and agrarian policy. The Education Reform Act of 1994 changed teacher qualifications,

---

[16] These included the Movimiento Bolivia Libre (an MIR splinter), the Partido Socialista, and Izquierda Unida (the United Left).

established merit hiring of superintendents, and mandated national testing for students, teachers, and school councils. It also introduced bilingual and inter-cultural education, teacher training and compensation based on performance. In 1996, major pension fund reform created privately managed funds and individual contributory accounts (Contreras 2003; Grindle 2003: 325). Negotiation with the CSUTCB over revisions to Bolivia's agrarian reform law had been under-way since 1984 and later involved lowland indigenous groups organized in the Confederación Indígena del Oriente, Chaco y Amazonía de Bolivia. In 1996 the legislature approved a bill that emphasized recognition of communal property.

In addition to these measures, faced with U.S. threats to withhold foreign aid, in early 1994 Sánchez de Lozada's government intensified coca eradication programs and their militarization. The Zero Option program contemplated the total eradication of illegal coca farms, voluntarily with compensation if possible or by force if necessary (Pinto Ocampo 2004: 11–18; Youngers and Rosin 2005). As part of the program, the United States oversaw the formation and training of special militarized antidrug units. Sánchez de Lozada also implemented ambi-tious political reforms focused on decentralization of the state and the inclusion of indigenous peoples in a multiethnic and pluricultural polity. From the neolib-eral perspective, decentralization further reduced the size and functions of the national state. It also diffused pressure on the national state because citizens would become involved in local politics. Engineering political pluralism, it was hoped, would generate multiple power centers and crosscutting cleavages to the ben-efit of political stability. Constitutional reforms in the interest of creating the "multiplural" polity aimed for the same effect.

The Popular Participation Law of 1994 was the centerpiece of decentral-ization. It established municipalities throughout the country along with direct elections for mayors and municipal councils empowered to make authoritative decisions and to administer revenue (20 percent of central government income was earmarked for municipalities). The law had several goals. It redistributed economic resources from urban departments (the largest territorial unit) to rural, predominately Indian campesino, areas. It placed decision making over the alloca-tion of those resources for projects in health, education, and infrastructure in the hands of local elites who were now more accountable to the local population. The framers of the law hoped that local accountability would reduce corruption. The decentralization law also eliminated the regional development corporations in an effort to break corporate mechanisms of representation judged to be undemo-cratic and corrupt. Party and electoral politics along with more accountable pub-lic administration procedures were to replace them (Grindle 2000; Grindle and Domingo 2003: 321–32; Van Cott 2000: 155).[17]

---

[17] The Administrative Decentralization Law of 1996 further strengthened the autonomy of muni-cipalities and tied departments to the central state, although it was more an administrative decon-centration measure than decentralization of policy decision making (Van Cott 2000: 173–74).

Constitutional reform complemented the Popular Participation Law's goal to incorporate predominately indigenous rural areas into a liberal conception of empowerment through local politics. In recognition of the growing importance of indigenous peoples in Bolivian political life, the 1967 Constitution was amended. Bolivia was not only "free, independent [and] sovereign," it was also "multiethnic and pluricultural." Other amendments gave legal recognition to indigenous territories, communities, peasant associations, and peasant unions. Ayllus and communities were guaranteed traditional land rights, rights to local traditional laws, and "the communal property rights of traditional rural communities" (Klein 2003: 261; Van Cott 2000: 76).[18] The proportional representation electoral system was also reformed to improve indigenous political participation. Uninominal single-member district seats were created in one half of the 130-member lower chamber of Congress (Van Cott: 2003: 22).

Power and Exclusion

Sánchez de Lozada built a political party coalition to win the presidency and to ensure legislative majorities. In the early 1990s new ethnic and regional parties had emerged, and he used them to stitch together Pacto por el Cambio, a coalition that included his own MNR, the Katarista ethnic party Movimiento Revolucionario Tupac Katari de Liberación, the Movimiento Bolivia Libre (a center-left party), and the Unión Cívica de Solidaridad (a populist party of lowland Santa Cruz) (see Tables 5.2 and 5.3). The Unión Cívica was a rapidly expanding party in Bolivia's most dynamic and economically burgeoning department. Indigenous identity was becoming increasingly important as a source of political organization. Sánchez de Lozada offered the Movimiento Revolucionario Tupac Katari the vice presidency because it supported a pluri-multicultural vision of society, one that melded Hispanic-"white" cultural practices and institutions with indigenous ones instead of advocating two separate Bolivias, one white and one indigenous. This fit well with liberal principles of tolerance and cultural coexistence. Because this coalition kept demands for "decommodification" off the political agenda, it ensured the popular sectors' political exclusion from policy making.

The consequences of the Popular Participation Law and the 1996 Agrarian Reform Act were complicated. From a neoliberal perspective they redressed the historical exclusion of indigenous peoples. The Popular Participation Law granted more resources and local control over their distribution to municipalities, especially heavily indigenous rural ones. Agrarian reform enabled land titling for communally held ancestral lands.

---

[18] In pre-Columbian times, ayllu referred to kin networks and the land they controlled. Today it usually means village community or part of a village community (Albó 2002; Ticona, Rojas, and Albó 1995).

Table 5.2. *Bolivia: Presidential Elections, 1985–2005*

Candidate	Party	1985	1989	1993	1997	2002	2005
Víctor Paz Estenssoro	**MNR**	26.4%[a]	–	–	–	–	–
Hugo Banzer	ADN	28.6%	–	–	–	–	–
Jaime Paz Zamora	**MIR**	–	19.6%[b]	–	–	–	–
Gonzalo Sánchez de Lozada	MNR	–	23.0%	–	–	–	–
Hugo Banzer	ADN	–	22.7%	–	–	–	–
Gonzalo Sánchez de Lozada	**MNR**	–	–	33.8%	–	–	–
Hugo Banzer	ADN	–	–	20.0%	–	–	–
Carlos Patenque Aviles	CONDEPA	–	–	13.6%	–	–	–
Max Fernández	UCS	–	–	13.1%	–	–	–
Antonio Aranibar Quiroga	MBL	–	–	5.1%	–	–	–
Hugo Banzer	**ADN**	–	–	–	22.3%	–	–
Juan Carlos Durán	MNR	–	–	–	17.7%	–	–
Jaime Paz Zamora	MIR	–	–	–	16.7%	–	–
Ivo Kuljis	UCS	–	–	–	15.9%	–	–
Remedios Loza	CONDEPA	–	–	–	15.9%	–	–
Gonzalo Sánchez de Lozada	**MNR**	–	–	–	–	22.5%[a]	–
Juan Evo Morales	MAS	–	–	–	–	20.9%	–
Manfred Reyes Villa	NFR	–	–	–	–	20.2%	–
Jaime Paz Zamora	MIR	–	–	–	–	16.3%	–
Felipe Quispe Huanca	MIP	–	–	–	–	6.1%	–
Juan Evo Morales	**MAS**	–	–	–	–	–	**53.7%**
Jorge Quiroga	PODEMOS	–	–	–	–	–	28.6%
Samuel Doria Medina	FUN	–	–	–	–	–	7.8%
Michiaki Nagatani	MNR	–	–	–	–	–	6.5%
Felipe Quispe	MIP	–	–	–	–	–	2.2%

Boldface indicates winning candidate, party, and percentage of the vote.
For the full name of political parties see the acronyms section.
[a] The Bolivian Congress stepped in and elected Paz Estenssoro president, even though he received fewer
   votes than Banzer.
[b] According to Article 90 of the Bolivian Constitution, if in the general elections none of the presidential
   formulas obtains an absolute majority of valid votes Congress will have to decide by absolute majority
   of valid votes between the two formulas that had obtained the highest number of valid votes.
Source: http://pdba.georgetown.edu/Electdata/Bolivia/pres. The Europa World Yearbook (1988–2006).

Second-generation neoliberal reforms pointedly excluded the interests of the
COB and the CSUTCB, the established organs of popular sector representation.
Aggressive privatization (and education reform) would destroy what was left of
once strong public sector unions and finish off a debilitated COB. By the same
token, the Popular Participation Law and the Agrarian Reform Act were a direct
attack on the CSUTCB. Historically, in the absence of other political institutions, the CSUTCB frequently functioned as local government. In a corporatist
system of interest articulation with the state – both at the department and the
national level – the CSUTCB represented the interests of highland peasants,
who were also overwhelmingly indigenous, and controlled the distribution of
the resources it obtained. The new municipalities, systems for the allocation of

Table 5.3. *Bolivia: Distribution of Seats in the Chamber of Deputies, 1985–2005*

Parties	1985	1989	1993	1997	2002	2005
AND	41	38	–	33	4	–
MNR	43	40	52	26	36	7
MIR	15	33	–	25	26	–
AP	–	–	35	–	–	–
CONDEPA	–	9	13	17	–	–
UCS	–	–	20	21	5	–
IU	–	10	–	4	–	–
MBL	–	–	7	4	–	–
ARBOL	–	–	1	–	–	–
MAS	–	–	–	–	27	72
MIP	–	–	–	–	6	–
NFR	–	–	–	–	25	–
PODEMOS	–	–	–	–	–	43
FUN	–	–	2	–	–	8
Others	31	–	–	–	1	–
TOTAL	130	130	130	130	130	130

For the full name of political parties see the acronyms section.
Source: The Europa World Yearbook (1984–2006)

resources, and the arrival of national political parties at the local level clearly threatened the CSUTCB (Yashar 2005). Meanwhile, the Agrarian Reform Act of 1996 favored lowland indigenous communities who still practiced traditional communal landownership.[19] Few highland indigenous communities, the very ones the CSUTCB organized, still did so. Most ownership was private, and the traditional problems of Latin American peasants – *minifundio* [small farms], lack of credit, adverse prices, landlessness, and proletarianization – plagued them. Moreover, highland indigenous were interested in protecting traditional systems that organized work obligations and use rights to dispersed plots of land, practices known as *usos y costumbres* [uses and customs]. Sánchez de Lozada's reforms deliberately excluded these issues – the very concerns the CSUTCB championed – from the policy agenda (Crabtree 2005; Healy and Paulson 2000).

Portentous Transformations in Anti-Neoliberal Contention, 1993–97

Sánchez de Lozada's sweeping second-generation neoliberal reforms affected a broad swath of Bolivian society: campesinos (mainly highland Quechua and Aymara), urban workers (including middle-class state employees, such as teachers), and lowland indigenous peoples. However, he successfully manipulated or repressed diverse campesino unions, lowland indigenous movement organizations, and a weakened COB. Consequently, anti-neoliberal mobilization failed

[19] This introduced a wedge between lowland and highland indigenous organizations.

to stop the deepening of market reforms; and, in the eyes of neoliberals, they were just so much background noise.

Such assessments missed what was new and distinctive about contentious politics during this cycle and how that affected the longer-term dynamics of associational and collective power building, which came to a head in the Water and Gas Wars of the early 2000s. First, the center of power within the COB shifted to the CSUTCB, now dominated by coca-grower federations, because the struggle against coca eradication initially was the most dynamic contentious issue. Resistance forced negotiation, which attracted the support of other social movement organizations thirsty for success. Second, anti-neoliberal movement organizations began to support each other when one or the other mobilized. Thus, although protests were rarely officially coordinated, they still had the effect of magnifying the impact of contentious action because they disrupted order in cities and the countryside simultaneously. This began to offset weaknesses created by the COB's irreversible decline. For example, the COB called general strikes in solidarity with coca-grower federations and CSUTCB-led mobilization against coca eradication. Urban workers and teachers added their own grievances over privatization and education reform to those of the coca growers revisiting U.S.-sponsored coca eradication policies. Meanwhile, the CSUTCB and the coca growers blocked roads to support COB and teachers unions' resistance to education reform. Third, the agrarian reform bill returned traditional agrarian issues (credit, infrastructure, prices, and protection of community-based work obligations) to the fore in the CSUTCB, thus expanding its appeal in the next cycle.

The second wave of anti-neoliberal contention began when Sánchez de Lozada launched three bold reforms in his first year: the Capitalization Law (privatization), the Popular Participation Law, and education reform. The COB and the CSUTCB mobilized against the first two without success. They failed to force the government to negotiate over their demands because the closed, tight-knit technocratic policy process left no chinks for the opposition to exploit and the legislative coalition held fast. Moreover, severance pay offers and early retirement incentives fragmented and weakened COB mobilization. CSUTCB resistance weakened because local leaders saw opportunities for personal political advancement.

Meanwhile, the dynamic pole of popular sector mobilization, the one that contributed to the expansion of collective power, had definitely shifted to resistance against to U.S.-led coca eradication policy. The Zero Coca program generated continuous mobilization in the Chapare beginning in 1994 that built on processes begun in the previous cycle. Coca-grower federation-led mobilization forced the government to the negotiating table. Although talks among coca growers, the COB, CSUTCB, and government representatives frequently broke down, coca growers – with Evo Morales, an energetic emergent leader who later became president of Bolivia, at their head – put revisions to antidrug Law 1008 and the industrialization of coca on the agenda.[20]

In those negotiations, the government's exclusionary tactics to isolate more militant coca growers caused an important transformation in anti-neoliberal contentious politics. On 17 May 1994 the government decreed the industrialization of coca in medicine, food, and cosmetics in the legal zones established by Law 1008. But transitional zones – such as the Chapare – were not included, and coca growers mobilized to defend their livelihood. These mobilizations strengthened the collective power of anti-neoliberal forces because they drew solidary support from other social sectors, culminating in the "March for Life, Coca, and National Sovereignty" from Villa Tunari to La Paz, beginning 29 August 1994. Demands included honoring the agreements of 23 March and 5 May 1994 and demilitarization of the lowlands, including removal of U.S. Drug Enforcement Agency presence. Although the government repressed the march, some 3,000 peasants began it and 1,500 reached La Paz on 19 September.[21] They got a warm welcome from inhabitants of La Paz.

The March for Life involved rural and urban popular sector organizations. The COB and separate member unions who had been demonstrating without much success throughout the year against privatization and education reform joined the coca growers in the protests of August and September 1994. These culminated in large-scale national demonstrations of teachers, students, COB, and coca producers. In short, battered and declining urban unions found renewed strength by supporting the ascendant coca-grower federations and the CSUTCB in their struggle against coca eradication. In a sure sign of coca-grower federation dominance in contentious politics, unrest subsided when the government pledged to end forcible eradication of coca and to withdraw forces gradually from the Chapare (Pinto Ocampo 2004).

A powerful innovation in issue framing contributed to the success of the march and surrounding mobilization. The organizing cry of "life, coca, and national sovereignty" drew participation from a broad spectrum of Bolivian popular sector – and even some middle-class – groups. "Coca" had become a symbol for indigenous culture, which meant the majority of the population regardless of whether they were rural or urban in origin. U.S.-led militarization of the Chapare symbolized Bolivia's lack of sovereignty, which extended to broader issues of denationalization through privatization in favor of international corporations and their domestic business allies. The assault on "life" followed from the negative consequences of privatization and other free-market policies for public sector unions, formal sector employment, and quality of life for the poor – who were the majority – because of price increases for goods and services. In other words,

[20] See Crabtree (2005: 37) for Law 1008.
[21] Evo Morales, one of the principal leaders, was arrested early on.

commodfication destroyed the economic, social, and cultural conditions that supported a way of life. It subjected people to hunger, misery, and alienation. The shift away from the language of class struggle and exploitation to the moral issue of the right to live with self-determination as authentic Bolivians was a major shift in the framing of the struggle against contemporary market society, one capable of attracting many different social groups and identities.[22]

This second wave of anti-neoliberal mobilization crested in March and April 1995 in urban-centered contentious action. In March, 80,000 teachers across the country protested privatization, education reform that restricted teachers' rights, and flex labor rules that weakened unionization. Later that month the COB called a general strike in support of 3,000 teachers beset by police and army. Meanwhile, coca growers in the Chapare independently continued to resist forcible eradication of coca farms. Thus the authorities faced protests, marches, strikes, hunger strikes, and roadblocks simultaneously on urban and rural fronts. In response to generalized unrest, the government resorted to repression, declaring a 90-day state of siege. However, teachers remained on strike and the government agreed to negotiate with them in April, marking the downswing of this cycle. Nevertheless, the government extended the state of siege for another 90 days because of violence in the Chapare.

In 1996, during the downswing of the second wave of anti-neoliberal contention, the locus of contentious politics shifted to the countryside over agrarian reform policy and traditional COB–CSUTCB modes of cooperation reemerged. In September, indigenous and peasant groups protested an agrarian reform bill, fearing it undermined their land rights. In early October, the COB called an indefinite general strike in support of a peasant-led hunger strike. Sánchez de Lozada defused the situation by meeting with Indian and peasant leaders and by making some concessions. He broke peasant–urban labor cooperation by excluding the COB from the negotiations, and the law was approved later that month. One concession ensured that the agrarian superintendency would not be authorized to rule on land tenure issues. However, the most significant concession favored lowland indigenous peoples. The bill recognized communal property, which was more prevalent in the lowlands. Highland indigenous had long established private ownership over minifundia, and their concerns turned more on credit, marketing, irrigation, and prices. They also worried that the bill undermined communal practices involving complicated reciprocal work and ritual obligations based on the kinship relationships of the ayllu. With these actions, Sánchez de Lozada

---

[22] "Life" as a framing mechanism emerged in 1986 when desperate tin miners staged a "March for Life" from Oruro to La Paz to protest the dismemberment of COMIBOL. On 22 August, over 5,000 miners, peasants, school teachers, students, housewives, and Roman Catholic clergy set out from Oruro. Along the way, the column swelled to 10,000. Many of the marchers emphasized the moral underpinnings of the march: "We are fighting for a just cause. With a salary of [about one U.S. dollar] a day we cannot live. It isn't enough to survive. That's why we are here." Quoted in Nash (1992: 279); also see Sanabria (1999).

demobilized the Confederación Indígena del Oriente, Chaco y Amazonía de Bolivia and drove a permanent wedge between lowland and highland indigenous organizations. However, he also set up continual struggles with the CSUTCB, especially after the coca federations lost their grip on it with the election of Felipe Quispe, who had a more highland peasant indiginist revival orientation.[23]

A Tale of Two "Wars"

A third wave of anti-neoliberal contention began during Hugo Banzer's and Vice President Jorge Quiroga's turbulent government (1997–2002) and ended in the truncated second presidency of Sánchez de Lozada who was forced to resign (2002–3). Deploying "battle-tested" tactics to politically exclude the popular sectors, both governments supported neoliberal reforms and implemented orthodox economic stabilization programs that reinforced patterns of economic exclusion. However, sustaining those policies proved more difficult. The political power of governing coalitions had declined, a process exacerbated by economic crisis. In this context, transformations in the associational and collective power of challengers to neoliberalism drove contentious politics to new heights over two major events, the "Water War" and the "Gas War." Innovations in framing and brokerage contributed to the vigor of these movements.

The Water War

Banzer and Quiroga, both from the ADN, headed a "megacoalition" that included the MIR, the Unión Cívica Conciencia de la Patria (Condepa, a highland populist party), and Nueva Fuerza Republicana. Because Condepa and Nueva Fuerza abandoned the governing coalition, Quiroga, who became president after Banzer resigned in 2001, was left with only the Unión Cívica and the MIR.[24] Their governments suffered two key weaknesses. First, the large governing coalition was unwieldy. This debilitated state power, as did the absence of a governing program (Grindle 2003: 325–26). Because Banzer had campaigned as a populist and lacked a governing program, he stimulated a "national dialogue" to establish policy priorities. But he was also the caretaker of the established neoliberal order. This contradiction cost him. Second, economic crisis – the Asian crisis and the Brazilian currency crisis – weakened their governments' functional power. Unemployment grew as did dependency on U.S., IMF, and World Bank aid. Given that dependency, the Banzer–Quiroga government ignored the policy recommendations of the "national dialogue" by implementing an orthodox stabilization program and

---

[23] The second wave ends with protests by miners of Potosí against new ownership (international mining companies) in December 1996 and January 1997. Troops repressed them, killing and wounding dozens.

[24] For coalition composition, see Gamarra (2003, 1994); Van Cott (2005); and Klein (2003, 1992).

deepening neoliberal programs. It raised taxes and prices, expanded privatization (water utilities and hydrocarbons), and reintroduced U.S.-sponsored militarized coca eradication policies (Assies and Salman 2003).

This persistent, stubborn, pointed will to exclude expressed popular sector interests provoked a third wave of anti-neoliberal contention that initially followed established patterns. After the government announced gas price increases and tax hikes in November 1997, the COB launched several strikes and demonstrations through early 1998. They had little impact given the COB's weakened and isolated condition. Meanwhile, the United States pressured the Bolivian government to revive coca eradication efforts on pain of losing foreign aid. Banzer dutifully launched Plan Dignity to eradicate all illegal plots. As a result, conflict raged with the coca growers, who mobilized against the plan throughout 1998. But they failed to link their struggle with that of urban popular sectors and obtained meager results.

Changes in the associational and collective power of anti-neoliberal popular sector forces were about to transform the character of mass protest. The "Water War" in Cochabamba from January to April 2000 was the opening salvo in this transformation. The privatization of water rights was a local issue with national resonance. The politics of its implementation was a microcosm of the willful exclusion of social groups opposed to neoliberal reforms and the corruption, duplicity, and manipulation that accompanied the politics. In this event, the politics of exclusion and the threat of economic harm created new organizations that built associational power and facilitated the emergence of a cross-class coalition that increased collective power along new axes. These new organizations framed issues in a way that invited solidary mobilization by more established anti-neoliberal movements. Leaders used those frames to broker transformations in mobilizing capacity. The Water War created a template for anti-neoliberal mobilization that replaced the old declining model centered on the COB.

Mass mobilization against the privatization of water utilities – the Water War – turned Cochabamba into a symbol of relatively successful resistance to neoliberalism. However, the dynamics and intensity of the event were influenced by the local political economy of water distribution and the simmering conflicts it created. These involved social organizations independent of the COB and the CSUTCB (Assies 2003: 20–21).

With close to a million inhabitants in the late 1990s, Cochabamba, the capital of its namesake department, was a fast-growing metropolitan area in the central Andean valley region that linked La Paz (Bolivia's traditional political center) with Santa Cruz, an emerging economic center in the eastern lowlands. Given rapid growth and lack of investment, the state water company could supply only about 50 percent of demand concentrated in mainly wealthy and middle-class sectors and at low subsidized rates. The rest of city relied on a network of cooperatives and individuals who managed private wells, family-owned cisterns, and water trucks (Laserna 2001).

This situation fed rural–urban tension. Most of the private wells were in nearby agricultural provinces and managed by community-centered customary legal rights over access and control of water (Crabtree 2005: 23–27). Owners and managers, known as *regantes*, had a history of defending their water rights against the public utility, which dug its own wells to supply the city and depleted aquifers for agricultural purposes (Assies 2003: 19–20). In the mid-1990s, well diggers and owners, water pump distributors, cistern builders, and truck distributors, and the individuals, cooperatives, and associations that controlled informal water supply, replaced old community-based defense committees with the Federación Departamental Cochabambina de Organizaciones de Regantes (FEDECOR; Cochabamba Department Federation of Irrigators' Organizations). By the end of the decade, mobilization in defense of regantes' rights was the main source of rural protest in Cochabamba outside of the coca-growing area (Assies 2003: 20–21; Laserna 2001).

In the middle of this conflict, the government decided to privatize the Cochabamba water system and put it up for competitive bid on coverage, quality, and price, with a tie-in to financing for a long-planned large dam and water distribution system – the Misicuni project. The actual sale conditions betrayed the original policy design that protected all stakeholders. Only one consortium was interested, Aguas de Tunari, with Bechtel as the principal partner. In June 1999 it negotiated directly with the national government and municipality, supported by a presidential decree. The contract they negotiated, signed in September, did not guarantee financing for the Misicuni project or for expansion of service coverage. It did specify rate increases and demanded legal changes to customary water rights to corner the market and ensure profitability.

On the heels of this murky deal, in November 1999, under pressure from the World Bank (which had been pushing water use reform for years) the government rushed Law 2029 through Congress without discussion, publicity, or consulting affected groups (Assies 2003; Crabtree 2005: 20–21). Law 2029 privatized water distribution. It granted 40-year concessions and 5-year licenses to any institution with legal status (public, nonprofit, or private) in the 41 urban areas with more than 10,000 inhabitants. However, conditions for receiving concessions disproportionately favored large private corporations, which would have exclusive rights over water resources. This meant that existing local cooperatives and neighborhood associations would be forced into contracts for water with the concessionaire (Assies 2003: 17).

Under these circumstances, the political and economic exclusion of social groups adversely affected by privatization drove mobilization and contributed to increases in the collective power of challengers. The policy process clearly excluded those who were to suffer exorbitant rate hikes and expropriation of water access rights. This united people from the rural areas around Cochabamba afraid of losing water rights with middle-class city dwellers who were connected to the state water utility company and were concerned about rising water bills. As early as

July 1999, middle-class local environmental organizations, the Cochabamba College of Engineering (which had crafted alternatives to water resource distribution during the 1990s), and FEDECOR protested the concession to both Aguas de Tunari and the Committee for the Defense of Water and the Household Economy. On 4 and 5 November, the Defense Committee organized a series of roadblocks to protest the new water law. They criticized the absence of transparency in policy making, lack of interest in discussing alternatives, and disinterest in expanding the distribution system (Assies 2003: 31–32; Crabtree 2005: 23; Olivera and Lewis 2004: 27). Uneasy with these popular sector demonstrations, city-elected officials (facing an election in December), local businesspeople, and notables (who had helped to broker the Aguas de Tuanri deal) formed a Civic Committee to mediate and deflect popular sector discontent over the issue (Olivera and Lewis 2004: 29).

Collective power quickly expanded in Cochabamba. Because national policy backed Aguas de Tunari, the Defense Committee understood that resistance required greater mobilization capacity. It turned to an innovative and combative local union for help, the Federación Departamental de Trabajadores Fabriles de Cochabamba (Departmental Federation of Factory Workers of Cochabamba). Unlike many COB-affiliated unions, the Fabriles responded to the decline of union power creatively. Like the CTA in Argentina, they brokered an expansion in the sources of mobilization and transformed the identity of their union. Oscar Olivera, the leader of the Fabriles, recalled how neoliberal policies had weakened them. As they pondered how to revitalize their union to avoid the COB's headlong decline, they found that individuals and groups from the informal sector, the unemployed, and urban self-help associations frequently sought their help. Instead of turning them away because they were not "proper workers," the Fabriles aided them. As the Fabriles learned about their world and struggles they forged linkages with many organizations opposed to neoliberalism. Olivera explained:

If there exists an invisible world of work [outside of the formal sector] what should we do? ... We have to organize, we have to strengthen organization, and we have to strengthen alliances. In this way the Fabriles became a kind of reference point for people. Everybody came around seeking solutions to their problems [and] ... we offered our support. (Olivera and Lewis 2004: 26)

In an assembly-style meeting on 12 November 1999 (following two days of protest against water privatization a week earlier), the Defense Committee and the Fabriles created the Coordinadora por la Defensa del Agua y la Vida (Coordinator for the Defense of Water and Life). "Life" framed the broadest possible spectrum of grievances against the indignities and hardships of life in neoliberal Bolivia. Olivera reminisced: "During the assembly, one peasant said, 'Let's not just have water in our name, but life as well, because they are taking everything away from us. All that's left to us are the water and the air'" (Olivera and Lewis 2004: 27).

Issue framing by the Fabriles also helped to consolidate and further expand the collective power of the social groups challenging neoliberal policies and exclusionary practices. They infused the Defense Committee's grievances with a discourse of traditional national-popular anti-imperialism. To this they grafted newer "elements of antiglobalism; protest against the societal and development model imposed by Decree 21060 of 1985; and criticism of the government's (non) policies, kleptocratic practices, and nepotism" (Assies 2003: 32). These were reformist platforms, not calls for armed revolution or even remotely suggestive of such action.

Rate hikes of up to 150 percent and Aguas de Tunari's plan to install water meters at private and cooperative wells triggered the Water War in January 2000. What the popular sectors feared had come to pass: The law thoroughly disrupted daily lives and threatened the livelihood of the regantes. Throughout, the Coordinadora carefully defined its targets: Aguas de Tunari for dispossessing the people in favor of foreign capital and the Civic Committee and municipal offices for their connivance (Assies 2003: 32; Olivera and Lewis 2004: 30). The government's persistent and willful exclusion of the Coordinadora and its substantive demands from negotiations, the Coordinadora's framing of the issue, and brokerage by movement leaders escalated mobilization. These turned the conflict into a "War," an all-out last-ditch stand against neoliberalism.

Over January and February, the Coordinadora and the Civic Committee vied for control of protest and negotiation over changes to the Aguas de Tunari contract and Law 2029. The Coordinadora demanded nullification of the contract, repeal of the water law, and reversal of the rate hikes (Olivera and Lewis 2004: 30). The Civic Committee stressed the rate question. Regantes, environmental groups, teachers, truck drivers, store owners, and neighborhood water committees blocked local roads, struck, marched on public buildings, and violent street battles broke out when police repressed them. Throughout, government negotiators met exclusively with the Civic Committee. The Coordinadora staged demonstrations, which were violently repressed, demanding inclusion in negotiations. Meanwhile, the government, vitally interested in maintaining a good business climate for international corporations, delayed by crafting agreements with the Civic Committee (Assies 2003; Crabtree 2005; Olivera and Lewis 2004).

The collective and disruptive power of mobilization escalated in April as other movements joined the fray. Frustrated and enraged that the government ignored an April deadline for negotiation set by a popular referendum the Coordinadora had organized in March, on 4 April 2000 the Coordinadora and the Civic Committee independently called for a general strike. The government reopened negotiations with the Civic Committee exclusively. In response, the Coordinadora organized roadblocks and massive demonstrations in the city center beginning on 5 April. Mobilization linked rural peasant irrigators, local water collectives, urban workers, middle classes, elderly men and women, and shantytown dwellers (water warriors), the traditional left, and anybody unhappy with the established order and its corruption and inefficiency. Coca growers under the leadership of Evo Morales, who were trying to break out of their isolation and renew their links with urban struggles, joined in; although the departmental branch of the COB did not. The coca growers blocked roads connecting Cochabamba to Santa Cruz. As they had in Argentina, demonstrators formed assemblies to make tactical and negotiating decisions. These included the occupation of Aguas de Tunari headquarters and surrounding the police prefecture where the Civic Committee, the mayor, and government negotiators were meeting. Coordinadora leaders forced their way into the meeting and were promptly arrested. Mobilization swelled as betrayed and infuriated residents took the city center. "Water Warriors" in the surrounding shantytowns blocked roads into the city, cutting it off from the rest of the nation. The CSUTCB added water rights to its list of grievances and set up roadblocks in the department of La Paz in solidary protest. The escalation of the struggle resembled that of the teacher's strike in March and April 1995, and the national government ordered a state of siege in the night of 7 April. This ultimate act of exclusion merely stiffened resistance, and tens of thousands turned out on the streets and blocked roads while their leaders prepared them to repel repression (Assies 2003: 26–27; Kohl and Farthing 2006: 162–68; Postero 2007: 193–96; Vargas and Kruse 2000: 10–13).

The rallying cries of the multitude and reminiscences of participants express the frustration, anger, and righteous indignation that motivated protestors. Everywhere, banners proclaimed the "Water Is Ours"; "Pachamama, Woracocha, and Tata Díos gave it to us to live, not to do business with"; "Aguas de Tunari Go Home!"; "Power to customary uses, long live water, die privatizers" (Crespo 2000: 21; Perreault 2006: 156; Postero 2007: 195). A retired village water regulator recalled:

Each community has someone whose job it is to regulate the use of water . . . it was never a problem because everybody respected *usos y costumbres* . . . Back in 2000, the leaders of the community decided to take part in the protests, because the government threatened to take our water away and give it to other people. Without water you cannot live. So we all manned the road blocks, taking it in turns . . . Then we marched to Cochabamba. (Crabtree 2005: 25–26)

A priest from a Catholic self-help association expressed feelings from the shantytowns:

All of a sudden it became illegal to have these sources of water [locally managed wells]. People would end up having to pay for water from sources in which they themselves had invested their meager earnings. Whole neighborhoods were therefore mobilized . . . Also, the idea of privatization doesn't square well with the way people think about water. Most . . . are of *campesino* origin, and have quite traditional ways of organizing themselves and their communities . . . it's not so easy to pull the wool over their eyes. (Crabtree 2005: 27)

Drawing on those feelings, the Coordinadora brokered transformations in the struggle over water, expanding participation and shaping demands. People flocked to the headquarters of the Fabriles and the Comité de Defensa del Agua to air their grievances over rate hikes and threats to livelihood. Daily, Coordinadora leaders attended neighborhood and community assemblies to discuss the water issue and organized local water defense committees where needed. Top Coordinadora leaders communicated directly with demonstrators during the mass demonstrations in the main Plaza, a massive popular assembly molding major decisions over strategy and tactics (Crespo 2000: 26; Olivera and Lewis 2004).

Cocaleros led by Evo Morales and the CSUTCB under Felipe Quispe supported the Water War for complex reasons. Competition between the two leaders was a significant factor. In a divisive and bruising conflict, Morales and the cocaleros had lost dominance of the CSUTCB to indigenous nationalist Quispe in 1998. Both needed to consolidate power in their respective union federations. Joining the Water War was an effective tactic (Albó 2002).

The CSUTCB's participation expanded regional protest to the national level. Innovations in framing and brokerage by the new leadership transformed the CSUTCB's mobilization capacity in 2000 and beyond. Quispe infused the CSUTCB with an indigenous Aymara nationalist framing for collective action. Kataristas of the pluricultural line had become identified with the establishment and declined. Quispe emphasized autonomy for the Aymara nation, the principal ethnic group in the Andean region where the CSUTCB was strongest (Albó 2002; Bolton 2007; García Linera 2005).

This framing breathed new life into the ayllu as the locus for social, political, and economic organization. In effect, the reconstituted ayllu became a key brokerage node that transformed the leaderships' framing of issues into local participation and facilitated horizontal linkage building across rural and urban communities. Ayllus were kinship networks that controlled and allocated land. Cultural codes defined reciprocal obligations in the organization of work, festivals, rituals, and politics. Males were expected to take on rotating leadership roles in public service. The life of the community, and of individuals, depended on participation in collective action and the community assembly was the decision-making center at the core of the concept of ayllu democracy. In many peasant communities the lines between ayllu and peasant unions blurred, being virtually indistinguishable in more remote areas (Albó 2002; Ticona, Rojas, Albó 1995).[25]

The revival of the ayllu and ayllu democracy in the communities reinvigorated the CSUTCB. More than ever, the peasant community general assembly became the locus of decision making for successful collective action and thus

---

[25] Ironically, laws passed during Sánchez de Lozada's government facilitated the success of Quispe's framing. These included the bilingual multicultural laws, legislation facilitating recognition of indigenous communities and their land, and even decentralization once indigenous organizations learned how to compete politically at the municipal level (Postero 2007).

the central brokerage node for strengthening associational and collective power. When the national or regional leadership decided to mobilize, effective collective action required agreement by union locals in community general assembly and their aggregation in larger assemblies called *ampliados* [amplified community meetings]. Local peasant union leaders could then legitimately draw on ayllu principles of reciprocal obligations to encourage and enforce participation. This was the task of "strike and blockade committees" who relied on customary rights to levies from families, including penalties for failure to comply. Roadblocks were organized along the lines and rhythms of Indian peasant labor. Rotating details of kin-group levies manned and supplied them (Albó 2002; García Linera 2004) The organization of marches closely paralleled that of festive parades, where every family knew their role and contributed accordingly (Lazar 2008).

Quispe and the national and regional CSUTCB leadership used these mechanisms to leverage massive turnouts of committed protestors for anti-neoliberal mobilization. Given the characteristics of ayllu democracy, this also required shaping community public opinion. Therefore the organization of seminars, workshops, and informative talks at the community level was a primary task of federation-level leadership. These promoted discussion of major issues and consensus building (García Linera 2004: 184). In the case of water privatization, the CSUTCB leadership organized numerous local seminars and informative talks (especially in the department of La Paz) regarding the impact of the law on daily community life (García Linera 2004: 134–35).

In April 2000, frustrated and angry peasant communities supported Quispe's call to mobilize against neoliberal agrarian policy and in support of their "brothers" customary claims over water rights, framed as an extension of neoliberal expropriation of indigenous livelihood. Demands included (Assies and Salman 2005: 280)

1. Suspension of the General Water Law project
2. CSUTCB participation in designing a sovereignty plan for coca production
3. CSUTCB monitoring of ministries to ensure implementation of hard-won concessions
4. The reestablishment of a peasant bank
5. Creation of an Agrarian University
6. Immediate titling of indigenous land
7. Direct administration of protected areas

Peasant–indigenous mobilization engulfed the departments of La Paz, Oruru, Cochabamba, Chuquisaca, and Tarija. Repression was especially strong in Achacachi (La Paz Department) after the declaration of the state of siege and Quispe's arrest. This was Quispe's personal stronghold (Assis and Salman 2005: 280). The deaths of two peasants spurred furor. Over an open radio microphone women railed: "They are massacring our children, our peasants, we cannot tolerate this!" (García, Gutiérrez, Prada and Tapia 2000: 143) Enra; redoubled their protests.

Battered by this storm of exponentially expanding mobilization the government signed an agreement with the Coordinadora that ʌguɑɔ ̄ Tunari would leave. The next day the government announced 36 changes to Law 2029 based on Coordinadora proposals. Highlights included the idea of forming a national water council with regante representation; five-year renewable-use licenses for indigenous organizations gave way to registration for the useful life of the service; concessionaries would not have a monopoly of water rights, customary rights of water committees, cooperatives, and other usos y costumbres would be recognized; and local government and organizations of "popular participation" would be included in establishing rate structures (Assies 2003: 30). The government also negotiated with the CSUTCB, released Quispe, ratified 1998 agreements over CSUTCB demands, and conceded union participation in the General Water Law (Assies and Salman 2005: 281).

The Water War marked a turning point in resistance to neoliberalism. It was a local issue with national resonance in which tried and true government mechanisms of political exclusion, manipulation, and repression only stiffened resolve and expanded mobilization by heterogeneous social groups that included middle classes who obtained significant concessions. Innovations in the characteristics of associational and collective power abounded. Movement organizations were independent of (or very different in orientation to) the traditional union structure; hence their strategies and tactics were not beholden to COB or CSUTCB hierarchy and their national political priorities. The Coordinadora was very open and tolerant; it welcomed any organization interested in joining the struggle; it helped interested groups, such as shantytown dwellers whom traditional unions had ignored, to organize. It promoted an assembly style of decision making to build confidence and support for its decisions. The Coordinadora introduced the idea of direct democracy to the policy agenda as a means to overcome persistent government neglect and denial of the legitimacy of popular sector organizations. Last, but not least, the Coordinadora framed the issue as an assault on the necessities of life for all in the interest of international capital and its domestic allies who were in cahoots with corrupt government officials (Assies 2003: 32–33; Olivera and Lewis 2004).

The issue and its framing drew support from other organizations, such as the coca growers and the CSUTCB. Challenges to neoliberalism now had the capacity to ignite mobilization across the land of a character and quality that was much more resistant to repression (Olivera and Lewis 2004: 47–49). A new form of coalitional politics was emerging. Although most protestors were poor Indians or urban migrants of Indian heritage, they united around a common idea of how market forces threatened cultural practices rather than a purely Indian identity. "Instead of organizing around class or ethnicity, the Cochabamba protesters came together around a shared notion of exploitation based on both culture and poverty" (Postero 2007:195).

The disruptive and irrepressible characteristics of this mobilization extracted concessions from the authorities because they threatened the business climate at a time when Bolivia needed foreign investment to consolidate neoliberal economic reforms. Differences within the "mega" governing coalition over how to deal with the threat contributed to concessions as did disagreements over the effects of mobilization on the expansion of rising opposition political parties.

The Gas War

The third wave of anti-neoliberal contention crested during the "Gas War" of October 2003 when, after just 13 months in office, massive protests forced Gonzalo Sánchez de Lozada to resign his second presidency. A drastic decline in the political power of neoliberal forces contributed to his ouster (see Table 5.3). Voter volatility and party system change during the 2002 presidential election caused the formation of an even more fragile governing coalition. The ADN garnered only 3.4 percent of the vote after obtaining over 22 percent in 1997. Condepa, a regional party that had been an important governing coalition partner in the 1990s, also collapsed. Thus Sánchez de Lozada, whose MNR party had received 22.5 percent of the vote, formed a coalition government with the MIR and the Unión Cívica (16.3 and 5.5 percent of the vote, respectively) and the tiny Movimiento Bolivia Libre. This was hardly a powerhouse coalition, made even weaker by the absence of the rapidly rising Nueva Fuerza Republicana (New Republican Force) party, which obtained 20.9 percent of votes. Nueva Fuerza, led by former Cochabamba Mayor Manfred Reyes (the incumbent during the Water War) was a natural ally of Sánchez de Lozada but refused to join him because he believed fraud had kept him from becoming the leading presidential candidate.

The 2002 elections also contributed to a positive shift in the political power of challengers to neoliberalism, which further debilitated the government by stiffening congressional opposition. Ironically, unintended consequences of Sánchez de Lozada's Popular Participation Law caused this change. The introduction of municipal electoral politics facilitated the formation of new political parties, such as Nueva Fuerza. But not all new parties were cut from the same cloth as the old ones. Evo Morales and the coca-grower federations appropriated the name of the moribund Movimeiento al Socialismo (MAS; Movement Toward Socialism). The MAS framed its politics in indigenist terms that made it popular with ethnic Quechua and Aymara, and with Evo Morales as its presidential candidate in 2002, MAS obtained second place with 20.9 percent of the vote.[26] Thus he

---

[26] Nueva Fuerza received only a few hundred votes less than the MAS, which was the source of Reyes' complaint (Assies and Salman 2003: 2).

and Sánchez de Lozada contested the run-off election for the presidency, which the latter won, 84 congressional votes to 43. Meanwhile, another new indigenist political party, the Movimiento Indígena Pachakuti (Pachakuti Indigenous Movement) organized by Felipe Quispe, won a fifth place, showing with 6.1 percent. Consequently, two of the major parties in Congress identified themselves as ethnic parties, had leaders in the forefront of anti-neoliberal mobilization seated in Congress, and rejected traditional parties because of their corruption, their opaque manipulation of the policy process, and their support for neoliberalism. These parties were not interested in the political deal making for government offices that consumed the traditional parties. These origins ensured their participation in contentious as well as institutional politics. (Albro 2005; Assies and Salman 2003; Mayorga 2005; Van Cott 2005, 2003).

Economic crisis further weakened the new government. Sánchez de Lozada had no intention of reforming the free-market economic model. But he understood the relative weakness of his political position and as a presidential candidate had run on a mildly populist platform, pledging to increase government spending, especially public works, to spur employment and demand-led economic growth. The Asian financial crisis-driven international recession put an end to those plans. It hit Bolivia hard, reducing domestic demand and exports and, consequently, fiscal receipts. With the fiscal deficit running at 9 percent of GDP, the government could not increase spending without feeding inflation, which the IMF would not allow. Faced with these pressures, the government implemented unpopular economic stabilization policies, mainly income tax increases and denying (once again) pay raises for public employees (except for high-ranking officials) (Assies and Salman 2003: 58–59).

The economic crisis and stabilization policies adopted in January and February 2002 sharply increased economic exclusion. Per-capita GDP shrank, unemployment rates climbed, informal employment jumped to almost 68 percent, and income concentration advanced unchecked. Despair and rage over Sánchez de Lozada's policy reversal, globalization, and IMF policies perceived to cause only misery fueled an upsurge of mobilization (Domingo 2005).

In similar fashion to Cochabamba, simmering conflicts ready to boil over preceded the Gas War. In January 2003 coca growers and the Coordinadora staged massive roadblocks and demonstrations against coca eradication in Cochabamba. More than 10,000 pensioners and retirees joined the struggle, marching 68 miles to La Paz to press demands for benefit adjustments. Income tax increases and public sector salary freezes decreed on 9 February sparked a tax revolt, the *impuestazo*. Feeling the full brunt of political and economic exclusion, private and public formal sector workers were incensed that the government had not raised corporate taxes, especially royalties on the burgeoning hydrocarbon sector, mainly natural gas.

The mobilization that followed turned Bolivia into a powder keg waiting to explode. In the midst of generalized discontent on 11 February, enraged policemen and firefighters of La Paz, protesting long-repressed wages struck, followed by police in Cochabamba and Santa Cruz. On 12 February striking La Paz police marched on the presidential palace and other government buildings joined by secondary school students. A spokesperson for lower-ranking police officers told reporters, "[We] vehemently reject the huge tax the government plans to levy. We're demanding a significant wage increase so our families can enjoy an adequate quality of life" (*World News Connection* 12 February 2003).[27]

The military guard around the palace fired on them, and a gun battle erupted during which the government quickly negotiated the withdrawal of the police. However, people who had joined the demonstration after hearing that the IMF was behind the tax increase became enraged and attacked, looted, and burned government ministries and the headquarters of the MNR, the MIR, and Nueva Fuerza. More than 30 people died and 170 were wounded in protests that took place in El Alto, Cochabamba, and other major cities (Olivera and Lewis 2004: 167–69). At the head of 3,000 protesters, a furious union leader exclaimed, "If the president wants to adhere to these policies, then he must go" (Associated Press, 17 February 2003). In the days that followed, pensioners and retirees protested the pittance they received, schoolteachers their salaries, and consumers high prices. MAS and Movimiento Indígena Pachakuti called for Sánchez de Lozada's resignation. Public opinion warned that reforms were necessary to halt the disintegration of the state (Assies 2004: 29; Assies and Salman 2003: 62–64; Crabtree 2005: 100–1).[28]

These events foreshadowed key characteristics of snowballing contentious action in the near future. The state's political power was eroding, and its insistence on the politics of exclusion to ram through orthodox stabilization programs to deal with the economic crisis motivated people from different walks of life all across major cities to protest. The demonstrations were no longer driven by more or less easily controlled urban trade unions. Moreover, protests found a strong political amplifying chamber in Morales' MAS and Quispe's Movimiento Indígena Pachakuti, who encouraged mobilization to support their oppositional role in Congress.

Sánchez de Lozada ignored the warning, and his government announced it would follow through on plans from Banzer's presidency to sell natural gas rights at low prices to a consortium of international companies who would export it to California via a Chilean port.[29] By 2003 natural gas had become Bolivia's leading export. Thus the terms of the concession to foreign capital, framed as a

[27] Other demands included social and institutional improvements, life insurance, pensions for widows and children of fallen police officers, changes to police law, and physical improvements to police stations.

[28] Also see "Month in Review: Bolivia" *Current History* 102, 663 (February, 2003).

[29] For details of this deal, see Assies (2004) and Hylton and Thomson (2006: 167). The fact that the gas would be exported through a Chilean port further fanned Bolivian nationalist indignation.

giveaway, turned the issue into a symbol of the popular sector's exclusion from contemporary market society and called attention to the president's prominent role in creating the nightmare of hunger that had engulfed them since 1985.

This announcement triggered the Gas War of September–October 2003. It engulfed the department of La Paz and its working-class suburb of El Alto, and spread to other depressed highland departments and cities, such as Oruru, Sucre, Potosí, and Cochabamba. Demonstrations also occurred in Santa Cruz, where coca growers protested U.S.-sponsored militarized eradication programs as well as neoliberal employment, social, and economic policies in general (Altamira 2003; Klein 2003; Mayorga 2005). During the Gas War, transformations in the associational and collective power of the social groups challenging neoliberalism that had been taking place in recent years came to a head, endowing it with unprecedented force. Therefore, an account of those transformations is given before we examine the Gas War proper.

To begin with, major transformations in popular sector associational and collective power had occurred in the city of El Alto, the emblematic epicenter of resistance during the Gas War. El Alto was a burgeoning working-class district perched above La Paz that became a city in 1985 and had a population of approximately 650,000, mostly indigenous Aymara and Quechua, by 2001. Well over half had rural origins and labored in the informal sector of the economy, and about 65 percent were poor or indigent with another 25 percent living on the verge of poverty (Lazar 2008, 2004; Villegas 1993). Unemployed miners and industrial workers had also made El Alto their home (Gómez 2004; Sandoval and Sostres 1989). The fact that the road system leading into La Paz necessarily passed through it allowed sustained mass mobilization and road blockages to cause food and supply shortages in the capitol. Moreover, as in the case of the Water War in Cochabamba, popular sectors had built significant associational power independent of the traditional union structure. Thus mobilization in El Alto had its own rhythm and reasons and was much harder to repress successfully once begun.

Over 30 years, El Alto had developed a dense, close-knit system of community associations organized mainly along territorial and geographic lines (district and neighborhood) to meet basic needs in the face of government neglect. The *junta vecinal* [neighborhood association] and the *sindicato* [union] were the principal forms. They mediated the relationship of members with the state and confronted the state. They also substituted for the state (Lazar 2008: 179).

The *juntas vecinales* were the most important local organizations, and the Federación de Juntas Vecinales (Fejuve; Federation of Neighborhood Committees) encompassed all 570 of them. The neighborhood associations were a major organizer of the informal sector. They had been born of urban dwellers' struggles for land titling, basic services (water and electricity), and infrastructure (roads and street lighting). Collective action focused on the municipality (Crabtree 2005: 96;

Lazar 2006; Sandoval and Sostres 1989). The Popular Participation Law sharpened that focus, because it empowered the neighborhood committees to oversee municipal spending. Thus the Fejuve had a history of pressing for public works, questioning local authorities, and resisting tax increases. It also had a tradition of linking local struggle to national politics.

Local *sindicatos* also organized people employed in the informal sector. As had been the case with the Fabriles in Cochabamba, the local branch of the COB, the Central Obrera Regional-El Alto (Regional Workers Central, or COR) represented local artisans and vendors in addition to industrial workers. After the restructuring of COMIBOL in the mid-1980s, displaced miners organized and created a National Committee of Unemployed Miners. The miners infused these organizations with their classic militancy and thought of themselves as the vanguard of popular sector collective action in El Alto (Lazar 2008).

Two more El Alto community organizations played a significant role in the Gas War. Women were prominent in the informal sector, and the Women's Federation organized a host of associations focused on food security, education, public services, production, and union activity. Youth, among whom Quispe and his indigenist nationalist discourse had made inroads, were organized into student federations, especially from the newly chartered University of El Alto, and a myriad of youth associations [*agrupaciones juveniles*] (Crabtree 2005: 96–97; Lazar 2006; Sandoval and Sostres 1989).

The characteristics of El Alto's popular sector organizations permitted leaders to broker transformations in contentious politics from purely local issues and effect to national questions and impact. The origins of most of the population, mixed with indigenous nationalist discourse, supported the functioning of ayllu democracy. Thus the open general assembly was the key to community decision making. They elected representatives, delegated voice and power, and retained the right to remove them. Leadership carried out the consensus of the community (and also influenced it).

Residents of El Alto understood that neoliberal reforms increasingly disrupted their daily lives. One street vendor complained:

Yes effectively things have changed radically; for example, before there were more sales, we had more income. In contrast, now because there is a lot more competition and more traders, the sales themselves have really lowered, too much. (Lazar 2008: 181)

After discussing these issues in general assemblies, mobilizing *alteños* clearly had a sense of the national origins and implications of their actions, as captured in these commentaries by two Fejuve members:

Everyone was the bravest: the artisans, the traders, [people from] the markets, from the schools, parents – that is to say, we all totally united. Those who had never before come together, came together. So there is no doubt that now, that is to say, since now we're united, I think that's given more force to the citizens of El Alto. Not only alteños, but we can say this at a national level, because bit by bit they have woken up. (Lazar 2008: 55)

I think that the alteño community has become conscious of many things. They've oppressed us for more than 500 years...Now...we've realized what's going on in this country (Lazar 2008: 54).

In short, leaders linked struggles to improve local conditions to defense against cuts in state expenditures for health, education, and pensions to service Bolivia's external debt and opposition to the use precious natural resources for the enrichment of international companies and their Bolivian cronies. Careful framing of the conflict as one between the Bolivian people ("us") and politicians and businessmen who were betraying the country ("them") strengthened collective action (Gómez 2004; Lazar 2008). From there leaders used ayllu understandings of reciprocal obligations to mobilize community members as previously discussed in the case of the CSUTCB, especially the transference of organization for parades to demonstrations and roadblocks. These leaders also drew on seemingly coercive means to ensure compliance. Community members could be fined if they did not attend general assemblies or participate in collective action, such as civic parades, demonstrations, and strikes (Lazar 2008: 187).

These tight-knit, face-to-face community networks also facilitated more spontaneous participation. For example, a resident described how she and all of her neighbors knew the local neighborhood association leaders because they had been working with their urban services self-help organization:

So when the uprising began, Doña Beatriz and her neighbors called on this network to get people into the streets. Each block had a leader who knocked on every door to make sure that the families were participating in the blockades...Everyone in the association was expected to do their part and to contribute to the fund for supplies and food (Postero 2007: 219).

In addition to these developments in El Alto, the collective power of the social organizations that had been challenging neoliberalism also expanded significantly at a national level thanks to the dedicated networking of key leaders. With the appropriation of the MAS political label, Evo Morales, now also a congressman, expanded the coca growers' federation and their struggles into a national electoral political movement framed around indigenous identity, economic nationalism, defense of popular sectors, and political renewal. He organized the MAS on CSUTCB-union lines, thus transforming the moribund party into a movement party that combined contentious and electoral politics capable of mobilizing large numbers of people.

After becoming the head of the CSUTCB in November 1998, Felipe Quispe melded a militant, nationalist, separatist, indigenous framing of the struggle against neoliberalism to traditional highland peasant demands for favorable land, credit, infrastructure, and pricing policies. This facilitated solidary support for protests on a wide range of issues. He also founded the Pachakuti party to give their issues national projection and lobbying power in the legislature and gained significant influence among popular sector organizations in El Alto.

The collective power of the social organizations challenging neoliberalism also expanded through coordination among them. As previously discussed, Oscar Olivera had been forging a closer relationship with Evo Morales and the coca growers ever since the formation of the Coordinadora del Agua during the Water War. He actively supported coca growers' struggles in 2000 and 2001. When President Quiroga maneuvered for a deal with international companies to export gas, Olivera brokered the creation of a Gas Coordinadora in mid-2002 (but it did not really become active until September 2003). The Gas Coordinadora linked the MAS and the coca growers with the Coordinadora del Agua. It opposed the sale of natural gas through Chile, demanded a referendum on the gas question, and advocated state control of gas resources. It also raised the question of a constituent assembly to promote inclusion of popular sector interests in national policy making and was against the Free Trade Area of the Americas (Assies 2004; Olivera and Lewis 2004). Olivera and Morales modeled the Gas Coordinadora after the original Water Coordinadora, which enhanced its capacity to build popular sector collective power: "[The Gas Coordinadora] would have as members any citizen, neighborhood group, housewife, or wage worker, and their goal would be to unite and to channel social discontent and collective demands" (Olivera and Lewis 2004: 158). This meant it was open to citizen's organizations (pensioners, environmentalists, professional associations, and business groups) critical of neoliberalism, labor unions, indigenous organizations, the women's movement, and neighborhood associations.

An Estado Mayor del Pueblo (Joint Chiefs of Staff of the People) formally capped collective power building. Formed in early 2003, it brought Evo Morales, MAS, and coca growers together with Oscar Olivera and the Water Coordinadora along with retired General Víctor Ramírez López (Assies 2004). However, according to its founders, it never played a leading role in either the February tax revolt or the Gas War. Those events took the leadership by surprise and they failed to devise a strategy to use the opportunity to push for greater change (Olivera and Lewis 2004: 147–48).

The framing of the gas issue also encouraged the expansion of anti-neoliberal collective power. Foreign exploitation of Bolivian natural resources (silver, nitrates, and tin) in alliance with the domestic oligarchy had left them with nothing (Hylton and Thomson 2006: 167). Gas was their last hope for underwriting national development, and the gas question became a symbol for all the abuses the popular sectors had suffered under neoliberalism. Thus the Gas War completed what the Water War started. It transformed demands from local, regional, or union-specific grievances (including the defense of coca) to national-level demands centered on sovereignty, state control of natural resources, pro-formal sector employment and worker's rights policies, agrarian reform, demilitarization of the drug war, and calls for a constituent assembly (Blanco 2001; Klein 2003; Mayorga, Klein, and Altamira 2003; Rivera-Cusicanqui 2006). This drew a wide variety of claimants and streams of movement together.

This unprecedented alliance of social movements advocated national scale mobilization around a common set of demands (Ballve 2006:155; Rivera-Cusicanqui 2006: 179). Its goal was to "break the political and economic order that caused ... abuses" (Olivera and Lewis 2004: 176). However, these did not orchestrate the events of October 2003, they only facilitated them. Anti-neoliberal mass mobilization was "a gradual convergence of fragmented protests around the banner of gas exports and then the ouster of Sánchez de Lozada" (Assies 2004: 34).

Following the events of February 2003 in La Paz, El Alto, and other cities, the Gas War, a term coined by the MAS in an August 2003 call for mobilization, began in the department of La Paz in mid-September 2003. Peasants of Warisata, organized by Quispe's CSUTCB-El Alto, had blocked roads in the Titicaca region by holding a tourist bus convoy hostage. They demanded liberation of imprisoned comrades, redress for peasant-related issues, and protested natural gas policy (Assies and Salman 2003: 65). Shortly afterwards, the Gas Coordinadora, with support from the COB who had just elected a new leadership independent of the governing coalition (the outgoing leadership was connected to the MIR) and had regained militancy, called for national mobilization on 19 September.[30] Support was massive. Between 500,000 and two million marched and blocked roads in La Paz, El Alto, Cochabamba, Oruro, Potosí, Sucre, and even Tarija (where the gas reserves in question were located) (Hylton and Thomson 2006: 168; Olivera and Lewis 2004: 178). Their demands included the following:

1. A referendum on energy policy
2. Industrialization of natural gas in Bolivia to increase value added
3. Convening a constituent assembly to reform political institutions
4. Withdrawing from free trade agreements with the United States.
5. Ending U.S.-mandated coca eradication.[31]

A colonizing peasant expressed the accumulated frustration and rage of the protestors against their political and economic exclusion. "On several occasions they [the authorities] have agreed to everything, but they never followed through. We want to see them here now, with the laws annulled and the decrees in our favor" (Gómez 2004: 34).

In the middle of this turmoil, on 20 September 2003, the government called the army to violently repress the peasants holding the buses in an attempt to free the tourists. Five peasants, including a little girl, and one soldier were killed. This set off a wave of peasant mobilization that blocked roads all around the altiplano. The COB called a general strike, mobilizing teachers, miners, university students

[30] See Crabtree (2005: 102) and Gómez (2004: 40).
[31] The Gas Coordinadora had held a national convention with delegates from over a hundred organizations on 5 September in Oruro, where they settled on a strategy of national mobilization demanding a referendum on the sale of gas (Olivera and Lewis 2004: 179).

and staff. Roadblocks called by Quispe's CSUTCB escalated in the Northern La Paz region.

Protestors and their leaders clearly directed their fury at persistent political and economic exclusion and repression. Asked how long their blockage of a road to La Paz would be in effect, a female peasant of Huaricana responded curtly: "Until they listen to us!" (Gómez 2004: 51). Speaking for the Coordinadora del Gas on a solidary march from Cochabamba to La Paz, Olivera made it clear that workers not only opposed neoliberal policies but the government of Sánchez de Lozada as well because "now he deigns to auction off all that is left to Bolivians: our gas" (Gómez 2004: 66).

Repression in Warisata encouraged popular sector movement coordinating organizations to cooperate and focused demands on Sánchez de Lozada's resignation. In a 4 October Manifest to the Bolivian People, the Coordinadora del Gas emphasized the need for unity among popular sector organizations to resist repression, defend against a possible coup d'état, to press for a national constitutional assembly, and to demand the president's resignation. On 13 October, MAS released a similar communiqué. The CSUTCB and the Movimiento Indígena Pachakuti party issued a joint resolution condemning repression of their long-held socioeconomic and political demands (the 72 points) and demanded the president's resignation.[32]

The turn to military repression also triggered the October uprising in El Alto that ultimately brought Sánchez de Lozada down. A participant, no doubt referring to the peasant migrant origins of the city, explained: "That was where the problem was born. The government sent the military and the police forces to Warisata, where . . . they unleashed a great fury to save the tourists. There were deaths, injuries, and the problem affected El Alto; and in El Alto we organized support for our peasant brothers" (Lazar 2008: 232). Note that the "peasant brothers" frame allowed rural and urban populations to make claims on indigenous authenticity rooted in kinship networks in opposition to Hispanic ruling elites (Lazar 2008: 232).

On 8 October the Fejuve and the COR-El Alto called a general strike supported by student associations, the women's federation, and unemployed miners. The disruptive power of protestors grew daily as demonstrations and roadblocks in El Alto and the department of La Paz cut the capitol off from supplies, especially fuel. By 10 October protests, marches, and strikes had spread to depressed highland departments, such as Oruru and Potosí, as well as to Sucre and Cochabamba where the Coordinadora mobilized tens of thousands. Evo Morales called for

[32] For details, see the "Manifiesto al pueblo Boliviano, Coordinadora Nacional de Recuperación y Defensa del Gas," "Defender la Democracia, Comunicado del MAS," and Resolución de la CSUTCB y el MIP," in *Observatorio Social de Latino América*, volume 12, numbers 69–73, 2003.

roadblocks by coca growers in the Chapare; northern Santa Cruz joined in. In addition to the natural gas issue, demonstrators now demanded president Sánchez de Lozada's resignation (Assies 2004; Assies and Salman 2003; Crabtree 2005; Gilly 2005; Hylton and Thomson 2006; Olivera and Lewis 2004).

An elderly man from the militant Rosas Pampa neighborhood of El Alto eloquently expressed the accumulated defiant fury of the multitude: "You know what, Mr. Journalist? We're going to resist to the last consequences . . . here we are, just us and our peasant brothers, resisting" (Gómez 2004: 73).

Events boiled over between 12 and 13 October. To open routes into La Paz and to crush the El Alto revolt, the government ordered the army to accompany a supply convoy on 12 October. The troops attacked and fired on demonstrators in a day of raging street battles, killing close to 30 protestors. Repression backfired, and protests surged around the country. The next day, 13 October, 150,000 marched from El Alto to occupy downtown La Paz. Twenty more died that day in the ensuing street battles. The next day, mass mobilization shook Sucre and Oruro. Cochabamba was closed as massive demonstrations erupted in the town center. Although not as dramatic, protests continued in La Paz and El Alto (Gómez 2004: 114–27).

Rage at the killings and indifference to the suffering of the popular sector had clearly stiffened the resolve of protestors to resist the military and sparked demands for the president's resignation. For example, after a bloody confrontation in El Alto, residents had to retreat from their roadblock. As they regrouped a few blocks away a youngster exclaimed, "They will not pass, even if they kill us" (Gómez 2004: 79). At another location a demonstrator shouted: "[we're] boiling [mad] over this government that's starving us" (Gómez 2004: 91). Over Radio Pachamama a defiant woman railed, "We demand the government's immediate resignation, otherwise we will continue to resist no matter the consequences." At his wits' end, a neighborhood leader cried, "What we want now is for Sánchez de Lozada to resign. Now that the armed forces have come to shoot at us . . . we will never give up . . . like good alteños" (Gómez 2004: 83). The leader of a CSUTCB community roadblock committee defiantly summed up the effects of military repression. "State of siege decrees have never scared us, the indigenous . . . other sectors maybe . . . workers may fear massacres . . . they give us more strength because we're different, we live differently in the communities, we're not afraid, we draw strength from it, more unity, more aggressiveness even" (García Linera 2004: 192).

The bloodbath caused Vice President Carlos Mesa to resign from the government, claiming that he opposed such disproportionate repression. Two days later Sánchez de Lozada, flanked by the leaders of his governing coalition (the MIR along with Nueva Fuerza that had opportunistically joined the government in August), announced some concessions (Assies and Salman 2003: 66; Gilly 2005; Hylton and Thomson 2006).

These concessions were too little and too late. Columns of miners and protestors from Oruro and Potosí, coca growers from Chapare, and peasants from the highlands, converged on La Paz. Demonstrators from El Alto and working-class neighborhoods of La Paz filled the capital, joined by middle-class personalities, intellectuals, NGO leaders, human rights advocates, and politicians organized a hunger strike in La Paz beginning 15 October. On 16 and 17 October, wave after wave of protests massing tens and hundreds of thousands of demonstrators in La Paz and across the country continued to rock Bolivia. Pressured by their rank and file, Paz Zamora (MIR) and Reyes (Nueva Fuerza) abandoned the government coalition, forcing Sánchez de Lozada to resign the presidency and flee the country on 17 October (Assies 2004: 30–31; Gilly 2005). Mesa formed a caretaker government pledged to addressing some of the popular movement's concerns, and Evo Morales won presidential elections in late 2005.

Aftermath

In Bolivia, political exclusion by means of party pacts, the betrayal of electoral mandates, and personal corruption involved in the construction of contemporary market society caused the citizenry to lose all patience with political elites. The popular sectors, and occasionally middle classes, mobilized repeatedly. They demanded greater independence from international capital and the United States; they wanted industrial policy, protection from markets, and a constituent assembly to design effective popular sector political participation. This impatience destroyed Mesa's government because he moved neither quickly nor decisively enough on a more nationalist agenda (Salman 2006). It helped elect Evo Morales who moved that leftist agenda along, although, as expected, not without political difficulties because his reforms challenge neoliberalism's strict interpretations of private property rights to a greater extent than in Argentina.

President Mesa, a respected politician, proposed revision of the zero coca policy, a referendum on energy policy, and the establishment of a constituent assembly. His coca policy focused on voluntary eradication and mollified militant coca growers, headed by Evo Morales, without alienating the United States. The energy referendum, held in July 2004, passed. It essentially abrogated Sánchez de Lozada's hydrocarbons law and approved greater state ownership in the oil and gas industry, and higher royalties and other regulations for international companies. However, regional elites in Santa Cruz and Tarija – departments in which oil and gas deposits were concentrated – supported by international energy companies and foreign governments, especially the United States, opposed the leftward trend. They feared lost development opportunities and greater revenue sharing with the highlands (Europa World 2007: 871; McNeish 2006). These concerns intensified maneuvering for greater regional autonomy among lowland departments and diluted the leftist cast of energy policy in the legislature.

As a result of these pressures, contentious politics intensified and polarized during Mesa's government. Elite-sponsored mobilization in lowland departments – led by Santa Cruz – plagued his government. This created a stream of leftist countermobilization in 2005 to defend the hard-won nationalist principles mandated in the referendum (McNeish 2006). Meanwhile, anger over raises in fuel and water prices caused El Alto to explode again. Peasants and the COB mobilized, and Evo Morales, as head of the MAS, assumed political leadership of this new wave of contentious politics. Mesa, plagued by this wave of protests, resigned in June 2005 (Cotler 2005). A new caretaker government took office and presidential elections were held in December.

Evo Morales and the MAS won those elections handily in first-round balloting with 53.7 percent of the vote to 28.6 for former president Quiroga and PODE-MOS (Poder Democrático y Social; Democratic and Social Power), a coalition of conservative parties and wealthy notables mainly from the eastern lowlands. MAS also won a majority in the house of deputies with PODEMOS as a strong second. The senate was almost evenly split between the two (Deheza 2007; Europa World 2007: 879–80).

Morales had emerged as the political leader of a heterogeneous mix of mestizo and indigenous popular sector groups brought together in their struggle against commodification and political exclusion over the past 20 years, and especially since 2000. Poverty, exploitation, and racial discrimination may have always characterized Bolivia, but neoliberalism destroyed even the principles upon which a more economically, socially, and politically inclusionary society might be imagined and built. Thus the election was a mandate to restore a measure of national economic and political autonomy, to open political participation and power to heretofore marginalized leftist and other popular sector leaders, and to protect the overwhelmingly poor and indigent mestizo and indigenous popular sectors from the ravages of the market (Dunkerley 2007).

Morales and the MAS campaigned on the promise of refounding the nation. Policy should focus in gaining state control over oil and gas development to generate revenue, decriminalizing coca production, land reform for peasants, subsistence subsidies, and a constituent assembly to draft a constitution to support nationalist and socioeconomically egalitarian policies (Deheza 2007; Mayorga 2006). Once in office, Morales quickly took steps in 2006 to make good on these campaign promises. In May he issued a decree to nationalize hydrocarbon production, although international companies would still be able to hold minority partnerships. The decree also raised royalties on foreign companies from 50 to 82 percent (Lettieri 2006). In June Morales decreed the state had the power to seize unproductive land and to distribute it to peasants. Landowners (especially from lowland eastern regions) opposed the measure but were defeated when in late 2006 the legislature enacted the measure along with new contracts for foreign oil firms (Europa World 2007: 872; Starr 2007). He also established a child food distribution program – *desnutrición cero* [zero malnutrition] – that combined clinics with popular sector organizations (Dunkerley 2007: 166).

Legalizing coca production brought Morales' administration into direct conflict with the United States. Pragmatism dictated walking a fine line between decriminalization and not antagonizing the United States to the point where it would decertify Bolivia and withhold aid. By negotiating with coca-grower associations, the government was able to ensure the voluntary eradication of coca fields in return for legalization of smaller plots per family. This mollified the United States sufficiently to stave off decertification but not enough to avoid a six-percent reduction in U.S. aid (Joseph 2006; Skog 2007). Nevertheless, tensions between Yungas coca-grower federations and Morales' government sharpened in April 2008. The Ministry of Social Defense announced the initiation of forced eradication where the negotiations for voluntary reduction had failed in seven regions of new coca plantings (Ledebur and Youngers 2008).

So far, regional cleavages between the highlands and the eastern lowlands based on racial and socioeconomic differences have been the major source of conflict. As noted earlier, the highlands are economically declining regions of traditional mining (tin) and production of crops for domestic consumption by largely indigenous peasants. The eastern lowlands are on the economic ascendant with agricultural export crops and oil and gas production. A larger percentage of the population is mestizo and agricultural workers and proletarianized migrant peasants labor on estates and farms.

Thus, in the face of Morales' reforms, eastern lowland political forces and notables – the core of PODEMOS – struggle for greater regional autonomy (Eaton 2007). That struggle played itself out in the constituent assembly. At issue were strict private property rights versus the mixed economy, land reform, and redistribution of state revenue, voting age changes (younger), a presidential reelection rule, and the right of departments to hold autonomy referenda.

In December 2007 the Constituent Assembly approved a draft constitutional charter along lines favorable to the government, but moderate. It proposed state control of oil, gas, and mineral reserves, consecutive election of presidents limited to two 5-year terms (Morales, if reelected, would serve to 2014), greater indigenous peoples' rights and autonomy, land reform, and autonomy to states over local issues. However, the voting process generated fierce conflict. The MAS controlled a majority of the assembly with 137 of 255 seats to PODEMOS' 60. But that fell short of the two-thirds majority needed to pass constitutional articles. Thus MAS had to negotiate with political parties outside of its traditional base to gain support for contested clauses. The upshot was that under controversial circumstances PODEMOS did not vote, although MAS garnered support form other representatives (Shah 2008; Sweeney 2008). Further deepening the crisis was the fact that, in May 2008, the government, after a ruling by the National

Electoral Court, suspended a national referendum to approve the constitution. This stymied efforts by lowland departments to hold autonomy referenda, which they did anyway illegally, proposing faculties far beyond what the draft constitution permitted, such as control over land distribution and oil and gas reserves (Sweeney 2008).

These tensions notwithstanding, between May 2008 and January 2009, Evo Morales' government won two important victories in its quest to reform neoliberalism. In May 2008 the conservative opposition in the legislature agreed to a recall referendum of President Morales initially proposed by the government in November 2007. Morales, who consistently enjoyed national approval ratings over 50 percent, accepted the challenge and won handily with 67 percent (up from 54 percent when he was elected president), strengthening his position in the highlands and coca-growing regions. He also made inroads in the secessionist provinces (Hylton 2008; Mokhtari 2007; Sweeney 2008; Wheeler 2007). Then, on 25 January 2009, voters overwhelmingly approved the new constitution by 61.4 percent to 38.6 percent, although the opposition won in the lowland provinces of Santa Cruz, Pando, Beni, and Tarija. Moreover, despite the fact that the prefects of these lowland provinces felt empowered to resist the central government, they entered into a dialogue of sorts with Morales' administration. This occurred after shocking, murderous local government-sanctioned violence in Pando provoked the central government to declare martial law and to arrest Pando's prefect. The administration also ejected the U.S. ambassador, accusing him of aiding secessionist forces (Hylton 2008).[33]

The victories in these referenda reflect the fact that Morales' administration held faith with its electoral mandate, a novelty in contemporary Bolivia. Improved economic conditions, in large part because of increases in world hydrocarbon prices, no doubt help, as does debt forgiveness under the IMF's December 2005 heavily indebted poor country's initiative (enacted after criticism of the IMF's role in aggravating the Asian financial crisis of the late 1990s) (Europa World 2007: 873). Moreover, Venezuela under Hugo Chávez has supported Bolivia with trade and aid, most flamboyantly with a new regional trade pact called the Bolivarian Alternative, which includes Cuba and Nicaragua. The idea is to create an alternative trading bloc outside of U.S. control and thus more supportive of national economic autonomy (Lettieri 2006; Skog 2007).

In conclusion, to a greater extent than Kirchner in Argentina, Morales and the MAS represented a reformist leftward decommodifying swing of Polanyi's double movement of capitalism. The goals are clear: to regain a measure of national economic autonomy, to reconstruct the mixed economy, to reintroduce industrial policy, to offer land reform for indigenous and mestizo peasants; to protect popular sectors from the market by providing services and subsidies; to construct institutions for a more participatory democracy; and to politically

---

[33] Simon Romero, *New York Times* 17 September 2008, 11 September 2008, 15 September 2008.

include intellectuals and popular sector thinkers and leaders in his administration. In this venture he commands a solid political majority, but not the overwhelming majority he needs, given the fact that his administration is undertaking reforms in a democratic polity. Moreover, conflict has not ended. It has shifted from concerted anti-neoliberalism writ large (anti-contemporary market society) to regional polarization as elites drum up support among popular sectors in eastern lowland departments to resist highland (and indigenous) designs on their property.

6

Ecuador

In contrast to Argentina and Bolivia, in Ecuador the national-populist impulse was weaker as were efforts to construct contemporary market society. Still, neoliberal programs threatened both the nonmarket instruments that supplemented the popular sectors' livelihood and the rights of organized labor and peasants. Relentless, willful, arrogant exclusion of their socioeconomic and political interests provided powerful motivation for anti-neoliberal contention and transformations in the associational and collective power of the popular sectors and indigenous peoples.

Similar to Argentina and Bolivia, in Ecuador anti-neoliberal contention spanned three waves, beginning with the administrations of León Febres (1984–88) and Rodrigo Borja (1988–92). Weak urban labor accomplished little during the opening wave, although the first indigenous "uprising" in 1990 announced the arrival of a new and powerful movement. A second wave engulfed President Sixto Durán (1992–96), who pursued neoliberal reforms with gusto. Increases in the associational power of urban movements and in collective power when they linked with the indigenous movement characterized this period. A third wave between 1996 and 2000, spearheaded by the indigenous movement, contributed to the resignation of two presidents committed to neoliberal reforms. A turbulent aftermath included the resignation of a president who betrayed his electoral mandate from the popular sectors and indigenous. It ended in the 2006 election of Rafael Correa who, at least, has not overtly given up on his "populist" campaign platform.

As in the previous two cases, the executive used the power of decree and other political maneuvers to neutralize congressional opposition. However, given Ecuador's fragmented and unstable multiparty system, party alliances never achieved the level of political exclusion through the pact making seen in Bolivia. Nor did Congress cede its responsibilities to the executive as in Argentina. Thus the politics of neoliberal reform was more contested in Congress, where opposition party coalitions could either dilute or terminally delay structural adjustment bills. This (in combination with mass mobilization) accounts for the piecemeal approach to neoliberalism. It also accounts for governments' penchant for fiscal policy to push neoliberal reform; it could be implemented by decree. Privatization and other structural reforms required legislation, a focal point for conflict in an unstable multiparty system.

Party politics were fluid because parties were not programmatic. Party politics were a matter of elite infighting and unstable party coalitions. Coastal commercial agroexport and financial elites, centered on Guayaquil, protected their earnings from a state dependent on them for much of its revenue. Highland hacienda-owning elites dominated the national government centered in Quito. Before agrarian reform their estates produced traditional crops such as potatoes, maize, and dairy products for domestic consumption. Afterward they diversified into commerce and finance. Amazonia was a frontier inhabited by indigenous peoples with, as of the 1960s, oil deposits developed by the state and international companies.

The characteristics of the social actors that mobilized against neoliberalism also differed from those of Argentina and Bolivia; yet they too built associational and collective power in a defensive reaction to relentless threats of economic and political exclusion. For example, the urban labor movement was weaker and more fragmented than in Argentina and Bolivia and had less independent impact on politics. Still, during the opening wave of contention, organized labor expanded collective power by timing mobilization to the political maneuverings of the congressional opposition to keep pro-neoliberal forces from passing legislation.

By contrast, the indigenous peoples' movements had greater direct impact. Like Bolivia, Ecuador has a large indigenous population (about 30 percent) concentrated in the highlands. Unlike Bolivia, it was much more organized. The Confederación Nacional de Indígenas Ecuatorianos (CONAIE; National Confederation of Indigenous Ecuadorians), the most successful indigenous movement in South America, contributed significantly to the associational power of the challengers to neoliberalism, and its capacity for disruption far exceeded that of urban labor. It also brought the authorities to the negotiating table.

Yet, if CONAIE was the most dynamic pole in anti-neoliberal contention, urban movements were not irrelevant. The development of collective power and thus disruptive capability, as the two linked up, transformed the dynamics of contention during the second and third waves of anti-neoliberal contention. The fact that CONAIE framed its movement in identity *and* class terms and was open to alliances helped.

National Populism in Ecuador

National populism was weaker than in the previous two cases because of the regionalism, elite conflicts, and political fragmentation of Ecuador's political economy. Ecuador and its state were poor because of the boom and bust cycles of its commodity export-led economy (cacao and bananas). Thus, even when a national development project emerged, the state had difficulty sustaining it and

Ecuadorian elites successfully watered down many of its components, especially social ones (Schodt 1987).

Within these limitations, building national populism in Ecuador was largely the work of military governments in the 1960s and 1970s when Amazonian oil gave the state revenue and relative autonomy from coastal agricultural export elites.[1] Although more attenuated, planning emphasized economic nationalism and stimulated import substitution industrialization. The state acquired substantial control over key industries such as oil, steel, fishing, and the national airline; it formed mixed enterprises in processed foods and chemical industries. Meanwhile, the army established a state agency to oversee investments in hardware, uniforms, munitions, and basic metal industries, and the navy acquired a commercial shipping fleet and a commercial airline. In a time-honored Ecuadorian populist tactic, the government increased spending on infrastructure (Isaacs 1993: 39). Industrialization also benefited from tariff protection and subsidies such as preferential credit, tax breaks, and foreign exchange.

Belated industrialization left a weak, fragmented urban labor movement. Labor legislation earlier in the century spurred the formation of two union confederations: the Christian Democratic Confederación Ecuatoriana de Organizaciones Clasistas in 1938 and the Confederación Ecuatoriana de Trabajadores in 1944 controlled by communists and socialists. With the Labor Code reform of 1973, union organizing expanded (Conaghan 1988: 100; Hurtado 1980: 235). Even then average unionization hovered only around 16 percent of the economically active population, and many unions, such as those of teachers and students, were unaffiliated with confederations (Conaghan 1988: 100). During this period, a third confederation, the Confederación Ecuatoriana de Organizaciones Sindicales Libres, linked to U.S. unionism, emerged. Differentiation between industrial labor, in the minority because of lack of industrialization, and artisan workers, a majority employed in small enterprises and linked to the informal sector, compounded fragmentation. So did the establishment of the cooperative movement, especially after the Cooperative Act of 1967, which emerged as the second largest form of popular sector organization (Hurtado 1980: 235–36; Middleton 1982).

In April 1974, the three major labor confederations joined forces to form the Frente Unitario de Trabajadores (FUT; United Workers Front) (Isaacs 1993: 86–87; Nurse 1989). Even with this advance in associational power, organized labors' small size, fragmentation, and restrictions on the right to strike kept it from exerting much political influence. It was too weak to support a regime. These characteristics, along with low militancy, translated into relatively low class conflict. Under these circumstances, in a country with significant restrictions on the franchise, neither political parties nor progressive military governments

---

[1] The pseudopopulism of José María Velasco Ibarra from the 1930s to the 1970s can be ignored because he never incorporated the masses or installed ISI (Drake and Hershberg 2006).

had much interest in formally incorporating labor into politics (Conaghan 1988: 100–1). Conversely, labor's weakness spared it from the onslaught it suffered in Argentina and Bolivia. There was no need to isolate or dismantle powerful unions.

As everywhere, national populism benefited middle classes and industrial labor. The expansion of state planning bureaus and agencies to administer public enterprises and programs in housing, cooperatives, health, and education provided formal employment and benefits to the middle classes and privileged sectors of labor. Cooperative banks for housing, industry, and artisans provided benefits to urban popular sectors who organized into legally recognized corporatist functional groups. Subsidized energy, transportation, and food staples along with wage policies further benefited the middle class and the popular sectors. In the Ecuadorian context, expenditure on public works was central to the benefits populist governments dispensed, such as employment and contracts. The popular sectors and middle classes also profited from expanding rights; they facilitated struggles to increase their share of the legal and material benefits of the political and economic system. The various agencies established to service all of these needs stimulated popular sector organization to access those benefits.

Peasants concentrated on land tenure security and rural working conditions. Agrarian reform during the military governments of the 1960s and 1970s brought the national-populist development program to the countryside. Land reform had greater impact in the highlands with a heavy concentration of Ecuador's indigenous population. They weakened landowner control over them and encouraged Indians to register as peasants (Zamosc 1994). Legally constituted peasant communities strengthened indigenous community authority structures and customary law (Guerrero 1993). Together with aid from peasant unions, mainly affiliated with the Federación Nacional de Organizaciones Campesinas, the communities organized along state corporatist lines to receive promised benefits: land redistribution, credit, and infrastructure improvement (especially irrigation) (Hurtado 1980; Isaacs 1993; Schodt 1987; Yashar 2005). The peasant union federation also brought indigenous communities in contact with leftist political parties (Korovkin 1997; Selverston-Scher 2001). As will be seen, these developments deeply affected indigenous mobilization at the end of the century. Oil development in the Amazon region, among other factors (colonists for example), stimulated organizing among lowland indigenous peoples, especially the Shuar.

In a pattern similar to Bolivia's, redemocratization in the late 1970s produced a center-left government. A coalition of the populist Concentración de Fuerzas Populares and Democracia Popular won the 1979 elections. When President Jaime Roldós died in an airplane crash in 1981, the Latin American debt crisis forced Vice President Osvaldo Hurtado of Democracia Popular to administer an economic stabilization package.

During the national-populist era, Latin America had a history of defensive mobilization against IMF-sponsored fiscal stabilization programs (Stallings

1978). Accordingly, the FUT – just formed in 1974 – organized two general strikes against Hurtado's stabilization policies in September and October 1982. However, the FUT's limited size and fragmentation dulled their impact.[2] The government repressed them, killing several protestors and wounding scores more, and, eventually, made some concessions.[3] The FUT abandoned plans for an indefinite general strike to sustain pressure on the government because of dissension among member organizations.[4]

Introducing Contemporary Market Society, 1982–92

If national populism was more attenuated in Ecuador, so was neoliberalism. As elsewhere, national populism collapsed with the onset of the Latin American debt crisis in 1982. Neoliberalism as a comprehensive economic, political, and social strategy for national renewal began in the administration of León Febres Cordero (1984–88), the presidential candidate of the Frente de Reconstrucción Nacional, a conservative electoral coalition (see Table 6.1).[5] Following that, fiscal constraints forced social democrat Rodrigo Borja (1988–92) of the Democratic Left Party to maintain the neoliberal policies of Febres Cordero.

Febres Cordero was a conservative Christian Democrat and wealthy businessman, avowedly antilabor and confrontational. Recognizing political limitations, his neoliberal reform program was not as sweeping as those of Víctor Paz Estenssoro in Bolivia or Carlos Menem in Argentina. It focused on exchange rate policy, principally gradual market-driven devaluation, financial sector liberalization, and deregulation of markets. Trade liberalization, mainly tariff reductions, was modest, and negotiated with the private sector. The government also negotiated foreign debt restructuring with the IMF, which required raising interest rates and taxes. Fiscal retrenchment mandated currency devaluation, the removal of most price controls, and subsidies to basic consumption items, such as gasoline, cooking oil, heating fuel, and staple foods, and keeping wage raises significantly below inflation (Conaghan and Malloy 1994).

State power was crucial for initiating neoliberal reforms. Febres accomplished as much as possible by decree because his coalition did not control the unicameral legislative branch. National populists, led by the Democratic Left Party (Bloque

[2] Not all of the labor confederations agreed to participate, and the strikes were not national in scope. For example, the more successful October strike, which garnered the support of the transportation sector and the independent teachers' union, really affected only Quito and Guayaquil (the two largest cities).
[3] It granted half of the wage raise the FUT demanded and a 50-percent reduction in the gasoline price hike.
[4] Accounts of these strikes were from *Latin America Weekly Reports* 24 September 1982; 1, 22, and 29 October 1982; and 12 November 1982. Additional information from *Facts on File World News Digest* 12 November 1982; *Financial Times*, 21 and 29 October 1982; and the *New York Times* 22 October 1982.
[5] For coalition partners, see Conaghan and Malloy (1994: 134).

Table 6.1. *Ecuador: Presidential Elections, 1984–2006*

Candidate	1984	1988	1992	1996	1998	2002	2006
León Febres Cordero	**52.2%**	–	–	–	–	–	–
Rodrigo Borja Cevallos	47.8%	–	–	–	–	–	–
Rodrigo Borja Cevallos	–	**51.3%**	–	–	–	–	–
Abdalá Bucaram Ortiz	–	48.7%	–	–	–	–	–
Sixto Durán Ballén	–	–	**58.0%**	–	–	–	–
Jaime Nebot Saadi	–	–	38.0%	–	–	–	–
Abdalá Bucaram Ortiz	–	–	–	**54.3%**	–	–	–
Jaime Nebot Saadi	–	–	–	45.7%	–	–	–
Jail Mahuad Witt	–	–	–	–	**51.2%**	–	–
Alvaro Fernando Noboa Pontón	–	–	–	–	48.8%	–	–
Lucio Edwin Gutiérrez Borboa	–	–	–	–	–	**54.4%**	–
Alvaro Fernando Noboa Pontón	–	–	–	–	–	45.6%	–
Rafael Correa Delgado	–	–	–	–	–	–	**56.7%**
Alvaro Fernando Noboa Pontón	–	–	–	–	–	–	43.3%

Boldface indicates winning candidate and percentage of the vote.

Sources: The Europa World Yearbook (1985–2007); http://pdba.georgetown.edu/Electdata/Ecuador.

Progresista), had the majority (see Table 6.2).[6] This set up a continual struggle for power between Congress and the presidency. The opposition-dominated Congress amended restrictive wage, price control, subsidy, and other bills. The president and his economic ministers vetoed them and ruled by decree when necessary, stretching the limits of constitutionality if required. This escalated conflict because the legislature had the right to impeach ministers of state (Conaghan and Malloy 1994; Isaacs 1993). The government also repressed protestors, frequently calling states of emergency, enforced by the military, which suspended constitutional rights to assembly and freedom of speech.

Ecuadorian neoliberals also relied on international economic and political support, especially from the IMF, with whom Ecuador signed agreements in 1983, 1984, 1985, 1986, and 1988 (García 2003: 77). The United States and other international financial institutions praised Febres Cordero's policies (North 2004: 198). International private capital, however, did not come flooding in, except partially in the petroleum sector, and high sustained economic growth rates did not materialize.

Although Febres' neoliberal program was not as sweeping as Argentina's and Bolivia's, it nonetheless hit the popular sectors and wage and salary earners hard. Devaluation in conjunction with wage reduction (by keeping raises well below inflation) hurt formal sector wage and salary earners in the public and the private sectors, including middle-class persons (especially those employed in the

---

[6] For the Progressive Bloc's composition, see Conaghan and Malloy (1994: 136). This bloc disintegrated by August 1985 because of the defection to the government of 11 deputies; but the opposition retook the majority in June 1986 elections. Febres Cordero enacted many important legal reforms during this period (Conaghan and Malloy 1994; Isaacs 1993).

Table 6.2. *Ecuador: Distribution of Seats in the Chamber of Deputies, 1986–2006*

Party	1986	1988	1990	1992	1994	1996	1998	2002	2006
Partido Social Cristiano – PSC	15	6	16	21	26	27	27	25	13
Partido Roldosista Ecuatoriano – PRE	5	4	13	15	11	21	24	15	6
Democracia Popular – DP	8	7	–	–	–	12	32	–	–
Movimiento Unidad Plurinacional Pachakutik – MUPP-NP	–	–	–	–	–	7	9	6	6
Frente Radical Alfarista – FRA	–	–	–	1	2	–	5	–	–
Movimiento Popular Democrático – MPD	4	4	1	–	–	–	–	5	3
Partido Conservador Ecuatoriano – PCE	–	–	–	5	6	–	3	–	–
Partido Izquierda Democrática – PID	17	27	14	3	8	–	18	16	–
Izquierda Democrática y RED Etica y Democrática – ID/RED	–	–	–	–	–	–	–	–	13
Partido Renovador Institucional Acción Nacional – PRIAN	–	–	–	–	–	–	–	10	28
Partido Sociedad Patriótica – PSP	–	–	–	–	–	–	–	9	23
Unión Demócrata Cristiana – UDC	–	–	7	6	4	–	–	–	5
Partido Unidad Republicana – PUR	–	–	–	12	3	–	–	–	–
Socialista Ecuatoriano – PSE	6	3	8	2	2	–	–	–	–
Concentración de Fuerzas Populares – CFP	4	6	3	–	–	–	–	–	–
Partido Republicano – PRA	3	1	2	–	–	–	–	–	–
Others	9	14	8	4	7	–	–	–	–
TOTAL	71	72	72	69	69	67	118	86	97

Sources: The Europa World Yearbook (1985–2007).

public sector). Cuts to subsidies (price increases) for consumption in energy, oil, food, transportation, and housing also affected formal and informal sector labor, peasants, and the middle class, deeply cutting into their purchasing power, and hence disrupting livelihood strategies. Moreover, beginning with Febres Cordero, deregulation weakened the fledgling manufacturing sector, and with it, industrial labor. Unemployment increased, as did the percentage of Ecuadorians laboring in the informal sector. Wages collapsed in this period, and wealth concentration rose, showing that modest increases in GDP and per-capita GDP were more unequally distributed.

Challenging Neoliberalism, 1984–92

As in Bolivia, urban labor, the highest expression of popular sector associational power at the time, mobilized. Building on the formative experience of the general strikes against Hurtado's stabilization policies, the FUT called seven general strikes against Febres Cordero protesting devaluation and price increases to basic consumer items (especially gasoline, fuels, transportation fares, and food staples). Three occurred in the first six months of the new administration (October 1984 and January and March 1985) with the rest concentrated in the second half of Febres Cordero's government (July 1986, March and October 1987, and June 1988). Demands centered on wage increases above the rate of price increases to maintain purchasing power, the reintroduction of price controls, and calls for the impeachment of various ministers.

Given its weakness, the FUT mobilized mainly in subordination to the rhythm of legislative conflicts. Most general strikes were timed to support the opposition-led legislature when it tangled with the executive-over-economic policy. Thus, although it did not play an independent leading role, the FUT nevertheless contributed to an expansion of the collective power of challengers to neoliberalism.[7] Mobilization also had a political purpose: to weaken the conservative government and boost the electoral fortunes of center-left political parties more sympathetic to the popular sector, especially the Democratic Left Party.

Despite organized labor's subordinate position in the opening wave of anti-neoliberal protest, Febres Cordero's unrelenting drive to implement neoliberal reforms began to change the characteristics of contentious politics in Ecuador over the course of those seven general strikes. First, it forged greater unity and militancy among the labor confederations of the FUT. This was not so true of the first four general strikes, but as of the fifth general strike, all three major member confederations participated. Transportation worker adherence from then on was also crucial, as was mobilizing by the independent teachers' and student unions. Second, although this did not build associational power, it enhanced the capabilities of existing organizations by modestly contributing to their

---

[7] General strikes abated when the opposition lost its majority in the congress.

collective power by linking blue-collar and middle-class organizations (the teachers, and to some extent the students, unions). Moreover, the transgressive quality of the demonstrations was high given their prohibition under states of siege, pronouncements of illegality, and significant repression (labor leaders and scores of protestors were routinely arrested, media was censured, and deaths were frequent). Transport worker strikes increased the disruptiveness of protests.

The results were, nevertheless, meager. The FUT had difficulty mounting truly national general strikes. They were most successful in Quito, Ecuador's political capital, and sometimes in Guayaquil, the largest city and financial and export center of the nation. This, and the fact that modern industry – the sector that the FUT represented – was a small component of the economy, limited the strikes' disruptiveness. The FUT's dependence on opposition control of Congress to successfully organize general strikes further limited it. Still, general strikes in support of opposition political parties that controlled Congress convinced the pragmatic Febres Cordero to shelve more radical economic reforms (Conaghan and Malloy 1994). They also helped the Democratic Left's candidate, Rodrigo Borja, to win the next presidential election.

Associational Power Surge

Rodrigo Borja of the social democratic Partido Izquierda Democrática became president in August 1988 in coalition with the Christian Democratic Party, giving him a working majority in Congress. He came into office committed to resisting the neoliberal trend, but the country's foreign debt, weak export earnings, and fiscal position forced him to announce an economic adjustment program that maintained the neoliberal line established by Febres Cordero. It proposed gradual trade liberalization by reducing tariff barriers, fiscal restraint by cutting social programs, sharp increases in state-controlled energy prices, stiff liberalization of price controls, wage controls to contain inflation, periodic minidevaluations, and export incentives. His government also signed a debt reprogramming agreement with the Club of Paris (García 2003: 86–87).

Feeling betrayed by a government they had helped elect, the FUT and transport unions mobilized. To attract greater support, the FUT framed the issue in terms of a war against an IMF-style economic package and the need to improve the lives of the poor.[8] This proved unsuccessful. The FUT called a general strike for November 1988, with mixed success in terms of disruptive capacity. In December a wave of work stoppages by public sector employees followed.[9] After failed attempts to organize another national work stoppage, the FUT's second general strike on 12 July 1989 flopped. Borjas' government was not as exclusionary as Febres Cordero's, who steadfastly refused to negotiate with the FUT and other unions, preferring to repress them. Borjas negotiated both with the FUT and

---

[8] *Latin America Weekly Report* 26 January 1989: 6; The *Globe and Mail* (Canada) 26 May 1989.
[9] *Latin America Weekly Report* 26 January 1989: 6; *Latin America Weekly Report* 3 August 1989: 12.

with individual unions, taking advantage of the movement's fragmentation to disrupt solidary mobilization.

A major surge in the associational power of rural Ecuadorian popular sectors shattered any perception that challenges to neoliberal reforms from contentious politics might be under control. The first "National Indian Uprising" in June 1990 catapulted the CONAIE into a national political actor and transformed it into Ecuador's leading social movement.[10] For 10 days, angry, determined indigenous peasants paralyzed six highland provinces. They blocked major roads, picketed roadsides, refused to deliver produce to market, and marched on government buildings in the provinces. Members of the FUT-affiliated peasant union also participated, as did the Federación Ecuatoriana de Indígenas Evangélicos and independent communities (Yahsar 2005: 142–43). They showed restraint in the face of police and army presence and avoided major violence. When the Borja administration agreed to negotiate, CONAIE ended the national protest (Zamosc 1994).

CONAIE had formed only four years earlier during Febres' administration when two strands of the indigenous peoples' movement joined forces in 1986. These were the highland indigenous confederation, ECUARUNARI (Ecuador Runacunapac Riccarimui; Awakening of the Ecuadorian Indian), and the lowland indigenous confederation, CONFENIAE (Confederación de Nationalidades Indígenas de la Amazonía Ecuatoriana; Confederation of Indigenous Nationalities of the Ecuadorian Amazon) – both of which had been organizing since the 1970s. Indeed, deepening economic and political exclusion due to Febres' neoliberal agenda were catalysts for the creation of CONAIE (Yashar 2005).

Although the social and cultural conditions of the highland and Amazonian indigenous differed substantially, the intertwining of land and cultural survival issues as key framing elements united them. ECUARUNARI's framing of the indigenous people's struggles melded peasant-class analysis (land, prices, subsidies, and working conditions) with indigenous ethnic and cultural consciousness; steadily displacing the FUT-affiliated, obstinately class-oriented Federación Nacional de Organizaciones Campesinas. Meanwhile, CONFENIAE developed as lowland Amazonian indigenous confronted landowners, colonizers, and oil companies that encroached on their land. In its framing, territorial security (land) was paramount because it was inseparable from ethnic and cultural survival (Benavides 2004: 140–41; Gerlach 2003; Luis Macas, CONAIE president, forward in Selverston-Scher 2001; Yashar 2005; Zamosc 2004).

Initially CONAIE pushed cultural issues, especially bilingual education, striking a deal early in the Borja government by patient lobbying instead of mobilization.[11] But CONAIE was very responsive to regional and local organizations,

---

[10] CONAIE called their mobilization an Indian "uprising" to connect the movement to insurrections dating back to colonial times (Zamosc 1994).

[11] The deal, struck in 1988, involved the establishment of an Intercultural Bilingual Education Program that CONAIE would help to run (Zamosc 1994).

and its highland members wanted CONAIE to press land issues and take a more combative stance toward the government. These grievances originated in the economic dislocation caused by neoliberal reforms and fiscal retrenchment. Many highland indigenous peasants, who owned tiny plots of land, supplemented their income with employment on public works projects, in construction, and hiring out as day laborers. Neoliberal reforms depressed all of these sources of income at a time of soaring prices. This increased poverty and turned attention back to land as a principal source of income. Meanwhile, government agencies in the peasant sector cut back services while the price of agricultural inputs soared, and gave preferential treatment for scarce resources to "white" landowners (Pallares 2002: 210–11; Zamosc 1994).[12] A Quichua nation leader summed the situation up this way: "A better distribution of land is a basic foundation if you want democracy... The land has been taken away so a part of our being has been taken away" (*Canadian Business and Current Affairs Catholic News Times* 31 March 1996).

The right to self-management and self-government in indigenous communities, and access to state resources for community development, was another key framing device. As will be seen later, CONAIE was the culmination of an active bottom-up process of community organization to obtain control over land, development, and cultural survival. These claims – common to most communities – were another thread that united the otherwise diverse groups CONAIE represented (Bebbington 1992: 147).

Success in cultural policy notwithstanding, land, self-determination, and a dispute over 72 unsettled land claims in particular, precipitated the First Indian Uprising. CONAIE leaders felt the Ecuadorian state was "exclusionary, hegemonic, antidemocratic, and repressive" (Collins 2006: 204). During the Febres Cordero and Borjas administration it became apparent that national political channels had been closed to them (Yashar 2005: 143–44). CONAIE president Luis Macas explained, "We [must] definitely abandon this system, so stifling, so aggressive and violent for the indigenous peoples – but not only in economic terms... They try to monopolize in their hands all the resources that in one way or another are also the conquest of our peoples" (Gerlach 2003: 71). These perceptions of political exclusion mirrored those of indigenous communities where Indians believed the local authority structure served foreign, mestizo society. An Indian peasant recalled that being turned away at government offices was a common experience. "The one with the poncho was always left to wait while the one wearing the tie went ahead" (Selverston-Scher 2001: 103).

From these perceptions of political, social, and economic exclusion during the "uprising," CONAIE pressed a list of 16 demands in three categories:

---

[12] Zamosc (1994) argues that this did not weaken local authority structures that mediated between the community and state development agencies set up by agrarian reform acts of the 1960s and 1970s because NGOs replaced the state. On this point also see Yashar (2005: 136–39).

(1) ethnicity, centered on recognition that Ecuador is a multiethnic population, all deserving of equal rights; (2) citizenship, meaning equal rights to services; (3) class, claiming that peasants have rights to land, fair prices, and decent working conditions (Zamosc 1994: 61).[13]

Leadership brokered the grievances and demands from diverse communities into a mass movement with national goals and a high degree of participation in contentious politics. Two factors facilitated leadership's brokerage function. First, because CONAIE was more of a bottom-up movement, local political authority, as in Bolivia, played a significant role in decision making. Second, leadership was open to collaboration with nonmember indigenous and nonindigenous social movement organizations.

Community authority structures were key brokerage nodes. As previously mentioned, agrarian reform during the 1960s and 1970s caused rapid expansion of legally registered Indian peasant communities and strengthened indigenous community authority structures – the *comunas*. Indian-peasant unions, cooperatives, and associations were central to comuna authority structure. Much like in Bolivia, authorities organized village life on remnants of ayllu principles of collective social organization: family-based work details for community service (such as the *minga* for school construction, irrigation ditches, roads, and the like), fiestas, parades, and local justice. With agrarian reform, community leaders became important mediators of conflicts and negotiators with government agencies responsible for the peasant sector. A generation of young indigenous adults who became leaders in the community councils and federations that created CONAIE grew up accustomed to state support for their communities in the form of agricultural inputs, credits, infrastructure, technical assistance, and education. Those leaders also struggled to achieve greater autonomy from the state. Indigenous activists wanted to increase the community's participation in and control over the process of agrarian change. These struggles strengthened the comuna as an administrative unit and pushed indigenous activists to form provincial and national federations in a process that culminated in the creation of ECUARUNARI first and then CONAIE (Bebbington 1992: 147–58; Korovkin 1998: 140; Pallares 2004; Selverston-Scher 2001: 103–7). Pressure from local-level organizations and their articulation through federations had a significant

---

[13] CONAIE's 16 points were as follows: (1) a public declaration that Ecuador is a plurinational country (to be ratified by the Constitution); (2) the government must grant lands and titles to lands to the nationalities; (3) solutions to water irrigation needs; (4) absolution of indigenous debts to FODERUMA and the National Development Bank; (5) freeze consumer prices; (6) conclusion of priority projects in Indian communities; (7) nonpayment of rural land taxes; (8) expulsion of the Summer Institute of Linguistics; (9) free commercial and handicraft activity; (10) CONAIE protection of archeological sites; (11) officialization of Indian medicine; (12) cancellation of government decree that created parallel land-reform-granting bodies; (13) the government should immediately grant funds to the nationalities; (14) the government should grant funds for bilingual education; (15) respect for the rights of the child; (16) the fixing of fair prices for products (Yashar 2005: 145).

impact on CONAIE decision making, especially in general assemblies. Indeed, as we saw, it was critical for the decision to launch the peaceful indigenous "uprising" of 1990.

In Ecuador, then, as in Bolivia, the local community was the key to mobilizing large numbers of indigenous in contentious politics in the 1990s and beyond. Assembly-style decision making facilitated consensus building. Community authority structures organized collective life based on reciprocal obligations among families and individuals (communal work, holiday celebrations, and parades), and adjudicated internal conflicts. These same structures and procedures ensured village participation in mass mobilization, as long as local authorities agreed with CONAIE on the rationale and timing. This was generally the case when CONAIE leadership framed calls for mass mobilization in terms of land, economic grievances of indigenous peasants, ethnic identity, and plurinationality as the basis for self-determination.[14]

A member of CONAIE's general council described the decision-making process: "All major resolutions are deliberated in the communities, and from there they pass to the next level [federation and CONAIE general assembly]. Because of that we are a little slow in making important decisions, but it is worth doing it that way because here individualism does not fit – we travel together" (Gerlach 2003: 73).

CONAIE's leadership used linkages between these organizational nodes to transform local claims for inclusion in agrarian development, access to state resources, cultural survival, and autonomy from the state into mass mobilization at the service of a national political strategy to realize those claims. Moreover, the leadership understood that accomplishing those goals required going beyond relatively narrow indigenous interests. The movement could accomplish its objectives only by linking indigenous struggles with those of all Ecuadorians and, because it was the strongest movement, by taking leadership (Zamosc 2004: 145–47). To accomplish these goals, CONAIE's second congress in 1988 developed the following strategic prescriptions: "negotiate demands with incumbent governments, take the initiative in national mobilizations to pressure the governments, have permanent public presence by taking stands on all relevant issues, combine forms of struggle, and put CONAIE at the center of a broad front of all exploited and marginalized sectors" (Zamosc 2004: 145).

These strategic prescriptions show that CONAIE's leadership was open to collaboration with nonmember and nonindigenous popular sector social movement organizations. In part, this posture stemmed from recognition of economic differences within the indigenous peoples movement. "We *indígenas* are immersed in the structure of Ecuadorian society and for that reason we are campesinos, workers, business people, artisans, etc; some of us work in the country, others in the city, some of us receive salaries, others do not" (Colloredo-Mansfield 2002: 638).

---

[14] Timing depended on agriculture and festival–work-related cycles.

Yashar (2005) argued that CONAIE's formative experience explains its proclivity for alliance formation. Its member organizations and local authorities had worked closely with a wide range of allies in their struggle to organize; these included Catholic orders, Christian base communities, international nongovernmental organizations, and labor unions (especially the peasant affiliate of the Confederación Ecuatoriana de Trabajadores and the Catholic Workers' Union). Class and ethnic-based roots commingled; and its leaders were used to negotiating with regional and national political authorities. This experience created lasting, expanding dense networks of activists, NGOS, and leaders from unions and center-left political parties. As these organizations (and their descendants) struggled against neoliberal reforms in the cities, CONAIE drew on those networks to lead the popular sectors' challenges to neoliberalism. Its first attempts at coalition building, however, were not successful, mostly because they did not involve those networks.

If the Indian uprising was the highpoint of this opening wave of anti-neoliberal contention, the downcycle included two failed general strikes and an unsuccessful attempt to build collective power by the FUT and CONAIE. The FUT recognized it needed links to other social movement organizations for mobilization to have a greater effect on national policy. Its own organization was too fragmented, and even when adherence to strikes was high, it reached only about a fifth of urban workers. Thus the FUT solicited CONAIE's support early on.[15] On 11 July 1990, a month after the First Indian Uprising, the FUT called a third general strike against Borja's economic policies and crafted demands to enlist support from the teachers union and from CONAIE.[16] Recently radicalized Indian organizations, however, did not participate in this event, despite their national leadership's exhortations. The regional and local grassroots affiliates of CONAIE (the ones that actually mobilized people) did not support the national leadership.[17] Indigenous peasants were unwilling to back urban movement-initiated mobilization without concrete grievances of their own. As urban mobilization fizzled, CONAIE settled into negotiating some of its 16 points with the government. Meanwhile, CONFENIAE negotiated a settlement over territorial rights with the government after staging a "March for Land and Life" from Amazonia (Pastaza) to the capital (Quito).

[15] CONAIE officially supported the seventh general strike against Febres Cordero (although that was probably only in principle as no major peasant mobilization was reported). *Latin America Weekly Report* 9 June 1988: 4.

[16] Demands included (1) increasing the minimum salary, (2) ending fuel and public service price increases, (3) price controls for basic consumer goods, (4) end to weekly devaluation of the currency (the Sucre), (5) integral agrarian reform, (6) government compliance with CONAIE's 16-point petition, (7) reverse privatization plans, (8) stopping plans to privatize social security, (9) strict observance of trade union rights, (10) passing a new law regulating the teaching profession. *Latin America Weekly Report* 19 July 1990: 9.

[17] *Latin America Weekly Report* 24 January 1991: 10; *Latin America Regional Reports: Andean Group* 6 September 1990: 4.

The March for Land and Life illustrates many of the points related to motivation and brokerage previously discussed. Leaders framed the march in the context of a series of contentious actions around the quincentennial of Spain's "encounter" with the new world symbolized in the slogan "After 500 hundred years of domination, self-determination in 1992!" In late 1991 and early 1992 leaders of the Organización de Pueblos Indígenas de Pastaza met repeatedly with community leaders to discuss strategy and tactics regarding land policy. They decided on, among other actions, a march to Quito, which they began planning in March 1992 with the establishment of a general coordinator and at least eight communal commissions. Instructions to participants included that each community send as many delegates as possible, men, women, children and elders; and participants should bring their own eating utensils, provisions, blankets and warm clothes for the march over the Andes, as well as musical instruments, lances, and adornments. The framing of the land issue to the communities was clear: "We either go to Quito now to present our proposals to the president of the republic, or we lose all our territory, and hence our livelihood." Those proposals were (1) the establishment of permanent territorial rights for indigenous people; (2) a share of the wealth of natural resource exploitation; (3) resolution of 117 specific land conflicts; and (4) constitutional reform to make Ecuador a multicultural, plurinational state. The march began in April and the 2,000 strong swelled to 10,000 by the time they crossed the Andes (Whitten, Whitten, and Chango 2003: 184–91).

Neoliberal Radicalization and Swelling Resistance, 1992–96

Sixto Durán's presidency (1992–96) radicalized neoliberalism. At the head of a conservative coalition he pushed an aggressive orthodox economic stabilization and structural adjustment program. Decrees sufficed to initiate the stabilization program. It stressed inflation control, currency devaluation, and fiscal restraint. This was accomplished by eliminating price subsidies to fuel and staple consumer goods (food, transport, and utilities that translated into drastically increased prices to consumers), cuts to public services (health, education, and credit to state development banks) and by slashing social insurance (North 2004).

The structural adjustment program required legislation. Major reforms contemplated deepening tariff reductions, total financial sector liberalization, complete liberalization of capital movement and foreign investment, and initiation of privatization of state enterprises by means of a state modernization plan.[18] Negotiations to refinance foreign debt, this time with the Brady Plan and the Club of Paris, preceded the structural program (García 2003: 87–88). In 1994, his government also proposed, and eventually passed, an Agrarian Development

---

[18] The 1994 general law of financial institutions set up the 2000 debacle because banks were left largely to regulate themselves (North 2004).

Law developed by a U.S. aid-sponsored think tank tied to Ecuadorian landowner interests. It guaranteed private property rights and land markets and rescinded the redistributive elements of previous agrarian reform efforts. It dismantled the Agrarian Reform Institute and replaced it with the National Institute of Agrarian Development (North 2004).

Durán's government, however, encountered the same implementation difficulties as Febres Cordero's because opposition parties controlled about two-thirds of seats in the legislature. Worse, his party coalition was undisciplined. Occasionally its members voted with the opposition (Conaghan and Malloy 1994: 228–29). Given this weakness, executive–legislative tensions stalled structural adjustment, but Durán's government forged ahead with the economic stabilization program. Durán's administration was also hampered by high inflation rates from the previous government and weak international oil prices, making him more dependent on international creditors and multilateral banks.

Transformations in Ecuadorian Contentious Politics

Durán's sweeping neoliberal reform program triggered a second, and more intense, wave of anti-neoliberal contention. Because the program was more ambitious than Febres Cordero's it threatened a much broader swath of urban popular sector, peasant–indigenous, and middle-class interests. The common threat of deepening economic exclusion caused a transformation in the associational and collective power of anti-neoliberal challengers and in its disruptive power. On the one hand, this time the FUT and the CONAIE successfully coordinated mobilization. On the other hand, now that privatization was on the policy agenda, public sector unions in the oil, electrical, and telecommunications sectors and the state employees union mobilized. Their disruptive power increased pressure on the government. They could stop the flow of oil for export on which the government depended for income and interrupt private and public business transactions. Nonpayment of salaries for months at a time of public sector employees (including teachers) spurred highly militant defensive mobilization by these groups.

The awakening of public sector unions over the threat of privatization also caused a significant transformation in the associational power of challengers to neoliberalism. Because this did not occur until the end of the second wave of anti-neoliberal contention, its full effect was not felt until the third wave. The FUT's unreliability during mobilization campaigns spurred the creation of the Coordinadora de Movimientos Sociales (CMS; Social Movements Coordinator) between 1994 and 1995 as an encompassing organization for nonindigenous social movements and unions linked to leftist political parties (Collins 2004: 38; García-Serrano 2003: 208, n. 25). As will be seen, the CMS expanded popular sector collective power. It coordinated contentious action with CONAIE, and together the two also formed a new political party to contest the 1996 elections.

Ecuador

In general, contentious politics between 1992 and 1996 followed a pattern similar to that of the previous period. Popular sectors frequently mobilized to support opposition political parties resisting the administration's reforms. This time, however, because of the aforementioned transformations in associational and collective power and the government's political weakness, expanded mobilization partially succeeded into pressuring the authorities to make changes, sometimes in negotiation with social movement organizations. A new pattern developed: The government announced price hikes or proposed economic reforms and following massive protests it negotiated. As elections drew closer, coordinated contentious action diminished as movement organizations concentrated on electoral politics.

The second wave of anti-neoliberal contentious politics began with a FUT-sponsored and CONAIE-supported general strike on 23 September 1992, barely 20 days after the announcement of price deregulation, privatization, and trade reform. Still, coordination between the two organizations was precarious. The urban labor movement's fragmentation left it, among other ills, susceptible to government manipulation through selective negotiation. The same held true for the CONAIE and for public sector unions. The government kept the transport and public sector unions from adhering by offering to negotiate separately with them. The strike had little disruptive effect because transport and government offices were not affected and because the CONAIE, already in negotiation with the government, limited itself to a few marches. The government's offer to negotiate with the FUT and with CONAIE further blunted cooperation. However, as the second wave of contention wore on, the government's capacity for this sort of manipulation declined because it habitually reneged on its commitments. It was also clear that, when CONAIE led contentious action, mobilization was much stronger.

In February 1993 the government introduced a Modernization Law in Congress that included provisions to give the executive extraordinary powers to implement neoliberal reforms. Faced with a strong threat of political exclusion, the FUT and CONAIE coordinated a second general strike in May to "fight government neoliberal policies to the end."[19] To demonstrate their seriousness, and with much fanfare, they announced an indefinite general strike, the first in 14 years. What followed revealed CONAIE's commitment to contentious politics, its disappointment in the FUT, and its pivotal role for generating disruptive capacity. The government repressed the strike with troops and arrested more than 100 protestors. The FUT ignominiously declared an end to the "indefinite" strike after the second day. The far more militant CONAIE, which was blocking highways in the highlands, criticized the FUT, accusing it of making separate arrangements with the government.[20] In any case, mobilization and continued strike threats had some effect. When Congress finally approved a Modernization

[19] Quoted in Inter Press Service 26 May 1993.
[20] *Latin America Weekly Report* 10 June 1993: 256–57 and 17 June 1993: 275–76.

Law, it contained concessions to organized labor. Gone was an original provision that would have given the president the power to fire public sector employees or to privatize state companies by decree; such measures would require legislation guaranteeing a congressional struggle backed by mobilization in each case (*Latin America Weekly Report* 11 November 1993: 520).

The buildup to the crest of the second wave of anti-neoliberal contention began with an indefinite national teacher's strike in October 1993 over pay raises. The government declared a state of emergency, brought in the army (two teachers were killed), invoked the national security law (permitting the government to dismiss or arrest all of them), and ordered teachers to return to work. They did so in December, accepting a settlement they had rejected in November.[21]

In early 1994 the government announced another stringent economic stabilization program that included staggering 70-percent fuel price increases. The economic threat touched all Ecuadorians because all consumed energy. This prompted massive nationwide demonstrations that evinced significant advances in popular sector (and middle-class) collective power. Protest began on 3 February 1994 with a call by the FUT for a third general strike against the government. Up to 500,000 participated in coastal and highland cities such as Guayaquil, Quito, and Cuenca with clashes between protestors and police (*The Washington Times* 8 February 1994: A14). CONAIE organized a 48-hour peaceful mobilization of its own, focused on roadblocks, on 8 February demanding repeal of fuel price hikes while students and workers continued to demonstrate in Quito.

CONAIE's framing of the issue articulated the common threat neoliberalism posed to all popular sectors and that the menace required a solidary response. In its call to action, CONAIE declared that the ruling class, the nation's oligarchy, was deliberately attacking "the union workers movement, the Indian-peasant movement, that is, all the Ecuadorian people [and therefore] we call on the people to join this struggle, which is a popular struggle. That is why this summons is coordinated through this nation's Indian-peasant, workers and peoples' organizations" (BBC Summary of World Broadcasts 4 February 1994).

Durán refused to negotiate. Teachers, oil, electrical, and telephone workers, and state employees threatened to join in, and CONAIE warned it would stage a full-scale uprising as in 1990. In the face of the presidency's intransigence, Ecuador's constitutional court, concerned about governability, intervened and declared the price increases unconstitutional (*Latin American Weekly Report* 24 February 1994: 77). Unrest roiled, however, as oil, electricity, and telecommunications workers struck against privatization in early April.

The crest of the second wave of anti-neoliberal contention occurred when CONAIE staged a Second Indian Uprising in mid-June 1994. The massive mobilization of highland and lowland indigenous peoples was a stark reminder that CONAIE was by far the most powerful movement in Ecuador. If urban unions,

---

[21] *Latin America Weekly Report* 2 December 1993: 556 and 9 December 1993: 573.

the informal sector, and other dissident movements ever joined such an uprising en masse, then challengers to neoliberalism would truly be a force to be reckoned with. However, such a confluence of forces did not take place until the third wave of anti-neoliberal contention.

A new agrarian reform law (the Agrarian Development Law) that strengthened land markets had been hastily passed, ignoring the recommendations of indigenous organizations. The bill threatened to place unproductive Indian community territory on the market claiming they were an obstacle to development (García-Serrano 2003: 205). Despite the shortcomings of land reform in the 1960s and 1970s, this law posed a clear and present danger because it "undermined the *intent* of earlier land reforms. It effectively stopped land redistribution, targeted large export-oriented farms for credit, privatized water rights, and created mechanisms (majority vote) for selling previously inalienable indigenous lands" (Yashar 2005: 147–48).

In response, CONAIE convened an Extraordinary Assembly between 7 and 8 June 1994, framed as a "Mobilization for Life." This framing resonated with core material (land) and cultural (survival) concerns of highland and lowland indigenous, thus contributing significantly to the success of the national protest. As occurred in Argentina and Bolivia, "life" literally meant defense of the bases for existence. Luis Macas, CONAIE president at the time, explained they rejected the agrarian law because it "eliminated the definition of the social function of the land and water at the same time that it opened doors for the disappearance of communal lands, the base and sustenance necessary for the survival of indigenous peoples. Definitely it was an instrument in favor of the landlords and worsened inequality, violence, and injustice in the countryside" (Yashar 2005: 148).

Demands specifically countered the perceived threat. They included, "(1) replacing the agrarian reform bill with an alternative one; (2) sufficient funds to resolve land disputes; (3) allocation of one percent of oil revenue to a fund for indigenous development managed by CONAIE and abrogation of unused oil concessions on indigenous lands; (4) reorganizing the management of the bilingual inter-cultural education program; (5) respect for human rights, prohibition of private security forces in the countryside; (6) funds for the reconstruction of Indian villages damaged by natural disasters; (7) official government recognition to CONAIE as the representative of indigenous and peasant interests" (Yashar 2005: 148). However, CONAIE also cast its proposals wider to include concerns common to all popular sectors and many in the middle class. It demanded a national referendum to convene a Constituent Assembly with representation for all social sectors and renunciation of privatization (including rural social insurance services) (CONAIE 1994).

Indigenous community councils and local CONAIE-affiliated associations considered the Extraordinary Council's call to action. The framing of the threat to the communities contributed to massive adherence. Communities and federations then organized local and provincial protests and roadblocks drawing on indigenous-peasant cultural and social norms of participation in communal life previously discussed. All across the central and south highlands and Amazonia, outraged indigenous people blocked roads, which interrupted the supply of agricultural goods to urban areas, cut access to major oil-producing regions, and marched on cities (*Latin America Weekly Report* 7 July 1994: 290). For 20 days CONAIE shut down large portions of Ecuador in highly disruptive protests. Protestors took over government buildings in some towns and marched up to 30,000 strong in city streets throughout Ecuador. In Amazonia, indigenous communities set up roadblocks and took over three oil wells, halting oil production for three days (Selverston-Scher 2001: 94).

The government responded by repressing them, calling a state of emergency, and mobilizing the army. Strong repression hindered the development of solidary, potentially crippling mobilization. The FUT attempted a sympathy general strike for the end of the month, but had to cancel the effort. Many member unions refused to participate, citing fear of repression from the army and jail for the leaders.

In a two-pronged strategy to defuse an explosive situation, and after initial refusals, the government negotiated with protestors. It gave small wage hikes and cost-of-living increases to urban workers and devoted considerably more attention to CONAIE (*Latin America Weekly Report* 14 July 1994: 309). The government formed a commission with strong CONAIE representation to negotiate changes to the Agrarian Development Law. Those included "credit for small farmers who produce for the local market, state control of water resources, continuation of land redistribution, development of indigenous agricultural knowledge, and a two thirds majority vote by indigenous communities to sell their community land" (Andolina 1999: 213; Yashar 2005: 148). These measures substantially *decommodified* essential resources such as credit, water, and land, all of which were crucial for the healthy reproduction of indigenous communities. Moreover, its success in forcing negotiation and obtaining favorable concessions consolidated CONAIE's status as the leading popular sector political actor.

Hostilities between Ecuador and Peru over oil-rich border regions dampened social protest in early 1995, but it picked up again in late May once the conflict ended. Undaunted by constant popular sector and congressional resistance to his neoliberal reforms, Durán persisted in efforts to pass legislation to privatize strategic economic areas such as electricity, oil, telecommunications and the rural social security agency. This particular bill also sought to limit the right to strike. This new threat rekindled efforts by CONAIE and the FUT to build collective power by calling a fourth general strike. Drawing on the framing of the previous year's Indian uprising, they dubbed their mobilization a "national uprising for life" because the bill directly affected the bases of existence for both urban labor and peasant-indigenous social groups. Nevertheless, in a reaffirmation of CONAIE's preeminence it was much more effective in disrupting commerce by means of roadblocks across the nation than the FUT was in urban areas. This fact was also a reminder of the difficulty in coordinating substantial disruption in town and country simultaneously.

The FUT's weaknesses and lack of commitment to coordinated mobilization with CONAIE impelled more militant, surging unions and nonunion groups to create an alternative organization. Threatened by privatization (including rural social security) and union busting during the second half of 1995, state workers in the oil, electrical, and telecom sectors, in addition to rural indigenous and nonindigenous peasants, teachers, and state employees, staged strikes and demonstrations monthly to the end of Durán's administration. These mobilizations contributed to a critical transformation in the associational and collective power of urban protest groups with the creation of the CMS. State unions understood that successful challenges to neoliberalism required a solid alliance with CONAIE (which was clearly interested in coalition building), and that the FUT was incapable of filling that role.[22] Hence, during 1995, oil and electrical workers organized union and nonunion groups independently of the FUT. That would make it much more difficult for the government to deflate mobilization by manipulating the FUT's fragmentation.

The CMS encompassed three distinct sectors. Organized labor included oil, electrical, cement, and professional unions such as teachers and university professors and the public employees union, many linked to leftist political parties. The informal labor sector encompassed vendors, retail merchants, neighborhood associations, rural sector retirees, urban self-help organizations, artisans, youth centers, and new social movements linked to NGOs in human rights, environment, gender, and citizen rights. Christian base communities comprised a third sector. All told, the CMS claimed affiliation from 80 national, 250 provincial, and 3,000 local and sectoral organizations (Andolina 2003: 730; Collins 2004; Zamosc 2004: 135).

The CMS coordinated contentious action among members, helped movements to develop, and shunned vertical leadership in favor of autonomous participation and internal democracy. In this it was similar to the CTA in Argentina and the Coordinadora del Agua and del Gas in Bolivia. It also rejected violence (armed revolt) for a combination of mobilization and negotiation within national institutional channels. The CMS framed issues to attract a broad spectrum of social groups and to support CONAIE. To expand political inclusion and defend against neoliberalism, it stressed the development of a more participatory democracy in the context of a plurinational society and state. Displaying a clear preference for Polanyi-like decommodification, it advocated an alternative economic model based on economic nationalism, a larger role for the state in economic development (including more control over the financial sector), more fiscal spending in social services and insurance, more state commitment to full

---

[22] *Latin America Weekly Report* 8 June 1995; BBC Summary of World Broadcasts 27 May 1995 and 30 May 1995; The Associated Press 7 June 1995.

employment and fair wages, and respect for ethnic and cultural diversity (Andolina 2003: 729–30).

The CMS's first victory in 1995 illustrates the mechanisms it used to encourage and coordinate contentious action among member organizations. To take the wind out of the sails of contentious politics, Durán's government organized a referendum for November to approve privatization, labor relations, and to extend presidential powers. To counter the big-business publicity campaign, in a style reminiscent of the CTA in Argentina, the "CMS and trade union federations organized public debates, presented alternative ideas for constitutional reform, and carried out an intense grassroots campaign to promote the 'no' vote" (Zamosc 2004: 135). They defeated all 11 questions.

In addition to attracting nonunion urban movements, the CMS expanded the collective power of challengers to neoliberalism in two significant ways. First, the CMS and CONAIE collaborated successfully, although they also welcomed FUT participation in strikes and protests. Second, the political power of movements challenging neoliberalism swelled in 1996 when CONAIE, along with the CMS, created a political party to participate in presidential, congressional, and local elections, the Movimiento de Unidad Plurinacional Pachakutik- Nuevo País. The CMS had created the Movimiento de Ciudadanos por Un Nuevo País to build on the success of the 1994–95 anti-neoliberal protests. They realized they needed the support of the indigenous movement to launch a presidential candidate. After holding a national convention to discuss the issue, CONAIE leaders agreed. Although CONAIE joined at the CMS's invitation, as the CMS itself expected, it was the dominant force. Moreover, alliances with leftist parties allowed Pachakutik to gain a significant amount of additional seats in districts where indigenous presence was weaker. Given the fragmented nature of Ecuador's multiparty system, Pachakutik quickly became a major political presence (Van Cott 2005: 121–24).

These developments set the stage for more intense collaboration between the CMS and CONAIE, brokered by dense overlapping organizational networks that connected their leadership at crucial nodal points (usually around specific campaigns). These included NGOs (especially human rights and environmental, but also legal and civic), Christian base communities, unions (CONAIE, for example, built on ample experience with peasant unions), and leftist political parties that supported urban movements and peasant unions (such as the Movimiento Democrático Popular (MDP; Popular Democratic Movement)[23] and that now interacted in Pachakutik.

Networks involving leaders of the urban, rural, and indigenous movements began to forge tighter linkages in the mid-1990s. For example, 1994 was a year in which both the urban and indigenous strands of social movement organizations began to develop alternative political projects to counter neoliberalism.

---

[23] For this connection see Korovkin (1997: 31) and Selverston-Scher (2001: 48).

CONAIE drafted a political platform that included a comprehensive proposal for a plurinational state and a mixed economy and submitted a constitutional reform project to Congress.[24] CMS's precursor, Democratic Forum, which drew from civic, professional, social movement, and interest groups, developed a similar project. Although CONAIE was not a member organization it maintained contact with the Forum (Andolina 2003: 729; Saltos 2001). Moreover, many of the Forum's organizations, or their forerunners, had supported the development of CONAIE's major indigenous confederations.

These connections expanded and deepened during the campaign against Durán's referendum in 1995 (Andolina 1999) and beyond as the CMS and CONAIE mounted urban and rural resistance against neoliberal reforms championed by the governments of Bucaram and Mahuad (Gerlach 2003:76).[25] Conferences and workshops where CMS and CONAIE leaders strategized for mobilization were significant brokerage nodes. These "strategy" conferences often entailed discussion and debate over the purposes of proposed actions in an ongoing dialectic between means and ends. Personal meetings and networks among leaders and activists also served these purposes. Meetings sometimes took place spontaneously over lunch or just outside of an ongoing larger conference or assembly. Meetings of Pachakutik's party assembly and executive council were another node that brought CONAIE and CMS leaders together, even if there were some tensions between them and elected Pachakutik figures.[26]

Neoliberal Hubris and Hypermobilization, 1996–2000

Brashly ignoring the swell in anti-neoliberal movements and their force, presidents stubbornly radicalized neoliberal reform programs. In reaction, mass mobilization swelled to new heights, eventually forcing the resignation of two presidents in a third wave of anti-neoliberal contention. What changed that popular sector contentious action developed such significant political effects beyond compelling temporary policy stalemate and winning small concessions? Economic crises had considerable negative impact on the political power of neoliberals. It

---

[24] Pallares (2002, especially in Chapter 7) supports the argument for the exhaustion of the pluricultural model of incorporation of indigenous peoples in the nation-state. This model focused primarily on the promotion of cultural policy such as bilingual education and artistic endeavors. The pluricultural approach ignored pressing material issues. The plurinational framing, first seen in the 1992 "March for Land and Life" defined the indigenous in terms of nations instead of cultures and ethnic groups. Plurinationalism adds economic and political dimensions to the question of the relationship of the indigenous to the nation-state. It demands land security, financial and infrastructural support, protection from predatory market behavior, and mechanisms of authentic participation in politics and the policy-making process.

[25] Agence France Presse 29 June 1995; *Latin America Weekly Report* 13 July 1995; BBC Summary of World Broadcasts 24 October 1995; *Latin America Weekly Report* 1 February 1996, 22 February 1996, and 14 March 1996.

[26] Personal communication with Robert Andolina, 4 September 2008.

reduced the functional power of the state – it could offer neither economic growth nor employment. This aggravated the chronic inability of presidents to forge policy coalitions in Congress. Economic crises also exacerbated economic exclusion, and hence the indignation, outrage, and desperation of urban and rural popular sectors and middle classes, motivating people to mobilize. More encompassing neoliberal reforms threatened a wide range of social groups facilitating issue framing that emphasized the common source of troubles and maximized solidarity. The social movements used the previously discussed mechanisms to promote participation and to transform the particular grievances into concentrated pressure for national policy and political change.

In the context of deepening economic hardship, mounting frustration at the government's insistence on neoliberal reforms in the face of massive resistance (political exclusion) caused the popular sectors to reinvigorate and expand the collective power created during the previous wave of anti-neoliberal mobilization. If the message had not been clear before, movement organizations unequivocally communicated that demobilization required incumbent politicians to give up their single-minded quest to impose contemporary market society in Ecuador. Huge, constant nationwide mobilization contributed to the political isolation of incumbent presidents, who, abandoned by their supporters, had no choice but to resign.

Anti-Neoliberal Uprising I: Ousting Bucaram

The first peak in this third wave of anti-neoliberal contention occurred when massive mobilization forced Abdalá Bucaram (August 1996 to February 1997) to resign barely six months into his presidency. Perceptions that he betrayed his electoral mandate contributed to the outcome. He had been elected on a populist platform as the candidate of the center-left Partido Roldoista de Ecuador, a splinter of the populist Concentración de Fuerzas Populares. His campaign stressed a mild, gradual approach to unavoidable economic stabilization (Lind 2004). With CONAIE support Bucaram won the highest popular vote percentage of any president since 1979.[27] To gain CONAIE's backing, Bucaram created a Ministry for Indigenous Affairs, and several CONAIE leaders served in his government. This created expectations that Bucaram would adopt parts of CONAIE's economic and social agenda (Van Cott 2005: 125).

Irrespective of Bucaram's intentions, looming economic problems dictated a policy reversal. He inherited a deepening financial crisis (caused by the previous administration's liberalization policy) and falling oil prices (Ecuador's principal foreign exchange earner). Faced with a serious fiscal shortfall, Bucaram abandoned his populist stance after meeting with international financial institutions

---

[27] CONAIE's candidate, who ran for the new MUPP (Movimiento de Unidad Plurinacional Pachakutik) party, came in a strong third, and thus was ineligible for the run-off vote.

and multilateral development banks (principally the World Bank). These emphasized fiscal discipline and market reforms as a condition for financing. In November 1996 he unveiled a strict fiscal stabilization package and free-market-oriented structural reforms. His program proposed state modernization focused on privatization of strategic economic sectors to promote a smaller, more efficient state, sharp reduction in public spending, tax and gasoline price hikes, more flexible labor laws, and a fixed foreign exchange regime – modeled after the Argentine convertibility plan.[28]

The new administration made the convertibility plan its highest priority and set its implementation for July 1997. Necessary preparations began immediately with decrees to eliminate subsidies to public services to bring the fiscal deficit under control. "Shock treatment" caused dizzying increases in prices such as 270 percent for gasoline, 1,000 percent for telephone, 300 percent for electricity, and 60 percent for public transport. These hikes dwarfed the 70-percent rise in fuel costs that sparked massive protest during Durán's government.

Bucaram suffered an immediate loss of political power because his sweeping neoliberal reform program alienated almost everyone and provoked a rift between coastal and highland business elites (mainly over tax reform but also over subsidies). His political coalition collapsed, and a broad opposition coalition prepared to defeat the convertibility plan. To top things off, Bucaram's nepotism and cronyism cost him support from the political class and elites.

Urban and rural popular sectors and the indigenous were deeply aggrieved by Bucaram's policy about-face, especially because Pachakutik, their party, had supported him in good faith. His deceit, refusal to adopt CONAIE's economic and social agendas, and insistence on free-market reforms lost him the support of urban and rural poor (Lind 2004: 629–30; Van Cott 2005: 125). The corruption caused by Bucaram's cronyism and nepotism further incensed the middle classes and popular sectors.

Feeling betrayed by the political establishment, contentious politics was the only means left to the popular sectors to challenge neoliberalism (Zamosc 2007). Defensive anti-neoliberal mobilization picked up where it had left off at the end of Durán's government. Indignant students and teachers struck, followed by transport workers. The FUT threatened a general strike and opposition political parties maneuvered to defeat the convertibility law. CONAIE, meanwhile, suffered internal divisions as Bucaram courted Amazonian indigenous by offering one of their leaders the new post of Minister of Indigenous Affairs.[29] By the end of the year, the frustrated and politically bruised leadership of CONAIE restored internal equilibrium and was ready to join the fray (Andolina 1999).

---

[28] Domingo Cavallo, the architect of the Argentine convertibility program, was a key consultant for Bucaram's currency policy (*Facts on File World News Digest* 13 February 1997: 82 A2).

[29] *Latin America Regional Reports: Andean Group* 10 October 1996: 6; *Latin America Weekly Report* 15 August 1996: 363

A significant expansion of and greater cohesion in the associational, political, and collective power of anti-neoliberal movements brought this third wave of contention to its first peak. It began in January 1997 when a small, militant, leftist political party, the Movimiento Democrático Popular, organized protests in Quito and seven other cities in alliance with the Frente Popular, which articulated students, teachers, and human rights organizations (Andolina 2003: 731). Government intransigence quickly caused a more significant spurt of collective power building. The FUT, CMS, CONAIE, and the Frente Popular formed the Patriotic Front to coordinate mass mobilization, principally a 24-hour general strike called for 5 February.[30] Business leaders from the Cámara de Productores met with the FUT and agreed to support the strike as did the journalists' union and women's and environmental groups. All pledged one united solidary front against Bucaram. As protestors laid the foundations for solidary action, throughout January students and teachers, municipal councils, CMS-affiliated groups (youths, human rights activists, and students), and eventually truck drivers struck and demonstrated.

Meanwhile, Bucaram's precarious political power plummeted. His stubborn refusal to acknowledge the political opposition's demands prompted calls for his resignation by three former presidents. Failing that, they urged Congress to impeach him. Social movement organizations amplified those demands.

The general strike began as planned on 5 February, and all of the organizations and groups that had pledged solidary action turned out in force. In all three of the country's major regions, hundreds of thousands of tired, angry, frustrated, and determined Ecuadorians (perhaps as many as two million) paralyzed the nation in all three regions (Gerlach 2003: 93–94; Lind 2004: 629–30). FUT-affiliated unions struck, 20,000 indigenous blocked main roads, stopping the flow of produce to the cities, shops closed, thousands marched on the Congress and government buildings around the nation (sometimes led by the city's mayor) demanding Bucaram's impeachment, middle-class women marched banging pots and pans. Taxi drivers, street vendors, truck drivers, and small and large businesses protested. Ouraged by the corruption of Bucaram's government and its blind eye to their suffering, striking workers outside, Congress demanded that legislators impeach him, chanting (to the tune of a well-known soccer chorus), "Olé, olé, olé! Thief, thief, thief!" All over the country the streets reverberated to the cry, "Out with him!"[31] Demonstrators ignored the fact that the government had called a state of emergency. The strike was so successful that organizers extended it to 48 hours.

CONAIE mobilized its people thanks to strong support from indigenous-peasant communities. CMS motivated its followers by holding meetings,

[30] Just prior to February CONAIE and the CMS had been planning to mobilize against corruption and the formation of a Ministry of Indian Affairs. They turned it into a mobilization for Bucaram's ouster (Zamosc 2004: 137).
[31] These quotes from Associated Press 5 February 1997 and *La Jornada* (Mexico) 6 February 1997.

seminars, talks, and the slogan, "No One Stays Home." Leaflets, with irony and humor, got the word out too. "We invite all Ecuadorians to the giant going-away party for Bucaram and his family on their one-way trip to Panama or wherever. This event will take place in the country's plazas and streets on February 5 and 6. Dress informally. The entrance fee is a street barricade, a burning tire, and the will to save the country's dignity" (Gerlach 2003: 94).

A budding People's Assembly movement – backed by CONAIE – provided an additional mechanism to mobilize people. Proliferating provincial assembly committees offered a space in which people congregated, debated issues, challenged state authority, and demanded government accountability. The provincial committees began to select delegates for local government positions, normally appointed by the central government (Andolina 2003: 736). They also bundled the grievances of particular social movements into common demands for a new government to "revoke Bucaram's economic adjustments, forbid corrupt politicians from returning to political office, and officially define unfulfilled campaign promises as electoral fraud" (Andolina 2003: 736). Radicalized participants committed to socioeconomic and political change no doubt fired up friends and neighbors from their respective social movement organizations to protest, adding a call for a constituent assembly to the list of demands.

On the second day of the strike Bucaram lost what remained of his political power when Congress impeached him. Bucaram relinquished office a few days later when he lost a key component of state power. It became clear that the military did not support him when they refused to carry out the state of emergency he had declared to repress demonstrators. In a deal of questionable constitutionality, in which the military participated, Congress allowed the vice president to take office for a few days while it drafted emergency legislation that permitted the president of the Congress, Fabián Alarcón, to become president of the republic. He would remain in office until completion of constitutional changes with general elections called for May 1998.

Interlude: The Constitutional Convention

The collective power of popular sector challenges to neoliberalism – embodied in the Patriotic Front and spearheaded by CONAIE – had played a crucial role in ousting Bucaram. Their demands included halting foreign debt payments (which would suspend economic stabilization programs) and channeling those resources into social and economic programs for the popular sectors. CONAIE's central demands remained on the table, and all wanted ironclad political commitments against privatization.[32] The demand for a Constituent Assembly was a strategy to strengthen legislation against privatization and to ensure mechanisms of popular

---

[32] *Latin America Regional Reports: Andean Group* 4 November 1997: 2; Agence France Presse 16 February 1997.

sector participation in policy making. CONAIE also saw the Constituent Assembly as a vehicle to obtain long sought constitutional measures favorable for indigenous peoples.

The movements of the Patriotic Front were (again) deeply disappointed by the political process. After political maneuvering, including Patriotic Front mobilization to ensure the formation of the Constituent Assembly when Alarcón attempted to shelve it, traditional political parties gained control of the 70-seat body.[33] The most ardent supporters of neoliberal reform, the Partido Social Cristiano, which also held the most seats in Congress, dominated a majority coalition. Jaime Nesbet, the Social Cristiano's presidential candidate, hailed the election for the assembly a personal triumph. Fabián Alarcón said his party, the Frente Radical Alfarista, would support the Social Cristiano's privatization plan with its eight seats as did former President Osvaldo Hurtado's Democracia Popular bloc.[34] Consequently the new constitution contained property rights clauses that facilitated privatization (García 2003: 89).[35]

Pachakutik had obtained seven seats (and three allied seats), making it the third largest voting bloc in the constituent assembly. Isolated, the delegation of this "upstart" party made no headway with its economic proposals. However, the relatively small Pachakutik delegation, in conjunction with lobbying by experienced CONAIE negotiators and the Pachakutik congressional bloc, obtained much of its indigenist agenda. Although the new constitution did not recognize Ecuador as a plurinational state, Article I declared it a pluricultural state (both were original CONAIE demands). Indigenous languages were recognized as official in indigenous areas and gave indigenous peoples who define themselves as a nation the right to practice customary law. The Constitution also established "special electoral districts for indigenous and Afro-Ecuadorian communities corresponding to newly recognized, self-governing indigenous and Afro-Ecuadorian territories." But implementing guidelines were left undefined.[36] The constitution also determined the indivisibility of communal land (Andolina 2003). Moreover, the process strengthened linkages among CMS member organizations and between CONAIE and the CMS (Andolina 2003).

---

[33] For political shenanigans around the Constitutional Convention see *Latin America Weekly Reports* 12 August 1997: 383 and 26 August 1997: 407. Also see *Latin America Regional Reports: Andean Group* 26 August 1997 and 4 November 1997: 2.

[34] *Latin America Regional Reports: Andean Group* 9 December 1997.

[35] These clauses ratified measures rammed through a special session of Congress by the Christian Social Party and its allies in November 1997. The Patriotic Front mobilized unsuccessfully to have those laws repealed. See *Latin America Regional Reports: Andean Group* 4 November 1997: 2; *Latin America Weekly Report* 25 November 1997; *Latin America Regional Reports: Andean Group* 9 December 1997: 4; BBC Summary of World Broadcasts 1 Decemebr 1997.

[36] See Van Cott (2005: 126). She also points out that Pachakutik deputies helped to pass International Labor Organization Convention 169 on the rights of indigenous peoples. On the constituent assembly also see Yashar (2005: 150).

Anti-Neoliberal Uprising II: Mahuad's Comeuppance

Intense frustration at the outcome of the Constituent Assembly with respect to its composition and stance on privatization reinforced the conviction that contentious politics was the principal, if not the only, means the popular sectors and the indigenous had to defend against commodification from neoliberal reforms. Established political parties were prepared to negotiate with CONAIE over cultural, ethnic, and local political administrative issues. But they would not compromise on economic and social policy, which were the material core of CONAIE's indigenous-peasant *and* national policy agenda and its linkage to nonindigenous popular sectors and middle classes. Popular sector and indigenous organizations remained firmly excluded from the political process where economic policy was concerned. It was an exasperating stalemate. Mammoth mobilization was sufficient to stall neoliberal reform but lacked the political capacity to establish a different agenda.

Jamil Mahuad's administration (1998–2000) was yet another iteration of this frustrating process. Aggravated by deepening economic crisis, its policies sparked a resurgence of anti-neoliberal contention. Each time swelling defensive mobilization forced the government to negotiate, it reneged on agreements once protest subsided. Political exclusion by deceit in the midst of skyrocketing economic exclusion caused an escalating spiral of contention that precipitated a crisis of Ecuadorian democracy and raised high hopes that the political stalemate against neoliberalism had been broken.

President Jamil Mahuad and Vice President Gustavo Noboa took office in August 1998 for a term to end in July 2002. Mahuad was from the Democracia Popular Party and a former mayor of Quito; Noboa, a wealthy businessman, had been the runner-up presidential candidate of the Social Christian Party. His administration embraced globalization and the neoliberal trend sweeping Latin America. Given Ecuador's fiscal and foreign debt crisis, in September 1998 Mahuad proposed a familiar IMF and World Bank-supported economic recovery program that stressed economic stabilization and free-market structural reforms. The economic blueprint attacked inflation by means of high interest rates to depress demand, maintained a floating foreign exchange rate with maxidevaluations, and emphasized fiscal restraint by eliminating subsidies for gasoline, cooking oil, heating fuels, electricity, and public transportation and by freezing salaries and cutting public sector employment. The program proposed accelerating privatization (in the oil, telecommunications, and electricity sectors), capital accounts liberalization, and a tax policy favorable for upper classes that suspended the income tax, increased value-added taxes from 10 to 15 percent, and introduced a 1-percent tax on financial transactions (García 2003: 88–89).

As customary in Ecuador, the executive implemented monetary and much of fiscal policy by decree. Taxation and privatization, however, required legislation. Mahuad came into office believing that his party's electoral alliance with the

Social Christians gave him a working majority in Congress to push his agenda through. Indeed, in late November 1998, Congress passed a law that eliminated the income tax and replaced it with a 1-percent tax on financial transactions (North 2004: 201).

However, economic crisis significantly undermined his power to pass legislation on value-added taxes and privatization or, as it turned out, to sustain economic stabilization decrees. The world economic slowdown of the late 1990s depressed prices for oil and bananas, Ecuador's traditional foreign exchange earning commodities. Devastation from El Niño (1997–98) hit the two principal nontraditional export products – cut flowers and shrimp – equally hard. This exacerbated Ecuador's perennial foreign debt servicing difficulties, raising pressure for draconian fiscal retrenchment to service international creditors and stabilize prices. These came in mid-September 1998 when the newly elected government decreed a currency maxidevaluation of nearly 100 percent and sharply raised prices of gasoline, electricity, cooking oil, and public transport, in many cases between 200 and 400 percent.[37]

Mahuad's shock-treatment-style stabilization policy, and his announcement of an aggressive privatization program, posed a clear threat of deepening economic exclusion for the popular sectors and the indigenous that immediately prompted familiar patterns of defensive mobilization. The CMS denounced the government's stark cutbacks: "Jamil Mahuad's administration has declared war. The electoral campaign lies [have been proved], the neoliberal model, which is declining in other areas, has been implemented" (BBC Summary of World Broadcasts 23 September 1998). The FUT called a general strike for 1 October that obtained partial support from the CMS (oil and electrical workers), a few CONAIE-affiliated organizations that blocked roads in the countryside, and from the Popular Front. They demanded an end to maxidevaluations of the currency, restoration of subsidies to basic consumer items, and no privatization.[38]

The government refused to compromise in the face of relatively weak contentious action by Ecuadorian standards, and popular sector organizations strove, unsuccessfully at first, to rebuild extensive collective power. In January 1999, the FUT planned a series of staggered protests intended to culminate in a second general strike on 5 February, the anniversary of the national mobilization that toppled Bucaram. FUT leaders stressed that government intransigence in the face of price increases that ravaged the already meager living standards of working people left no option but to mobilize. As one union leader emphatically declared, "We oppose the increase in fuel prices and the 35 percent increase in energy bills, which will trigger inflation and will make people's living standards deteriorate... The

---

[37] Associated Press 30 September 1998; *Latin America Weekly Report* 6 October 1998.
[38] BBC Summary of World News 23 September 1998; Associated Press 30 September 1998; *Latin America Regional Reports: Andean Group* 6 October 1998; *Latin America Weekly Report* 6 October 1998.

economic situation is distressing to people who have no choice but to protest" (BBC Summary of World Broadcasts 15 January 1999). The Popular Front called on teachers and students to join in. Strikes by the FUT and the Popular Front began as planned, but did not reach expected levels. CONAIE's absence – it was still in the process of raising necessary local community support for mass mobilization – was felt. Meanwhile, in the Congress, the Izquierda Democrática, Pachakutik, and the Partido Roldoista Ecuatoriano did their best to oppose economic adjustment policies.[39]

Economic crisis and willful, arrogant acts of political exclusion quickly changed this panorama. The collapse of Ecuador's private banking sector, which began in August 1998, deepened the country's economic crisis and required a policy response. After financial liberalization in 1994, predatory and corrupt business practices precipitated the insolvency of Ecuador's major banks in 1998 and 1999. Congress intervened to rescue the financial system by establishing the Deposit Guarantee Agency in November 1998. The state committed itself to protecting all deposits and rescued Ecuador's largest bank, Filanbanco, from bankruptcy, with a 700-million-dollar package, the equivalent of Ecuador's education budget for that year.

These measures, however, proved insufficient to save the financial system. On 8 March 1998, Mahuad (in a preview of Argentina's financial meltdown) issued a decree that "froze half of all deposits in savings and checking accounts and all monies in long-term deposits, taking two thirds of the money supply out of circulation and effectively confiscating the personal savings of several million Ecuadorians to shore up the financial institutions owned by a few dozen families" (North 2004: 201).

International power sources promoted ancillary measures (Agence France Presse 12 March 1999). It was public knowledge that Ecuador was negotiating standby loans with the IMF, as well as receiving advice from the World Bank and a private think tank linked to Domingo Cavallo that promoted currency board solutions similar to Argentina's.[40] From their advice, the government introduced bills to increase the value-added tax from 10 to 15 percent and to privatize the oil, telecommunications, and electricity sectors. The government also proposed freezing public sector wages and labor law reforms to flexiblize the labor code along with further reductions of subsidies.

To get these measures passed, Mahuad probably calculated that his congressional coalition would hold together and that the popular sectors were too exhausted to mobilize. He miscalculated. The freeze on bank accounts and the rescue package for bank owners, in conjunction with the measures introduced

---

[39] BBC World News Summary 15 January 1999 and 9 February 1999; Associated Press 21 January 1999.

[40] There was speculation that austerity measures and privatization were preparatory to establishing a currency board to ensure price stability (Inter Press Service 12 March 1999).

in Congress, threatened tremendous economic hardship for the popular sectors and indigenous who were to disproportionately bear the burden of adjustment; and all to protect international and domestic economic elites. Of course, the bank holiday also affected popular sector organizations directly; they lost access to payroll and operating funds. Mobilization followed immediately with rapid reconstitution of the collective power created during Bucaram's administration, but it was a turbulent, drawn-out struggle.

In the opening clash, the Patriotic Front reemerged in all its strength. On 10 March 1999, in the midst of a 40-day-old national teachers' strike, the FUT and equally inflamed union allies in the public transportation sector, taxi drivers, and oil workers staged a 48-hour nationwide general strike against the bank rescue and fiscal austerity. The strike paralyzed much of Ecuador, shutting down most commerce, especially in major cities such as Quito, Guayaquil, and Cuenca, where banks were already closed because of a government-mandated bank holiday to avoid a run on them. The CMS and student groups and indigenous and peasants affiliated with the rural social security agency, organized by the Popular Front, also struck. Indigenous organizations blocked roads in the highlands and Amazonia.[41] The Patriotic Front promised more mobilization, including a campaign of civil disobedience, to be followed by a "popular uprising" (*Latin America Weekly Reports* 16 March 1999).

The government responded by declaring a 60-day state of emergency and calling out the army and police to maintain order.[42] By the second day, up to 324 protestors had been detained nationwide. This "maximum expression" of political exclusion in a democratic polity radicalized protestors. The Patriotic Front, the "maximum expression" of popular sector collective power, which coordinated the CONAIE, CMS, FUT, and still striking teachers organized by the Popular Front, called a national strike for the week of 15 March to force Mahuad to back down.[43]

---

[41] On 12 March CONAIE convoked local community organizations and the National Assembly for 15 March to define "mandates and actions for the next *Indigenous Uprising*" (emphasis in the original, CONAIE 12 March 1999). On 15 March CONAIE issued a press release in which it "informed the nation of the initiation of an Uprising of Indigenous Nations and Peoples' against the government's measures. *This action is indefinite and decreed by the Indigenous Peoples' and Nations to confront the state of Social and Economic upheaval caused by President Jamil Mahuad, Jaime Nesbot, and the big bankers*" (emphasis in the original, CONAIE press release 15 March 1999). Demands included revocation of the state of emergency, revocation of economic measures, immediate restitution of funds transferred to the banking sector, liquidation of bankrupt banks and criminal penalties for mismanagement of citizen funds, removal of pending bills in Congress and insurance that all legislative initiatives involve consensual civil society participation. The press release concluded: "CONAIE invites all sectors of civil society, *all the people to rise up*, to join in these expressions of *indignation*, and protest by blocking roads, striking pots and pans, lights out for ten minutes at 7 pm, wearing black, convocating on street corners, to sing and chant their indignation, call radios, television stations, and periodicals, etc."

[42] Associated Press 12 March 1999; *Washington Post* 11 March 1999; Inter Press Service 12 March 1999.

[43] Inter Press Service 18 March 1999; Associated Press 12 March 1999; Agence France Presse 19 March 1999.

On Monday 15 March, desperate, fed-up, and angry taxi drivers across the nation struck for two days, protesting a 100-percent increase in gasoline prices. Oil workers struck against privatization. About a million indigenous blocked roads in 10 provinces in the highlands and 6 in Amazonia to disrupt food supplies to the cities (Agence France Presse 17 March 1999; Bretón 2003: 205). Residents from poor neighborhoods in Quito and Guayaquil clashed with police and looted (Inter Press Service 18 March 1999).

The feelings of rage, desperation, and frustration against policies that deepened people's misery and motivated them to mobilize are captured in the following quotes. Taxi drivers protesting bank closings and sharp gas price increases exclaimed to the press, "We can't live anymore. The government wants to kill us" (Associated Press 15 March 1999). "It's not profitable to run a taxi anymore. It costs more to fill up the tank than we can possibly make in a day" (*National Post*, Canada, 16 March 1999, C11). "This is not about politics. This is about being able to make a living, and we are not backing down until the government rescinds these measures, which are crippling the middle class and the poor" (*New York Times* 16 March 1999). Similar sentiments reverberated in other social sectors. A housewife angrily stated, "I don't trust the banks and I don't trust the government" (*National Post*, Canada, 16 March 1999, C11). A mechanic plaintively explained, "I took everything out, every last cent [the account had less than $200 and was not subject to withdrawal restrictions]. I have no confidence in any of the banks ... since no one can guarantee to me they won't collapse (*New York Times* 16 March 1999). A union technician for the state oil company (who earned $400 a month) railed against government free-market zealots "who want to sell out our country and let us all starve ... We don't want any part of [the U.S.-supported economic] system. Before we let [Mahuad] sell our lives to foreigners, we'll cause total chaos here – we'll close this country down" (*The Washington Post* 24 March 1999). A supervisor for the state oil company defiantly stated, "There is no way we are going to let the same [widespread privatizations] that happened in Chile and Argentina happen here. If they privatize and I get fired, what is a 46-year-old oil technician going to do for a living? Find another job? Doing what?" (*The Washington Post* 24 March 1999).

The sweeping, decidedly defensive, and reformist demands of CONAIE and participating organizations included repealing the economic measures announced on 8 March; immediate return to state coffers of moneys transferred to the private banking sector or confiscation of their assets if that were not possible; state intervention of insolvent banks; and legal proceedings against corrupt and criminal bankers (Inter Press Service 18 March 1999; CONAIE press release 15 March 1999; also see footnote 39). They also demanded lowering fuel prices, withdrawal of 10 bills in Congress, and a lifting of the state of emergency (Zamosc 2004: 139). Some of the more radical elements in the Frente Popular (especially the Movimiento Democrático Popular) called for the resignation, voluntary or otherwise, of the president (*Latin America Weekly Reports* 16 March 1999).

Issue framing stressed the common threat the government's sweeping neoliberal reform package posed to all Ecuadorians not of the socioeconomic elite. Protestors claimed neoliberalism favored an alliance of international economic interests and their domestic allies at their expense. Bank policy saved private financiers by sacrificing common folk; privatization, driven by international capital, thrust unemployment and hunger on the popular sectors and the indigenous. In short, neoliberal policies promoted starvation and misery while enriching foreign economic interests and domestic elites. Neoliberalism, the protest leadership stressed, had to be replaced with economic nationalism, the necessary foundation for policies favoring the popular sectors.[44]

Mahuad's government suffered a significant loss of political power between 8 and 15 March. First, the 60-day state of emergency (the maximum permissible repression in democratic Ecuador) failed to break up massive nationwide mobilization. Second, the president's party suddenly found itself in a minority in Congress. Its coalition partner, the Social Christian Party, abandoned it over tax policy (value-added tax increases added to the cost of products) and the bank freeze, which adversely affected commerce. Calls for the impeachment of the finance minister and others abounded.

Unable to bludgeon protestors into submission, the government opened negotiations with the core of the Patriotic Front: the CONAIE, nonindigenous sectors, and social movements affected by the bank holiday and associated measures (Bretón 2003: 205). It established a National Consensus-Building Commission (Mesa de Acuerdo Nacional) to deliberate socioeconomic policy. Immediate concessions were significant. They included an agreement to lower fuel prices increases to 39 percent, but not to prereform levels; making the freeze on bank deposits more flexible; withdrawal of the privatization bill; and consideration of opposition proposals for tax reforms (Inter Press Service 18 March 1999). The government also promised to lift the state of emergency and free protestors and leaders arrested without due process. In a separate agreement with CONAIE, the government promised to establish a fund for rural development, to allow CONAIE access to frozen bank funds ahead of schedule, eliminate surcharges on electric services not provided to indigenous communities, reorganize the Indian social development fund run by the World Bank; and control prices on essential foods (BBC Monitoring Latin America 21 March 1999).

In the midst of these struggles, international economic weakness, coupled with domestic economic crisis, generated the worst Ecuadorian economic depression since the 1930s. The livelihoods of the popular sector and middle classes suffered accordingly. In 1999 GDP and GDP per capita contracted a dramatic 9.5 percent and 11.2 percent, respectively. Official unemployment shot up to over 15 percent,

---

[44] Agence France Presse 16 March 1999; *New York Times* 21 March 1999: A3; *Washington Post* 24 March 1999.

and employment in the informal sector shot up to all time highs at close to 57 percent. Wage indexes plummeted as inflation picked up. Meanwhile, official Ecuadorian statistics showed that poverty had been increasing over the 1980s and 1990s, reaching 62.6 of the population in 1998 (82 percent in rural areas and 48.6 percent in urban areas) and shot up to 68 percent in 1999 (91 and 53 percent in rural and urban areas, respectively) (North 2004: 202) (and see Table 6.3).

Deepening economic exclusion, government duplicity, and backpedaling on the March agreements inflamed an enraged mobilized popular sector and indigenous masses.[45] Throughout April and June unrest simmered as public health workers, including doctors and teachers (many in the middle class) led by the Popular Front, struck over unpaid public sector salaries. In early July, after Mahuad raised gasoline prices 13 percent in line with currency devaluation, tempers boiled over. Issue framing was direct, simple, and underscored the popular sector's cognition of its political exclusion. They were outraged over the government's deafness to the country's social problems (Agence France Presse 7 July and 14 July 1999).

Over the next two weeks, challengers to neoliberalism once again unleashed the full weight of their collective power against a government that refused to take them seriously. One more time, indigenous social movements allied with class-based social groups (unions) and other social movements (informal sector). On 5 July 1999, in the midst of ongoing health workers' and teachers' protests, 50,000 bus and taxi drivers called a national strike. They demanded repeal of the price hike, a freeze on gas rates at the prehike level, and permission to raise fares. As the national strike got underway, CONAIE called an indigenous uprising (their fourth), paralyzing the highlands with roadblocks that caused food shortages in the cities. Disruption mounted as the indigenous protestors took over "cities, water treatment plants, power stations, and radio and television relay stations in several provinces of the Ecuadorian sierra" (Inter Press Service 16 July 1999). The FUT joined the struggle on 7 July when "hundreds of [its] workers [marched] on government headquarters to ask President Jamil Mahuad to roll back the gasoline price increases" (Agence France Presse 7 July 1999). Oil workers and the CMS (street vendors and small-scale banana producers) added their considerable numbers on 11 July.[46] Unlike in the March mobilization, indigenous organizations from the central and northern highlands staged a march on Quito (beginning 12 July) to force the president to negotiate in the very capital, the very center of political power in Ecuador. About 12,000 to 20,000 indigenous met in Quito for two days between 15 and 17 July (García-Serrano 2003: 206).

Reporters captured the anger and frustration of protesters against intolerable levels of economic and political exclusion and their determination to resist. In

[45] For more details on socioeconomic exclusion during the economic crisis, see North (2004: 202).
[46] Agence France Presse 12 July 1999; Inter Press Service 16 July 1999.

Table 6.3. *Ecuador: Economic and Social Indicators*

	1980	1990	1991	1992	1993	1994	1995	1996	1997	1998	1999	2000	2001	2002	2003	2004	2005	2006	2007[a]
GDP	4.8	3.2	5.0	3.0	2.2	4.4	3.0	2.3	3.9	1.0	-9.5	0.9	5.5	3.8	2.5	8.0	6.0	3.9	2.7
GDP/CAP		0.8	3.0	1.4	0.3	2.5	0.5	0.2	1.8	-0.9	-11.2	-0.1	-0.7	-2.0	-0.3	6.5	4.5	2.4	1.2
Income Distribution[b]																			
D1	2.1					1.5				2.3				1.8				1.3	
D2	3.0					3.5				3.5				3.4				2.5	
Q2	11.3					10.6				11.2				10.3				7.6	
Q3	15.5					15.8				15.1				15.2				11.9	
Q4	21.5					22.2				21.6				20.5				19.2	
D9	15.3					14.7				14.4				14.6				15.4	
D10	30.5					31.7				31.9				34.3				42.1	
Unemployment	5.7	6.1	8.5	8.9	8.3	7.1	6.9	10.4	9.2	11.5	15.1	14.1	10.4	8.6	9.8	11.0	10.7	10.1	9.8
Informal[c]		53.4	57.8	58.3	57.3	56.1	56.7	57.0	53.2	58.6		57.0	57.4	55.0	56.5	57.4			
Poverty																			
Total		62.1								56.2				49.0		51.2	48.3	43.0	
Urban																47.5	45.2	39.9	
Rural																58.5	54.5	49.0	
Average Wage Index[d]	88.3	65.4	68.4	74.2	83.5	90.9	100.0	105.4	103.0	98.9	90.7	*132.1*	*134.7*	*161.0*	*151.7*	*160.8*	*151.4*	*172.1*	
Minimum Wage Index[e]	209.8	72.8	63.4	72.8	84.4	100.0	100.0	109.7	105.8	98.3	87.7	*100.0*	*111.5*	*112.5*	*119.3*	*122.2*	*125.9*	*130.0*	*135.1*

[a] Estimated.

[b] D9 and D10 = richest quintile; D1 and D2 = poorest quintile. Data not reported for all years.

[c] Informal sector data reported only from 1990 to 2004 in constant format. Data not reported for all years.

[d] Average wage index between 1980 and 2000 based on 1995 = 100; 2000–2007 not reported by ECLAC. These figures based on 1990 = 100 and only for manufacturing in *Labor Outlook 2007*-ILO.

[e] Minimum wage index between 1980 and 1999 based on 1995 = 100; 2000–2007 based on 2000 = 100 (in italics).

Sources: Economic Commission for Latin America and the Caribbean, *Statistical Yearbook* (Santiago: ECLAC, 1980–2007) and *Economic Survey of Latin America* (Santiago: ECLAC, 1980–2007). Labor Statistics from International Labor Organization, Labor Overview: *Latin America and the Caribbean* (Lima: ILO, 1994–2007). For comparability of data, I have not filled in years these sources omitted with other sources, except in the case of the average wage index.

Quito, a worker declared, "I favor the strike because the government doesn't understand [our anger] any other way." Another worker defiantly stated, "We might have to walk, but it is not just for the government to raise gasoline prices because us poor people [then also] pay more for meat, milk and bread" (Agence France Presse 5 July 1999). A striking hospital worker poignantly echoed, "We can't work while we're hungry" (Agence France Presse, 7 July 1999). A determined oil union leader impugned the duplicitous president: "We will not work until Mahuad's government becomes sensitive to and pays attention to the suggestions from the country's different political and social groups. We [oil workers] want the government to freeze electric, telephone, water and household oil taxes for two years. We also hope the government will reject the 'recommendations' of the IMF" (Agence France Presse 12 July 1999).

Deepening economic hardship, political exclusion, and repression clearly motivated indigenous protestors as well. In reference to Mahuad's 14 July promise to freeze gasoline prices and create an Indigenous Nations' Development Fund, indigenous protestors who marched peacefully to Quito and were repressed by the army indignantly exclaimed: "Where is Mahuad's sensitivity? The president is used to lying to us. We won't believe his announcements until they take effect. He has not lifted the state of emergency which is a fundamental measure for any dialogues to begin" (Inter Press Service 16 July 1999).

Reporters from *The Globe and Mail* of Canada (6 August 1999) interviewed in their mountain villages indigenous peasants who participated in the demonstrations. An elderly peasant couple had marched to Quito because "It's tough here. It's difficult." Expressing his anger over steep electric rate hikes another indigenous peasant exclaimed, "A very tremendous robbery"; adding, "We Indians are not happy because children do not have what they need for school. We cannot buy books. They should not raise prices. The mestizos have always exploited us Indians, so the people feel they are going to explode." A woman who had marched two days to Quito summed up: "We are waking up from a long dream of being oppressed and enslaved. We allowed ourselves to be ordered around, and now we have realized we should act together. The police tried to stop us marching and the army as well. We never carry arms, our hands were empty, and in spite of that, they fired tear gas at us."

Reformist defensive demands against commodification dominated the protest agenda. In addition to rolling back gasoline price hikes, demonstrators wanted a two-year price freeze on electric, telephone, water, and cooking oil prices (Agence France Presse 12 July 1999). They insisted the government permanently withdraw the privatization law (Inter Press Service 16 July 1999); that it renegotiate the foreign debt on favorable terms to Ecuador (or declare a moratorium); and that it modernize state enterprises instead of privatizing them. Political demands included the impeachment of the ministers of finance, energy, defense, and interior. CONAIE, terminally frustrated with seeing the government ignore its petitions, also demanded Mahuad's resignation.[47]

Mahuad responded to this challenge as ever. He tried to suppress mobilization by imposing a state of emergency and called out the troops to restore order, especially in the countryside. The army also tried to stop marchers from entering the city – but the marchers found back roads. Repression resulted in at least two deaths and over 500 arrests, including those of 56 movement leaders (Inter Press Service 16 July 1999). However, as in March, the army was unable to squelch protest.

Mass mobilization and Mahuad's ritualistic and unsuccessful attempt to repress it further eroded his government's political power. Congress voted 64–26 to lift the state of emergency because repression only stiffened resistance. The military, however, supported the president (Agence France Presse 14 July 1999). Here were portents of dangerous rifts at the very heart of state power. Meanwhile, the president's erstwhile coalition partner, the Social Christian Party, self-servingly sensed an opportunity to press its own demands. Mostly it urged Mahuad to pursue more radical market solutions to Ecuador's economic problems. These included terminating subsidies for health care in state hospitals; cleaning up the banking system; reducing Ecuador's foreign debt burden by means of swaps, repurchase, or capitalization (read privatization); and the implementation of a new foreign exchange system. Ominously, in a sign of growing presidential isolation, some on the right also wanted Mahuad's resignation (*Latin America Weekly Reports* 20 July 1999: 326).

Beset on all sides and unable to suppress mobilization, Mahuad once again gave in and negotiated with the protestors. Twelve days after the strike began, he acquiesced to the transport workers' (and everybody else's) major demand by agreeing to roll back fuel price hikes. The next day his government reached an accord with CONAIE; it lifted the state of emergency (a precondition for negotiation set by CONAIE) and unfroze CONAIE bank accounts. In addition, the authorities promised to consider a more gradual approach to economic stabilization and austerity measures (especially regarding the price of electricity).[48] In a novel development, the government acquiesced to establish a dialogue mechanism that allowed CONAIE to monitor progress on the agreement with the state that had ended mobilization (García-Serrano 2003: 206, fn. 22).

Yet Ecuador's economic crisis had not yet reached bottom, and Mahuad's government desperately needed revenue to shore up its distressed fiscal position and to service its foreign debt. In the absence of new revenue (partially because of agreements struck to end the July mobilization) it financed the fiscal deficit

---

[47] Agence France Presse 14 July 1999; Inter Press Service 16 July 1999; *New York Times* 19 July 1999; *Latin American Weekly Reports* 20 July 1999: 326.
[48] *New York Times* 19 July 1999; *Latin America Weekly Reports* 20 July 1999: 326.

through inflation, which triggered steeper currency devaluation and sharp price increases for basic consumer goods (North 2004). Meanwhile, in a desperate attempt to shore up vanishing foreign investor confidence, in November 1999 Mahuad's administration unveiled a debt restructuring plan it had negotiated with the international financial sector. As usual, conditions included stark orthodox stabilization policies to generate forced savings and value-added tax increases to raise revenue with which to repay international creditors (*Latin American Weekly Reports* 16 November 1999).

The loose alliance of popular sector organizations under the umbrella of the Patriotic Front – CONAIE, the unions, the CMS, and associated social movements – interpreted these developments as yet another exercise in willful political exclusion by the government, a deliberate, arrogant, and offensive betrayal of hard-won agreements. It seemed impossible to get social questions on the political agenda through established institutions. Time and time again, presidents, political parties, and jurists reneged on agreements struck with social movements following protests.

Frustration with this pattern radicalized CONAIE. In its sixth National Assembly held in November 1999, CONAIE moved to break off dialogue with the government (García-Serrano 2003: 206). During the conclave, CONAIE reaffirmed long-standing ethnic and economic claims, as well as demands for Mahuad's resignation. CONAIE also concluded there was no reasonable way to work within the established order; it had to be changed. Thus it called for the dissolution of the three branches of government and their replacement with an alternative democratic system that was more direct and participatory (García-Serrano 2003: 206). This program pushed the envelope of reformism. CONAIE leaders argued it should be interpreted as a call for radical reform of the existing system to ensure the inclusion of popular sector and indigenous in the political process.

COANIE also developed a strategy to accomplish those goals. Building on the experience of 1997, it proposed the establishment of provincial popular assemblies and a national popular assembly in Quito to act as a shadow government. The assemblies would include delegates from the social organizations aggregated by the CMS and the Frente Popular and coordinated by the Patriotic Front. They also planned to march on Congress and take it over, as they had done in the uprising against Bucaram (García-Serrano 2003: 206).

As unrest roiled over the government's actions, a sharp devaluation of the currency incited the Frente Popular and the FUT to mobilize in Ecuador's three major cities: Guayaquil, Quito, and Cuenca on 6 January 2000. One-thousand protestors marched on the presidential palace demanding Mahuad's resignation and the dissolution of the three branches of government. The demonstrations failed to garner spontaneous support from CONAIE and the CMS, and hence were much smaller in size and impact than desired. Anticipating larger demonstrations, the government called a 60-day state of emergency (Agence France Presse 4 January 2000; Associated Press 6 January 2000).

The government's announcement on 9 January 2000 that Ecuador would adopt the U.S. dollar as the national currency precipitated matters. CONAIE mobilized 11 January, spearheading a massive upsurge in mobilization (García-Serrano 2003:206). Dollarization proved that "the government only listened to bankers and large agro-exporters who were calling for the measure" (Inter Press Service 11 January 2000). Indigenous streamed into Quito while public sector unions and informal sector workers joined in as the CMS and the Frente Popular rallied in support.[49]

On 11 January CONAIE and the Frente Popular set up a People's National Congress in Quito to develop an alternative political and economic blueprint for Ecuador and threatened to demonstrate until all three branches of the government resigned. The People's National Congress aggregated 21 Provincial Assemblies and innumerable community, parish, and neighborhood congresses. It was seen as the only means to reassert sovereignty over a political and economic class that threatened the Ecuadorian people with ruin and arrogantly dismissed years of determined mobilization against it. Thus CONAIE announced that it planned to take power in conjunction with other popular sector forces (CONAIE press release 16 January 2000). Meanwhile, using state of emergency powers, the government arrested leaders of the Frente Popular, CONAIE, and the FUT. Instead of dispersing, Indians rose up all over Ecuador and converged on Quito (Gerlach 2003: 163–66). The FUT, however, appeared crippled.

Protesters expressed their indignation, rage, frustration, and determination to challenge the government's economic policies, political exclusion, and repression to the international press. These expressions reflected a keen understanding of the need for unity against Mahuad's administration. In the coastal city of Porto Viejo, a leader of the National Peasant Council said peasants would maintain protests indefinitely alongside indigenous peoples "in addition to blocking highways, we will continue occupying government and municipal buildings nationwide" (Inter Press Service 20 January 2000). A protestor in Quito exclaimed, "This government must prioritize the country's monetary sovereignty and put aside the dollarization plan. [The government should] assist the productive sector, modernize state enterprises to be more efficient without privatization, reduce payments on the foreign debt, create an emergency fund to fight poverty and imprison all the bankers who pillaged the nation" (Inter Press Service 20 January 2000). Meanwhile, after deadly repression of mass demonstrations in Quito, an indigenous hunger striker declared: "I'm prepared to give my life; we're here to the end, to victory" (Agence France Presse 5 February 2001). A demonstrator from the Patriotic Front explained: "We feel that the struggle for the indigenous peoples is also that of all Ecuadorians and so we need to press our demands through this type

---

[49] See García (2003); North (2004); Collins (2004)

of mobilizations...Our main goal is to radicalize the protests against the government's economic measures and demand freedom for the 150 people detained around the country" (EFE News Service 7 February 2001; Agence France Presse 7 February 2001).

CONAIE and its popular sector allies – the CMS and the Frente Popular – won their immediate goal of ousting Mahuad on 21 January 2000, albeit in a manner that caused a crisis of Ecuadorian democracy. Convinced that nothing useful could be accomplished within the current institutions of Ecuadorian democracy, the dominant sector of CONAIE's leadership allied with 400 dissident officers of the Ecuadorian army (headed by Colonel Lucio Gutiérrez) and attempted a coup d'état. The military had erected protective cordons around Congress and the presidential palace. However, when protestors stormed Congress, the guard was under orders to let them break through, highlighting the ambivalence the high command felt toward their president.

Having taken Congress by force, CONAIE leaders and participating military under Colonel Gutiérrez established a Government of National Salvation (O'Conner 2003). CONAIE demanded the dissolution of the presidency, legislature, and judiciary and the establishment of a National People's Parliament along with provincial and district parliaments. They also demanded a "total change" from neoliberal economic policies to a "fair, responsible, environmentally sustainable economy that recognizes plurinationality and cultural diversity [and is] productive and democratic [and] directed toward human development; and democracy...under the principles of AMA KILLA, AMA LLULLA, AMA SHUA" (don't steal, don't lie, and don't be lazy) (North 2004: 190).[50] Colonel Gutiérrez's demands were vaguer, referring to a "tenacious and implacable Pacific Junta against a new form of slavery to break the chains that bind us to the most appalling corruption. We are here to overthrow that disgraceful model in order to change the structures of the state and strengthen democratic institutions. We are acting peacefully in order to recover the self esteem, pride, and honesty of the Ecuadorian people, to check the corruption and impunity sponsored by the government" (North 2004: 190).

Protestors then stormed the presidential palace, where the protective cordon also allowed them to pass, forcing Mahauad to flee. The head of the Joint Chiefs of Staff, Carlos Mendoza, took over command of the military occupying Congress, raising the hopes of the CONAIE and the CMS that the rest of armed forces would support the coup. They felt betrayed when the following day General Mendoza negotiated the reestablishment of constitutional order with the

[50] Economic demands included restitution of state subsidies, capitalization of state credit agencies for poor farmers and peasants, and closing the U.S. Plan Colombia-related base at Manta. Indigenous-based demands included increasing the budget of state agencies that had been created to deal with indigenous affairs, funding for an irrigation system, resolution of pending land, natural resources, and water rights conflicts, and establishing various commissions to ensure that the government followed through on accords (Bretón 2003: 210–11).

congressional leadership, who agreed to depose Mahuad and let Vice President Gustavo Noboa finish the term (Gerlach 2003).

In sum, President Jamil Mahuad was forced out of office by an indigenous uprising allied with nonindigenous social organizations and leftist political parties in the CMS and the Frente Popular, with approximately 400 officers from lieutenants to colonels in support. They framed the crisis in terms of corrupt politicians in the pockets of national and international bankers who pushed neoliberal reforms that hurt all popular sectors, indigenous and nonindigenous. Grievances expressed by protestors echoed that framing, and leaders mobilized their people by mechanisms discussed earlier.[51]

Mobilization in the context of economic crisis also precipitated a sharp decline in Mahuad's political power, essential for his ouster. Conservatives and center-left politicians were unhappy with Mahuad, and the military suffered a split. Although the high command, in the end, sided with constitutional order, they too wanted him out (as evidenced by the fact that that the protective cordons around the Congress and the presidential palace let the protestors though). He had become the major polarizing factor in the protests. Forcing him out might restore order without a bloodbath. After all, the protestors and their military allies were not armed and were not calling for a violent revolutionary uprising.[52]

The Government of National Salvation lasted barely 24 hours. CONAIE, the CMS, the Frente Popular, and their handful of military allies failed to generate support from broader society, i.e., middle classes and business sectors, the political establishment, or, most important, from the military high command. By most accounts, intense pressure from international sources convinced General Mendoza to resign and hand over government to Vice President Noboa and continue constitutional succession. The U.S. government, the Organization of American States, and international financial institutions made it clear to the generals (who had demanded Mahuad's resignation) that they would be cut off from the loans Ecuador needed (North 2004; Zamosc 2007).

Aftermath

Mahuad's ouster and the short-lived coup d'état marked the end of Ecuador's protracted episode of anti-neoliberal contention. After his ouster, popular sector outrage and frustration found electoral options to challenge neoliberalism. The political trajectory of elected presidents that followed differed markedly from those of traditional Ecuadorian politicians and political parties. They were clearly identified with newer political movements that advocated economic nationalism

---

[51] For a similar argument, see North (2004: 200).
[52] General Mendoza claimed he accepted leadership of the Government of National Salvation to return political control to the Congress and Vice President Noboa without precipitating a bloodbath (North 2004).

and that ran on platforms pledged to address popular sector demands neglected during the past 20 years. They offered a better hope for political renewal.[53] Even so, the next six years were, sadly, as turbulent as ever and marred by the same frustrating policy reversals practiced in the recent past. This occurred with the appointed caretaker government of Gustavo Noboa, Mahuad's vice president, and, most galling, that of Lucio Gutiérrez elected as a professed anti-neoliberal reformer. It was not until the election of Rafael Correa in 2006, a fresh figure on the political scene, that Ecuador finally found a president committed to reforming neoliberalism.

After the putschist adventure and Mahuad's ouster, Congress nominated former Vice President Gustavo Noboa (2000–2), who was cut from the same ideological cloth as Mahuad, to be president. With congressional consent, the new government approved the dollarization plan, fiscal adjustment, and an accelerated privatization plan in February 2000 (North 2004). Continuing with the pattern established in the previous period, CONAIE and the FUT strenuously protested the measures. Although they could not thwart dollarization, the government raised the minimum wage (Europa World Encyclopedia 2007: 1593).[54]

The last hurrah for concerted CONAIE-led popular sector anti-neoliberal mobilization came in February 2001 against government-mandated increases in the price of energy (natural gas for domestic consumption, gasoline, and public transportation fares) (Bretón 2003: 207). Protests and work stoppages lasted for 15 days. One set of demands focused on social and economic grievances of the Ecuadorian poor in general. These included restitution of energy subsidies, capitalization of state agencies that gave credit to poor farmers and peasants, and closure of the U.S. Plan Colombia-related base at Manta. A second set of demands emanated from specific welfare grievances of the indigenous. These included increasing the budget of newly created indigenous affairs state agencies, funding for an irrigation system, resolution of pending conflicts over land, natural resources, and water rights, and establishing commissions to ensure that the government followed through on accords. (Bretón 2003: 210–11).

This mobilization had some success. In March 2001, the government and indigenous organizations renewed negotiations. By September the government compromised on five demands: the cost of fuels, the cost of public transportation, capitalization of the Banco Nacional de Fomento to service peasants and poor farmers, support for population that had emigrated from Ecuador, and diplomatic opposition to Plan Colombia. To the indigenous the government offered a process to resolve land conflicts and the establishment of an irrigation fund (Bretón 2003: 211).

[53] For electoral change see Tables 6.1 and 6.2.
[54] Noboa's lack of a policy coalition in Congress caused him to attempt labor code reform, privatization, and reform of the petroleum sector by decree. Popular sectors and CONAIE mobilized, but CONAIE, especially, had difficulty generating massive participation (Europa World Encyclopedia 2007: 1593).

The biggest disappointment, however, was yet to come. In October 2002, with support from the popular sectors and the indigenous, Colonel Lucio Gutiérrez (2002–5), who had participated in the 2000 Indian uprising and coup d'état, was elected as a progressive, corruption-fighting populist with 59 percent of the vote at the head of a newly formed political party, the Partido Sociedad Partiótica. He invited Pachakutik to join the government along with CONAIE, assuring them important government posts. Thus the new government politically included representatives of the indigenous and the popular sectors (Wolff 2007).

However, once in office in January 2003, he turned on his mandate, announced negotiation over foreign debt repayment with the IMF, and proposed an economic stabilization and structural adjustment program. It included a freeze on public sector wages and fuel and electricity price hikes (35 and 10 percent, respectively). Later in the year, the administration backed privatization of the state oil company and significant civil service labor code reforms (Europa World Encyclopedia 2007: 1593).

This turnaround, as one might expect, generated strikes from public sector workers (including teachers) and protests from numerous organizations, including the FUT that roiled over the year and beyond. CONAIE also mobilized. However, it lost its capacity to lead. It no longer secured massive support from the communities and could not coordinate contentious action with other social movement organizations.

The main reason for CONAIE's sudden weakness was its involvement in the government, which brought to the fore problems that began with its participation in the January 2000 coup d'état attempt. First, it generated significant tensions and conflicts among the leadership of the various confederations (and within them) that formed CONAIE. They squabbled over strategy, tactics, and government posts. Gutiérrez skillfully exploited these cleavages and manipulated organizations to his purposes. Second, indigenous communities, the core of successful mobilization, viewed their national directorship's incursion into politics with suspicion and were reluctant to follow where they led. The astute Gutiérrez also provided job relief to Indian communities (*picos y palas* [picks and shovels]). Third, unions, CMS social organizations, and citizens in general believed that CONAIE had lost its capacity to represent Ecuadorian society; instead, it had become a narrow indigenist interest group. Fourth, the economy had begun to recover. Stabilization policies were not as severe as in the past, and the government compensated with social policy (Collins 2004; Wolff 2007; Zamosc 2007).

Thus, while protests, demonstrations, and strikes plagued Guitiérrez's government, these were not the primary force behind his resignation in April 2005 because they could not muster the collective power they possessed in the late 1990s. It was the government's own political weakness and a confluence of progressive and conservative opposition parties that brought him down. As usual in Ecuador, Gutiérrez lacked a working congressional policy coalition. Once he embraced neoliberal economic policies, small leftist parties abandoned him and joined other center-left parties in opposition. The conservative Social Christian Party gave him contingent support on specific policies but opposed him when it was to their advantage. In the end, a struggle over Supreme Court appointments cost Gutiérrez the presidency when he tried to put his own nominees in by decree over Congress' preferences. Fearing a Fujimori-style self-coup, congressional parties, supported by street protests, forced his resignation (Europa World Encyclopedia 2007: 1594; Wolff 2007; Zamosc 2007).

The volatile caretaker government of Vice President Alfredo Palacios (2005–6) tried to address some of the economic, social, and political issues that created such discontent among subordinate social groups. Although it did not have much success, it catapulted economy minister Rafael Correa into the public limelight. He was an unusual independent technocrat who believed in the mixed economy and advocated socioeconomic rights and political inclusion for the popular sectors and middle classes instead of neoliberalism (Europa World Encyclopedia 2007: 1594–95).

Rafael Correa ran for president in October–November 2006 and won with 56.7 percent of the vote against a conservative candidate in second-round balloting. His campaign pledged to deliver a referendum on a Constituent Assembly that would have the power to dissolve the Congress, the Supreme Court, and to rewrite the constitution. This was also a strategy to overcome his weakness in Congress and therefore thwart conservative parties' traditional ability to veto progressive legislation. Furthermore, his campaign stressed a Correa government would sever ties with the IMF and the World Bank and reject a free trade agreement with the United States in favor of strengthening ties with Latin American trading partners. Correa also proposed to renegotiate international company contracts with the state oil firm and to invest increased revenue in Ecuador's social sector (Europa World Encyclopedia 2007: 1595). This platform clearly reflected policy trends and influences from Venezuela and Bolivia.

During his first year and half in office, Correa has followed through on many of these pledges. His government has also kept a high profile with its nationalist economic agenda. Although it has not actually severed ties with the IMF, it threatens such action constantly; it also asked the World Bank representative to leave the country and cancelled an investments treaty with the United States. More important, Correa's administration is working diligently to restructure the country's foreign debt payments to generate revenue for domestic spending. Correa's boldest move has been to become a founding member of a South American development bank created in November 2007 that has no U.S., IMF, or World Bank involvement. Spearheaded by Venezuela, in addition to Ecuador, the Banco del Sur includes Argentina, Bolivia, Brazil, Paraguay, and Uruguay.[55] Moreover,

---

[55] Associated Press 8 October 2007 and 1 February 2007; BBC Monitoring International Reports 23 February 2007 and 8 May 2007; Lucien Chauvin, "Ecuador Plays the Markets," *Latin Finance* 1 July 2007; *The Banker* 1 October 2007.

reaching out to the Middle East, Ecuador has rejoined OPEC and diversified investment sources by partnering with Venezuela, Iran, and China (Conaghan 2008:56).

Correa's administration has also moved forward with nationalist development plans. In 2007, for the first time in 25 years, Ecuador released a comprehensive national development plan. Correa signaled his commitment to business regulation by hiking taxes on foreign oil companies. Like Venezuela, Ecuador restructured royalties to generate more revenues, increasing windfall profits from 50 to 99 percent (Conaghan 2008: 55; Seelke 2008). In response to the public's perception that neoliberal governments had protected banks over people during the financial meltdown of the late 1990s, Congress also passed a bank reform. It targeted usurious interest rates, especially for small loans, among many other unstable features of the banking sector.[56] His government is also considering an agrarian reform directed at the distribution of abandoned, idle, fallow, and "improperly farmed" land. It would not touch productive land, environmental reserves, or "efficient" farmers. Protection for domestic industry, creating jobs, and redistributing income are also on the agenda of the Correa administration's economic program.[57]

On the basis of revenues from windfall oil profits, Correa made a show of keeping his promises to a variety of constituencies by issuing a series of executive decrees on social policy. For example, Correa raised public sector salaries and reestablished subsidies for fuel prices. In addition, Correa

doubled the regular welfare payments to poor households from US$15 to US$30 a month, a move that benefited nearly a tenth of all Ecuadorians. Correa also doubled the amount available for individual housing loans to $3,600. The poor got another boost when Correa enacted subsidies that halved the price of electricity for low wage consumers. A variety of other programs expanded credit to micobusinesses, youth, and women . . . From January to July 2007, Correa dispensed $215 million by declaring emergencies in ten sectors, ranging from education and health to the prison system. Emergency road construction, assigned to the army corps of engineers, has been a boon to the military, helping to strengthen ties between Correa and the armed forces. (Conaghan 2008: 55)

In tandem with these measures, Correa launched a series of substantive and symbolic administrative reforms to build support for his project among heretofore excluded constituencies. The Secretariat of Peoples, Social Movements, and Citizen Participation coordinates programs for social movements and indigenous communities. The new National Secretariat of the Migrant emphasizes Correa's concern for the troubles of Ecuadorians living abroad. He renamed the Welfare Ministry the Ministry of Economic and Social Inclusion to emphasize his administration's commitment to citizen rights. To counteract the powerful

---

[56] The Congress significantly modified the president's bill (*The Banker* 1 October 2007).
[57] BBC Monitoring International Reports 23 February 2007; Agence France Presse 17 January 2007; *The Banker* 1 October 2007.

municipal political machine of Guayaquil Mayor, and arch rival, Jaime Nesbot, Correa established a new Ministry of the Littoral. It coordinates the operations of all central government ministries in Guayaquil – Ecuador's largest city and its commercial and financial center – and President Correa has an office there that he uses frequently (Conaghan 2008: 55).

Correa also kept his campaign promise to convene a constituent assembly capable of assuming full legislative power, a key component of his reform project. It was his bid to bypass the institutions that had destroyed former presidencies, to recast Ecuadorian politics, and to consolidate the necessary power to push a policy agenda for planning and socialization. The process unfolded swiftly and successfully in three phases between April 2007 and September 2008.

After taking office in January 2007, Correa immediately organized a referendum to convene a constituent assembly for 15 April 2007. The political opposition in Congress and among Supreme Court justices maneuvered to derail the process. Although Correa lacked strong backing in Congress, he relied on supportive mass demonstrations to ensure the referendum took place. It passed by an overwhelming majority – 82 percent of voters approved (Ribando Seelke 2008).[58]

Voting for constituent assembly seats was scheduled for 30 September 2007, and in the intervening months the opposition resorted to more shenanigans to derail the process, especially because the April referendum vested the Constituent Assembly with the power to dissolve Congress. They were unsuccessful, and on 30 September Correa delegates, running under the newly formed Alianza País Party, swept the voting, garnering 80 of 130 constituent assembly seats. The Constituent Assembly convened on 29 November, immediately dissolved the Congress, and assumed legislative functions, sweeping away entrenched traditional "corrupt" politicians and crafting a constitution that supported a nationalist economic program (Conaghan 2008; Machado Puertas 2008; Ribando Seelke 2008).

On 28 September 2008, Ecuadorians approved the new constitution with 64 percent voting for it to 28 percent against.[59] The new constitution strengthens the presidency and permits increased state control over the economy. It allows presidents to run for a second term, which the previous constitution prohibited, thus paving the way for Correa's reelection. It also enables the presidency to stack courts, dissolve Congress, control monetary policy, and, although private property is protected, the executive gains greater powers to expropriate (Serrano and Tamayo 2008).[60] The constitution responds to the planning and socialization preferences of the movements and political forces that challenged

---

[58] Europa World Book 2007; Simon Romero, "Ecuador Appears Likely to Rewrite Constitution, *New York Times* 16 April 2007; and *Turkish Daily News* 2 October 2007.

[59] Seven percent of the ballots were invalid and 0.7 percent left blank, according to the Supreme Electoral Tribunal.

[60] John Lyons, *Wall Street Journal* 27 September 2008; Simon Romero, *The New York Times* 29 September 2008.

neoliberalism. The state reserves the right to administer, regulate, control, and manage "strategic sectors of the economy, such as energy, telecommunications, non-renewable natural resources, transportation, and refining of hydrocarbons, biodiversity, genetic heritage, and water" (Serrano and Tamayo 2008: 2). The constitution ends the agreement that allowed the United States to operate military bases in Manta. It promotes agrarian reform (especially of fallow and under-utilized land), and reestablishes public sector investment in health care, education, housing, and water supply (Serrano and Tamayo 2008). Although not a supporter of dollarization, after the referendum Correa declared that the dollar would remain Ecuador's currency (Diario La Hora 9 October 2008). Last but not least, the constitution makes Quichua Ecuador's second official language; it grants equality to all regardless of race, creed, gender, or sexual orientation; and it is much more liberal with respect to reproductive rights in general. General elections are expected in December 2009.

In conclusion, the fact that a president stayed true to the main outlines of his campaign platform has earned Correa consistently high approval ratings by erstwhile discontented masses, even though actual policies so far have not been earth-shattering departures from the past. Instead of bringing governments down, for the most part Correa turned popular sector mobilization that helped to elect him into a source of support against obstructionist traditional socioeconomic elites defending their privileges. Localized contentious action continues, especially in the oil sector. In some oil fields, communities protest and demonstrate against international corporations whom they accuse of falling short on contractual obligations to them. A commitment to political and socioeconomic inclusion within the confines of a capitalist domestic and international economy has changed the character of mobilization (it is no longer anti-neoliberal) and, for now, calmed the fires of mass mobilization. It remains to be seen what policies Correa and Congress actually craft, given their technically sweeping powers and how opposition develops.

7

Venezuela

Venezuela's episode of anti-neoliberal contention, which spanned two distinct waves, began in February 1989 during the second presidency of Carlos Andrés Pérez and ended with the election of Hugo Chávez in December 1998. However, the characteristics of contentious politics in this case were different. In the previous cases, persistent political and economic exclusion in the construction of contemporary market society created new popular sector organizations – or radicalized existing ones – that patiently strengthened associational power and built collective power by coordinating mobilization and protest with other emerging or existing organizations. In Venezuela, unlike Bolivia and Ecuador, the principal labor confederation never sustained leadership or coordination of mass anti-neoliberal mobilization, although it called several general strikes at crucial moments. Neither did factions of the established labor movement break away to develop a strategy of contentious and electoral politics based on the organization and coordination of excluded popular sector groups as occurred in Argentina.

Instead, nearly constant anti-neoliberal contention involved highly decentralized and uncoordinated groups. Anti-neoliberal protests, strikes, marches, demonstrations, and violent disturbances of varying magnitudes (some affecting much or all of the country) occurred almost daily. Most were sharp, short-lived actions. Participants included state employees, public sector industrial unions, transport workers, community associations and activists, students, teachers, professors, and doctors; thus spanning popular sector and middle-class social groups. Their demands usually involved satisfaction of immediate material interests threatened by free-market economic reforms, which the state mollified with real or promised concessions, frequently of small magnitude. Within this pattern, anti-neoliberal mobilization brought significant associational power to bear when large public sector unions, such as state employees, teachers, and doctors, protested.

Despite the lack of overarching organization and strategic purpose, surges in contentious politics had powerful effects. Daily protests of varying magnitude, punctuated by general strikes, were ever-present indicators of widespread dissatisfaction with public policy and the party system that dominated it. It emboldened military putschists and engendered new political parties and alignments, including Hugo Chávez's in 1997 and 1998. Indeed, in the midst of deepening economic crisis, Chávez, a charismatic leader of the February 1992 coup attempt, won the December 1998 presidential elections, thus ending Venezuela's episode of anti-neoliberal contention.

Why did Venezuela follow this different pattern? Venezuela is most similar to Argentina: largely urban, with a centralized organized labor movement integrated into a successful labor party in which it traditionally had a lot of influence.[1] However, as will be seen, it differed from Argentina on three critical dimensions. The first two strongly inhibited the formation of a breakaway confederation. First, the principal labor confederation was more inclusive of dissident factions. Second, although the president was of the labor party, he had less power than Menem because he did not dominate it. The labor party, which had a strong plurality in Congress, resisted the president's efforts to exclude it from policy making to the point where it openly opposed him. Hence, across the spectrum, unions believed they could negotiate with the government. Third, with two bloody failed coup d'état attempts in 1992, Venezuela had much higher levels of political violence than Argentina. This caused the labor party and the labor confederation to suspend hostile opposition for fear of destroying the democratic regime their existence depended on.

National Populism, Inclusion, and Crisis

Oil has dominated Venezuela's political economy since the 1920s. As the oil sector expanded with an influx of foreign direct investment, it provided an abundance of foreign exchange to fund national populism beginning in the mid-1940s. The state "sowed the oil," under the explicit assumption, as early as 1946 and until 1989, that there was something for everyone (Thorp and Durand 1997: 229–30).[2] It did so under authoritarian and military governments alike. With the income from petroleum, the state promoted import substitution industrialization providing easy credit and tariff protection. It built infrastructure, basic industries in iron and steel, hydroelectric power, petrochemicals, and aluminum, and ran telecommunications and air transport. Investment increased in social policy, such as public education and health services (including clean water and sanitation), housing, and transportation, as did pensions and worker-friendly labor rights. As everywhere under national populism, the state was a major employer (Gómez-Calcaño 1998: 214–15). Price controls and subsidies to basic food items, cooking

---

[1] Also, like Argentina, it lacks a significant indigenous population that could be mobilized on the basis of identity and socioeconomic exclusion.

[2] In 1946, the government created the Venezuelan Development Corporation (Corporación Venezolana de Fomento, CVF), a state investment and holding agency, to plan and fund industrialization. Under President Hugo Chávez (1998–present) the principle of sowing the oil has returned, along with a new oil boom.

oil, and, especially, fuel (gasoline) and transportation supplemented monetary income and had their greatest impact on the popular sectors. With low inflation, real incomes rose.

Venezuela, a founding member of OPEC in 1960, received generous influxes of foreign currency when international oil prices skyrocketed in the 1970s, augmented by the nationalization, with compensation, of foreign oil companies (Sigmund 1980). During this period the public sector expanded rapidly as the state boosted investment in basic industry, spent freely on social services (especially in health and education), and public sector employment swelled. Under these conditions, "the popular sectors of Venezuelan society, especially the new urban majority of the population, expected continued upward social mobility. A 'modern' integrated society appeared possible in the not too distant future" (Lander 2005: 26). Social harmony prevailed because the economic and social inclusion of the popular sectors did not threaten middle and upper classes. Oil made it possible for the state to increase spending and provide good public services and jobs without taxing the wealthy (Buxton 2003: 114–15).[3]

These conditions supported the consolidation of Venezuelan democracy after 1958. In that year, an agreement among the main political parties, the military, and business sectors – known as the Pact of Punto Fijo – cemented the underlying political understandings that underpinned Venezuelan democracy into the 1980s. The major political parties, Acción Democrática, COPEI (Comité de Organización Política Electoral Independiente; Committee for the Organization of Independent Electoral Politics), and the Unión Republicana Democrática (URD; Republican Democratic Union), pledged to respect each other's right to compete for political power and permitted them to isolate radical leftists (especially communists) and the extreme right, which had just been defeated with the ouster of Marcos Pérez Jiménez's 10-year dictatorship. Acción Democrática, a reformist populist political party formed in the 1930s, controlled most of organized labor and dominated elections. COPEI was a center-right Christian Democratic party originally created to counteract Acción Democrática.[4] Third-place URD was a middle-class centrist secular party that collapsed in the early 1970s. The Catholic Church accepted the pact because COPEI represented its interests. The military acquiesced to civilian oversight, especially congressional approval of promotions to higher ranks, in return for operational autonomy and ample funding for the armed forces. Business leaders recognized unions and regulation of the economy in return for the state's commitment to maintain macroeconomic stability and support for import substitution industrialization, mainly cheap and

---

[3] Public spending increased by 96.9 percent between 1973 and 1978 (Buxton 2003: 115).
[4] These two political parties had their origins in the 1930s. Acción Democrática headed the government during Venezuela's first brief three-year democratic interlude known as the Triennio. The Pacto Punto Fijo explicitly addressed the conditions that destabilized the Triennio and installed Pérez Jimenéz's dictatorship. For an early study of Acción Democrática, see Martz (1966).

abundant credit and protection (Hellinger 2006: 477).[5] The regime had the full support of the United States.

Acción Democrática and COPEI dominated electoral politics, and candidates from both parties became president. Smaller parties generated by the exclusion of the radical left also existed. These were, most notably, the Movement Toward Socialism (Movimiento al Socialismo, or MAS) and Causa R (Radical Cause). MAS attracted intellectuals, and Causa R organized shantytown dwellers in Caracas and workers in new state industries. Even smaller left parties included the Communist Party of Venezuela and the Electoral Movement of the People. These had even greater difficulty winning congressional seats (Ellner 1993; Hellinger 1991; López Maya 1997).

Under national populism, Acción Democrática was the principal vehicle for the inclusion of labor into the political system (Collier and Collier 1991). In its first short-lived administration (1946–48) Acción Democrática promoted peasant and urban labor organization and encouraged social mobilization (part of the reason for the coup against it). Union leaders affiliated with the party gained control of the Venezuelan Workers Confederation (Confederación de Trabajadores Venezolanos, or CTV), and Acción Democrática's Labor Bureau incorporated union leaders into the party. Until the end of the 1980s, "Unions provided [Acción Democrática] with political machines while channeling workers' loyalty and supporting [Acción Democrática's] development policies based on state intervention and import substitution industrialization. In return [Acción Democrática] administrations provided workers with social and labor benefits, and union leaders with political influence" (Murillo 2000: 140). Moreover, the CTV also spoke for the popular sectors in general, especially in earlier times (Collier and Collier 1991: 251–70). Its highly infrequent general strikes were politically devastating, such as the one that brought down the dictatorship of Pérez Jiménez in 1958 (Ellner 1993: 3–5).

The dominance of Acción Democrática labor leaders in the CTV secured organized labor's support for the party's political line. Strikes were far more frequent during the two COPEI administrations (Coppedge 1994: 34). General strikes never occurred between 1959 and 1989 because they were considered political weapons to destabilize political regimes, such as that of Pérez Jiménez. Bread-and-butter issues could always be negotiated or forced to the bargaining table by partial strikes. The CTV also exercised a high degree of centralized control over affiliates (Murillo 2001: 37). Partisan loyalty, in turn, depended on (1) significant labor influence over Acción Democrática policies and patronage through the party's Labor Bureau, by appointments to ministries (especially labor and social security), the election of labor deputies to Congress; and (2) national-populist policies that directly and indirectly protected and promoted labor.

---

[5] For more detailed accounts of Venezuelan political history and the founding of Venezuelan democracy, see Martz (1966); Martz and Myers (1977); Blank (1984); Bond (1977).

Although Acción Democrática union leaders dominated the CTV they did not exert exclusive control. Unlike the Argentine CGT, the CTV was more pluralistic and permitted partisan competition for control of unions. Thus more radical leftist parties, especially the MAS, the Movimiento Electoral del Pueblo, and the Communist Party, but also COPEI on the center right, controlled unions and had representation on its executive board (Murillo 2001: 33–38). Causa R, representing a "new unionism," gained control of the steel and textile unions in the state of Bolívar during the 1970s and 1980s. From that base, Causa R built a strong electoral machine (Ellner 1993: 53–162; Murillo 2001: 37). Causa R also organized informal workers and the unemployed in shantytowns and working-class districts, especially the sprawling Catia in Caracas, until the early 1980s.[6] In addition to the CTV, three minor union confederations appeared in the 1960s. One was largely communist – the Central United Venezuelan Workers' Confederation. The remaining two were controlled by COPEI (Ellner 1995; Urquijo-García 2000).

Economic crisis shattered the illusion of Venezuela as a wealthy country with an inclusive political economy that permitted upward social mobility and class harmony. The treasury had borrowed heavily against high oil prices to finance that perception. Their decline in the early 1980s precipitated Venezuela's entry into the Latin American debt crisis. The economy shrank by over four percent per year in 1982 and 1983; 28 February 1983, "Black Friday," became the symbol for the beginning of the end. On that day, having exhausted foreign exchange reserves, Venezuela implemented a maxidevaluation, ending the iconic foreign exchange regime of Bs. 4.3 to the U.S. dollar of the 1970s. In a multiple exchange rate system, the cheapest rate was seven to one, compounding debt servicing difficulties. The poverty rate climbed as unemployment rose because of the collapse in public spending, per capita income fell, the informal sector expanded, and public services and institutions deteriorated as did real wages. Inequality, as measured by the distribution of income, was accentuated (Buxton 2003: 116; Grindle 2000: 55; Roberts 2003a: 59–60). All the while, the fiscal deficit continued to grow and capital flight ravaged international reserves and investment (Frieden 1991; Maxfield 1989).

The economic crisis also corroded the system of clientelism that distributed oil income. Politicians from the two main parties (Acción Democrática and COPEI) stood at the epicenter of a vast patron–client network encompassing public contracts, public sector employment (from high bureaucratic office to elevator operators), and access to privileged information and subsidies. As long as oil income was plentiful, expanding corruption was tolerated because the spoils trickled down to everyone. But when international oil prices collapsed, the inherent inequalities of the spoils system became intolerable. The money no longer filtered down to the

---

[6] For example, Causa R organized the Popular Movement of Catia (Pro-Catia), known for strengthening community affairs.

middle classes and the popular sector. Only politicians and the rich, powerful, and well-born benefited (Buxton 2003: 116). A notorious example occurred with the creation of an agency to manage a preferential dollar exchange system adopted in the second half of the 1980s. It was formed to make foreign debt repayment less onerous for the private sector so that it could continue to perform its investment and employment functions. However, business interests essentially looted the fund, shipping large quantities of reserves to safe havens abroad in collusion with key politicians who received generous payoffs (Hillman 1994).

The Great Turnaround, Power, and Exclusion

Venezuelans elected Carlos Andrés Pérez president in December 1988 after campaigning on a traditional Acción Democrática populist platform and raising expectations for a return to the economic good times of the 1970s. During his first administration (1974–79) he had presided over an expansion of social spending and public sector investment along with generous severance pay rules for private sector workers and the growing number of state employees. Candidate Pérez played on those perceptions and promised gradual adjustment to the debt crisis (without outlining a specific program) to be followed by renewed prosperity for everyone (Hillman 1994: 118). Instead, barely two weeks after taking office on 2 February 1989, President Pérez announced a neoliberal economic austerity and structural adjustment program titled "The Great Turnaround."

President-elect Pérez faced a grave economic crisis. International reserves were all but exhausted, fiscal and balance-of-trade deficits ravaged the treasury, and repayment of substantial international debt obligations was near unmanageable. Low oil prices, the unavailability of commercial loans, and low taxation in Venezuela eliminated alternative sources of revenue. Given this situation, Pérez decided he had no alternative but to adopt an IMF-sponsored economic stabilization and adjustment program.[7]

On 16 February, Pérez announced the Great Turnaround to the general public. The program outlined a shock therapy approach to economic stabilization in the interest of international debt servicing and restoration of macroeconomic stability. It emphasized deep cuts in public spending (including wages and salaries), deregulation of prices on most private sector goods and services (including food and transport), eliminating price controls on public sector goods and services (including gasoline), deregulation of interest rates, devaluation of the national currency and introduction of a unitary foreign exchange rate, establishment of a value-added tax and a more effective tax system, and a restructuring of the foreign debt. Meanwhile, to ensure the subordination of politics to the market, the program called for privatization of banks, airlines, telecommunications, ports, and

---

[7] An IMF mission conducted a country study of Venezuela in 1987. The Great Turnaround program adopted its main recommendations (Lander 1996).

other activities. Trade liberalization was also recommended (Crisp 1998; Naím 1993). In short, the sweeping neoliberal reform program proposed establishing contemporary market society in Venezuela.

State power and the exclusion of most of the Venezuelan political and economic establishment from sensitive policy-making teams were central to the design and implementation of neoliberal reforms, which aimed at a fundamental restructuring of political relationships from the national populist era. As in the other cases, a close-knit group of free-market technocrats crafted them.[8] Similar to Carlos Menem (and around the same time), Pérez appointed a narrow group of free-market-oriented business people and technocrats to top cabinet positions. He also planned to push as many of the reforms as possible (mainly fiscal and monetary policy) through by decree (Naím 1993; Silva 1997: 182). This prevented Acción Democrática party leaders from obtaining expected cabinet postings, as was customary in Venezuelan politics. It was also a first step in restructuring the state to separate politics (political party leadership and their clients) from economic policy making (Lander 1996).

The popular sectors and middle classes (especially those employed by the state) understood the implications of the Great Turnaround only too well. They were to bear the brunt of economic adjustment. Instead of the relief they had voted for after seven years of economic hardship and growing misery, a sharp and permanent spike in economic exclusion loomed. The prices of most goods and services were to rise substantially and quickly while their incomes and working conditions were guaranteed to deteriorate rapidly and probably permanently.

That plunge, in fact, occurred, causing significant changes in the class situation of many Venezuelans (see Table 7.1). Although economic immiseration began in the 1980s with the debt crisis, as Kenneth Roberts (2003a: 59) argued, it "accelerated rapidly in the wake of structural adjustment policies at the end of the decade." He found that, by the mid-1990s, per-capita GDP had declined by 20 percent from its peak in the late 1970s to levels of the 1960s. Critical indicators for popular sector living standards fell even more rapidly. By the end of the 1990s, minimum wages were more than 60 percent lower than in the 1980s, public sector per-capita spending was 40 percent lower than in 1980. Especially noteworthy were declines of 40 percent in education, 70 percent in housing and urban development, 37 percent in health care, and 56 percent in social development and participation (República de Venezuela 1995: 40).[9] Spending cuts were especially sharp between the late 1980s and 1994.

Roberts (2003a: 59–60) shows how the cuts in wages and social spending correlated with rising poverty, a trend that spiked after 1988. The percentage of

---

[8] Many of the framers of the Great Turnaround had been associated with a working group established in the early 1980s called the Grupo Roraima, dedicated to finding a neoliberal solution to the crisis of national populism (Silva 1997: 182).

[9] For a detailed account of social policies during this early period of adjustment, see Gómez-Calcaño (1998).

Table 7.1. *Venezuela: Economic and Social Indicators*

	1980	1990	1991	1992	1993	1994	1995	1996	1997	1998	1999	2000	2001	2002	2003	2004	2005	2006	2007[a]
GDP	-1.2	7.0	10.5	7.0	-0.4	-3.7	5.9	-0.4	7.4	0.7	-5.8	3.8	3.5	-9.0	-9.3	18.3	10.3	10.3	8.4
GDP/CAP		4.4	7.1	3.6	-1.6	-4.8	1.3	-2.5	5.2	-1.3	-7.7	-1.0	3.5	-10.7	-14.6	16.2	8.4	8.5	6.6
Income Distribution[b]																			
D1	2.5	2.0				2.5			1.8		1.1			1.2				1.5	
D2	4.4	3.7				3.7			3.2		2.5			3.1				3.1	
Q2	13.2	11.1				10.5			9.7		8.2			10.0				9.4	
Q3	17.1	15.9				15.6			14.4		13.1			15.0				14.3	
Q4	24.9	22.8				21.3			21.4		20.7			22.5				21.9	
D9	16.0	16.2				15.0			16.8		16.6			17.0				16.4	
D10	21.8	28.4				31.4			32.8		37.8			31.3				33.4	
Unemployment	6.6	11.0	10.1	8.1	6.1	8.9	10.3	11.8	11.4	11.3	15.0	13.9	13.3	15.9	18.0	15.3	12.3	10.0	9.0
Informal[c]		38.8	38.3	37.4	38.4	44.8	46.9	47.7	48.1			50.6	49.2	51.8	53.8				
Poverty																			
Total	21.0			37.1		38.0			36.0					48.6		45.4	37.1	30.2	
Urban	19.5			35.8															
Rural	43.0			43.5		32.0			30.0										
Average Wage Index[d]	302.0	138.1	130.1	136.5	124.4	104.8	100.0	76.7	93.3	101.5	96.8	*100.0*	*106.9*	*95.1*	*78.4*	*78.6*	*80.7*	*84.8*	*85.8*
Minimum Wage Index[e]	209.8	72.8	63.4	72.8		84.4	100.0	109.7	105.8	98.3	87.7	*100.0*	*94.5*	*92.7*	*103.7*	*113.9*	*114.4*		

[a] Estimated.

[b] *D9* and *D10* = richest quintile; *D1* and *D2* = poorest quintile. Data not reported for all years.

[c] Informal sector data reported only from 1990 to 2003 in constant format. Data not reported for all years.

[d] Average wage index between 1980 and 2003 based on 1995 = 100; 2000–2007 based on 2000 = 100 (in italics).

[e] Minimum wage index between 1980 and 1999 based on 1995 = 100; 2000–2007 based on 2000 = 100 (in italics).

Sources: Economic Commission for Latin America and the Caribbean, *Statistical Yearbook* (Santiago: ECLAC, 1980–2007) and Economic Survey of Latin America (Santiago: ECLAC, 1980–2007). Labor Statistics from International Labor Organization, Labor Overview: *Latin America and the Caribbean* (Lima: ILO, 1994–2007). For comparability of data, I have not filled in missing years with other sources.

Venezuela

people living in poverty rose from 36 to 66 percent between 1984 and 1995, and those living in extreme poverty increased from 11 to 36 percent, more than tripling. In 1989, the year in which shock therapy was applied and GDP contracted by more than 10 percent, poverty levels jumped from 46 to 62 percent and the figure for those living in extreme poverty doubled from 14 to 30 percent. After the introduction of structural adjustment policies, poverty was no longer limited to a minority of the population who had yet to benefit from the sowing of the oil. It now affected a majority of the population that was systematically excluded from any real benefits of the socioeconomic model.[10]

Structural adjustment also accelerated changes in the employment structure. These revealed expanding economic exclusion from the fruits of the development model not only for the popular sectors but for growing numbers of the middle class as well. The migratory trend from the countryside to the cities that began in 1980 accelerated rapidly with the implementation of structural adjustment between 1989 and 1992 (CEPAL 2000: 26; Venezuela 2000: 4008). At that same time, formal sector employment in the private and public sectors was also contracting. Rural migrants and out-of-work urbanites swelled the ranks of the informal sector of employment from 34.5 percent in 1980 to over 50 percent in the late 1990s (Economist Intelligence Unit 2000: 16; Sunkel 1994: 155). Average wages in this sector were about 30 percent lower than in the formal sector. Meanwhile, urban unemployment more than doubled between 1980 and 1999, from 6.6 percent to 15.4 percent (CEPAL 2000).

From the "Caracazo" to Ignominious Exit

Following the announcement of a shock-therapy-style neoliberal reform package, President Pérez quickly implemented deep fiscal spending cuts, liberated price controls for most private sector goods and services, and decreed sharp price increases for most public sector goods and services. Given his presidential campaign, Venezuelans dubbed the Great Turnaround the Great Trick. Discontent roiled in the few days in between announcement and implementation.

Blatant political exclusion and the threat of certain economic hardship had immediate effect. The opening salvo in the wave of anti-neoliberal contention that followed, and that ended when Congress cut Pérez' presidency short by six months, was very different from that of the other cases.[11] It began with the "Caracazo," widespread spontaneous rioting and looting that erupted on 27 February 1989, quickly spread to other cities, and lasted for nearly a week. After

[10] The more conservative data from the UN Economic Commission for Latin America and the Caribbean (ECLAC) in Table 7.3 confirm the more than doubling of poverty rates in Venezuela.
[11] López Maya (1999a) argues that the cycle spanned to the election of Caldera. In keeping with the criteria established in Chapter 2 and applied to the other cases (that the ouster of presidents who support neoliberal reform generally marks the end of a cycle) I have settled for the end of Pérez's presidency.

initial inaction, the government suspended constitutional guarantees and sent 10,000 army troops into working-class neighborhoods and downtown to repress the looting. Somewhere between 246 and 1,500 persons lost their lives.[12] The riots began as angry protests against a 100-percent increase in gasoline prices and unscrupulous price-gouging bus drivers who illegally doubled fares (only 30 percent increases had been authorized). Inflamed protestors quickly turned their fury and frustration against small shopkeepers who had been hoarding goods in anticipation of price increases and sold them at sharp markups after the Great Turnaround freed prices. A long decline in policing over the 1980s – the front line of the state's coercive power – facilitated looting. Underpaid police forces in parts of Caracas had recently been on strike, demanding raises, and seemed uninterested in intervening and in some cases even organized looting (Hellinger 2006: 481). For example, a metropolitan police officer philosophically advised looters, "Just take a little so there'll be enough for everyone." To the reporter he said, "We [the police] are the people too." Another policeman explained, "It's impossible to take action. If I try to stop the looting and am forced to shoot my comrades will start shooting too and then this turns into a tragedy" (*El Nacional* 1 March 1989). After the Caracazo, the government established a curfew that lasted to early March and froze prices on some basic goods.

Statements to the press by rioters and looters link their motivation to the perceived effect of the neoliberal economic restructuring package after a decade of growing hardship; hunger lurked. Caracas residents in general blamed rising food prices and hoarding of food. A clerk from a downtown Caracas shop despaired, "We cannot stand this... We are already half-starving... The new rates condemn us to eat nothing" (The Associated Press 27 February 1989). One looter gruffly explained, "Everything but food can be in short supply...you don't play with the people's hunger." Another added pragmatically, "*Mi'ja*, what's a person to do? We have to eat" (*El Nacional* 1 March 1989). A third looter offered this justification, "We ran out of food and have to forage" (*El Nacional* 2 March 1989). An indignant neighborhood leader summed up the Caracazo this way: "It was about time something like this happened...People finally got fed up and came down from the hills to protest" (The Associated Press 28 February 1989).[13] As the army moved in, a resident observed angry crowds shouting at the soldiers, "We prefer to be killed by bullets than to die from starvation." Troops promptly fired on them and three fell (The Associated Press 1 March 1989). A middle-aged woman who had experienced the era of economic stability succinctly explained:

---

[12] For the Caracazo and the buildup to it, see López Maya (1999a); Briceño (1993); Kornblith (1998); Hillman (1994). The Caracazo was not completely unprecedented; riots over perceived government abuses, impunity, corruption, and violence had already occurred in outlying states; see Coronil and Skurski (1991).

[13] Many of Caracas' poor live in slums built on the hills surrounding the city's long east–west valley, with concentrations at each end, and with few or no services.

"Add it up – what it costs to buy cooking oil, to buy milk, to buy rice. The money people make isn't enough. Finally people just came down [the hills] to take the food because they were hungry" (*The Washington Post* 6 March 1989).

The Caracazo was also a sign of the profound indignation and frustration most Venezuelans felt at their political exclusion from the policy-making process and their declining faith in the political system's capacity to solve public problems equitably. For example, during the riots a desperate mother had cried, "I've got two little children and the country is paralyzed" (The Associated Press 1 March 1989). A looter explained, "This [the looting] is proof of the people's discontent with the government. It has forced many [economic] measures like these on us before . . . Something like this has to happen for them [the government] to notice us" (*El Nacional* 2 March 1989). An angry clerk offered, "You may not believe it, but there is a deep feeling of unbearable rage, social hate, and ill will provoked by the accumulation of so many aggressions [against the people] and no means of defense" (*El Nacional* 3 March 1989).

These expressions of discontent reveal that the popular sector rejected Venezuela's centralized political system controlled by the presidency, political party bosses, and their patron–client networks. In a time of collapsing public services, ordinary Venezuelans no longer benefited from a system in which they had no institutional channels to influence policy (Grindle 2000: 70–71). Even the CTV, which had once represented popular sector interests, was perceived to have lost that capacity, relying on its political ties to Acción Democrática to negotiate deals for a "labor aristocracy" (Ellner 1995). Indeed, the CTV initially acquiesced to the neoliberal program on the understanding that it would negoti-ate programs to soften the blow of fiscal retrenchment (Burgess 2004). Organized public opposition to the reform package appeared nonexistent, except perhaps from university students (McCaughan 2004: 65).

The floodgates to anti-neoliberal contentious politics opened after the Cara-cazo with some 5,000 protests recorded in the three years that followed (López Maya 1999b; Roberts 2003a: 61). However, the characteristics of this open-ing cycle of contention differed significantly from those of the preceding cases. The associational power and collective power brought to bear were cumula-tively weaker. The CTV managed only fleeting attempts to lead a cycle of anti-neoliberal contention, as the COB and the FUT had done in Bolivia and Ecuador. After a successful general strike in May 1989, a ginger effort to sustain con-tentious politics died as a consequence of escalating violence when two failed coups d'état threatened the democratic regime itself. Moreover, in contrast to Argentina, an alternative union movement did not split from the CTV and orga-nize associational and collective power. There was, however, plenty of uncoordi-nated contentious action by individual public sector unions, independent unions, and decentralized community-based organizations. In conjunction with a second CTV general strike in November 1991, constant protest emboldened military putschists.

The grievances expressed attest to the Polanyi-like defensive character of mobilization during this period. They focused on reinstating (or maintaining) protections from the market enshrined under national populism and threatened by the neoliberal reform program. In this sense, mobilization was decidedly reformist, not revolutionary or even putschist (the CTV had nothing to do with the military coup attempts). Demands overwhelmingly focused on protecting jobs and severance pay, work rules, wages and salaries, subsidies, and price controls (especially for gasoline, transportation, and food).

Escalating Anti-Neoliberal Contention

The CTV was the highest expression of worker associational power. That it had become the labor arm of Acción Democrática deeply influenced its response to President Pérez' neoliberal reform package. The CTV had grown accustomed to working through Acción Democrática to influence policy and to amass resources. Thus Pérez's overtures to bargain with the CTV consistently undermined its capacity to sustain a leadership role in anti-neoliberal contention. For example, following Acción Democrática's lead, immediately after the December 1989 presidential elections the CTV initially accepted Pérez's economic reform proposals on the understanding that the government would take measures to soften the blow for the popular sectors.

The Caracazo, however, severely challenged the CTV. It had always maintained that it represented the interests of the popular sector in general as well as those of union members.[14] But the Caracazo proved that over time the CTV had lost the capacity to channel the discontent of the popular sectors not represented by organized labor (Burgess 2004: 132; Ellner 1993: 102). These factors, sharpened by internal pressure and competition from minority leftist parties in the CTV, moved the CTV to action to reclaim its leadership role. Fearing the labor movement was about to escape CTV control, over March and April 1989 Acción Democrática union leaders in the CTV and in the party's Labor Bureau agreed to take a more autonomous, independent, critical, rebellious stance toward the party and the government (Burgess 2004: 133; Murillo 2001: 68).

The decision to stage a general strike in May 1989, first proposed at a conclave of all of the CTV's party factions called in early March, became final by unanimous vote in a special congress of the CTV held on 25 April (only the second special congress in its history). The call for a general strike was a momentous decision because the CTV had not staged one since January 1958 against the dictatorship of Pérez Jiménez. The general strike was considered a political weapon drawn

---

[14] Indeed, it had done so from the 1940s through, perhaps, the 1960s. For example, in the 1950s, during the Pérez Jiménez dictatorship, and while it was in exile, the CTV fought for the rights of the unemployed (Ellner 1995). Even as late as the early 1980s the CTV supported across-the-board wage increases and the enactment of a new labor code that extended their benefits to unorganized workers Ellner (1993: 102).

only against illegitimate governments, not for economic grievances. However, in the wake of the Caracazo, political exclusion in the decision-making process, emphasized by the refusal of either President Pérez or Acción Democrática's congressional bench to revise the economic program, contributed to the CTV's decision to mobilize.[15] Otherwise it would lose control of the labor movement and forfeit its claim to represent the popular sectors.

The CTV's demands focused on repeal of stringent austerity measures rather than a direct attack on the government itself. These included (1) a price freeze on basic services (transportation and electricity), food, and gasoline; (2) periodic wage increases indexed to inflation; (3) consumer legislation punishing merchandise hoarders; (4) adoption of a CTV-sponsored labor code bill; and (5) a moratorium on repayment of Venezuela's foreign debt (Ellner 1993: 83; *The Globe and Mail* 17 May 1989; Xinhua General Overseas News Service 18 May 1989).

In addition to flexing its associational power, the CTV brokered a temporary surge in collective power. During the 25 April special congress, it resolved to coordinate the strike with Venezuela's three significantly smaller labor confederations, one controlled by leftist parties and the other two dominated by COPEI. CTV executives also pledged to orchestrate a longer-term plan of action with them.

The CTV framed the events of 27 February to reclaim its role as spokesperson for all popular sectors. The "foreign-inspired" neoliberal program threatened to aggravate the steady erosion of general living conditions since 1983 that caused the Caracazo. It would intensify merchandise hoarding, unemployment, and price increases in gasoline, transport, food, and electricity (Ellner 1993: 82–83; *Financial Times* 27 April 1989; *The Globe and Mail* 17 May 1989). CTV President Juan José Delpino encapsulated that framing: "[T]he insanity would be to fail to respond to this economic package that has caused grave harm to the working class and to all the popular sectors."[16]

The expressed grievances of striking workers and protestors echoed that framing. During the general strike, angry demonstrators outside a McDonald's restaurant shouted, "Close it down! Down with the gringos!" (The Associated Press 18 May 1989). Frustrated court clerks striking over pay arrears indignantly exclaimed, "Never mind a pay raise . . . We just want the raise that was already promised us" (The Associated Press 2 May 1989).

The framing of this call to contentious politics underscored perceptions of political exclusion. Demanding a new direction to economic policy, CTV President Delpino argued the confederation had to take action to end its treatment "as a simple receptor of information – often partial – regarding policies already decided and negotiated" (Burgess 2004: 133). He added that "when a collectivity

---

[15] In a typical hard line statement on 18 May 1989 in a nationally televised speech President Pérez declared, "Our economic policy will continue to be developed with full firmness. This is the only path open to us" (Facts on File World News Digest 9 June 1989).

[16] *El Nacional* 22 April 1989, quoted in Burgess (2004: 133).

decides to carry out its demands in direct form, it is because the institutions that represent or defend it are not adequately fulfilling their function of channeling their demands" (Burgess 2004: 133). With near total adherence by CTV affiliates and the three smaller labor confederations (along with "dissuasive brigades" to ensure businesses remained closed), the peaceful general strike of 18 May 1989 was a huge success.[17] Economic activity ceased in industry, commerce, and agriculture across the country (United Press International 18 May 1989; Associated Press 18 May 1989).

However, the CTV was not ready to break with the government and sustain leadership of anti-neoliberal contention. Instead, its Acción Democrática-dominated leadership expected that the show of strength and its political symbolism would force the president and the party to negotiate. According to Ellner (1993: 83), "the general strike signaled a measured distancing of the labor movement from Acción Democrática and the government." It was not framed as an attack on the government. There were no demands for the resignation of the president or any of his ministers. Moreover, both the presidency and Acción Democrática's congressional bench declared their tolerance of the strike as a legitimate expression of labor's rights. The complicated relationship among the CTV, Acción Democrática's Labor Bureau and congressional bench, and a president from the same party kept the confederation from assuming sustained leadership of popular sector resistance to neoliberalism (Burgess 2004: 134–35). That would have required organizing "successive strikes [over] months, that is to say, an open war against the government."[18] They were not prepared to risk that.

Nevertheless, nine months later, in mid-February 1990, a dormant CTV mired in party politics roused itself sufficiently to organize strikes, marches, and demonstrations in eight major cities in protest of announced increases in gasoline prices.[19] According to Murillo (2001: 70), the need of Acción Democrática's CTV leadership to counteract mounting internal competition from leftist political parties heavily influenced this mobilization. In any event, it was not as successful as the May 1989 general strike. Fewer numbers turned out, and an outbreak of rioting and looting reminiscent of the Caracazo, but on a smaller scale, tarnished the event (Ellner 1993: 83; The Associated Press 21 February 1990). After this the CTV was content to allow Acción Democrática's Labor Bureau to represent it in legislative wrangling over reforms such as privatization.

---

[17] A month earlier, a civic strike [*paro cívico*] against the Great Turnaround and government corruption in Mérida was called by neighborhood associations, the state branch of the CTV, transport associations, students, professionals, and housewives (López Maya 1999a: 225).

[18] Delpino, quoted in Burgess (2004: 135). This was, of course, the strategy that the CTA, the COB, and the FUT adopted in Argentina, Bolivia, and Ecuador.

[19] High subsidies kept gasoline prices well below world prices (among the lowest in the world). Venezuelans believed low gasoline prices to be virtually an inalienable right and defended it fiercely.

The CTV's sporadic, and ultimately waning, forays into contentious politics did not mean public order prevailed the rest of the time. To achieve fiscal stabilization targets, President Pérez let public sector wages and benefits erode to inflation, and payment arrears accumulated. Public services also declined, especially in police protection, sanitation, health, education, and general infrastructure maintenance such as roads and water delivery. By the same token, the informal sector was growing rapidly and union membership was declining (Roberts 2003b). These conditions spurred mobilization by social groups not controlled or mollified by the CTV's successes at the negotiating table in defense of union privileges.

Decentralized, uncoordinated strikes, marches, demonstrations, and disturbances, in which each group protested for its own specific grievances, occurred almost daily. These events created a constant drumbeat of publicly expressed and increasingly violent discontent. They involved public sector unions, either given leave by the CTV to take independent action or that were not affiliated with the CTV. These included middle-class state employees, such as teachers at all educational levels, doctors, court employees, and transportation workers (some of whom were controlled by a small leftist labor confederation or by leftist political parties in the CTV).[20] Occasionally police forces would strike, and, significantly, petroleum workers, who had not struck in decades, began to protest. By contrast, unions operating in the private sector struck infrequently (López Maya 1999a: 224).[21] Polanyi-like defensive demands centered on wage adjustments, job security, and subsidies to cover price increases in transportation and other essential goods and services. Secondary and university students were also very active, as were highly decentralized territorially based community organizations. Contentious action by the latter usually erupted in poor neighborhoods and city districts. Protest involved road and street blockages, occupation of property, rioting, and looting (López Maya 1999a: 223; Roberts 2003a: 61–62). Over time, the frequency of violence (small-scale looting and rioting) rose (Ellner 1993: 84; López Maya and Lander 2005).

The major difference with the other cases was that these protests did not generate more coordinated efforts that built into larger waves of contention over time. Why did organizations and cooperation comparable to the CTA–Federación Tierra y Vivienda–Corriente Combativa Clasista coalition in Argentina, who framed and brokered such transformations, not emerge? First, the politically more inclusive nature of the CTV kept dissident factions from breaking away. Discontent with Acción Democrática benefited dissident leftist parties in internal CTV elections, and so they opted to struggle for influence within the

---

[20] Professional associations, such as those for doctors, medical technicians, university professors, some teachers unions, and court employees (including judges) were not in the CTV, neither were student federations or many community-based organizations (Ellner 1995: 141).

[21] Public sector workers rarely faced penalties for their work stoppages even when they were illegal, whereas private sector ones did (López Maya 1999a: 224).

confederation.[22] Second, larger leftist parties, such as MAS and Causa R, focused on national, state, and municipal elections to gain political power and used it to influence policy. Indeed, their electoral fortunes improved as discontent mounted over neoliberal policies and Acción Democrática's politics as usual stance. Given these leftist parties' posture in the labor movement, their elected political officials lacked significant incentive to coordinate community-based organizations and public sector unions (as Frepaso had done in Argentina) (Buxton 2001: 168–73). Third, with a (growing) voice in the CTV for non-Acción Democrática unions, and, as we shall see, with Acción Democrática in no mood to give the president a blank check, the chances of negotiating within the system were good. In other words, the political exclusion of labor in Venezuela was less stark than in Argentina. Nevertheless, competition between Acción Democrática and non-Acción Democrática unions encouraged their generally disjointed mobilization (Murillo 2001).

Thinking he could manipulate Acción Democrática and therefore continue to control popular sector mobilization by dividing it, President Pérez pushed neoliberal reforms. He persisted on economic stabilization and trade liberalization. These he could implement by decree (Carey and Shugart 1998; Crisp and Levine 1998). He also introduced bills in Congress for privatization, labor code reform (including reduction of generous severance pay clauses), social security reform; and tax and banking reform (Crisp and Levine 1998; Murillo 2001; Roberts 2003a).

However, President Pérez had significantly less political power in relation to the legislature than was the case in either Argentina or Bolivia. First, although Acción Democrática still possessed a strong plurality, his party had lost an absolute majority in Congress in the December 1988 national elections (see Tables 7.2 and 7.3). Party leaders were angry that he had gone outside the party for important ministerial appointments, robbing them of influence and patronage resources. Hence they opposed Pérez whenever they could in an escalating spiral. Second, Acción Democrática and COPEI did not grant Pérez extraordinary powers to solve economic problems. Third, in December 1989 Venezuela had its very first elections for governors and mayors in which left-wing political parties (MAS and Causa R) did well, as did COPEI. Causa R astonished the nation by winning the important governorship of Bolívar, its union stronghold. Acción Democrática barely won a majority of these elected positions (Grindle 2000: 88; Hellinger

---

[22] In 1991 Acción Democrática union leaders lost elections to leftist parties in local union elections, especially to Causa R but also to MEP and MAS (Murillo 2001: 70). MAS and MEP also increased the overall number of posts they held in the CTV administration between 1985 and 1995 (although in relative terms MEP lost strength while MAS gained) and the PCV won posts in 1990 and increased them again in 1995 (Urquijo-García 2000). The experience of the PCV and MAS's lack of success after breaking away from the CTV to form the Central United Venezuelan Workers' Confederation in the 1960s colored their calculations as well (Ellner 1995, 1993; Urquijo-García 2000).

Venezuela

Table 7.2. *Venezuela: Distribution of Seats in the Chamber of Deputies, 1988–2000*

Party	1988	1993	1998	2000
Movimiento Quinta República – MVR	–	–	46	76
Acción Democrática – AD	97	55	62	29
Social Cristiano – COPEI	67	53	28	5
Alianza – AD/COPEI	–	–	–	5
Convergencia	–	26	4	–
Convergencia Nacional	–	–	–	1
La Causa Radical – LCR	3	40	6	5
Movimiento al Socialismo – MAS	18	24	17	21
Movimiento de Integración Nacional – MIN	–	1	1	–
Unión Republicana Democrática – URD	2	1	1	–
Organización Renovador Autentica – ORA	2	1	1	–
Movimiento Electoral del Pueblo – MEP	2	1	1	–
Proyecto Venezuela – Proven	–	–	–	7
PRVZL	–	–	20	–
Prim. Justica	–	–	–	5
Conive	–	–	–	3
Lapy	–	–	–	3
Polo	–	–	–	1
ABP	–	–	–	1
Patria para Todos	–	–	7	1
Migato	–	–	–	1
PUAMA	–	–	–	1
Others	10	1	13	2
Total	**201**	**203**	**207**	**167**

For full party names see the acronyms section.

Sources: http://www.cne.gov.ve/estadisticas, http//pdba.georgetown.edu/Electdata/Venezuela.

1996: 122).[23] It blamed the president's insistence on neoliberal reforms for the poor electoral showing. These tensions between Pérez and his party broke into public struggle that intensified throughout 1990 and 1991, culminating in the victory of Pérez's opponents (the "orthodox" faction) in the party's October 1991 internal elections (Corrales 2002; Burgess 2004: 136).

Thus fears of electoral decline and loss of patronage positions because of the president's neoliberal reforms and his efforts to exclude them politically drove Acción Democrática to behave like an opposition political party in Congress. These same tensions permeated the Acción Democrática-dominated CTV leadership. Acción Democrática's break with the president freed Acción Democrática

---

[23] Electoral reforms and state decentralization in 1984 contributed to the success of these political parties and to the formation and success of new political parties and movements through 1998. Those reforms involved the direct election of governors, creation of the office of mayor, and the devolution of service provision to the municipalities (which increased their political autonomy). Laws that weakened slate (straight list) ballots also opened electoral competition (Corrales 2002; Grindle 2000; López Maya 1997).

Table 7.3. *Venezuela: Presidential Elections, 1988–2006*

Candidate	1988	%	1993	%	1998	%	2000	%	2006	%
Carlos Andrés Pérez	**3,868.843**	**52.89%**	–	–	–	–	–	–	–	–
Eduardo Fernández	2,955.061	40.40%	–	–	–	–	–	–	–	–
Teodoro Petkoff	198,361	2.71%	–	–	–	–	–	–	–	–
Godofredo Marín	63,795	0.87%	–	–	–	–	–	–	–	–
Ismenia Villalba	61,732	0.84%	–	–	–	–	–	–	–	–
Rafael Caldera	–	–	**1,710.722**	**30.46%**	–	–	–	–	–	–
Claudio Fermín	–	–	1,325.287	23.60%	–	–	–	–	–	–
Osvaldo Alvarez Paz	–	–	1,276.506	22.73%	–	–	–	–	–	–
Andres Velásquez	–	–	1,232.653	21.95%	–	–	–	–	–	–
Modesto Rivero	–	–	20,814	0.37%	–	–	–	–	–	–
Hugo Chávez	–	–	–	–	**3,673.685**	**56.20%**	–	–	–	–
Henrique Salas Romer	–	–	–	–	2,613.161	39.97%	–	–	–	–
Irene Saez Conde	–	–	–	–	184,568	2.82%	–	–	–	–
Luis Afaro Ucero	–	–	–	–	27,586	0.42%	–	–	–	–
Hugo Chávez	–	–	–	–	–	–	**3,757.773**	**59.76%**	–	–
Francisco Arias Cardenas	–	–	–	–	–	–	2,359.459	37.52%	–	–
Claudio Fermín	–	–	–	–	–	–	171,346	2.72%	–	–
Hugo Chávez	–	–	–	–	–	–	–	–	**7,309.080**	**62.84%**
Manuel Rosales	–	–	–	–	–	–	–	–	4,292.466	36.90%
Luis Reyes	–	–	–	–	–	–	–	–	4,807	0.04%
Venezuela Da Silva	–	–	–	–	–	–	–	–	3,980	0.03%

Boldface indicates winning candidate and percentage of the vote.

Sources: http://www.cne.gov.ve/estadisticas, http://www.cne.gov.ve/divulgacionPresidencial/resultado_nacional.php.

union leaders of their loyalty constraints. They followed their party's cue and formulated – however gingerly – a strategy for sustained anti-neoliberal contention to force President Pérez to revise his free-market economic reform program, especially with respect to labor reform and stabilization policy.[24] They were prepared to bring the full weight of the CTV's associational power to bear against the president and sought to build collective power by coordinating with independent union confederations.[25]

Against a background of escalating independent, decentralized, and uncoordinated mobilization, the CTV planned its campaign. It opened in April when Acción Democrática labor congressmen, with full public CTV support, defied the presidency by introducing a bill for higher wages and pensions and a 180-day freeze on employment termination (*Financial Times* 12 April 1991). On the heels of this legislative insurrection, in June 1991 the national CTV and its regional CTV federations, together with the national and regional organizations of the three smaller labor confederations, agreed on a joint mobilization program. They formed a "union action commando" and staged joint protests in several states. On 18 June they demonstrated in front of Congress and threatened another general strike when the president refused concessions (Burgess 2004: 137). The framing focused on a thoroughly Polanyi-like defensive posture against the threat of severance pay losses, wage reductions through inflation, and job instability. Hence they demanded (1) wage hikes, (2) wage indexation, (3) job stability in the public sector, and (4) the resignation of the labor minister. They also rejected reform of the severance pay system (Murillo 2001: 70–71).

Anti-neoliberal contention intensified as independent mobilization escalated in August when announced increases in gasoline prices sparked widespread demonstrations and strikes. These could bring significant associational and disruptive power to bear, even without CTV participation. One-million transport workers struck across the country in conjunction with a "civic strike," referring to protests by mixed union and community organizations; they included neighborhood associations, artist associations, local notables, and activist unions controlled by MAS and Causa R. The government narrowly averted a national general strike by opening negotiations with the CTV over its demand for a freeze on dismissals and by repealing a decree that denied state employees the right to collective bargaining (López Maya 1999a: 226).[26]

However, in October the government backpedaled and the CTV called a second massive general strike for 7 November 1991. The trade unions demanded (1) wage increases, (2) the reintroduction of price controls on basic goods and

---

[24] The CTV was not mollified by the president's concession in 1989 (Murillo 2001).

[25] Throughout most of 1989 and 1990 the CTV and Acción Democrática used established institutions (Congress) to force the president to accept their labor reform law, which was anything but market-oriented (Burgess 2004: 136).

[26] Europa Yearbook (2004); The Associated Press 12 August 1991; Agence France Presse 14 August 1991.

services, (3) an end to plans to fire 300,000 state employees, and (4) the resignation of the labor minister. Again, the weight of massed associational power in the CTV and allied labor confederations paralyzed the country. The CTV threatened a follow-up general strike for 14 November, a clear choice to escalate and sustain confrontation with the government. Meanwhile, independent mobilization continued with a massive teachers' strike on 12 November and many uncoordinated actions by students and community groups (The Associated Press 7 November 1991, Murillo 2001: 68; Venezuela 2004; The Xinhua General Overseas News Service 12 November 1991).

The government averted the follow-up general strike by making concessions to the CTV and Acción Democrática. Given their strength, Pérez contemplated *inclusion* of their interests rather than risk deepening political isolation and electoral defeat of Acción Democrática – the government's potential ally – in future elections. Pérez replaced the labor minister with a CTV-sponsored one, raised the transportation bonus, and suspended severance pay reform, later adopting a labor-friendly bill introduced by Acción Democrática–CTV. He also promised to restrain layoffs and to ensure CTV participation in the policy process (Murillo 2001: 71). The CTV, characteristically, backed away from its hard-line posture after obtaining concessions.

Nevertheless, anti-neoliberal contention continued unabated. Protests, marches, demonstrations, and strikes by independent, decentralized, and uncoordinated groups occurred practically on a daily basis. A number of public sector unions were not mollified by the government's concessions. Public sector doctors and health technicians and workers struck and demonstrated frequently against reform of the Venezuelan Social Security Institute. The CTV, which also opposed the reform, supported them tacitly by not using its centralized administrative power to stop them.[27] Fiscal retrenchment continued unabated, eroding public sector wages, pensions, and social security benefits sharply through inflation and payments arrears as job insecurity mounted. A new form of more violent contentious action also gained ground. "Disturbances," many led by students and with participation by masked protestors [*encapuchados*], became more common. Those protests developed into street blockages, vandalizing autos, trucks, and buses, setting up barricades, and violent confrontations with riot police (López Maya 1999a: 228–29). These events escalated after the 7 November general strike and continued through December (López Maya and Lander 2005).[28]

Protestors clearly linked the erosion of material well-being and perception of political exclusion to their actions. A demonstrating high school student

---

[27] The CTV relied on its congressional delegation to fight the social security reform bill in the legislature, with support from the rest of Acción Democrática and other opposition parties. They held up the law indefinitely, and after the failed coups of 1992 the Pérez administration dropped it (Murillo 2001).

[28] The Associated Press 4 December 1991; *Latin America Weekly Report* 5 December 1991: 1; *Latin America Regional Reports* 19 December 1991: 6.

explained, "We want to put pressure on the government to lower prices; to make life better for people. And we can do it." Another student added, "My family does not have much money. When the government raises the prices it hurts. We want them to stop." A university student elaborated, "The dominant political and economic groups are getting what they want [from the changes], while 95 percent of the population is dominated. They're using their policies as vehicles of oppression on the people. The future of Venezuela looks terrible."[29] Arturo Uslar Pietri, a respected essayist and humanist, summed up the mood. "We have in Venezuela a feeling of suffocation. The government doesn't function. The institutions don't function. There are no mechanisms to provide for minimum living standards" (The Associated Press 4 December 1991).

Political Collapse of Carlos Andrés Pérez

Two unsuccessful military coup attempts in February and November 1992 decisively altered the dynamics of anti-neoliberal contention in Venezuela. They foreclosed the possibility that the CTV could take a more active leadership role.[30] They also caused a serious erosion of the president's political power, indeed, of the very foundations of Venezuelan democracy.

The conjuncture of open Acción Democrática opposition to a president of the same party, CTV mobilization, and strikes, protests, and riots by independent unions, students, and community-based groups convinced rebellious military officers that an insurrectionary moment was at hand. Thus widespread, constant, and escalating anti-neoliberal mobilization in 1991 contributed to a failed coup attempt on 4 February 1992 by midlevel army officers from the MBR-200 group (Movimiento Revolucionario Bolivariano-200; Bolivarian Revolutionary Movement).[31] The officers involved, who began organizing in the 1970s as study groups of Venezuelan political and economic history, felt that the Punto Fijo Pact, especially during the 1980s, had become corrupted and significantly excluded the interests of the popular sectors. Lieutenant Colonel Hugo Chávez Frías emerged as a prominent national anti-neoliberal and populist leader. President Pérez's attempt to construct market society contributed heavily to the decision to rebel. Insurgent officers stressed concerns over increasing social polarization and concentration of wealth at the top resulting from structural adjustment and stabilization policies, as well as corruption in government and the lack of representativeness of established political institutions, especially the two main political parties. They, and the CTV, excluded the concerns of the popular sectors from their political and economic agendas. Hugo Chávez and others were particularly

---

[29] All quotes in The Associated Press 23 November 1991.
[30] Ellner (1995) argued that they never had the capacity.
[31] The "200" commemorates the founding oath of membership said to have been taken on the 200th birthday of Simón Bolívar (López Maya 2003: 75). For a broader analysis of civil–military relations during the period, see Burggraaff and Millett (1995).

shocked at having been ordered to repress looters with deadly force during the Caracazo (Gott 2000; López Maya 2003; McCaughan 2004; Norden 1998).[32]

Coordinated from Caracas, the rebellion also engulfed the cities of Maracaibo, Maracay, and Valencia. The objectives of the coup had been to capture or kill the president and to control major military installations in Caracas. Their assaults failed. Less than 10 percent of army units took part, and practically none from the air force or navy; neither did any high-ranking officers. Units loyal to the constitution quickly put the rebellion down, and Chávez surrendered. Rebellious military had more success in Zulia where they took over the state government, the oil fields, and the airport. They also had some successes in the states of Aragua and Carabobo (Burggraaf and Millett 1995; López Maya 2003). Although the coup had been a military failure, Chávez electrified the country and propelled himself into the national limelight with a televised one-minute speech, a condition of his surrender. Thirty-two officers and 1000 soldiers were arrested and more than 70 people had lost their lives in the adventure.

The turn to violent insurrection ended any chance that Acción Democrática and the CTV might lead anti-neoliberal contention on a more sustained basis in the event that the president reneged on agreements and persisted with his original plans for neoliberal reforms. After all, the few times the CTV contributed to anti-neoliberal mass mobilization, it did so from a resolutely reformist stance. It never framed contentious action as a violent challenge to Venezuela's democratic regime. The general strikes of 1989 and 1991 were not antisystem in their framing as had been the case against Pérez Jiménez in the late 1950s. Thus, after the coup, the CTV and Acción Democrática closed ranks in support of Venezuelan democracy and refrained from mobilization so as not to contribute to an insurrectionary climate and further destabilize the political system on which it depended (Corrales 2002; Murillo 2001). In the final analysis, the major political parties, the CTV, the majority of the military high command, and even large swaths of the general public still preferred a democratic regime over military government.

Nevertheless, the attempted coup severely weakened President Pérez's political power, including the state's power of coercion. Many MBR-200 officers and sympathetic soldiers were still on active duty, fueling putschist sentiment and concocting plots. The army had to be mollified, and Pérez could not implicitly rely on the armed forces to obey him. But the coup also showed that Pérez had lost control of the political process; his leadership style in pursuit of neoliberal reforms was not up to the task of neutralizing centrifugal forces. He personally had become the problem because of his insistence on an exclusionary leadership style without the necessary institutional capacity to carry it off. COPEI openly

---

[32] McCaughan (2004: 66–67) reports conflicting versions over whether or not a civilian uprising led by Causa R cadres was supposed to have accompanied the coup. McCaughan concluded that, regardless, for Chávez this marked the beginning of an uneasy relationship with the left.

called for his resignation and early elections to solve Venezuela's political crisis, further reducing his political power. So did the public. Because martial law was in effect, people organized massive pot banging and whistle blowing, campaigns to show their support for Pérez's resignation.

Pérez ignored demands for his resignation now that Acción Democrática (and therefore the CTV) had come back into the fold. The party, however, extracted a high price from the president for its support: inclusion in policy making and ending neoliberal reforms. Pérez replaced most of the technocrats in the cabinet with Acción Democrática ministers. He allowed major party leaders to formulate policy for the executive branch and negotiate with the opposition. Major reform efforts requiring legislation ended, including social security, privatization, and tax and banking code revisions. He also reinstated some price controls (Corrales 2002: 157).[33]

Whatever agreements Pérez, Acción Democrática, and the CTV came to did little to ameliorate the economic exclusion of many Venezuelans. These included state employees (a large share of the workforce), the popular sectors in general (especially those in the burgeoning informal sector), and middle-class groups dependent on state employment. The state continued to cut employment-related costs (especially salaries, wages, and pensions), inflation eroded everyone's livelihood, and public services deteriorated further. Moreover, they still felt politically excluded. They mistrusted what they considered to be opaque back room deals among politicians of the establishment (Corrales 2004). Hence the organizations that drove decentralized, uncoordinated anti-neoliberal contentious action mobilized once martial law was lifted in early April, beginning with a pot-banging and whistle-blowing campaign.

Although protests were generally constant, peaks occurred, such as the "hot week" in mid-May – called by leftist parties (MAS and Causa R) that stretched into early June. Dozens of public sector unions declared strikes. Impromptu, often short-lived, community organizations, and sometimes official neighborhood associations, joined in, as did students and teachers. The unions protested for wages, back pay, pensions, and job security; community organizations demanded improvement in public services; students and teachers claimed to speak for all popular sectors (and some middle classes) by demanding an end to neoliberal economic reforms all together. During this period popular support for a return to the previous economic model surged to nearly 60 percent (Roberts 2003c: 261). Although the CTV did not participate in the strikes, it defended their legitimacy (Inter Press Service 13 May 1992; López Maya 1999a; Roberts 2003a: 61).

---

[33] After the February coup attempt the government suspended constitutional guarantees and introduced press censorship. President Pérez also announced a 50-percent raise in the minimum wage and 30-percent pay increase for midlevel officers in the armed forces. In March he proposed political and economic changes, including reform of the constitution, suspension of increases in gasoline and electricity prices, and price controls on basic foods and medicine. Pérez also added some *Copeiyanos* to the cabinet (council of ministers), but they resigned a couple of months later.

Violent "disturbances," looting, and rioting became more common and, Caracazo-like, erupted in many major cities in June, including Caracas.

Thus anti-neoliberal protest, even if decentralized, led to conjunctures in which independent, decentralized, and diverse organizations demonstrated, struck, marched, burned, looted, and rioted more or less simultaneously. These impromptu confluences of associational and collective power could be highly disruptive.[34] They showed that people all across Venezuela and from many different social backgrounds wanted Pérez to resign and longed for political forces committed to a more national-populist political and socioeconomic development model.

Protestors expressed their outrage and frustration over economic and political exclusion (the plunge in living standards and corruption in government) quite directly. A demonstrator summed up the feeling during the pot-banging and whistle-blowing campaign that swept Caracas, Maracaibo, Valencia, Barquesimeto, and Mérida immediately after the government lifted the state of siege in April 1992: "Listen to everyone taking their noise to the streets. They're angry with the government... They want a change" (The Associated Press 8 April 1992). Striking teachers (symbols of middle-class resistance along with doctors) indignantly declared, "It should not be possible that these officers [the coup plotters] are prisoners while the corrupt ones are free" (Agence France Presse 11 May 1992). Cries of support for Chávez were a repudiation of neoliberal reforms and the politicians implementing them; for example, when demonstrators wearing red berets chanted: "Long live Chávez! The people are with you!" (The Associated Press 5 May 1992).

Roiling, constant, sometimes violent, and expanding protests led disgruntled military officers to believe that the insurrectionary moment was still alive. In this context, a second failed coup attempt by the air force and navy on 27 November 1992 shattered President Pérez's tenuous hold on political power. Unlike the previous coup, this one involved high-ranking military officers and it was much more violent – air attacks were the principal shock force. Although the putschists called on popular sector organizations to join in the uprising, not many entered the fray. Loyal army units again put down the military insurrection, which was not too difficult because it did not mobilize many ground troops (López Maya 2003; Norden 2003, 1998). After this second coup attempt, President Pérez lost all political support. Decentralized popular sector and middle-class mobilization continued unabated, and its violence rose. The ferocity and lethality of the second coup (hundreds died), however, dampened support for another putschist adventure. For example, during interviews in working-class and slum neighborhoods an unemployed metalworker said, "I hate those bastards [the government]. They're

---

[34] The collective power dimension comes from the temporary, independent, more or less simultaneous mobilization of formal sector workers, informal sector workers, middle-class professionals, and students.

corrupt and life has just gotten worse. But I don't see what the military would do that would be better." A beautician repulsed by the violence confided, "When I heard about the brutality [of the rebels] I could not follow them" (*The Record* Canada 1 December 1992).

Most Venezuelans wanted to work out political conflict through constitutional means, which was reflected in the 6 December 1992 local and state elections. MAS and Causa R on the left made significant gains, but so did COPEI on the right after blunt anti-neoliberal speeches by former President Caldera. By May 1993 all political parties wanted Pérez out. Impeachment proceedings began against him on charges of corruption; then, with Acción Democrática participation, Congress shortened his presidential term by six months, and a caretaker government headed by independent Ramón Velásquez finished out his term (Coppedge 1996; Grindle 2000: 75).[35]

Dashed Hopes, Mobilization, and the Rise of Hugo Chávez

The impeachment of President Pérez crowned four years of resistance against neoliberal reforms and the patterns of political and economic exclusion that accompanied them. Although the characteristics of anti-neoliberal contention differed markedly from those of the previous cases, it contributed to the outcome. Even in its decentralized and uncoordinated form, the confluence of different strands of protest at critical moments brought significant associational and, at times, some (mostly unplanned) collective power to bear. The unintended consequence was to embolden military putschists. Their two failed coups d'état changed the course of contentious and institutional politics. They truncated any possibility of coordinated, strategically oriented anti-neoliberal contention allied with political movements offering alternatives to neoliberalism. Moreover, the coups reinforced the commitment of most Venezuelans to work out their political and economic problems within constitutional, democratic institutions.

This situation had three consequences. First, electoral volatility directed against the two-party system, along with changes in electoral rules, facilitated the emergence of a multiparty system. This permitted the election of Rafael Caldera to his second presidency, campaigning on an anti-neoliberal platform he had established as early as 1992 in the wake of the military uprisings. Second, when economic crisis and mounting fiscal deficits forced him to reintroduce orthodox stabilization and free-market structural adjustment policies, a second wave of even more decentralized anti-neoliberal contentious politics ensued. However, given its uncoordinated nature, it failed to promote either a strategic political or an

---

[35] Congress granted Velásquez what it denied Pérez, an emergency economic policy enabling law. He used it to enact terminally blocked market-oriented tax and banking reforms (Corrales 2002: 61–62). Mostly, however, he used these powers to "reverse major elements of the neoliberal model by reimposing price and exchange controls, restoring trade protection for agriculture, and suspending the privatization initiative" (Roberts 2003c: 262).

economic vision of an alternative to neoliberalism. Protests were mainly a means to obtain concessions for the immediate economic grievances of specific groups (Salamanca 1999). Third, despite these shortcomings, the protests encouraged former MBR-200 putschists to form a political party to take advantage of expanding electoral volatility and party system change initiated in the previous period. They interpreted the steady drumbeat of mobilization as public discontent and yearnings for change. Thus they formed a political party to contest the December 1988 presidential elections with Hugo Chávez as their candidate and won. Chávez embodied those decentralized demands for an alternative to neoliberalism by running on a platform that promised to overhaul Venezuela's democratic institutions and the political economy to encourage the political and economic inclusion of the popular sectors.

Caldera, Contentious Politics, and the MVR

The popular sector and middle-class groups that had participated in decentralized, uncoordinated anti-neoliberal protests had sent clear signals that support for the old Acción Democrática–COPEI two-party dominant system was rapidly waning. Electoral volatility encouraged a shift to a working multiparty system as small new and old leftist political parties, and new political movements, gained at the ballot box or allied (see Tables 7.2 and 7.3). By the same token, erstwhile dominant political parties struggled to renew their image by presenting fresh faces for the December 1994 presidential election.

These changes permitted Rafael Caldera to cobble together a coalition of 16 small left- and right-wing political parties, Convergencia Nacional (National Convergence), as an electoral vehicle to contest the 5 December 1993 presidential election. This event signaled the further decay of the political system Acción Democrática and COPEI had anchored. Caldera had been a founder of COPEI, and as the party's leader had served as president of Venezuela (1968–73).

However, his candidacy was also an attempt to equilibrate Venezuela's badly battered political system (Romero 1997: 28). He personally symbolized continuity with the principles of the Punto Fijo pact, to which he had been a signatory. His choice of coalition partners and his alliance with the MAS for the presidential race symbolized its renewal: heretofore politically excluded voices of the old system would be heard. He ran on an antimarket economic platform that promised relief for battered popular sectors and middle classes (as well as domestic market-oriented business sectors) from neoliberal policies. He also held out hope for greater inclusion in policy making by means of the legislature and reconciliation with disgruntled military factions and their civilian supporters.

In the context of a 40-percent abstention rate Caldera won the presidential election with 30.45 percent of the vote to 24, 23, and 22 percent, respectively, for the candidates of Acción Democrática, COPEI, and Causa R (Coppedge 1996). Not only was Caldera a minority president, but his support in Congress was tenuous. Although Acción Democrática and COPEI's representation had declined precipitously from past levels, together they still held a majority of the seats. Their support for Caldera's initiatives generally vacillated between cooperation and confrontation (McCoy et al. 1995: 258).

Following through on his campaign pledges, in an effort to stabilize civil–military relations, on 4 February 1994 Caldera pardoned the rebellious junior officers of two years earlier, including Hugo Chávez.[36] Also true to his campaign promise, in the first two years Caldera adopted a heterodox economic stabilization and recovery program. His administration fixed foreign exchange rates and rationed hard currency, reintroduced price controls on 40 articles of primary necessity, and halted privatization. However, he also faced a serious economic crisis when several banks collapsed in 1994 and the state placed them in receivership.[37] These policies had the support of the legislature. Congress amended laws or wrote new ones to give the president the power to fix prices, to set foreign exchange rates, and to intervene in the management of banks during financial crises (Crisp 2000: 186, 1998: 29).[38]

Mounting outlays for subsidies, price controls, and the bank bailout, in the context of low international oil prices, pushed the fiscal deficit and inflation far above government targets (McCoy and Smith 1995: 258). Embroiled in this expanding economic crisis, in April 1996 Caldera announced his government had reached an agreement with the IMF on a U.S.$3.3 billion structural adjustment plan. It was a sweeping turnaround. The program included a 500-percent increase in gasoline prices, return to a unitary foreign exchange rate, the abolition of controls over foreign exchange, interest rates, and consumer prices, an increase in sales taxes, and renewed commitment to privatization in the aluminum, airline, and even petroleum industries to expand production (Kelly and Palma 2004: 216).

A second wave of anti-neoliberal contention gripped Venezuela during Caldera's presidency. Although the number of protest events between 1994 and 1997 declined to about half of the previous cycle (around 500 per year) the characteristics remained similar to those of the post-coup period during Pérez's administration. First, public sector unions, teachers, students, transport workers, and neighborhood protests dominated this second wave of anti-neoliberal contention. Oil workers occasionally joined in as did militant unions controlled by Causa R; even the CTV joined the fray and eventually staged another general strike. Second, demands again focused on (1) pay (arrears, raises, better pensions,

[36] Seventy were still in Venezuelan prisons and 52 were in exile in Peru and Ecuador (Coppedge 1996: 16).
[37] Ten banks were closed permanently; the rest were to be returned to private sector.
[38] Getting the support involved a strong confrontation with Congress. In June 1994 he gave himself extraordinary powers to deal with intensifying economic crisis. When Congress balked he threatened to dissolve it and establish a constituent assembly. Congress gave in and negotiated the necessary laws in return for policy input and patronage positions (Coppedge 1996: 13–14; Weyland 2002: 215–16).

government compliance with promised bonuses); (2) the poor quality of public services; (3) high transportation fares; (4) general economic policy; (5) the high cost of living in the face of diminishing purchasing power; (6) evictions; (7) police violence; and (8) crime.

Third, as in the previous wave, protest was decentralized. The demands of the various organizations and social actors involved focused on material grievances specific to them. They took to the streets because that appeared to be the only means to be heard and, perhaps, to have their demands met. But none developed the capacity to coordinate action or to frame mobilization around larger strategic objectives, either in terms of economic policy or an electoral strategy to defeat neoliberalism (Salamanca 1999).

Although the number of protest events per year was fairly constant through 1997 (with the exception of 1994), the reintroduction of neoliberal economic reforms caused a strong upsurge in their intensity, beginning with the lead up to the March 1996 IMF mission that prescribed them.[39] From then on the public sector unions staged a series of massive protests where on several occasions more than a million went on strike across Venezuela, paralyzing public administration. These were punctuated by marches, demonstrations, and disturbances led by doctors, judicial system workers, teachers, university professors and, of course, students accompanied by hooded hooligans. Evident to all was the participation of middle-class groups. During this same period, the CTV reemerged taking a more militant stance, but still not leading a long-term protest movement even though it staged a general strike in August 1997.

Thus, decentralized as these protests were, they signaled widespread dissatisfaction with neoliberal policies among popular sectors and middle-class professionals employed by the state. Moreover, the associational power they brought to bear was occasionally formidable, as was the case with nationwide strikes by public sector employees and teachers. Associational power expanded even more when the CTV began to get involved again. Its decision probably hinged on intensifying leftist party competition in union elections and on the fact that the former insurrectionary military movement (the MBR-200) was entering electoral politics; thus CTV contentious action was unlikely to create conditions for another coup.[40] Collective power, however, never emerged. Still, the disruptive power of strikes, marches, demonstrations, and disturbances caused by the larger unions undertaking national action could be formidable.

To illustrate the shape of this upsurge in contention, in August 1996 over a million state employees walked off the job. In October the CTV threatened a

---

[39] From September to October Salamanca (1999: 245) counted the following number of protest events: 1993–94, 1,099; 1994–95, 561; 1995–96, 534; 1996–97, 550.

[40] Ellner (2003: 168) reported that in the 1993 congressional elections not a single Acción Democrática-sponsored unionist won office, whereas some Causa R ones did. Also see Urquijo-García (2000) for details on increased leftist party competition inside the CTV in the 1995 XIth National Congress, partially driven by new democratizing electoral rules in the confederation.

general strike over unpaid bonuses the government had promised in compensation for rising consumer prices caused by the elimination of subsidies, not an insignificant gesture given the political as well as economic impact of rare general strikes. Public sector unions struck *en masse* again in November for two weeks over pay arrears and unpaid bonuses, which the government agreed to pay. Public health service doctors (symbols of the middle class) struck over pay raises in January 1997 to which the government acquiesced. The CTV again threatened a general strike, this time linking their own pay raise demands to those of teachers and university professors. The CTV settled for a fraction of what it had demanded in February. In August 1997, after new gas price hikes, the CTV staged a general strike over pay and for protection from massive layoffs in the private sector. Economic exclusion in the form of growing misery forced the action. However, so did pressure within the CTV by more leftist political parties that continued to gain ground because the Acción Democrática leadership had given away too much in labor reform negotiations with the government. In November 1997 over a million public sectors workers struck yet again over back pay, wage increases, and privatization.[41] At the same time Causa R-led iron and aluminum workers struck against privatization in Bolívar.

Grassroots grievances during this wave of anti-neoliberal contention expressed popular sector and middle-class feelings of abuse, indignation, anger, and frustration over their economic and political exclusion. During a 200,000-strong May-day union parade in Caracas, an oil worker declared, "We are demanding more determination on the part of the government to fight price speculation, which is drowning us" (United Press International 1 May 1995.) Informal sector workers were stretched to the breaking point. An angry ice cream vendor, with assenting interjections by sympathetic companions, told the press, "If they devalue there will be killing and looting in the streets [by us, the people]." A distraught informal sector factory worker explained, "We're spending more than we make. Even if you have a good job, you have to go out and sell gum on the street after work just to survive." Another frustrated factory worker added, "To get sick here is a luxury. You can't afford to take the time off, no matter how bad it is. Go to a hospital? Forget it."[42] An indignant motorist grumbled over constantly rising gas prices, "I think it's terrible, it's an abuse" (The Associated Press 31 July 1997). Meanwhile, in the wake of the August 1997 CTV general strike for wage increases, a union leader declared, "The fundamental goal of the strike has been achieved, the workers have shown that they are not satisfied and we disagree with the attitude of the private sector [it did not implement agreed upon salary hikes]" (Agence France Presse 6 August 1997). Striking oil workers, outraged over a wave of firings and the authorities' deaf ears, explained, "We want to get the government's attention. They plan to do away with at least 54 drilling

[41] For the effects of privatization on labor, see Ellner (1999).
[42] Both quotes were from *The Washington Post* 2 October 1995.

rigs in the states of Anzoátegui, Monagas, Apure, and Zulia [each rig employs between 50 and 60 workers]" (*Calgary Sun* 30 July 1998). By the same token, doctors on a massive nationwide strike for salary raises, better funding for hospitals, and rejection of hospital privatization when faced with official pressure to stop public demonstrations, declared, "We want it to be known that this is a struggle in defense of free speech and the dignity of medicine" (Agence France Presse 16 September 1998).

Decentralized, uncoordinated, and without strategic purpose as those challenges to neoliberalism were, popular sector discontent had diffuse effects, which worked themselves out in the electoral arena. First, they contributed to the failure of Caldera's bid to reequilibrate a Punto Fijo-based democratic regime. The administration's political base crumbled as coalition partners abandoned it. The electoral base of traditional political parties (Acción Democrática and COPEI) eroded even further. Second, the constant drumbeat of protests helped convince Hugo Chávez and his closest political allies to create a political vehicle to channel discontent into votes and propel them to political power. In July 1997, they founded the Movimiento Quinta República (MVR; Movement of the Fifth Republic), controlled by the MBR-200, to contest the December 1998 presidential elections (López Maya 2003: 82).[43]

In midst of these developments, international economic crisis hit Venezuela hard at the end of 1997. The fall of international oil prices aggravated the state's fiscal deficit, forcing even more strenuous orthodox economic stabilization efforts. This impoverished the population further, discredited the Caldera administration's economic performance, and gave a strong boost to Chávez's electoral prospects (López Maya 2003: 83). Economic crisis, the backdrop of constant protests, and voter volatility made Chávez's candidacy attractive to other leftist political parties, permitting the creation of an electoral alliance called the Polo Patriótico. It included the MVR, MAS, and Patria Para Todos, the larger portion of a split in Causa R, and the Communist Party.[44] Smaller political parties such as the Nuevo Régimen Democrático, the Movimiento Primero de Mayo, and even the far-left Bandera Roja participated. Chávez and his coalition won the election handily, putting an end to Venezuela's episode of anti-neoliberal contention (see Table 7.2).

Aftermath: President Chávez, 1998–Present

Hugo Chávez ran on an anti-neoliberal platform. It stressed economic nationalism to reclaim Venezuelan sovereignty, specifically rejecting free trade

---

[43] The MBR-200 national assembly voted for this strategy in December 1996 (McCaughan 2004: 84). The MVR was not initially conceived as a political party, but rather as a political movement to support Chávez and the MBR-200. But by 2000, the MVR's electoral successes caused the MBR-200 to wane and disappear (López Maya 2003: 82–88).

[44] For the evolution of this split, see Hellinger (1996); Buxton (2001).

agreements with the United States and repudiating the oil sector's opening to private investment.[45] It promised expansion of state economic and social programs for the popular sector (especially informal labor). It vowed to hold a constitutional convention that ensured representation of popular sector interests and destroyed the capacity of traditional political parties to make deals that consistently excluded those interests. These reforms would "pave the way for a Fifth Republic where citizens would enjoy equality and fair government managed by honest, competent *compañeros*" (McCaughan 2004: 85).

Chávez and the Polo Patriótico won the presidential election with 56.2 percent of the vote against the opposition Proyecto Venezuela coalition's 40 percent (Roberts 2003b). Polo Patriótico candidates also won 70 of 189 seats in the chamber of deputies and 18 of 48 in the Senate along with 8 of 23 governorships. However, Acción Democrática and COPEI still had a strong presence in Congress, governorships, and local elections (McCaughan 2004: 39).

Chávez has enjoyed considerable political success. He won every election until 2007, when he lost a plebiscite on proposed constitutional amendments.[46] Chávez held a special election (the "megaelection") in July 2000 in which all elected positions, including his, were to be renewed. He and his supporters won big, and Acción Democrática and COPEI lost big (Hellinger 2003: 44). Chávez also survived a coup d'état attempt in April 2002 and a recall referendum in 2004.[47] Venezuelans reelected him to the presidency in December 2006, and Chávez quickly crafted a referendum to amend the 1999 Bolivarian Constitution. The most controversial clause was the elimination of two-term limits for the presidency and extension of the presidential period from six to seven years. Another clause proposed a new branch of government centered on communes as central building blocks of popular power for a new socialist state. And, although private property remained guaranteed, the reform project proposed creating several forms of collective property. The opposition, which included Chávez supporters, narrowly defeated the government's constitutional reform project in a December 2007 referendum. Chávez accepted the outcome, blunting persistent attempts to discredit him for his authoritarianism (Hellinger 2009: 480–81).

---

[45] For an overview of the position on foreign private oil interests, see Hellinger (2006); Parker (2005).
[46] The abstention rate for this election, at 36.5 percent, was high. It was even higher for the mega-election, 43.5 percent.
[47] A very strong anti-Chávez opposition movement quickly formed, and Venezuelan society became polarized. It included business groups, middle-class professionals, and, eventually, the CTV. Protests, demonstrations, strikes; and road blockages were frequent. In 2001 these groups, and Acción Democrática and COPEI, formed the Coordinadora Democrática. The CTV staged several general strikes; one in April 2002 (in conjunction with other anti-Chávez demonstrations) was apparently coordinated to support an attempted coup d'état in which the U.S. government was implicated. Its failure allowed Chávez to purge the armed forces of disloyal officers. The Coordinadora organized the presidential recall referendum, which it lost (Hellinger 2006; Norden 2003).

In office, Chávez set out to craft an alternative to neoliberalism that he calls 21st-century socialism. He began by reorganizing political institutions (the state). Upon his election, he immediately fulfilled a campaign promise by convening a constitutional convention in which his supporters won overwhelming representation. The new constitution encouraged more direct democracy, thus, over time, further weakening institutionalized political power of the old regime (mainly Acción Democrática, COPEI, and business circles) (Alvarez 2003). The promotion of direct democracy opened opportunities for the political inclusion of heretofore excluded and largely popular sector voices. These had to be organized by new political parties, such as the MVR, by grassroots organizations, and by reorganizing the labor movement.

With respect to the popular sectors, Chávez used the state to build forms of associational and collective power that had emerged from below in the other cases. With respect to grassroots organizing, Chávez's regime stimulated the proliferation of Bolivarian Circles. The movement had begun in the mid-1990s with small cell-like study groups, generally in poor and working-class neighborhoods. By the late 1990s they had a loose, and probably sketchy, structure of municipal and regional coordinators. In 2001 they received a boost, and by 2004 nearly 10 percent of the adult population (1.5 million persons) are said to have registered in them. Some did so out of conviction, others to obtain material benefits distributed by the municipality (García-Guadilla 2003: 190–92; López Maya 2003: 80–81; McCaughan 2004: 108–9; Ramírez 2007). Moreover, despite the defeat of the December 2007 constitutional referendum, communes already legally existed as part of municipalities and states. The law permits them to receive funds directly from the central government and to disburse them. It remains unclear how elected municipal officials and spokespersons from the communes – authorized officers – will interact (Hellinger 2009: 480).

In the labor movement, Chávez encouraged the formation of a rival confederation with a referendum on labor code reform in December 2000 (held simultaneously with municipal elections). Chavista labor leaders initially created the Fuerza Bolivariana de Trabajadores (Bolivarian Workers' Force) current inside the CTV, but in a CTV constituent assembly vote, Fuerza Bolivariana failed to win enough support to dissolve the CTV and form a new labor federation. After that defeat, the Chavista current formed a competing labor confederation, the Unión Nacional de Trabajadores (National Workers Union) in 2003. A large factor in the creation of Unión Nacional was the CTV's turn to open opposition to the Chávez government, staging several general strikes, one of which helped precipitate the failed coup in 2002 (Ellner 2005, 2003). The new unionists were also interested in organizing informal sector workers (McCaughan 2004: 105).

Socioeconomic policy emphasized inclusion of the popular sectors and economic nationalism. First Chávez created a Unified Social Fund directly managed by the armed forces in the Plan Bolívar 2000 to implement programs in health, sanitation, care for the indigent, public transport, and housing among others (Hellinger 2003: 44). Later the Chávez administration established *misiones* [missions] to address the same problems. Only this time, the effort involved cooperation with better trained and experienced Cuban personnel in exchange for oil to the island nation (McCaughan 2004). For example, Misión Barrio Adentro provided health care to shantytowns across the nation. In 2004, 13,586 doctors participated in the program that reached four million people. Misión Robinson was a literacy campaign that applied tested Cuban techniques to reach marginalized urban and rural populations. Over 100,000 facilitators reached more than a million citizens in 2004. A poorly designed and implemented *misión* focused on educational scholarships followed, as did another to issue national identity cards necessary to access services. Misión Mercal distributed subsidized food at discount stores to the poor that serviced 9.3 million persons in 2004. This quickly became a very popular program (Penfold-Becerra 2007: 72–74). The misiones are directly funded by the state petroleum corporation, largely from windfall profits of oil revenue, about 13 billion dollars in 2006 (Hellinger 2008: 487).[48] Although these programs have yet to be institutionalized, expenditures as a percentage of GDP for health, education, and housing outside of misión spending have increased. The government also opened access to education by prohibiting public school enrollment fees and providing meals (Parker 2005).

Economic policy has taken a nationalist turn as well as a third-world perspective on economic cooperation. Early on, the Chávez administration passed a land reform act (Buxton 2003). However, regaining control over the state oil corporation, which had been increasingly managed as an independent transnational firm, was perhaps the highest priority and successfully accomplished by 2006. This permitted Venezuela to revive its leadership in OPEC and to use it as a means to stabilize what had been declining oil prices (Hellinger 2003; Parker 2005).[49] This, coupled with a world increase in demand for oil, generated an oil boom, which has allowed Chávez to extend and expand domestic social programs, establish independence from the IMF, and help other Latin American countries, such as Argentina, Uruguay, and Bolivia to gain more breathing room with their international creditors. The administration also promoted local, nationally owned suppliers for state companies and transnational corporations (Buxton 2003).

Chávez has also reasserted the state's role in economic planning and socialization. As previously mentioned, his administration passed a land reform act implemented on public lands shortly after taking office. Turbulent economic and political times up to 2004 probably kept him from addressing the question of private property more broadly. He claimed to respect private property in

---

[48] Concern among scholars exists that new and recycled client–patron networks will replicate some of the problems of the "old regime" (Penfold-Becerra 2007). For a critical assessment of the missions' impact, and Venezuelan social policy in general, see Rodríguez (2008).

[49] For an overview of the Venezuelan oil industry up to the Punto Fijo Pact, see Tinker Salas (2005).

general, but did not believe it was an absolute right. In 2005 he applied the 2001 Land Reform Act to private estates with substantial fallow acreage (Ellner 2007). After his coalition swept the December 2005 National Assembly elections, he began a more aggressive nationalization program. In 2006 the state bought controlling shares in the major telephone (privatized in 1991) and electric (always private) companies owned by international firms. The Venezuelan government also tightened regulation over foreign companies in the oil sector increasing royalty payments and limiting their exploitation rights. Furthermore, the state took over bankrupt firms and turned them over to worker cooperatives (Ellner 2007). In 2007 and 2008 the government nationalized a major steel company privatized in the early 1990s, a dairy firm, and intervened in a large Spanish-owned bank.[50]

Last, but not least, Chavez's government took a strong anti-Free Trade Association of the Americas (FTAA) stance, helping to derail the World Trade Organization's Cancún talks. Venezuela's government links this position with a defense of sovereignty; it sees the FTAA as tool of U.S. and international hegemony over Latin American states. Instead, Venezuelan foreign policy has focused on economic integration measures to create a Latin American bloc to counteract U.S. hegemony. Telsur broadcasts Latin American-produced satellite television programs. Petrosur and Petrocaribe develop joint energy programs. The Bolivarian Alternative for the Americas provides an alternative to the U.S.-sponsored FTAA, featuring a "social charter on labor and human rights and an investment fund for least developed areas. The Bank of the South initiative of 2007 is a major step in that direction intended to counteract the IMF and the World Bank (Hellinger 2008: 490). Last, but not least, as has been reported in the press, Venezuela has intensified ties with China, Russia, and Iran in an effort to shift a U.S.-dominated unipolar world to a multipolar one.

Looking back, the Bolivarian revolution has gone through several stages over its first 10 years. The early stages focused on survival and consolidation of power; social and economic policies were not very radical. This period spanned Chávez's first election, the Constitutional Assembly, the revolt of the Venezuelan state oil company and traditional organized labor, and the economic downturn in 2003. During this period, Chavez's government and its reforms met significant opposition. Contentious politics in the form of pro-Chávez and anti-Chávez demonstrations, protests, and strikes abounded. It culminated in a failed coup d'état in 2002 with U.S. complicity. With political power firmly in his grasp, Chávez began a more ambitious social and economic reform program as reelection loomed. He expanded the misiones, which significantly increased his sagging popularity for the 2005 and 2006 elections. After reelection, he began a more aggressive nationalization program to reassert more direct state involvement in the economy. In

[50] Simon Romero, *The New York Times* 6 August 2008: A13.

August 2008, he also issued decrees to advance political and socioeconomic measures defeated in the December 2007 constitutional referendum, although they fell short of permitting Chávez to stand for reelection. Exactly what kind of socialism his government is building remains unclear.[51] But a highly visible commitment to the poor and excluded – regardless of the efficiency of delivery – has generated a strong base of support. It remains to be seen if the effort can survive a downturn in oil revenues.

---

[51] For assessments, see Zúquete (2008); Hellinger (2008); Lebowitz (2007); Ellner and Tinker Salas (2007); Penfold-Becerra (2007); Ellner (2007).

8

Peru and Chile

If efforts to construct contemporary market society in Argentina, Bolivia, Ecuador, and Venezuela contributed to Polanyian backlashes in the form of nationwide episodes of anti-neoliberal contention between 1989 and 2003, why did these not occur in Peru and Chile during the same period? In Peru, Alberto Fujimori aggressively implemented a cohesive neoliberal reform program between 1990 and 2000. Much like Carlos Menem and Carlos Andrés Pérez, he too ran a populist presidential campaign and "betrayed" his electoral mandate by turning to Washington Consensus prescriptions. Yet mobilization during this period was practically at an all-time low. Meanwhile, Chile was the original market society experiment. At the head of a ruthless labor repressive military dictatorship, General Augusto Pinochet (1973–89) stabilized the economy, privatized, deregulated, and liberalized financial and trade regimes to an extent never seen in South America. After redemocratization in 1990, successive administrations of a political party coalition that had opposed the dictatorship consolidated the dictatorship's neoliberal model *and* democracy under conditions of popular sector quiescence.

The puzzle runs deeper because of Peru's similarities to Bolivia and Ecuador and of Chile to Argentina. Like Ecuador and Bolivia, Peru lies in the central Andes and has a significant indigenous population.[1] It too was late in developing national populism and, as in Ecuador, an inclusionary corporatist military government implemented it to overcome social tensions generated in a democratic regime dominated by traditional commercial and landowning elites. Moreover, as in the rest of the central Andes, Peru's political party system was weak and fragmented. Meanwhile, Chile and Argentina shared the same geographic area, the Southern Cone; lacked a significant indigenous population; implemented import-substitution industrialization and national populism early; and had relatively strong political parties linked to the popular sectors.

The previous chapters showed that the negative effects of structural adjustment on organized labor and the rise of identity politics were insufficient to explain

---

[1] About 30 to 40 percent of Peru's population is estimated to be indigenous (Yashar 2005: 225–26).

episodes of anti-neoliberal mobilization or quiescence – all suffered them. What was noteworthy, especially, in Argentina, Bolivia, and Ecuador, was the transformation of diverse movement organizations (some new, some old). In the context of relatively open associational space, the political and economic exclusion inherent in constructing market society, punctuated by economic crisis, facilitated expansion of associational power. From there, framing along reformist lines and brokerage efforts by leaders contributed to the formation of horizontal linkages (collective power).

This conjuncture of necessary conditions did not occur in Peru and Chile. In Peru, significant insurrectionary movements and a turn to authoritarianism that closed political space during Fujimori's presidency inhibited the formation of associational power and horizontal linkages among social movement organizations. In Chile a highly repressive military regime constructed a contemporary version of market society. After redemocratization in 1990, an unbroken succession of governments by a center-left party coalition implemented public policies to provide protection from the free-market economy to ever greater numbers of citizens. Thus, although Chilean public policy since the end of the dictatorship has supported a market economy, Chile has strongly moved away from market society – a key necessary condition for episodes of anti-neoliberal contention experienced in the other cases. Ironically, however, for reasons supported by the general argument of this book, Chile experienced an episode of anti-neoliberal contention in the mid-1980s. Two conditions distinguished this period from the 1970s. First, to legitimate its rule, in 1980 the military began a process of political liberalization that opened political associational space. Second, in the context of this political opening, economic crisis and high levels of exclusion in 1983 contributed to the eruption of reform-oriented mass mobilization with significant collective power.

Peru

In Peru, as in Ecuador, an inclusionary corporatist military government led by General Juan Velasco built national populism from 1968 to 1975. The military acted against traditional socioeconomic elites that manipulated the fragmented structure of Peru's democratic regime to block state-led import-substitution industrialization and policies that addressed glaring social inequities. The military, supported by leftist political figures, believed these to be the keys to reviving Peru's stagnating economy and to defuse mounting social tensions that favored radical left revolutionary movements. Velasco quickly increased state enterprise from 1 percent of GDP in 1968 to nearly 20 percent by 1975, largely by nationalizing foreign firms (oil and mining) and by expanding existing state-owned companies in mining, steel, and electricity. The state also protected domestic industry, invested in public infrastructure, controlled prices, and created development banks for various economic and social sectors to distribute credit raised largely through public sector borrowing (Wise 1997: 74–78). The government's investments were concentrated in basic industries and natural resources and therefore did not crowd out private domestic investment, which was expected to flow into manufacturing, commerce, and finance (Conaghan and Malloy 1994: 58–59).[2]

More important for our purposes, Velasco's government facilitated the rapid development of leftist popular sector associational power because it actively promoted the proliferation of industrial unions, urban squatter settlement organization, and peasant unions (Roberts 1998: 203). In pursuit of greater equity with social control, Velasco encouraged the corporatist inclusion of the popular sectors to the state by sponsoring the vertical integration of authorized organizations to economic redistribution channels and, to a lesser extent, to policy making (Stepan 1978). To stimulate popular sector participation and its linkages to the state, the government set up SINAMOS (Sistema Nacional de Apoyo a la Movilización Social; National System for the Support of Social Mobilization).

Inclusionary corporatism was also a strategy to isolate the Alianza Popular Revolucionaria Americana (APRA; American Popular Revolutionary Alliance) and its union arm, the Confederación de Trabajadores Peruanos (Confederation of Peruvian Workers), APRA emerged in the 1930s as a national-populist party and became Peru's oldest institutionalized party. Conflicts with the military led to its exclusion from presidential politics since the early 1930s. APRA's success in other areas, however, crowded out the left until the 1960s when APRA moved to the right and made alliances with the oligarchy in the pragmatic pursuit of political power (Conaghan and Malloy 1994: 32–33; Haworth 1993: 42). To undercut the APRA-dominated union confederation, the Velasco government strengthened the communist-controlled Confederación General de Trabajadores del Perú (CGTP; General Confederation of Workers of Peru), which quickly eclipsed APRA's unions (Huber 1983).[3] During the 1970s, CGTP ideological pluralism expanded with the admission of unions controlled by other leftist parties (Haworth 1993: 43).

In the countryside the military government began an extensive agrarian reform program in 1969 and established an Agrarian Bank to finance it. Land reform was intense on the coast, the site of the most productive lands. As elsewhere in the central Andes, indigenous peasants concentrated in the highlands (Yashar 2005: 231–32). Although the extent of land distribution may be disputed, the reform effectively eliminated the extensive haciendas, pillars of the traditional Peruvian oligarchy (McClintock 1981: 60). Agrarian reform distributed land and credit to small holders organized into several forms of cooperative enterprises. The state then sponsored peasant organizations with vertical linkages to the Ministry of

---

[2] Conaghan and Malloy (1994) argue that private sector mistrust thwarted investment in those areas.
[3] The Velasco government also encouraged competing union confederations (Huber 1983).

Agriculture: the Communist Party-controlled Peruvian Peasant Confederation and the National Agrarian Confederation (Hunefeldt 1997).[4]

Land reform was also an integral component of a plan to restructure ethnic relations in Peru by redefining Indians as peasants and peasant communities.[5] In addition to redefining Indians as peasants, it reorganized indigenous communities into cooperatives and distinguished them from rural day laborers. In short, the government encouraged the class identification and organization of indigenous with controlled vertical links to the state as a means to integrate Indians as citizens into modernizing Peru (Yashar 2005: 232–35).

In practice, these reforms generated tensions in the countryside. Indigenous communities adapted traditional ways to new organizational forms and retained a measure of autonomy (Yashar 2005: 234–35). Further, land reform benefited only about 10 to 15 percent of Peru's peasants who worked or resided on coastal and highland haciendas. Most landless rural laborers and poor indigenous communities outside of the haciendas, especially those in the highlands, did not receive land or join cooperatives. Their land hunger was unmet, and claims to community land usurped by the haciendas remained unsatisfied (McClintock 1981: 62–63). Because APRA had concentrated on organizing rural workers on coastal sugar plantations, radical left parties took advantage of tensions and conflicts in the central and southern highlands to organize a militant peasantry into local, regional, and national federations. Splinters of the Communist Party eventually controlled the Peruvian Peasant Confederation (Roberts 1998: 212).

In addition to workers and peasants, SINAMOS fomented the proliferation of urban shantytown dweller organizations in the "new towns" that had sprung up around Lima (the capital) and other major cities since the 1940s because of massive migration from rural populations in search of opportunity.[6] As elsewhere in Latin America, grassroots community associations pressed for land titles, housing, and urban services. Many of them, however, rejected the imposition of rigid corporatist controls, bureaucratic routines, and interference in leadership selection. This provided proliferating radical leftist political parties an opening to establish linkages with them. These parties encouraged popular sector organizations to maintain an autonomous and confrontational stance toward the government to maximize the impact of their demands (Roberts 1998: 213). However, community organizations retained a measure of autonomy from leftist political parties, and community mobilization did not always coincide with the strategies of the left. Shantytown dwellers supported whichever parties seemed capable of fulfilling their demands, irrespective of ideology (Haworth 1993: 48).

---

[4] A Maoist faction of the Communist Party gained control of the PCC (Roberts 1998: 206).

[5] The term peasant communities applied to Andean indigenous and the term native communities referred to the Amazon (Yashar 2005: 231).

[6] Before SINAMOS, time-honored patron–client mechanisms had been the urban squatters' main recourse; they received some benefits in return for political loyalty to the patron (Roberts 1998: 215).

Political Shifts, Economic Stabilization, and Contentious Politics, 1975–80

Velasco's revolutionary military government suffered from many difficulties, but three were especially salient. First, economic nationalism, agrarian reform, and redistributive social policies in general created fiscal imbalances. These fueled a domestic economic crisis aggravated by the world recession of 1973–75 (Thorp 1979; Wise 1997). Second, having sponsored popular sector organization through corporatist institutions, these tended to resist corporatist controls and were penetrated by militant leftist parties ready to exploit old and new contradictions, conflicts, and tensions that government reforms exacerbated or created. Third, the military high command split over what to do about these problems. The more conservative faction of Francisco Morales Bermúdez staged a bloodless coup d'état in August 1975 and moved the military regime rightward (Stepan 1978).

Morales Bermúdez's military administration dismantled Peru's fledgling national-populist order. Orthodox economic stabilization policies cut back or eliminated funding for state-led economic and social development programs (Thorp 1979; Wise 1997). It also repaired relations with the international business community. By cutting subsidies, stabilization policy doubled as a tool to demobilize the popular sectors. It weakened or dismantled many of the organizations and institutions that supported them. Successive devaluations, price increases, tax levies, and budget cuts between 1976 and 1978 ravaged popular sector consumption capacity heretofore supported by the state (Conaghan and Malloy 1994: 102–6).

The orthodox economic stabilization program did not develop into full-fledged neoliberal reform. This was because, with the exception of timid trade liberalization policies, it "stopped short of a wholesale attack on the directive role of the state in the economy" (Conaghan and Malloy 1994: 105). Still, the turn to more closed authoritarianism and the attack on the subsidy functions of state enterprises that supported popular consumption generated significant economic and political exclusion for the popular sectors that, if unchecked, threatened much worse.

Although SINAMOS had had promoted significant associational power in all three branches of the popular sectors – urban labor, shantytown dwellers, and peasants – they nevertheless harbored autonomous economic and political demands because corporatism had not fully co-opted them. Thus economic and political exclusion after 1975 in the wake of the breakdown of traditional patron–client relationships during the Velasco government awakened greater militancy and a turn to contentious politics (Mauceri 1997: 24–26). Moreover, the dismantlement of corporative institutions that had segmented popular sector organizations facilitated the development of horizontal linkages among them (Roberts 1998: 213–14). In other words, in the midst of deepening economic and political exclusion, relatively well-organized popular sectors built *collective power* to more effectively press their claims on the government as the vertical ties to the state that had kept them apart weakened.

The Communist Party-controlled sector of organized labor played a leading role in social mobilization against the military government, which peaked in the general strikes of 1977 and 1978. As Roberts (1998: 215) argued, "With its organizing experience, national direction, and political ties the labor movement served as a practical school for the diffusion of collective identities and organizational lessons." The labor movement *framed* resistance to the rightward turn in the military government in class-based terms that included shantytown dwellers. Labor organizers brokered collaborative relations with community associations sharing organizing expertise and resources (Roberts 1998: 215). In conjunction with leftist political parties, the labor movement coordinated strikes and demonstrations with community organizations and rural cooperatives (Mauceri 1997: 26). In this way, "organized labor has managed to reach out to the unemployed, the marginally self-employed, and the peasantry, and thus to enlarge the popular movement" (Huber 1983: 61–62). Demands centered on wage adjustments, food subsidies, and rescinding austerity measures in order to protect popular sector consumption levels (Conaghan and Malloy 1994: 104; Huber 1983: 61).

General strikes are labor's maximum expression of economic and political power. In July 1977 the CGTP staged the first general strike in Peruvian history, coordinating demonstrations and protests with other popular sectors. The general strike contributed to an announcement nine days later that the military government would begin a transition to democracy. The CGTP organized a second general strike in May 1978 to force the military to keep its word and craft a transition program whereby it would relinquish political power (Haworth 1993: 43–45). Elections for a constituent assembly were scheduled for that same year with general elections in 1980.

Political and economic weaknesses of the military government also contributed to the emergence of mass leftist popular sector mobilization. Although the inclusionary military regime had taken an authoritarian turn and repressed mobilization, it never did so to the extent of military governments such as Chile's beginning in 1973. This was partially due to two factors. First, the military as an institution was divided over the question of inclusionary national populism and more closed authoritarianism following the Argentine model of 1966 and Chile as of 1973. Hence the "closure" of the military regime was accomplished more by statute than by repression. Second, managing Peru's economic crisis drove even more wedges among the high command, further weakening the military as an institution. In this context, the military did not want the added burden of managing sociopolitical stability. Crafting a transition to democracy whereby the military could turn over political power to center-right parties committed to continuing conservative economic policies and demobilizing popular sectors seemed an attractive option to preserve the institutional integrity of the armed forces.

Peru's Neoliberal Turn and the Puzzle of Declining Leftist Popular Mobilization

Like Bolivia and Ecuador during the same period, in Peru an IMF orthodox economic stabilization program under "soft" military rule contributed to the eruption of leftist mass popular sector mobilization led by urban labor. If the popular sectors created significant collective power in the late 1970s, why did their capacity for coordinated mobilization crumble during the imposition of "full-blown" neoliberalism after redemocratization? More to the point, even if neoliberal reforms weakened organized labor, why did other nodes of resistance not develop in poor urban neighborhoods and among indigenous peasants and reconstitute horizontal linkages (including with the remnants of the labor movement) as they had in Argentina, Bolivia, and Ecuador? Indeed, popular sector mobilization practically disappeared at the height of neoliberalism under Fujimori in the first half of the 1990s. The answer lay in two distinctive factors: the development of insurrectionary movements and Fujimori's authoritarian turn in 1992.

Neoliberalism in Peru, 1980–2000

Efforts to construct a Peruvian version of market society after redemocratization spanned two administrations with a neostructuralist interlude between them. They began under Fernando Belaúnde's presidency (1980–85), suffered a hiatus with the ascent of Alan García's APRA government (1985–90), and returned with a vengeance in the presidency of Alberto Fujimori (1990–2000). What were the major policy initiatives and the sources of political, economic, and military power that supported them?

Peru emerged from military rule with a multiparty system that had three poles. The Partido Popular Cristiano and Acción Popular occupied the right and center right, APRA the center, and Izquierda Unida anchored the left. Belaúnde, of Acción Popular, won the double round presidential election in coalition with the Partido Popular Cristiano (Stokes 1996: 59). Belaúnde, as did García and Fujimori after him, relied on state power to design and initiate economic policy. Technocratic teams and rule by decree were the norm. However, his party coalition also obtained a majority in Congress, minimizing friction with a pliant legislature (Conaghan and Malloy 1994).

Belaúnde deepened stabilization policy and introduced or intensified structural reforms. He opened debt negotiation with the IMF, reduced income taxes, and held periodic small devaluations of the currency. He also removed price controls, reduced subsidies to consumption on food and gas, and kept wage increases below inflation. To promote the private sector he expanded credit to business. Structural reforms included aggressive tariff reduction (from 115 percent to 30 percent); new foreign investment rules to attract international capital, especially in mining, oil, and banking. His government also initiated privatization (Conaghan and Malloy 1994: 140; Wise 1997: 75).

Under Alan García APRA revived its center-left populist heritage and won presidential elections in 1985. APRA obtained a majority in Congress, and Izquierda Unida on the left became the second largest bloc (Haworth 1993: 51– 53; Stokes 1996; 59). In contrast to Belaúnde, he pursued a neostructuralist and populist economic program. He reintroduced wage and price controls, encouraged consumer-led economic reactivation, increased trade protection, overvalued the exchange rate, followed expansionary monetary and fiscal policy, and, in defiance of the IMF and international financial institutions, established a unilateral debt moratorium (Wise 1997: 75).

Beginning in 1982, international economic recession and the Latin American debt crunch precipitated a prolonged economic crisis in Peru aggravated by poor domestic policy choices. These derailed Belaúnde's economic program and destroyed García's. By 1990, Peru was South America's worst economic performer in terms of GDP growth, real wages, and consumption growth (Stokes 1996: 61). Between 1983 and 1990 the fiscal deficit as a percentage of GDP mushroomed from a staggering 46.3 percent to a crushing 60.7 percent and yearly inflation skyrocketed from 90 percent to 7,650 percent (Wise 1997: 72).

Poor economic performance and rising political violence contributed to electoral volatility that began as swings within the established party system and ended with its disintegration by the end of García's term.[7] The magnitude of the economic crisis and allegations of corruption in the executive branch drove voters to the presidential candidacy of Alberto Fujimori in 1990. He ran as a political outsider with a vaguely populist campaign and an improvised electoral organization, Cambio 90. In second round balloting he won with 56.5 percent of the vote against conservative Mario Vargas Llosa, an acclaimed novelist (see Table 8.1) (Cameron and Mauceri 1997; Conaghan 2005; Crabtree and Thomas 1998; Dietz and Myers 2007; Roberts 2006).

Once in office, Fujimori, from a tour of Washington D.C. was convinced that shock treatment and free-market structural economic reforms were the only viable paths to economic stabilization and renewed growth.[8] The new president quickly introduced a draconian program of neoliberal reforms going far beyond Belaúnde's (Cameron 1997: 48). He used technocrats and plans from Vargas Llosa's economic team. On 8 August he announced a shock-treatment-style stabilization program that liberated prices and removed subsidies for many basic food products as well as a tight monetary policy and resumption of foreign

---

[7] AP was discredited in the Belaúnde period; APRA and IU were discredited in the García administration. This opened the opportunity for Fujimori with Cambio 90. Cameron (1997: 46) argues that Fujimori was the only candidate who connected with the informal sector and this helped him to come in second in first-round voting and to win the second round. The IU was too aloof, too focused on a class-oriented approach.

[8] For an overview of key policy reforms and their social impact, see Arce (2006).

Table 8.1. *Peru: Presidential Elections, 1980–2006*

Candidate	1980	1985	1990	2000	2001[a]	2006[a]
Fernando Belaúnde Terry	**45.2%**	–	–	–	–	–
Armando Villanueva del Campo	27.4%	–	–	–	–	–
Luis Bedoya Reyes	9.6%	–	–	–	–	–
Hugo Blanco Galdós	3.9%	–	–	–	–	–
Horacio Zevallos Gámez	3.3%	–	–	–	–	–
Leonidas Rodríguez Figueroa	2.8%	–	–	–	–	–
Alan García	–	**45.7%**	–	–	–	–
Alfonso Barrantes	–	21.2%	–	–	–	–
Luis Bedoya	–	10.2%	–	–	–	–
Javier A. Orlandini	–	6.2%	–	–	–	–
Roger Cáceres	–	1.2%	–	–	–	–
Alberto Fujimori	–	–	**56.5%**	–	–	–
Mario Vargas Llosa	–	–	33.9%	–	–	–
Null Votes	–	–	9.5%	–	–	–
Alberto Fujimori	–	–	–	**51.2%**	–	–
Alejandro Toledo	–	–	–	17.6%	–	–
Null Votes	–	–	–	29.9%	–	–
Alejandro Toledo	–	–	–	–	**53.1%**	–
Alan García	–	–	–	–	46.9%	–
Alan Garcia	–	–	–	–	–	**52.6%**
Ollanta Humala	–	–	–	–	–	47.4%

Boldface indicates winning candidate and percentage of the vote.
[a] Second-round results.
Sources: http://pdba.georgetown.edu/Electdata/Peru, The Europa World Yearbook (1981–2007).

debt repayments (Stokes 1996: 62; Wise 1997). Structural reforms in the first 18 months (before Fujimori's palace coup) included foreign exchange rate unification and liberalization, deeper trade liberalization, removal of export taxes, capital market liberalization, state employment cuts, elimination of employment security laws, elimination of wage indexation, and flexibilization of labor relations. Tax and banking reform, an aggressive privatization program, and the dismantling of agrarian reform and strengthening land markets followed (Stokes 1996; Wise 2006).[9]

Fujimori relied on decrees to pass most of the early reforms but, unlike Belaúnde and García, his party did not control the legislature (see Table 8.2). Cambio 90 had less than a quarter of seats in the lower chamber and less than a fifth in the Senate (Cameron 1997: 49). Nevertheless, the economic crisis was so severe that, like Menem in Argentina, he was granted by Congress an enabling law that delegated legislative power to him (Cameron 1997: 38).

Nevertheless, tension erupted in September 1991 when Fujimori presented a slate of 126 decrees to implement structural adjustment and to give the military

[9] For details, see Crabtree and Thomas (1998); Wise and Roett (2003); Sheahan (1999).

Table 8.2. *Peru: Distribution of Seats in the Chamber of Deputies, 1980–2006*

Party	1980	1985	1990	1995	2000	2001	2006
Partido Acción Popular – AP	98	11	–	4	–	3	36
Partido Aprista Peruano – PAP	58	107	53	8	3	28	–
Partido Popular Cristiano – PPC	10	–	–	3	–	–	–
Unión de Izquierda Revolucionaria – UNIR	3	–	–	–	–	–	–
Partido Revolucionario de los Trabajadores – PRT	3	–	–	–	–	–	–
Unidad de Izquierda	2	48	16	–	–	–	–
Frente Nacional de Trabajadores y Campesinos – FNTC	2	–	–	–	–	–	–
Frentre Obrero, Campesino, Estudiantil y Popular – FOCEP	1	–	–	–	–	–	–
Convergencia Democrática – CODE	–	12	–	5	–	–	–
Izquierda Nacionalista – IN	–	2	–	–	–	–	–
Frente Democrático – FREDEMO	–	–	62	–	–	–	–
CAMBIO 90	–	–	33	67	–	3	–
IS	–	–	4	–	–	–	–
Union por el Perú – UP	–	–	–	17	3	11	45
Frente Independiente Moralizador – FIM	–	–	–	6	9	–	–
Renovación	–	–	–	3	–	–	–
Movimiento Cívico Nacional – OBRAS	–	–	–	2	–	–	–
Frente Popular Agrícola – FIA del Perú	–	–	–	1	2	–	–
Movimiento Independiente Agrario	–	–	–	1	–	–	–
Alianza Popular Revolucionaria Americana – APRA	–	–	–	–	6	–	–
Avancemos – AV	–	–	–	–	4	–	–
Perú 2000 – P2000	–	–	–	–	52	–	–
Perú Posible- PP	–	–	–	–	26	45	2
Solidaridad Nacional – SN	–	–	–	–	5	–	–
Somos Perú	–	–	–	–	–	4	–
Todos por la Victoria – TpV	–	–	–	–	–	1	–
Partido Renacimiento Andino – PRA	–	–	–	–	–	1	–
Alianza Electoral Solución Popular- SP	–	–	–	–	–	1	–
Agrupación Independiente Unión por el Perú – UpP	–	–	–	–	–	6	–
Alianza Electoral Unidad Nacional	–	–	–	–	–	17	–
Alianza por el Futuro	–	–	–	–	–	–	13
Frente de Centro	–	–	–	–	–	–	5
Restauración Nacional	–	–	–	–	120	–	2
Unidad Nacional – UN	–	–	–	–	–	–	17
Total seats	**180**	**180**	**180**	**120**	**120**	**120**	**120**

Sources: http://psephos.adam-carr.net/countries/p/peru; http://georgetown.edu/Electdata/Peru.

expanded powers to combat the insurgencies of the Shining Path and the Movimiento Revolucionario Tupac Amaru (MRTA; Revolutionary Movement of Tupac Amaru) (Mauceri 1995). Congress balked, as did some Supreme Court justices. Fujimori, however, had cultivated ever-closer relations with the military since he became president. Because of his mistrust of political parties, the minority status of the inchoate Cambio 90, and his own desire to concentrate power, the military became his main source of organized political support. After launching a public relations campaign to discredit political parties and the other two branches of government, Fujimori, with the military's backing, launched a palace coup on 5 April 1992 in which he dissolved Congress, purged the judiciary, and established press censorship (Kenney 1996; McClintock 1996; Stokes 1996: 64).

After the palace coup Fujimori concentrated state and military power, despite the fact that the Organization of American States and foreign governments pressed him to reestablish democracy (McClintock and Vallas 2003: 136–39; Muñoz 1994: 195–96). To deflect those pressures he eventually convened a Democratic Constitutional Council, and constitutional rule returned in November 1993. However, Fujimori kept only the veneer of democracy. Under the surface, his was still an authoritarian government; Fujimori and his intelligence advisor, Vladimir Montecinos, manipulated the system to their advantage. There was little respect for the rule of law; intimidation and buying of congressional votes and of the press and opponents in general was rampant. Political parties collapsed as effective organizations for the intermediation of interests between state and society (Roberts 2006; Weyland 2006). There were many security and human rights violations in the prosecution of counterinsurgency warfare. In short, Fujimori and his supporters used the extralegal authoritarian concentration of state and military power to ram through a neoliberal structural adjustment program and to fight the Shining Path and the MRTA (Belaúnde 1998; Conaghan 2005; Mauceri 2006; Obando 1998; Roberts and Peceny 1997).

Exclusion, Declining Mobilization, Authoritarianism, and Violence

The cumulative effects of economic crises and stabilization policies under Belaúnde and García had devastating consequences for the popular sectors.[10] The situation did not improve under Fujimori, although macroeconomic conditions did (Wise 2006). Real wages lost approximately two thirds of their 1979 value by 1992 (Balbi 1997: 141; Stokes 1995: 46). Although private sector real wages recovered somewhat by 1995, they were still less than half those of 1980, and minimum wages simply continued to plummet; in 1995 they had lost 80 percent of their 1979 value (Figueroa 1998: 136). Meanwhile the prices of basic

---

[10] Peru suffered two devastating recessions during that period: (1) 1982–83, GDP contraction of 12.3 percent; (2) 1988–90, GDP contractions of 8.4, 11.4, and 4.9 percent (Mauceri 1997: 41).

foodstuffs, transportation, cooking essentials, and medicine rose dramatically because of cuts and eventual elimination of subsidies.[11] From 1981 to 1991 formal sector employment fell steadily each year, from 61 percent to 47 percent of the economically active population. During the same period the informal sector expanded from 33 percent to 48 percent of the economically active population. In just five years (from 1987 to 1993) the percentage of the adequately employed as a percentage of the economically active population in Lima plunged from 60 to 13 percent, and the underemployed who labored in temporary jobs or under otherwise precarious job conditions jumped from 35 to 77 percent (Roberts 1998: 239–40).[12] The situation had not improved by 1993. Meanwhile, national poverty levels, which stood at nearly 42 percent of the population, rose to 53 percent in 1994, dipped to 51 percent in 1997, and climbed to 54 percent in 2000 (Sheahan 2006:187). During the same period, rural poverty climbed from almost 54 percent to 68 percent (Figueroa 1998: 137–38). Table 8.3, drawing from different sources, corroborates the shift in class situation for Peruvians.

In Argentina, Bolivia, and Ecuador, comparably long neoliberal periods with high levels of political and economic exclusion generated contentious politics in which, after the initial decline of the labor movement, new movement and protest organizations in cooperation with the labor movement eventually built collective power, forced out presidents committed to neoliberalism, and helped usher in alternatives. In Venezuela, such a trend was cut short by violent military coups d'états attempts; nevertheless, high levels of decentralized anti-neoliberal protest continued.

Peru was different. From high levels of collective power in the late 1970s (in a situation similar to Bolivia's) protest steadily declined. First, horizontal linkages among different movements eroded during Belaúnde and García's presidencies. When Fujimori began to construct market society, protest was meek. What accounts for this inability to reconstruct collective power?

One explanation focused on the negative effects of neoliberal reforms and economic crisis on the labor movement, which contributed to the severing of cooperation with the shantytown and peasant movements. It points out that the decline of formal sector employment in the private and public sector decimated organized labor, destroying its capacity to lead, and cut links with shantytown and peasant movements. In Belaúnde's and, to a lesser extent, García's, presidency there were nine national and many regional strikes, protests by squatters, women, and youth movements. But coordination within and among them was generally lacking, and thus they did not achieve the power of the massive strike waves of 1977–78. By Fujimori's presidency, anti-neoliberal mobilization was decidedly

---

[11] Immediately after Fujimori took office, gasoline rose 3,140 percent, kerosene for cooking jumped by 6,946 percent, bread by 1,567 percent, cooking oil by 639 percent, sugar by 552 percent, rice increased by 533 percent, and medicine by 1,385 percent (Stokes 1996: 62).

[12] For a detailed examination of Peruvian labor markets under Fujimori, see Thomas (1998).

241

Table 8.3. *Peru: Economic and Social Indicators*

	1980	1990	1991	1992	1993	1994	1995	1996	1997	1998	1999	2000	2001	2002	2003	2004	2005	2006	2007[a]
GDP	3.8	-4.9	2.8	-0.9	5.8	13.9	8.6	2.5	6.8	-0.6	0.9	2.8	0.3	4.9	4.1	5.1	6.7	7.6	8.9
GDP/CAP	1.0	-6.8	0.9	-2.6	4.0	12.0	6.7	0.7	5.0	-2.3	-0.8	1.2	-1.3	3.3	2.5	3.9	5.5	6.3	7.6
Income Distribution[b]																			
D1									1.0		1.0		1.1		1.4				
D2									2.0		2.0		2.2		2.4				
Q2									7.0		7.0		7.5		7.9				
Q3									12.1		11.5		12.4		20.6				
Q4									20.0		18.9		20.2		16.0				
D9									16.3		15.1		16.0		39.2				
D10									41.6		44.6		40.6		9.4				
Unemployment	7.1	8.3	5.9	9.4	9.9	8.8	7.1	7.2	8.6	6.9	9.4	7.8	9.3	9.4	9.4	9.4	9.6	8.5	8.7
Informal[c]			60.2				63.8					58.8			57.9				
Poverty																			
Total													54.8		54.7	48.6	48.7	44.5	
Urban													42.0		43.1	37.1	36.8	31.2	
Rural													78.4		76.0	69.8	70.9	69.3	
Average Wage Index[d]	265.0	85.7	98.7	95.2	94.4	109.2	100.	095.2	94.5	92.7	90.8	100.0	99.1	103.7	105.3	106.5	104.4	105.7	103.8
Minimum Wage Index[e]	676.1	158.0	107.4	107.4	75.5	97.8	100.0	103.2	181.2	200.9	90.0	100.0	101.2	101.0	102.2	106.9	105.1	112.0	111.7

[a] Estimated.

[b] *D9* and *D10* = richest quintile; *D1* and *D2* = poorest quintile. Data not reported for all years.

[c] Informal sector data reported only from 1991 to 2003 in constant format. Data not reported for all years.

[d] Average wage index between 1980 and 1999 based on 1995 = 100; 2000–2007 based on 2000 = 100 (in italics).

[e] Minimum wage index between 1980 and 1999 based on 1995 = 100; 2000–2007 based on 2000 = 100 (in italics).

Sources: Economic Commission for Latin America and the Caribbean, *Statistical Yearbook* (Santiago: ECLAC, 1980–2007) and *Economic Survey of Latin America* (Santiago: ECLAC, 1980–2007). Labor Statistics from International Labor Organization, Labor Overview: *Latin America and the Caribbean* (Lima: ILO, 1994–2007). For comparability of data, I have not filled in missing years with other sources.

mild. Between 1990 and 1992 the CGTP called three general strikes that were completely ineffective because of changes in the class situation of the rank and file. Workers did not support them because they believed the leadership fought for the rights of only a tiny labor aristocracy in the formal sector of the economy and therefore no longer represented their interests. Shantytown dwellers, overwhelmingly employed in the informal sector of the economy, felt and acted the same way (Balbi 1997; Cook 2007; Huber 1983; Roberts 1998; Tanaka 1998).

In addition to these factors, Mauceri (1997: 26–29) argued that anti-popular sector statutory changes established during the transition to democracy intensified under Fujimori. These measures imposed legal sanctions to mobilization on labor leaders and union members. Further, Morales Bermúdez's military administration denied legal recognition to the two major peasant confederations. It also radically reduced subsidies to "new towns" and channeled remaining services to municipalities. These measures broke up horizontal linkages and weakened the impact of mobilization by deflecting them to the local level.

These conditions were certainly important but insufficient because they were present in all of our cases. The labor movement declined everywhere because of neoliberal stabilization and adjustment policies. Bolivia and Ecuador introduced laws restricting labor organization. Argentina and Bolivia devolved the provision of public services and emergency relief to the departmental, provincial, and municipal levels. Nevertheless, collective power, with the participation of urban labor but not under its leadership, reconstituted in Argentina, Bolivia, and Ecuador; and it might have done so in Venezuela too if not for the attempted coups d'état. If these conditions were present in other cases where popular sectors mobilized and built horizontal linkages, what, then, accounts for the difference in outcome?

As most of the literature on Peru explicitly or implicitly recognizes, the rise of insurrectionary guerrilla movements, unique to this case, helps to explain why associational and collective power in opposition to the construction of market society did not develop. These were the Shining Path and the smaller MRTA. Of the two, the Shining Path was the most significant. Its origins can be traced to the Velasco era when Maoist splinters of the Communist Party in the poor southern highlands formed a revolutionary arm that rejected all reformism (Degregori 1994). After redemocratization in 1980, they expanded quickly among poor, land-hungry central-south highland peasant communities in the departments of Ayacucho, Huancavelica, and Apurímac, whose grievances governments consistently ignored and made inroads in Junín and Cuzco. The Shining Path also grew progressively ruthless, violent, and brutal as it turned to armed conflict to sharpen the contradictions of dependent capitalism and precipitate spontaneous mass uprising against the Peruvian state (McClintock 1989).

Although the Shining Path had been organizing in the shantytowns of major cities – especially Lima – for some time, insurrectionary violence escalated notably beginning in 1988. The Shining Path believed that the economic crisis that engulfed García's administration, and the mobilization that accompanied it, presented an opportunity to launch a destabilizing offensive to force the ultimate crisis of the state. By 1992, the Shining Path had made significant inroads in a number of large "new towns" (shantytowns) and military presence in them increased dramatically. Lima was under siege, and the guerillas planned a major national offensive to overturn the state (Burt 1997: 284; Palmer 1994: 3).

In short, between 1980 and 1992, the Shining Path built significant associational power by organizing peasants and shantytown dwellers. However, its emphasis on cell-based organization for security purposes limited the emergence of horizontal linkages among them. Its sectarianism, intolerance of reformism, and emphasis on armed conflict and indiscriminate violence inhibited the development of an anti-neoliberal episode of contention in Peru. These characteristics drove a wedge between the Shining Path and other popular sector organizations, "merely" demanding reform of neoliberal capitalism. Moreover, they corroded and disarticulated shantytown dwellers' and indigenous peoples' movements by infiltrating their organizations and by threatening and killing their leaders to eliminate competition (Roberts 1998; Yashar 2005).[13] Many peasant communities, some initially sympathetic to the Shining Path, defended themselves from these vicious onslaughts by organizing civil defense units. Shantytown organizations, because of urban density, had difficulty responding in the same manner, and the Shining Path penetrated and weakened even former bastions of the Izquierda Unida (Burt 1997).

The state's counterinsurgency campaign in the 1980s and 1990s effectively closed political associational space for reformist anti-neoliberal organizing by placing large swaths of highland Peru under military control (Yashar 2005). By the late 1980s three departments (Ayacucho, Apurímac, and Huancavelica) were declared emergency zones and placed under martial law (Palmer 1994). Political associational space constricted even more when Fujimori, supported by the military, carried out a coup d'état by dissolving Congress and dismantling the judiciary. He used the authoritarian turn to prosecute the war against the Shining Path and the MRTA vigorously. By 1993, the number of provinces under a state of emergency expanded from 52 to 66, and in 1994 nearly half of Peru's population lived in such zones, where the security forces repressed leftist organizations in general. By the end of 1995, insurgents, state security forces, drug traffickers, death squads, and civilian paramilitaries had killed more than 27,000 Peruvians (Roberts and Peceny 1997). The figure was probably substantially higher given that the Peruvian Truth and Reconciliation Commission estimated over 69,000 victims between 1980 and 2000.[14] Equally important, Fujimori exploited the

[13] The Shining Path saw itself in competition with left groups and political parties and attacked them viciously (Woy-Hazelton and Hazelton 1994).
[14] Truth and Reconciliation Commission, República del Perú, final report delivered to President Toledo on 28 August, 2003.

authoritarian turn to decree highly constrictive if not repressive labor laws that demolished whatever remained of organized labors' capacity for contentious politics (Cook 2007).

Anti-neoliberal popular sector mobilization never really recovered from the combination of violence and authoritarianism under Fujimori. The CGTP ill-advisedly called a general strike to protest neoliberal economic policy at the height of the insurgency in 1992. It received very little support from union rank and file (Balbi 1997: 146). The state-owned oil company's union struck in 1996 to oppose privatization, and leaders of APRA and some leftist parties, along with the CGTP, attempted to force a referendum on the issue. The effort failed when Fujimori supporters in Congress (many of them literally bought) amended referendum rules (Conaghan 2005: 123–24). These, and a few other isolated actions, did not constitute a cycle of anti-neoliberal contention.[15]

Contentious politics intensified in the wake of the fraud-tarnished 2000 presidential elections that gave Fujimori a third term in office; but again not at a level to characterize them as an anti-market society wave of contention. Opposition candidate Alejandro Toledo and his supporters tried to force an annulment. They organized a large demonstration – March of the Four Suyos – to support their effort, an event set to coincide with Fujimori's inauguration on 28 July 2000. Indeed, the march briefly reconnected horizontal linkages between the labor movement, peasant associations, youth groups, and political parties. An estimated 250,000 demonstrators converged on central Lima. To a large extent the strong presence of international election observers and the OAS who were investigating claims of numerous election irregularities afforded the protestors the capability to organize the march. They ensured a minimum of political space in Fujimori's authoritarian democracy to operate. Fujimori, however, unperturbed by their presence, used the usual underhanded mechanisms to weather the storm, and mobilization could not be sustained (Conaghan 2005: 203–19).

Aftermath

In the end, Fujimori's regime fell under the weight of its own corruption when videos of congressional influence-buying became public on 14 September 2000.[16] Fujimori and Valdemir Montecinos, the shadowy architect and manager of corruption, were forced to resign in November. Cycles of anti-neoliberal contention – coordinated or decentralized – did not contribute significantly to Fujimori's fall because mass mobilization erupted only *after* Fujimori's regime had

---

[15] In one such isolated action on 28 April 1999, with the country fully pacified, the CGTP called a general strike with support of political parties and Lima community organizations. The strike was reasonalbly successful, also in provinces such as Iquitos in the Amazon and Cuzco, Arequipa, and Ayacucho in the central-south highlands. They were protesting the cumulative effects of free-market economic policies (Associated Press 28 April 1999).

[16] The videos themselves were bought for $100,000 (Conaghan 2005)

been fatally weakened (Conaghan 2005: 247). The revival of democratic freedoms and accountability in the wake of the corruption scandals opened political associational space for contentious politics. A spasm of mobilization reminiscent of the 1977–78 general strikes erupted; demonstrators protested neoliberal policies and demanded Fujimori's immediate resignation. On 11 October a million and a half peasants and farmers of the CNA and other associations began a 48-hour national action, demanding relief from neoliberal agrarian policies. On 12 October the CGTP, 250,000 teachers, public employee unions, and community groups joined them.[17] In the final analysis, mass mobilization probably hastened a finished dictator's decision to flee but it did not contribute to systematic weakening of his regime.

Following a brief interim government, Alejandro Toledo and his newly formed political party, Peru Posible, won second-round presidential elections against APRA's Alan García in June 2001. Drawing attention to his indigenous background and rags-to-middle-class-respectability story, Toledo's campaign emphasized socioeconomic inclusion. It promised to reduce shockingly high poverty levels (one in two Peruvians were officially poor or indigent), two million jobs to tackle unemployment and underemployment, improved budgets for health and education, and 100-percent raises in salaries for teachers and doctors. He also vowed to stamp out government corruption (González 2004; Macbeth 2005; Ministry of Economy and Finance 2005).

Unfortunately, once in office Toledo betrayed his mandate. Corruption continued unabated, he did nothing to reform the deplorable justice system inherited from Fujimori, and human rights violations that occurred during the Shining Path insurgency were not prosecuted.[18] Toledo continued to institutionalize structural adjustment programs (including privatization) advocated by the World Bank, the IMF, and international investors. These lauded him for Peru's strong macroeconomic recovery: rapid sustained GDP growth (over 5 percent per year between 2002 and 2006), low inflation (down to 2 percent in 2004), expanding exports, positive trade balances, and positive current account balances in 2004 and 2005 (Ministry of Economy and Finance 2005).

But macroeconomic success came at the price of continued grinding socioeconomic exclusion. In 2004, 52 percent of the economically active population lived in poverty and 20.7 percent in extreme poverty. Rural poverty and extreme poverty were even more appalling at 75 and 45 percent, respectively. The figures for the rural highlands were a crushing 80-percent poor and 50-percent indigent. In some impoverished provinces, such as Huancavelica, those staggering rates

---

[17] Indigenous peasant associations and unions precipitated the action on 11 October. The protest's peak was set for Columbus Day, 12 October (Agence France Presse 10, 11, 12 October 2000).

[18] Toledo did establish a Truth and Reconciliation Commission that submitted its final report in August 2003, see Hite (2007).

stood at an unimaginable 90 and 75 percent, respectively (Ministry of Economy and Finance 2005). Job creation and shifts in the ratio of formal to informal sector jobs remained flat and official open unemployment did not really improve.

With democracy restored and in the absence of armed insurgencies, contentious politics surged, driven by Toledo's policy about-face, sustained political exclusion, and persistent high levels of socioeconomic exclusion. Four waves of anti-neoliberal protest swept over Peru between 2002 and 2005; roughly one per year (Arce 2008). They were largely decentralized mobilizations, but disparate social forces tentatively built some collective power in the first three by forging horizontal linkages. This was especially true regionally in southern Peru around the country's second largest city, Arequipa. Protests occurred in Lima as well (and frequently) but a sustained national level of coordination among popular sector organizations never emerged. By 2005, anti-neoliberal contention, while frequent, was thoroughly decentralized. This can be explained by the absence of economic crisis to focus discontent, concessions by the government (partial inclusion), and the lack of a movement to lead in replacement of structurally weakened organized labor, probably because of lingering memories of recent violence.

The presidential election of April 2006 channeled much of this discontent. As 2005 drew to a close, it catapulted the candidacy of a political outsider, Ollanta Humala, an outspoken nationalist and former army officer who had led failed nonviolent coup against Fujimori in October 2000. In early 2006, his Partido Nacionalista del Perú (PNP, or Nationalist Party of Peru) was doing well in the polls, vowing to "fight to build the great Latin American nation, as a new power with sovereignty in the global world [following] the integrationist struggles by the liberators Simón Bolívar and José de San Martín"(Sánchez 2006: 4). In classic style, his vague populist platform excoriated traditional oligarchs and free trade agreements with the United States. It also promised to break coca eradication agreements and forge links with Chávez's Venezuela. Millions of impoverished Peruvians flocked to his tumultuous rallies.[19]

However, in June 2006 Humala, in second-round ballot, lost the election to APRA's Alan García, whose political star had risen, phoenixlike, from the ashes of a seemingly unrecoverable state of disgrace (Schmidt 2007).[20] He cast himself in the mold of Chile's center left, promising to retain neoliberal reforms that reinvigorated economic growth but with an emphasis on greater social equity. This won him the support of the middle class, and his pledge to retain free trade agreements with the United States gained him backing from the north.[21]

---

[19] Council on Hemispheric Affairs, "Peru's 2006 Presidential Elections," 7 April 2006.
[20] In first-round balloting Humala received 30.6 percent of the votes to García's 24.3 percent. In the second round, García won 52.6 percent to Humala's 47.4 percent.
[21] Council on Hemispheric Affairs, "Peruvians Face a Difficult Choice," 1 June 2006.

In office, García, so far, has followed through on this platform. With just under a third of the seats in Congress, his party, APRA, has alternately forged policy coalitions with center-left and center-right parties. In August 2006, Congress approved the government's five-year plan, which focused heavily on poverty alleviation (11 social welfare programs), education, health, job creation (300,000), investment in rural infrastructure, and support for export-oriented agriculture in the highlands. To calm unrest in coca-growing areas, García's government shifted emphasis from eradication to crop replacement and prosecution of cocaine production and trafficking. Finally, President García has also remained true to his pledge of fiscal responsibility and to ratification of a free trade agreement with the United States (Europa World Book 2007: 3609–12). These socioeconomic and politically inclusionary measures have, to date, restored a measure of stability to Peru's volatile politics and society (Jasper and Ribando Seelke 2008).

Chile

Chile was *the* original experiment in free-market economics. A ruthless, repressive military dictatorship under General Augusto Pinochet imposed an authoritarian version of contemporary market society between 1975 and 1989. The armed forces had intervened to resolve the crisis of Chilean national populism during the socialist administration of Salvador Allende (1970–73). At the head of an unwieldy coalition of left parties (Popular Unity), Allende attempted radical reform of Chile's political economy that provoked sharp class conflict. On 11 September 1973, a military coup d'état, supported by the United States, ended 43 years of democratic rule.

The subsequent construction of market society obliterated the remnants of national populism in Chile. To regain control of a chaotic economy between 1975 and 1978, the military government implemented a radical orthodox economic stabilization and restructuring program. It lifted price controls, liberated interest rates that then rose rapidly, and slashed fiscal spending that drastically reduced contributions to health, education, and welfare. It also privatized most of Chile's considerable number of public enterprises – especially in the financial and industrial sectors but not in mining, Chile's principal export sector – and deregulated the financial system. The military government executed a trade reform that restructured Chile's economy from protected industries producing for domestic markets toward those with comparative advantage in mining, fishing, fruits, and timber. The commercial, financial, and construction sectors also boomed, and a generous foreign investment code lured international capital back. Starting in 1979, second-stage neoliberal reforms privatized the pension system and turned it over to Pension Fund Administrator, health care insurance by creating Private Health Insurance Plans, and the educational system by means of school vouchers. The military government also instituted a labor code reform that institutionalized the emasculation of organized labor that occurred after the coup. To decentralize political administration, Pinochet's technocrats gave regions and municipalities more authority over local issues.[22]

The combined weight of state and military power initiated Chile's neoliberal transformation. Power was extraordinarily concentrated. Pinochet, commander in chief of the army, quickly centralized power in his person. By April 1975, he relied on a close-knit team of free-market economists – the so-called Chicago boys because many had studied economics at the University of Chicago – to direct economic and social policy. The armed forces, the militarized police force, and the feared Directorate of National Intelligence squelched opposition and ruled by terror. The record of human rights violations was particularly harrowing to 1977 and, although violent repression abated, it was always present and kept the population in fear and quiescent.[23]

In short, the junta imposed market society at the cost of massive political exclusion and terror. The junta established a highly centralized nonporous authoritarian military government. It closed Congress indefinitely, banned all political parties, and purged state institutions and universities. The consolidated intelligence services of the armed forces and the national police mercilessly persecuted socialists, communists, and other far-left groups that had been active in political parties, in the student movement, and in the urban and rural labor and shantytown organizing movements. Thousands of activists died or simply disappeared. Thousands more were tortured, imprisoned, exiled, or blacklisted.

Following recessionary or stagnant years immediately after the coup, the Chilean economy began to recover, with strong economic growth from 1977 to 1981.[24] Rapid growth occurred in the financial sector, fishing, forest products, fruits, mining, and construction (while the manufacturing sector declined). International investment poured in, and GDP per capita recovered to 1970 levels in 1979. Real wages did the same in 1981 (Larraín 1991: 283); and inflation was under control.[25]

Under the gloss of success, Chile's economic transformation came at a high price in terms of socioeconomic exclusion. Open unemployment never fell below

---

[22] For general texts on this period, see Edwards and Cox Edwards (1987); Foxley (1983); Angell and Pollack (1993). For second-generation reforms, see Borzutzky (2002); Raczynski (2000, 1983). For labor code reform, see Campero and Valenzuela (1984); Ruiz-Tagle (1985); Drake (1996); Angell (1991).

[23] For state structure under military rule, see Valenzuela (1991); Valenzuela and Valenzuela (1976); Valenzuela and Valenzuela (1986); Garretón (1989); Loveman (1993). For the Chicago boys, see Puryear (1994); Fontaine (1988). For human rights violations, see Verdugo (2001); de Brito (1998); White (1974).

[24] Although economic growth began to decelerate in 1981, it was still a respectable 5.5 percent (Marcel and Meller 1986: 125).

[25] For an overview of economic transformation, see Ffrench-Davis (1999); Foxley (1983); Edwards and Cox Edwards (1987).

10 percent in its best year (1981); if we include people on minimal employment relief plans (established in 1975) it never fell below 15 percent.[26] Wages dropped sharply by more than 30 percent in the first few years relative to 1970, inching their way back to 1970 levels in 1981.[27] Income inequality as measured by the Gini coefficient worsened substantially; from a low of.45 in 1974 it shot to.54 in 1976 and remained there in 1981 (Larraín 1991). In 1981 expenditures on aid to families and per capita spending for health and education were 19, 25, and 8 percent lower than in 1970 (Ffrench-Davis 1999: 266). In the face of appalling socioeconomic exclusion, military rule with high levels of repression kept the popular sectors and middle classes from resisting neoliberalism through contentious politics. Meanwhile, the controlled media suppressed this reality and saturated the public sphere with news of Chile's macroeconomic success and achievements in sectoral transformation.

Riding the economic upturn and a mood of propaganda-generated optimism, Pinochet and his supporters, who heretofore had relied exclusively on force, began a process of *political liberalization* to legitimate authoritarian rule. They submitted a new constitution for ratification by plebiscite in 1980 (Varas 1991). The framers designed the Constitution of 1980 to guide Chile through a transition from military rule to a protected democracy. The transition was to begin in 1988 with another plebiscite to decide whether Pinochet should continue to be president for eight more years (to 1997). If "yes" there would be an election for Congress in 1989. If "no" national elections for president would also be held. Regardless of whether Pinochet or the political opposition won the plebiscite, the 1980 Constitution established military guardianship over the political system and protected the interests of property holders by making it virtually impossible to reform the free-market economic system imposed by the dictatorship without the consent of conservative interests (Garretón 1989).[28]

Compared with the depths of closed authoritarianism, political liberalization, however limited and arbitrary in its implementation, opened political associational space for opposition. Banned political parties resurfaced in a gray area of tolerated campaigning to oppose the 1980 Constitution, although the military's manipulated and overwhelming victory left them dispirited and in disarray. By the same token, the labor code reform of 1979 provided associational space – albeit constrained – for struggling unions to operate. Even though the regime carefully

---

[26] Worst years were 1975–76 with nearly 20 percent (including relief employment) declining to 17 percent in 1980; open unemployment went from nearly 17 percent in 1976 to nearly 12 percent in 1980 (Jadresic 1986: 151).

[27] On average, wages were 25 percent lower between 1974 and 1981 than in 1970 (Ffrench-Davis 1999: 84).

[28] In a protected democracy, a national security council with majority military representation would advise presidents. The legislature and the electoral system overrepresented conservatives, and amending the constitution required extraordinary majorities, making it impossible to change without approval of conservatives. This was especially true in the Senate, which exercised veto power over all bills.

controlled political liberalization to limit and emasculate opposition, the political associational space it offered became significant when other key conditions changed.

Economic Crisis, Political Liberalization, and Anti-Market Society Mobilization

Selective repression, economic good times, an aggressive propaganda-saturated controlled press, and defeat in the 1980 constitutional plebiscite left banned and disorganized opposition political parties resigned to suffering Pinochet for another 17 years. The recently legalized labor movement struggled to rebuild under difficult conditions. Shantytown dweller organizations did their best to establish clientelist relationships with Pinochetista mayors and the expanding political machines of proregime protopolitical parties. All battled for survival in deep isolation from each other.

Economic crisis from 1982 to 1983 in the context of limited *political liberalization* changed all this. The Latin American debt crisis combined with overexposure in the highly concentrated domestic financial sector to unleash a devastating recession, the worst since the Great Depression of the 1930s. Between 1982 and 1983 GDP contracted violently by 15 percent. Necessary devaluation contributed to financial system collapse and forced the government to place many financial institutions in receivership (Edwards and Cox Edwards 1987; Vergara 1985).

Because the military regime initially responded with procyclical economic policies, it aggravated the recession and therefore *socioeconomic exclusion*. Unemployment including people in minimum relief programs soared to 26 and 31 percent in 1982 and 1983, respectively; open unemployment averaged approximately 19 percent (Jadresic 1986: 151). In 1984 almost half the population in greater Santiago – 49 percent – was estimated to live in poverty (Larraín 1991: 285). In 1985, after a few years of economic recovery, a staggering 45 percent of Chileans still lived in poverty (Oppenheim 2007: 190). Real wages, for those who were still earning them, had contracted 15 percent by 1984 (meaning they had again fallen below 1970 levels) and the Gini coefficient climbed to .55 (Larraín 1991: 283).

The dictatorship insisted on orthodox economic procyclical responses to the crisis with total disregard for its socioeconomic effects, which reached beyond the popular sectors to include middle classes and business. In 1982, this stance weakened state cohesion by creating tension between it and business sectors, demanding countercyclical policy and relief from crushing debt burdens. The junta ignored them (Silva 1996). In May 1983, however, the government's arrogant intransigence and the desperation of social groups suffering from profound political and socioeconomic exclusion sparked an episode of anti-neoliberal contention that ended in 1986.

In addition to economic hard times and the regime's slavish orthodox prescriptions to overcome them, the dictatorship's efforts to legitimate its rule beyond the use of force – to liberalize authoritarian rule no matter how controlled – opened a sliver of political associational space that permitted the resurgence of contentious politics. Three aspects of the new political institutional setting were particularly important. First, the new labor code permitted space for the legal, and therefore open, reconstitution of the labor movement, albeit under highly restrictive conditions. Labor leaders, spearheaded by the historically militant copper miners' union (Confederación de Trajadores del Cobre), began the arduous and dangerous task of rebuilding, that is, of recreating associational power.[29] Second, however limited, imperfect, and manipulated the political liberalization process was, it allowed opposition political parties, especially the centrist Christian Democratic Party, to reemerge in an odd gray zone. They were not legal, but neither were they severely repressed for holding semiclandestine meetings and setting up think tanks to publish papers and books of limited circulation sustained by funding from international sources. (This, of course, did not apply to leftist parties of Marxist inspiration.) Third, repression eased; although the government's more strategic exercise of that tool kept Chileans in fear.

The consolidation of market society, controlled political liberalization, and economic crisis detonated massive reform-oriented anti-neoliberal mobilization. This involved a rapid buildup of associational and collective power that was due, to a large extent, to the *brokerage* of political parties. In Chilean democracy, political parties had deeply penetrated urban and rural unions and shantytown organizations. They were the "backbone" of social movements (Garretón 1983). As the labor movement and shantytown organizations revived in the late 1970s, so did links between them and political parties. Indeed, political parties (and international labor, relief, human rights organizations, and the Catholic Church) helped to reconstitute them (Drake 1996).

The opening wave of anti-market society contention began in May 1983, and ended in October 1984. It started when the influential copper miners' union – under Christian Democratic Party leadership – with support from other labor federations called for a national day of protest on 11 May 1983, encouraging absenteeism, work slowdowns, and demonstrations. Largely through the brokerage of political party leaderships, university students simultaneously held assemblies and demonstrations. Residents of middle- and working-class neighborhoods boycotted stores; at night they turned out the lights and banged pots. Organized by the Communist Party, some poorer districts set up barricades (Roberts 1998: 122).

Following up on the success of the May mobilization, the labor movement built collective power by forming the Comando Nacional de Trabajadores that brought together unions and middle-class professional associations [*gremios*] – and through them political parties, especially the Christian Democrats and a reformed sector of the Socialist Party (Barrera and Valenzuela 1986: 261). However, they

[29] For the labor movement under Pinochet, see Drake (1996); Campero and Valenzuela (1984); Frías (1989); Barrera and Valenzuela (1986); Roberts (1998); Cook (2007); Ruiz-Tagle (1985).

did not include shantytown organizations. These protested simultaneously but independently. A radicalized Communist Party (and smaller leftist parties) had been patiently working to rebuild popular sector power in sprawling poor neighborhoods. They led the shantytown organizations they had penetrated in more transgressive (meaning violent), contentious action (Oxhorn 1995). However, given the decentralization and diversity of shantytown associations, they did not form a unified movement. Indeed, many were not politically oriented and therefore did not participate in anti-neoliberal contention (Salman 1994).

Emboldened, these two strands of opposition to the dictatorship staged similar protests almost every month to October 1984. Demonstrators repudiated the dictatorship's economic policies, protested their effects, demanded relief, and clamored for Pinochet's removal and reform of the 1980 Constitution to ensure a speedy transition to full democracy (Martínez and Díaz 1996; Oxhorn 1995; Roberts 1998). Ending the dictatorship and returning to democratic rule was a necessary condition for economic policy reforms that would protect people more from the effects of the market.

Collective and associational power built on two tracks that emerged during the first three protest events. By the fourth month of national protests in August, the demonstrations were getting larger and the more moderate reformist opposition movement, with the Christian Democrats and the Comando Nacional de Trabajadores at the core, formed the Democratic Alliance (Alianza Democrática, or AD). AD advocated Keynesian demand stimulus policies and industrial policy to overcome the economic crisis along with reform of the 1980 Constitution for an earlier return to full political democracy. Within AD, political parties gained control of participating movements and social organizations and subordinated their actions to party strategy. Thus AD proposed a strategy of peaceful mobilization involving labor, middle-class associations, new social movements, and civic groups to put pressure on the military. Seeking broader cross-class alliances, AD also made overtures to disgruntled business sectors and traditional conservative political party figures, linking their shared need for countercyclical economic policy to AD's desire for redemocratization (Silva 1996: 187). Peaceful mobilization was also important to allay the fears of regime softliners that democratization was not synonymous with a resurgence of the "chaos" that had precipitated military rule.

Meanwhile, by the fifth national day of protest, the Communist Party and several smaller radial leftist parties (including a minority splinter of the Socialist Party) formed the Movimiento Democrático Popular (MDP; Popular Democratic Movement). As previously mentioned, these parties were particularly strong in lower-income neighborhoods. In part, as was later the case in Argentina, their organizing was the fruit of formal sector workers who had been let go and, as members of the expanding informal sector or the unemployed, organized neighbors in similar conditions along territorial bases. They proposed a much more transgressive repertoire of contention to induce confrontation with the forces of order and therefore insurrectionary conditions (Oxhorn 1995). The MDP believed "popular rebellion" was the only strategy capable of ousting Pinochet, compelling reform of the 1980 Constitution, and forcing redemocratization (Martínez and Díaz 1996; Roberts 1998).

The opposition's split into these two camps undermined further collective power building to force major economic and political change. AD pointedly excluded the MDP in order to calm the fears of reform-minded regime softliners it wished to win over. The MDP rejected AD's negotiating strategy, believing it futile. Nevertheless, the two collaborated indirectly by coordinating independent but simultaneously held mobilizations on what had become routine monthly days of protest. This first wave of anti-neoliberal–prodemocracy contention ended shortly after the 11th protest in October 1984, which turned into a near-general strike. The military regime responded by declaring a six-month state of siege to suppress further mass mobilization (Cavallo, Salazar, and Sepúlveda 1988: 339).

Although the state of siege ended in mid-1985, it was not until later in the year that anti-neoliberal mobilization resumed. Since early 1985, under the auspices and protection of the Catholic Church, AD had been seeking to expand the anti-Pinochet coalition of political parties and notables to include conservatives who had initially supported the military government and the emerging social democratic left. In September 1985 they crafted a National Accord for a Transition to Full Democracy, which outlined necessary conditions for true redemocratization (Martínez and Díaz 1996: 38). Pinochet rejected it out of hand. Over the next few months the opposition mounted several demonstrations in support of the National Accord, culminating in a large concentration in the Parque O'Higgins in November, but to no avail (Oxhorn 1995: 77).

Faced with this stonewall, AD rebuilt collective power and revived mass mobilization as a tool to force Pinochet to the negotiating table in 1986. To this end, a number of social movement organizations formed a Civic Assembly supported by political parties. For once, it even included shantytown dweller organizations represented by the Unitary Pobladores Command, itself a strengthening of shantytown dweller associational power (Oxhorn 1995: 219, 1994: 59–61). The Civic Assembly hammered out "Demands of Chile" – an accounting of the grievances of participating social groups – as a platform to negotiate with the regime in April (Oxhorn 1995: 78).

When Pinochet dismissed the document out of hand, the Civic Assembly organized a mass demonstration for July 1986. On 2 July protests reminiscent of the early massive turnouts of 1983 erupted all over Santiago, and especially in the low-income neighborhoods that ringed the city. Contentious action in the shantytowns was transgressive and violent. Police and military responded in kind, although with much greater capability and ruthlessness. Whereas in the past military, police and plainclothesmen had shot people in the shanties, now they deliberately set two on fire. This brought mass mobilization to an end (Cavallo, Salazar, and Sepúlveda 1988).

Here we see again how violence and the presence, or perception, of insurrectionary forces committed to popular rebellion prevent the construction of broadly inclusive coordinating organizations essential for collective power building. It may also disarticulate partial advances in collective power building. From the early 1980s on, a radicalized Communist Party advocated armed conflict and insurrectionary tactics as legitimate tools in the struggle against the dictatorship.[30] This, in addition to the Christian Democrats reflexive anticommunism, drove a wedge between AD and the MDP. As long as the MDP supported "popular rebellion," AD had to exclude them; otherwise it could not hope to be the opposition's interlocutor with the military government. Moreover, protests in the low-income neighborhoods that ringed Santiago turned increasingly violent as of August 1983. Fear of escalating violence in the cordons around Santiago and by shantytown agitators in other areas made middle-class demonstrators nervous and eventually kept many from participating in later demonstrations (Garretón 1991).

Violence also inhibited collective power building – and eventually ended Chile's episode of anti-neoliberal contention – because it brought the weight of the formidable repressive capacity of the military government down on protestors. From the beginning, the regime exercised a "two-track" policy. In downtown, middle-class, and sometimes even upper-class, areas, the forces of order measured their repression. However, it was fierce in the shantytowns. Protestors erected barricades, set fires, and threw rocks and other projectiles while women taunted police and soldiers. The forces of order responded by rounding up residents, ransacking their homes, and carrying out mass arrests in operations similar to those of the first years after the coup. They fired their weapons indiscriminately, killing and wounding people, mostly innocents in their homes as bullets pierced flimsy walls. Plainclothesmen in unmarked cars roamed the mean streets, intimidating and shooting (Oxhorn 1995, 1994).

Violence in the shanties and the fierce repressive response scared middle-class and even working-class protestors. The repressive response brought back searing memories of the deadly horror-filled post-coup period. It was a reminder that, given sufficient "chaos," the military was capable of ruthless brutality and that with sufficient provocation (or quite arbitrarily) it could be brought to bear against them (Garretón 1989; Oxhorn 1995). Many shantytown leaders and militants from AD-affiliated parties – or simply gainfully employed residents with strong party identities – calculated that the costs of losing one's livelihood, freedom, or even life was not worth the potential gain. Indeed, there was no potential gain. The military government simply refused to budge (Salman 1994; Angell 1991).

The horror of the live burning of two unarmed, nonthreatening young protestors caused a soul-searching reevaluation of mass mobilization as a strategy to force economic reform and an early transition to full democracy. The

---

[30] To this end they created the Frente Patriótico Manuel Rodríguez.

danger of unleashing a repressive reaction that would extend to them and close the option of a negotiated transition was too great. The discovery of an arms cache for the revolutionary arm of the Communist Party and an attempt on Pinochet's life that very nearly succeeded that same year convinced AD to abandon mass mobilization. Instead, it opted to turn the very rules of the transition process crafted by the military government against it, and, specifically, against Pinochet. That meant ensuring the 1988 plebiscite would be held and that the vote would be sufficiently fair and free for the opposition parties to win (Garretón 1991).

In the end, contentious politics could not bring down a military government that after a few brief months of disorientation rebuilt internal cohesion, rearticulated its supporting coalition among business interests and political conservatives, and efficiently repressed the citizenry (Silva 1996). But it did bring politics back into the public sphere: People lost their fear. Mobilization expanded political associational space initially opened by the regime, allowing dormant political parties to challenge the dictatorship, rebuild their networks, and learn how to engage the military regime in a discussion over a transition to democracy (Garretón 1989).

Between 1987 and 1988, AD, which changed its name to Concertación de Partidos por el NO (Coalition of Parties for the NO Vote), organized to defeat Pinochet at the polls and succeeded on 5 October 1988. However, another key condition for the success of the transition was the Concertación's acceptance of the dictatorship's free-market economic system. This allayed the fears of capitalists and military softliners concerned that Pinochet had become a polarizing figure and for whom continuity of the neoliberal socioeconomic model was the key issue. The Concertación – which in 1983–85 had favored a mixed economy and industrial policy – conceded the point for a number of reasons. The failure of mass mobilization to dislodge Pinochet meant the Concertación did not have the power to do otherwise. But its economic advisors also believed in the value of economic growth for overcoming poverty and recognized that adjustments to the neoliberal economic model after the 1982–83 depression had spurred strong sustained economic recovery. The spectacular failure of "heterodox" economic policies in Argentina, Bolivia, and Peru in the early 1980s sobered them too. After winning the plebiscite, the Concertación and conservative political forces prepared for general elections in December 1989. The Concertación, now named Concertación de Partidos por la Democracia (CPD; Coalition of Parties for Democracy), triumphed and has governed uninterruptedly since 1990 (see Tables 8.4 and 8.5).

Democracy, Market Economics, and Quiescence

The conditions of Chile's transition to democracy set up a puzzle. If the Concertación preserved the neoliberal socioeconomic model, why has it not

Table 8.4. *Chile: Presidential Elections, 1989–2005*

Candidate	1989	%	1993	%	1999	%	2005	%
Patricio Aylwin Azócar	**3,850.571**	**55.17%**	–	–	–	–	–	–
Hernan Büchi Buc	2,052.116	29.40%	–	–	–	–	–	–
Francisco Javier Errázuriz Talavera	1,077.172	15.43%	–	–	–	–	–	–
Eduardo Frei Ruiz-Tagle	–	–	**4,040.497**	**57.98%**	–	–	–	–
Manfred Max Neef	–	–	387,102	5.55%	–	–	–	–
Eugenio Pizarro Poblete	–	–	327,402	4.70%	–	–	–	–
Cristián Reíste Campos	–	–	81,675	1.17%	–	–	–	–
Arturo Alessandri Besa	–	–	1,701.324	24.41%	–	–	–	–
Jose Piñera Echeñique	–	–	430,950	6.18%	–	–	–	–
Ricardo Lagos Escobar	–	–	–	–	**3,683.158**	**51.31%**	–	–
Joaquín Lavín Infante	–	–	–	–	3,495.569	48.69%	–	–
Michelle Bachelet Jeria	–	–	–	–	–	–	**3,723.019**	**53.50%**
Sebastián Piñera Echeñique	–	–	–	–	–	–	3,236.394	46.50%

Boldface indicates winning candidate and percentage of the vote.

Sources: http://www.elecciones.gov.cl/SitioHistorico.

Table 8.5. *Chile: Distribution of Seats in the Chamber of Deputies, 1989–2005*

Party	1989	1993	1997	2001	2005
Concertación de Partidos por la Democracia (CPD)	–	–	–	62	65
Alianza por Chile	–	–	–	57	54
Partido del Sur	–	–	1	–	–
Partido Demócrata Cristiano (PDC)	39	37	39	–	–
Renovación Nacional (RN)	29	29	23	–	–
Partido por la Democracia (PPD)	16	15	16	–	–
Unión Demócrata Independiente (UDI)	11	15	17	–	–
Partido Socialista de Chile (PS de C)	7	15	11	–	–
Partido Radical	5	2	–	–	–
Independents of the Center-Right	8	4	–	–	–
Unión de Centro	–	2	1	–	–
Partido Radical Socialdemócrata	–	–	4	–	–
Independientes (Fuera de Pacto)	–	–	8	1	1
Others	5	1	–	–	–
TOTAL	**120**	**120**	**120**	**120**	**120**

Sources: http://www.elecciones.gov.cl/SitioHistorico, The Europa World Yearbook (1988–2006).

generated a Polanyi-like backlash as it did in the other cases? Indeed, for a society that mobilized against neoliberalism under politically liberalizing authoritarianism, why was there such a conspicuous absence of contentious politics, let alone mass mobilization, in democracy?

Three factors have often been cited. First, the political parties of the Concertación demobilized labor and the popular sectors in the interest of governability. Historically in Chile, political parties had penetrated and directed social movement organizations. The redemocratization process was no different. Thus movements lacked a political amplifying chamber for protests (Baldez 1999; Jelin and Hershberg 1996; Oxhorn 1995, 1994; Paley 2001).[31] Second, movement leaders exercised restraint because they feared a climate of "ungovernability" could give military and civilian conservative hardliners an excuse to destabilize fledgling democracy. Third, the labor movement, which historically led mobilization, had been so weakened structurally by the dictatorship that it was incapable of organizing effective resistance against neoliberal continuity. Moreover, as elsewhere in Latin America, the decline of industry and flexibility-induced changes in the labor market turned industrial unions into defenders of a privileged labor aristocracy with whom other workers and popular sector groups felt little connection or affinity. Hence they could not articulate and lead protest (Angell 1991; Cook 2007; Posner 2007; Roberts 1998; Sehnbruch 2006).

[31] Observers constantly note how the Concertación brought the most energetic, enterprising, and successful movement leaders (frequently based in foreign-funded NGOs) into the government at the national, regional, and local levels. Moreover, much of the funding for movement organizations (especially from international sources) dried up.

These factors were important to be sure. However, they wash out in a comparative perspective for in one form or another they also afflicted the cases that developed Polanyi-like backlashes to the construction of contemporary market society. In those instances, the political exclusion necessary to impose and consolidate neoliberalism generated new opposition political movements and parties. These took the place of parties that favored demobilization. Industrial-based unionism declined everywhere too. However, other social sectors organized along mixtures of identity, class-based, and territorial lines to fill the vacuum. Weakened industrial unions then worked with them.

The major difference in relation to the other cases lay elsewhere. The Concertación tempered market economics with a commitment to *socioeconomic and political inclusion*. Thus, although market oriented, Chile after Pinochet was not consolidating market society, the ruthless subjection of people to commodification and systematic subjugation of politics and society to the efficiency of the market. Successive governments of the CPD consolidated a market economy *and* introduced or expanded significant protections from the market for many Chileans who had suffered far more profound socioeconomic exclusion during the dictatorship. Under Concertación rule, the Chilean state steadily expanded its welfare function, albeit on a liberal rather than a social democratic model.[32] The Concertación's commitment to ridding Chile's "protected democracy" of the authoritarian features inherited from the military – and to tackling human rights abuses by the military – slowly but consistently liberated Chile from the worst aspects of political exclusion. The Concertación also created a complex of government agencies that interface with virtually every sector of Chilean society. This dense inclusionary network of state–society interaction deflects tensions that might otherwise propel groups to contentious action.

Competent macroeconomic management by Concertación economic teams over four successive governments contributed to the continuation of uninterrupted high economic growth with low inflation that had begun in the mid-1980s. True, GDP expansion slowed significantly during the international recession at the turn of the century, with temporary negative effects on employment, but it resumed afterward. Although the governments of the Concertación have emphasized economic growth, they also considered it a tool to deal with poverty and social equity. Thus, although overall income distribution has not improved (indeed it has worsened somewhat), growth has contributed to substantial increases in the income and welfare of the population (Angell 2007: 192–93; Oppenheim 2007: 205–7).

The Concertación, from its earliest days as AD under Pinochet, stressed democracy and economic growth with social equity. Once in government, it moved quickly with respect to social policy. Forming a legislative coalition with one of two major conservative political parties, it slightly raised the corporate tax

---

[32] For an examination of models of welfare-statism see, Esping-Andersen (1990).

rate, income tax for the wealthy, and value-added taxes for the general population to pay for massive expansion of social services. Government investment in public hospitals and primary care units jumped tenfold from US$10 million to US$100 million per year. Between 1990 and 2000, expenditures for health services increased by 9.4 percent per year. As a result, public health care on which 75 percent of Chileans rely has improved.[33] By the same token, over the same period, spending on education increased by 10.6 percent per year and housing subsidies, especially targeted for low-income and rural families, leaped by 160 percent (Angell 2007: 193; Foxley 2004). The first Concertación government, under President Patricio Aylwin, also established a social investment fund to channel resources to social projects for poverty alleviation (Oppenheim 2007: 191).

Economic growth and social policy raised incomes and dramatically reduced unemployment and poverty. Immediately after taking office, the Concertación, committed to the concept of a minimum salary, substantially raised the minimum wage (17 percent in real terms between 1989 and 1991) and adjusted it yearly for inflation (Oppenheim 2007: 191). Real wages increased by 3.3 percent yearly between 1990 and 2000. Meanwhile, during the same period, employment grew by 1.7 percent annually and unemployment fell to a low of 6.1 percent, although it increased to about 9 percent during the international recession of the late 1990s and early 2000 (Angell 2007: 193). Better yet, formal sector employment expanded whereas the informal sector contracted.[34]

Dramatic poverty reduction has been one of the Concertación's greatest successes. In 1970, 23 percent of the population was classified poor or indigent. Government expenditure cuts during the dictatorship had contributed to a staggering 45 percent poverty rate in 1987, of which 17.4 percent were indigent. Overall poverty stood just below 40 percent when the Concertación took office in 1990. By 2000 those appalling figures were slashed to 20.6 percent, of which 5.7 percent were indigent, and dipped even lower in 2003 to 18.8 and 4.7 percent, respectively (Oppenheim 2007: 190). By 2006 those figures dipped to 13.7 percent under the official poverty line, of which 3.2 were classified indigent (see Table 8.6).

Political inclusion was another priority of Concertación rule. First, the Concertación by its very nature promised extensive representation. It was a broad center-left coalition that included leftist parties (albeit reformed, i.e. no longer radically socialist) that had formed part of Salvador Allende's Unidad Popular.

---

[33] The private health insurance system remained unaffected by Concertación policies until the Lagos administration in the early 2000s. Policy analysts had concluded that both the public and private systems were underfunded. Thus the Lagos administration shepherded a bill through Congress (Plan AUGE, Guaranteed Universal Health Access Plan) that affected both public and private delivery of health care services with an eye toward making quality service near universal (Borzutzky 2002; Borzutzky and Oppenheim 2006).

[34] For a fine-grained analysis of the Chilean labor market, see Sehnbruch (2006).

Table 8.6. *Chile: Economic and Social Indicators*

	1980	1990	1991	1992	1993	1994	1995	1996	1997	1998	1999	2000	2001	2002	2003	2004	2005	2006	2007[a]
GDP	7.5	2.0	7.1	10.5	6.0	4.1	8.2	7.2	6.6	3.2	−0.8	4.5	3.4	2.2	3.9	6.0	5.6	4.3	5.1
GDP/CAP	5.7	0.3	5.4	8.7	4.2	2.5	6.5	5.6	5.1	1.9	−2.0	3.2	2.2	1.0	2.8	4.9	4.5	3.3	4.0
Income Distribution[b]																			
D1	1.2											1.2			1.3			1.5	
D2	2.3											2.2			2.4			2.6	
Q2	7.0											6.9			7.2			7.8	
Q3	11.0											10.7			11.0			11.8	
Q4	17.9											17.6			17.8			18.7	
D9	15.5											15.2			15.0			15.5	
D10	45.1											46.3			45.4			42.2	
Unemployment	7.4	7.1		6.2	6.4	7.8	6.6	5.4	5.3	6.4	9.8	9.2	9.1	9.0	8.5	10.0	9.2	7.8	7.1
Informal[c]	37.9							34.3		37.5		31.9			31.9				
Poverty																			
Total	38.6											20.2			18.7			13.7	
Urban	38.5											19.7			18.5			16.0	
Rural	38.8											23.7			20.0			12.3	
Average Wage Index[d]		80.9	84.9	88.7	91.8	96.1	100.0	104.1	106.6	109.5	112.1	*100.0*	*101.7*	*103.7*	*104.6*	*106.5*	*108.5*	*110.6*	*113.7*
Minimum Wage Index[e]	87.9	76.9		87.9	92.2	95.6	100.0	104.2	107.9	114.1	93.4	*100.0*	*103.8*	*106.8*	*108.3*	*111.3*	*113.4*	*116.3*	*118.5*

[a] Estimated.

[b] *D9* and *D10* = richest quintile; *D1* and *D2* = poorest quintile. Data not reported for all years.

[c] Informal sector data reported only from 1990 to 2003 in constant format. Data not reported for all years.

[d] Average wage index between 1980 and 1999 based on 1995 = 100; 2000–2007 based on 2000 = 100 (in italics).

[e] Minimum wage index between 1980 and 1999 based on 1995 = 100; 2000–2007 based on 2000 = 100 (in italics).

Sources: Economic Commission for Latin America and the Caribbean, *Statistical Yearbook* (Santiago: ECLAC, 1980–2007) and *Economic Survey of Latin America* (Santiago: ECLAC, 1980–2007). Labor Statistics from International Labor Organization, Labor Overview: *Latin America and the Caribbean* (Lima: ILO, 1994–2007). For comparability of data, I have not filled in missing years with other sources.

Presidents have included two from the center right of the coalition (Christian Democrats Patricio Aylwin and Eduardo Frei) and two have been from the center left (Socialists Ricardo Lagos and Michelle Bachelet).

Second, successive governments of the Concertación patiently chipped away at authoritarian "tethers" of Chile's protected democracy. The two main ones were appointed seats in the Senate that gave conservative forces a majority, and therewith an absolute veto power over legislation and a binomial electoral system overrepresented conservatives in the lower chamber. The military also retained reserve domains of power. These and other authoritarian enclaves required constitutional amendments. Because two-thirds majorities are necessary, the cooperation of conservative political parties is necessary. Thus eliminating them is difficult.

The Concertación negotiated a first set of 54, mostly minor, constitutional reforms with the conservative Renovación Nacional Party in 1989 to ensure free and fair elections and reduce some of the presidency's more arbitrary powers.[35] In 1991, mayors became elected rather than appointed officials, substantially democratizing local government. Other changes occurred, such as shortening presidential terms (now four years) and rescinding their right to become ex officio senators for life. A significant change transpired in 2006 with the elimination of designated senators.

Third, the Concertación patiently and steadfastly addressed human rights violations of the military government. Alywin established a Truth and Reconciliation Commission to give a full accounting of deaths and disappeared persons; his administration also pushed through pardons for most remaining political prisoners. In a strange twist of fate, during the Lagos administration (2000–2006) Pinochet found himself under house arrest and threatened with prosecution for human rights violations. The discrediting of Pincohet permitted the government to negotiate with the military further discovery of the full extent of human rights violations, including the whereabouts of victims and their perpetrators with the possibility of trials for the latter. Reparations were paid to the families of victims, and the army issued a public acknowledgement of complicity and pledged "never again" (Lira 2006).

Political inclusion and participation also expanded significantly with careful restructuring of state–society intermediation. The Aylwin administration began what became two signature practices. First, when policy issues become heated, the Concertación establishes a blue-ribbon commission to study the problem that includes representatives from all sides. Negotiation absorbs energy otherwise

---

[35] These included the restoration to full electoral competition by lifting the ban on the communist and other leftist parties. Political party affiliation was permitted to labor and professional organization leaders. The number of elected senators was increased from 26 to 38 to reduce the weight of designated senators. The president would no longer have the power to dissolve the Chamber of Deputies, and civilian representation was increased to parity with military officers on the National Security Council (Silva 2006).

directed toward contentious action. This has occurred with human rights, conflicts over environment and development, the incorporation of indigenous peoples into national life, and most recently (2006) with student protests. Of course, the fact that some reforms occur – even if only at the margin – helps make the mechanism work.

Second, and perhaps most important, the Concertación has built a dense network of government agencies to service diverse social groups and movements. Equally significant, those groups and movement organizations established sustained linkages to government agencies. The fact that many of the agency, department, and division heads – as well as the upper management of those administrative units – came from those movements strengthens their reciprocal relationship. The most notable examples have been the women's movement and the Servicio Nacional de la Mujer (SERNAM; Women's National Service); the environmental movement with the creation of the Comisión Nacional del Medio Ambiente (CONAMA; National Commission for the Environment); and the Corporación Nacional de Desarrollo Indígena (CONADI; National Corporation for Indigenous Development).[36] By the same token, low-income neighborhood residents and shantytown dwellers are enmeshed in a dense network of government agencies (usually at the municipal and regional level). Municipalities and regional governments distribute funds allocated by the central government targeted for community development-based proposals submitted by community organizations. The government agencies establish long-term relationships with community organizations, teaching them how to write successful proposals, how to follow up on success and to improve on failure, and by monitoring project implementation. These efforts absorb the energies of community organizations with at least some rewards. The system also isolates them from each other because each organization enters into an individual contract with the state. There are few, if any, incentives to establish horizontal linkages (Greaves 2007; Oxhorn 1995; Paley 2001).

So far these conditions and mechanisms of socioeconomic and political inclusion offer sufficient rewards and channels of participation to defuse discontent over the shortcomings of Chile's political and economic system. All across the spectrum of subordinate social groups, they structure incentives in ways that compartmentalize tensions, isolate conflicts, and snuff out contentious politics on those occasions when it occurs.

This has been the plight of Chile's labor movement. Merciless political persecution, deindustrialization, the flexibilization of labor, and the emasculation of the right to collective bargaining and the strike left it structurally and organizationally weak coming out of the dictatorship. During redemocratization, the labor movement reconstructed connections with political parties and built up membership. Its leaders felt politically included once again. Over all four Concertación

---

[36] For SERNAM, see Baldez (2002); for CONAMA and CONADI, see Silva (2006, 1997).

administrations the labor confederation (Unitary Workers Confederation; Confederation Unitaria de Trabajadores or CUT) has pushed for labor code reform to strengthen organizational capability and collective bargaining and strike rights. However, the Concertación has not delivered. Having kept the dictatorship's free-market economy, it was also necessary to hold wages down and preserve labor-market flexibility to ensure the international competitiveness of Chilean commodities (Cook 2007; Drake 1996; Roberts 1998; Winn 2004). Thus the Concertación did not fight employer association and conservative political party resistance as hard as it could have; particularly later as Concertación appointments to the Senate and the loss of Pinochet's seat in the Senate weakened conservative veto power. In the final analysis, relatively minor adjustments to the labor code were made over the years, but none that addressed the CUT's core demands (Frank 2002; Haagh 2002; Oppenheim 2007; Posner 2007).

It took the CUT some time to conclude that, despite its linkages to the Concertación's center-left parties, its central demands were effectively excluded from the policy agenda. Although the Concertación tried to push a more labor-friendly code bill through Congress, when it became necessary to vigorously support labor's agenda the Concertación pulled back and capitulated to capitalist and conservative party resistance. The CUT's attempts to mount national strikes and demonstrations failed both in terms of turnout and capacity to attract participation from other social groups. More recently, under President Lagos' administration (2000–2006), and, after a brief warming, again under President Bachelet (2006–present), the CUT distanced itself from the Concertación and it remains isolated.

For reasons previously discussed, conditions for building horizontal linkages among movements in Chile have been poor. The mechanisms for political, socioeconomic, and postmodern movements' inclusion have sufficed to maintain relative social peace in the face of serious problems with Chile's development model. Some of those problems are rising to the top of the policy agenda as social groups, citizens, policy analysts, and political leaders push to have them addressed. These include the extraordinary high rates of income concentration, among the worst in the world. Economic growth and market-friendly social policy have improved poverty figures; achieving a more equitable distribution of income will be harder. The privatized pension system is also facing difficulties as the Chilean population ages and it becomes increasingly clear that many citizens will have inadequate coverage. This despite President Bachelet's recently passed universal minimum pension program. The same holds true for the private health care system and the pressure it places on the public system, Plan AUGE (a recently approved quasi-universal health care program for legally recognized illnesses) notwithstanding. University students have already begun clamoring for more thorough reform of the education system they inherited from the dictatorship. Unions, especially for copper miners, struck in 2006 to protest subcontracting rules. Indigenous peoples, especially the Mapuche, have mobilized around land claims in the south. Under the right conditions these stirrings might spark a resurrection of contentious politics – with the reconstruction of horizontal linkages between movements – as people try to defend themselves from the market's inherent inequalities. One of those conditions might well be the ascent of a conservative government less interested in maintaining mechanisms of socioeconomic and political inclusion.

9

Conclusion

This book argued that episodes of anti-neoliberal contention in Argentina, Bolivia, Ecuador, and Venezuela, from the 1980s to the early 2000s, were Polanyian backlashes to the construction of contemporary market society. First- and second-generation neoliberal reforms recommodified labor and land by dis- mantling the national-populist order and by restructuring the state in support of market efficiency to the exclusion of other values. Free-market policies severed the connections of organized subaltern social groups to the state, leaving them to fend for themselves against capital in the market. The process of recommodi- fication swept aside the mixed economy and brought domestic prices, regulatory environments, and practices in line with the world economy.

Urban popular sectors, peasants, the indigenous, and some middle-class groups – especially those dependent on state employment – experienced this process as economic, political, and social exclusion and injustice. Herein lay the motivation for anti-neoliberal mobilization. The all-encompassing, society-wide nature of the neoliberal project – an effort to reconstruct contemporary market society – helped to link a wide variety of grievances. Although many groups lim- ited protest to policies that specifically affected them, and often in a localized manner, the fact that so many neoliberal reforms were enacted simultaneously (or in compressed time frames) helped bring protest streams together. Further- more, some reforms, such as stabilization policy, affected everyone, which is why reduction or elimination of subsidies caused such huge displays of public outrage. These intersected with the particular struggles of public sector workers, teachers, and private sector-organized labor fighting to hold on to hard-earned privileges, and indigenous or mestizo peasants.

Emphasizing the common origins of grievances as a unifying element for diverse protest groups was not just an analytic construct. Governments aggres- sively publicized policy reforms as comprehensive programs designed to set their countries back on the path to modernity and renewed economic growth and prosperity for all. This helped many protestors, and protest leaders in particular, to pinpoint the common source of their myriad grievances. Thus, in the context of favorable political associational space, a reformist thrust to demands rather than insurrectionary violence, and persistent economic crises, protest leaders in Argentina, Bolivia, and Ecuador applied framing and brokerage mechanisms to mobilize individuals and connect organizations. In Venezuela, failed armed insurrection by anti-neoliberal military elements ended early efforts to build popular sector collective power. Nevertheless, its episode of anti-neoliberal mobilization continued with constant decentralized demonstrations. In all four cases the political power of neoliberal forces declined as parties collapsed and that of challengers increased as new political parties (or factions of political parties) capitalized on voter volatility. Meanwhile, the closing of political associational space and armed insurrection in Peru inhibited the development of an episode of anti-neoliberal contention, despite many similarities with Bolivia and Ecuador. Finally, although democratic Chile basically kept the free-market economic model imposed by military dictatorship, a center-left ruling coalition steadily *reformed* market society. The expansion of *economic and political inclusion* blunted motivation for massive nationwide anti-neoliberal protests. Chile has a market economy, but not a market society.[1]

These episodes of anti-neoliberal contention suggest the dawning of a Polanyian countermovement to contemporary market society in Latin America. This countermovement reasserts the legitimacy of principles that decommodify labor and land and advocates a greater degree of state intervention to achieve those goals. To varying degrees the new governments are turning to classic policy instruments to control markets – planning and socialization – to reform neoliberalism (Gourevitch 1986). Resurgent economic nationalism strives to extract a larger share of the resources that international companies produce (revenue, technology, and managerial know-how) to invest in the development of the domestic economy. A greater emphasis on social equity addresses the clamor for decommodification on the part of popular sectors, peasants, indigenous peoples, and even sectors of the middle classes. The question then becomes one of how much "planning and socialization" and with what, if any, innovations in policy instruments to avoid the pitfalls of the past?

This, at least in part, is the meaning of the "leftist turn" in the governments of Venezuela, Bolivia, Argentina, and Ecuador. Other countries have followed suit recently, although more through electoral politics than mass mobilization, such as Nicaragua, Uruguay, and Paraguay.[2] Strong electoral challenges to free-market economics also appeared in Peru. Chile, I argued earlier, followed its own path to socioeconomic and political inclusion with mild (but sufficient) reforms to what had been an authoritarian version of contemporary market society.

---

[1] See Chapter 3 for a full summary exposition of the explanation.

[2] This opens another line of inquiry suggested by Kenneth Roberts at the 2007 LASA international convention in Montreal, Canada. What factors account for the channeling of anti-neoliberal sentiment mainly through elections instead of mass mobilization? This book suggests that earlier patterns of political inclusion are one factor. (Nicaragua won that inclusion through revolution in the 1970s; Chile, as we saw, in part, by mass mobilization in the early to mid-1980s.)

Understandably, hope, uncertainty, and healthy skepticism abound regarding what anti-neoliberal mobilization accomplished. How robust are the social and political movements that drove anti-neoliberal contentious politics? Have new movements with the capacity to lead societal transformation emerged to replace the labor movement? Have meaningful shifts occurred in the popular sectors' repertoire of contention to replace the classic strike? What was the impact of transnational movements on anti-neoliberal mobilization? To what extent do the policies of new governments really challenge neoliberalism? What are the prospects for the construction of a more inclusionary and just social order? Obviously, these questions launch new research agendas that deserve books of their own. However, because they are a logical extension of this one, I offer my own reflections.

On the Emergence of Transformative Movements

In our cases, new organizationally cohesive and vigorous social movements capable of supporting a transformative national development project – a role, perhaps erroneously, ascribed to the labor movement in the previous century – have not yet emerged from the struggle.[3] The indigenous movement, especially Ecuador's CONAIE, had raised hopes. However, the tensions, discord, and internal conflicts caused by its putschist adventures and ill-fated forays into electoral politics have, by all accounts, weakened it. The leadership of the major confederations fight among each other, and the community organizations at the base no longer trust them (Wolff 2007; Zamosc 2007). Meanwhile, Bolivia's indigenous movement never came close to the promise of Ecuador's. It is uncertain whether the MAS can fulfill that function as a party–movement organization (Yashar 2005). By the same token, the Argentine piquetero movement – and related community organizations such as the FTV – also quickly unraveled after 2001 (Svampa and Pereyra 2003; Wolff 2007). Venezuela, as we saw, never developed new movements remotely close in size and organizational capacity to the indigenous movements in Ecuador and Bolivia and the piqueteros in Argentina.

The absence of a rising social movement capable of sustaining a society-wide transformative project to take up the banner from the faltering labor movement has caused dismay and disappointment in some quarters (Petras and Veltmeyer 2005). Yet students of contentious politics have long recognized that movements and movement organizations tend to wane after initial objectives have been achieved and they become included in institutional political processes. This is the norm, and new developments follow: movements reconstitute, transform, or collapse; it is too early to tell which might transpire (Tarrow 1998).

---

[3] Rueschemeyer, Stephens, and Stephens (1992) argued that, unlike Europe, in Latin America labor lacked the power to deepen democracy and extend social insurance, that is, to create the modern capitalist welfare state. In Latin America that role fell to an uneasy alliance of middle-class movements and labor.

Conclusion

This introduces a historically grounded theme to which I return later. It seems premature, even if it were possible, to expect the rise of such a Promethian movement in such a short time. It is worth remembering that in the early 1900s – a comparable period of societal transformation with the rise of the "social question" – the Latin American labor movement hardly seemed a likely candidate to transform society and peasants made revolutions. Yet, whatever its shortcomings, over time the labor movement developed into a key component of Latin America's original Polanyian countermovement to market society. After uncertain starts, and with great variety in timing, it consolidated, contributed to progressive change, and allied with center-left populist political movements (Cardoso and Faletto 1979; Collier and Collier 1991).

I would argue we are in a historically comparable moment: the stirrings of a Polanyian countermovement to a second wave of global capitalist expansion and market society building. Thus, disappointment over power deflation among key protagonists in our episodes of anti-neoliberal contention should not tempt us to dismiss or overlook evolving trends regarding the construction of a longer-term Polanyian countermovement to contemporary market society. The rise of territory- or community-centered organization to complement production-based labor movements decimated by globalization is a phenomenon worth exploring. People come together around a shared identity of place (village, indigenous community, working-class neighborhood or barrio) intertwined with shared cultural and material concerns. Equally novel is the fact that these organizations joined streams of national mobilization and that their contentious action has significance beyond the locality. Their emergence challenges theories that argue that their heterogeneity and precarious livelihood strategies absolutely prevent the development of their associational, not to mention collective, power.

To be sure whether they have the "staying power" of the labor movement remains to be seen. Nevertheless, this may not necessarily be the most relevant issue. This book showed that absent the presence of a transformative social movement (overwhelming associative power) amassing popular sector collective power is the key to change.[4] This involved forging horizontal linkages between the myriad territorially and identity-based movements and the traditional union movement. From there connections to political parties also become important. Herein, at present, lies any hope for the transformative capability of movement, at least in South America. From this perspective, even though these organizations weakened after the massive mobilization of the 1990s and early 2000s, they have not disappeared and therefore are available for reconstituting popular sector collective power.

---

[4] A growing body of work supports this position: see Arrighi and Silver (1999); Tarrow (1998); McAdam, Tarrow, and Tilly (2001); Roberts (2003b); Howard (2002). More important, movement leaders themselves understand the necessity.

If we ask which of these movements might lead such efforts to construct collective power, no clear pattern suggests itself from our cases. What quickly becomes apparent is that such "leadership" has heterogeneous and changing sources. In Ecuador it was CONAIE, in Bolivia it may have been the CSUTCB and the coca-grower federations and their appropriation of the MAS, a political party (Yashar 2005; Zamosc 2007, 1994). In Argentina the CTA may have played that central role, fleetingly with Frepaso, and in conjunction with the Federación Tierra y Vivienda (Svampa and Pereyra 2003). After the relative decline of CONAIE in Ecuador, the urban-based CMS and the traditional labor federation (FUT) spearheaded collective power formation after 2002 (Wolff 2007).

Nor should we in our haste to discover and embrace the "new" overlook the contributions of the structurally challenged and declining union movement. It may not be glamorous and lead, it may be "tired," but it can still be a vital component of popular sector collective power; this, despite the onus of its contemporary lack of "purity of purpose" given its ties to political parties and the state. In Bolivia the COB and some of its regional federations transmitted important organizational and negotiating know-how to *cocaleros* and were integral members of the *coordinadoras*. In Argentina, the CTA was union based, and CGT general strikes made a difference. In Ecuador a strong FUT showing contributed to the success of the urban component of national mobilization, as did the public union core of the CMS. Last, but not least, despite all of its contradictory and self-serving actions, CTV national strikes in Venezuela carried decisive weight. It may be worth keeping an eye on the extent to which and the mechanisms by which the labor movement directs its strategic thinking and organization building toward playing a constructive role in collective power building. Equally noticeable, in most of these cases public sector unions were the most militant and instrumental for building popular sector associational and collective power.

On a related point, the fluidity of contemporary developments suggests we may be at a new critical juncture with respect to the incorporation of the popular sectors in politics, as a number of analysts have proposed (Centeno 2002; Collier and Collier 1991; Mahoney 2001). This approach draws attention to a different, but related, set of research questions. What forms will the rearticulation of the popular sectors to political parties and the state take? What policy impact might they have? In Venezuela under Chávez, for example, it appears the state leads the process with the expansion of Bolivarian circles, community organization, and the creation of an alternative labor confederation. In Bolivia it seems a more bottom-up process with the creation of the MAS, which has modeled its organizational form after that of the CSUTCB. With the resurgence of economic nationalism under Morales, will new institutional linkages to the state be created? How would they differ from past practices? Moreover, will the MAS institutionalize? Argentina's story may be one of the reequilibration of Peronism, with the bulk of the piquetero movement absorbed into more or less traditional ties to the Peronist party machine (Auyero 2007; Svampa and Pereyra 2003; Wolff 2007).

Conclusion

These cases and questions reveal tremendous variation, which raises even more issues. Are discernable patterns emerging? If so, will institutional versus clientelist modes of articulation of new popular sector organizations to political parties and the state result in the consequences posited by Collier and Collier (1991), Centeno (2002), and Mahoney (2001) for earlier historical critical junctures? Before returning to some of those questions, the following two sections explore emerging changes in Latin American movement as suggested by our cases of anti-neoliberal mobilization. These are shifts in the logic of movement organization, developments in the repertoire of contention, and transnational influences.

Theory, Territorial Organization, and Repertoires of Contention

At a general theoretical level, the organizational logic for protest movements, shifts in the repertoire of contention, and allied political movements support a key hypothesis of Polanyi. The spread of territorially based forms of popular sector and indigenous organization in conjunction with the prominence of the roadblock (and other forms of contentious action) emphasize the growing importance of exchange as the principle for organization and struggle. This is a direct response to the decline of struggle based on the point of production, meaning industrial labor (Silver 2003).[5] Crucial rallying cries for mobilization (among others) were jobs, unemployment relief, social insurance, subsidies, local development opportunities, land, and prices in general – all of which involve exchange. This allowed individuals differently located in the structure of production to identify with each other. Recognition of shared problems created solidary bonds among people regardless of whether they were employed or not and despite the type of employment (factory, informal sector, or various types of rural labor and farming).

The roadblock emerged as the most novel form of struggle during our episodes of anti-neoliberal contention. It too was exchange based because it disrupted national, regional, and local commerce. True, it was not an entirely new invention; farmers and peasants had resorted to it in the past. However, its massive application to urban areas and coordinated use across a nation was an innovation.

Roadblocks were highly transgressive and disruptive; the tool of urban and rural protestors, they were always illegal. Their economic effects lay in the disruption of commerce. However, as used by indigenous peasants in Ecuador and Bolivia, roadblocks had highly political purposes. They were a means to lay siege to urban areas, causing or threatening shortages of fuel, water, food supplies,

---

[5] This raises critical questions over the primacy of the point of exchange versus the point of production as the strategic node for exploiting the contradictions of capitalism to reform or transform it. It also raises more readily researchable midrange research questions about the interaction between them in specific conflicts. Such a research agenda may help us to make sense of the "messiness" of historical developments rather than impose overly rigid grand-theoretical designs on them (Centeno and López-Alves 2001).

and medicines. At all levels, the transgressive and disruptive characteristics of the roadblock provoked a repressive response by the authorities. Because this only inflamed protestors and strengthened their resolve, roadblocks put pressure on authorities to negotiate. That was because governability – hence their jobs as elected officials – was at stake. The p-uebladas in Argentina had much the same effect at the provincial and local level.

Other forms of contention also disrupted exchange, mainly of public services. The mass demonstration terminating at major government buildings and plazas was a tried-and-true one in Latin American contentious politics. Its significance, however, had evolved. As the feasibility and impact of strikes waned, they became a quasi-substitute for them. Movement leaders organized them to draw people who had lost their jobs into contentious politics or, if they had jobs, who could not strike for one reason or another, as well as individuals in the informal sector of the economy for whom striking made no sense (shopkeepers, artisans, street vendors, clerks) or pensioners and retirees. Mass demonstrations allowed all to express their frustration, indignation, and outrage and to share in the warmth, joy, festival, spectacle, and catharsis of solidary action.

The transgressive and disruptive capacity of mass demonstrations expanded geometrically when they transmuted into attacks on government buildings and their occupation, as they frequently did in Argentina, Bolivia, and Ecuador. Again, the novelty lay in the relative frequency of the occurrence as a culmination to massive demonstrations, often accompanied by other forms of contention such as roadblocks, marches, and strikes. Always, repression inflamed the passions of protestors and emboldened them to take more extreme measures.

Such attacks, as well as peaceful demonstrations, marches, and the banging of pots and pans clearly expressed the focus of popular sector and middle-class demands – the state. Contrary to theoretical expectation among neoliberals, mar-ketization (taking the state out of economic transactions) did nothing to weaken that impulse. The popular sectors and indigenous peasantry understood that state power was their best hope for countering private economic power in markets.

In sum, forms of struggle that emphasized disruption at the point of exchange rather than through strikes at the point of production gained prominence dur-ing these episodes of anti-neoliberal contention. They attracted media attention, encouraged individuals to join in, and frequently invited repression, which rein-forced resistance and often forced negotiation. Traditional strikes did not dis-appear. However, public sector strikes became more effective than strikes from unions in the private sector. This involved public employees, teachers, health care workers (including doctors), and in Ecuador, hydrocarbon and telecommunica-tions workers. The state had greater difficulty downsizing and flexiblizing public sector unions than private companies, where market conditions made it much easier for them to control unions and their labor force. Argentina was a partial exception with the hydrocarbon and telecommunications sector and Bolivia with tin mines. Still, private sector unions could be highly effective, especially when they affected exchange, such as transport sector workers (buses, taxis, railroads, and trucking).

The intercity march, especially from the periphery to the capitol, also became a much more frequent event during anti-neoliberal episodes of contention in Argentina, Bolivia and Ecuador. It was not a disruptive event and usually was not repressed by the authorities. The main object was to publicize grievances and demands, a tool to raise public awareness. Media attention and the direct experience of onlookers in the towns and villages along the way accomplished those goals. As noted in the country cases, frequently they were marches for "life" to highlight the devastating consequences of neoliberal reforms.

Roadblocks (especially in and around urban areas) and intercity marches, along with the framing of their cause, also created solidary bonds among diverse participants, thus helping to link different groups and organizations. As the leadership hoped, struggle itself promoted solidarity. The roadblock required cooperation to man day and night, to supply, to transport people and leaders, and to make decisions in popular assemblies. Repression strengthened and enlarged those bonds by drawing in more people to defend friends and neighbors. The intercity march engaged (or created) sympathizers along the way who offered food, drink, shelter, and encouragement. Mass demonstrations had some of the same effects (as did encampments before government buildings), especially when the authorities repressed them.

Two other forms of struggle made more limited appearances on a large scale. One was riots and looting in major cities, principally in Argentina and Venezuela. These events occurred in comparatively wealthy countries after periods of sharp socioeconomic decline. In Venezuela they initiated an episode of anti-neoliberal contention and seemed spontaneous. In Argentina they largely capped an episode of anti-neoliberal contention and were frequently directed by grassroots political operators [punteros]. In both cases the relative complicity of underpaid police forces played a role, through their absence, negligence, or direct involvement.

The other form was a largely symbolic middle-class expression of struggle, the banging of pots and pans. Its most significant occurrence was in Argentina in December 2001, although it also appeared on a lesser scale in other cases. Its origins lie in conservative antisocialist middle-class mobilization in Chile during the early 1970s. It usually begins with a call by political parties or movement organizations to start banging pots and pans at a certain date and time to repudiate government policies and politicians that support them. Descriptions typically mention how they begin with timid efforts by isolated individuals fearful of retaliation (public snubbing, vandalism, or being informed on to authorities by neighbors) should they be the only ones from their building or block to participate. Once it becomes clear that many are heeding the call (especially direct neighbors), the banging raises to a crescendo throughout the city. Participants describe an exhilarating release of tension and a joyful, liberating sense of solidarity in finding out they are not the only ones overwhelmed by intolerable public policy-induced private troubles. This type of contentious action conveys clear political consequences. Political parties receive unequivocal signals that they are losing significant middle-class support. The blackout, also called for a specific time, has the same effect, although it may involve popular sectors as well.

The centrality in several cases of heretofore secondary forms of struggle, such as the roadblock and intercity marches framed around "Life," raises the question of diffusion. There is some evidence for it in the case of intercity marches. For example, indigenous organizations from Ecuador shared their experience with their Bolivian counterparts (Brysk 2000). Videotapes also circulated, and Argentines may have seen them as well, even in the major news media perhaps. The evidence of diffusion for roadblocks is less clear. In Argentina historically they had been a tool in the repertoire of contention of farmers and peasants. Their transference to urban settings beginning in remote provinces seems to have been a local invention born of desperation that diffused nationally because of its success.

Roadblocks historically had been a traditional tool in the Andean indigenous peasants' repertoire of contention. More recently, Bolivian indigenous peasants applied them during the democratization campaign of the late 1970s and in the early stages of anti-neoliberal mobilization in the 1980s. However, they were not the pivotal form of struggle as they became in the 1990s and early 2000s. Meanwhile in Ecuador they made their first modern massive appearance in the 1990 indigenous uprising. Did they learn from the Bolivian experience? Did the Bolivians learn from Ecuadorian events? Although I have not found direct supporting evidence, the answer to both questions is probably yes to some extent, if nothing else due to media (audio-visual, radio, Internet, and print) and cross-national contacts among indigenous organizations. However, perhaps to a larger extent, they were also autonomous responses within countries built on the shared cross-border historical traditions of ethnically related highland and mountain valley indigenous peoples. They recognized the power the disruption of exchange gave them to force negotiation.

The simultaneous use of all of these forms of struggle in the repertoire of contention of diverse popular sector and middle-class movement organizations was, perhaps, the signature development of major, often climactic, anti-neoliberal mass mobilizations. Massive roadblocks, demonstrations, marches, strikes (including transport and public sector strikes), occupation of and attacks on government buildings, pot-and-pan banging, and blackouts convulsed nations. They turned into nodes of harsh, sometimes murderous, confrontation with the forces of order sent to repress them, feeding the outrage of indignant demonstrators, and steeling their resolve to resist. This concatenation of forms of struggle wrought by the fragmentation inherent in globalization may well be the contemporary replacement for the general strike of yesteryear.

Conclusion

Transnational Influences and Movements

The development of international regimes on rights-based issues beginning in the 1980s and the rapid expansion in transnational activism from the 1990s to the present raise important questions regarding their impact on the genesis and evolution of our episodes of anti-neoliberal contention. In Chapter 3 I posited we should expect them to strengthen mobilizing popular sector, peasant, indigenous, and middle-class groups. Yet how, exactly, did they contribute to the growth and intensification of critical associational and collective power from the late 1980s to the early 2000s? This is a difficult question to answer given a paucity of research on the effects of transnational activism on key movement organizations relevant to this book – particularly urban ones. Most research has focused on the creation of international regimes along with transnational movement organizations, coalitions among them, and the international campaigns they have mounted (Ayres 2004; Keck and Sikkink 1998; Legler 2000; Munck 2007; Routledge 2004; Saguier 2007; Seoane and Taddei 2002; Tarrow 2005). Indigenous peoples' movements in Ecuador and Bolivia are significant exceptions, which is why I begin with them. I then raise questions for future research regarding the possible role of transnational movements as brokerage nodes that contribute to the diffusion of strategies, tactics, and material support for national movements that participate in them.

It is well established that multilateral organizations and transnational movement organizations and the international regimes they create can have significant impact on the development of local or national movements. They provide support to construct movement organization, such as building leadership, technical aid, and material resources. They construct frames and provide brokerage nodes for movement building. This is generally accomplished by organizing conferences, working groups, seminars, sharing information, and helping people to travel. These mechanisms bring people together, form networks, and generate ideas (Keck and Sikkink 1998).

The impact of the international indigenous peoples' rights and environmental movement on the formation of CONAIE and the revitalization of the CSUTCB are, perhaps, the clearest examples. Yashar (2005), Brysk (2000), and others have analyzed how from 1983 forward the United Nations built an international regime to support indigenous peoples' rights, beginning with the "working group on indigenous populations." The UN then focused on the 500th anniversary of Spanish conquest from 1989 to 1992. The working group framed indigenous rights issues and created a network for regional and national organizations by sponsoring a permanent working group, conferences, and workshops. It also publicized the issue worldwide and gave it legitimacy. The UN extended the effort by declaring 1995–2005 to be the decade of indigenous people. The International Labor Organization (ILO) complemented the undertaking with its Convention 169 and campaigns for national government ratification.

The UN, the ILO, and international NGOs created norms, principles, institutions and procedures – international regimes – highly supportive of indigenous peoples' organizing. The attention it generated brought the issue into sharp focus at the national level and legitimated state action on behalf of indigenous rights. In the context of democratizing and democratic governments this facilitated legislative initiatives favorable to the indigenous and permitted their organization (bilingual education, land demarcation, and constitutional recognition of pluriculturalism among others) (Brysk 2000; Van Cott 2005; Yashar 2005).

The dovetailing of environmental and human rights international movements, in particular, strengthened the organization of Amazonian indigenous. In Ecuador this facilitated the formation of the Shuar Federation and CONFE-NIAE. In Bolivia it made the Indigenous Confederation of the East and Amazonia possible. The complementary action of liberation theology Christian base communities and international advocacy and development NGOs contributed to those developments in both Amazonia and in the highlands. In the aggregate, all of these international organizations contributed to framing the indigenous question in terms of citizenship rights, social justice, land security, and cultural survival (Yashar 2005). Transnational movements and international regimes also offer material and technical support to indigenous peoples' movements.[6]

An important drop-off in research occurs outside of the indigenous peoples, environmental, and human rights issue areas. This hampers data gathering regarding the influence of international movements and regimes on the CMS in Ecuador, the CTA, the Corriente Classista Combativa, and the Federación Tierra y Vivienda in Argentina, not to mention the myriad organizations involved in Venezuela's anti-neoliberal episode. A few clues exist, but this is an area open to significant research.

The scant evidence on the CMS suggests influence by international urban-focused human rights, citizen rights, and social justice movements with strong connections to domestic NGOs and Ecuadorian academic institutions. Prominent examples were the Democratic Forum (which debated constitutional reform strategies) and the campaign in support of petroleum workers' who had chained themselves to pipelines to disrupt supply in demonstration against privatization [los ecadenados del oleoducto]. Many of the urban popular sector and middle-class social organizations that made up the CMS began to network and build horizontal linkages around these issues (Andolina 1999). Yet, exactly which transnational organizations participated, with what linkages to domestic NGOs and popular sector urban movements, and how they contributed to the formation and

---

[6] The legal case of CONFENIAE versus Texaco is a famous example of what Tarrow (2005) calls externalization, in which domestic movements cannot find redress for their grievances and enlist the help of transnational movements and regimes to get a hearing (Sawyer 2002; 2001). The global anti-World Bank campaign in Brazilian Amazonia in the 1980s is another famous example (Schwartzman 1991).

approach of the CMS remains unclear.[7] Similarly, Argentina's CTA is a member of the Regional Interamerican Labor Organization. One might expect that the CTA drew framing and perhaps organizational resources from it, but it is not known if it did or to what extent. Whether and to what extent local branches of international development and human rights NGOs directed by "rooted cosmopolitans" were involved in supporting key components of the Federación Tierra y Vivienda, the Corriente Clasista, or the Polo Obrero is also not known.[8] Conversely, In Chile the role of the Catholic Church and of international foundations (Ford and major European social democratic foundations) in supporting opposition think tanks and center-left political parties (including funding for party-specific weekly news magazines) during the dictatorship has been well documented (Puryear 1994).

The evidence becomes even thinner when researching an even more critical theme in the relationship between transnational movements and our national episodes of anti-neoliberal contention.[9] How did participation in transnational movements affect the framing, strategic thinking, and brokerage opportunities for the major national movement organizations? Brysk (2000) suggests the UN working group on indigenous peoples influenced the inclusion of land issues on CONFENIAE's agenda. Moreover, human rights organizations clearly publicized excessive force during repression and helped release prisoners in Ecuador, Bolivia, and Argentina. Brysk (2000) reports that Oxfam and the Rainbow Action Network helped organize marches from Amazonia to capital cities in Bolivia and Ecuador in the early 1990s. These gained important national publicity and government concessions. Moreover, the Catholic Church (bishops and archbishops) formed part of multisectoriales in Argentine pueblladas and interceded on behalf of protestors when repression escalated (Svampa and Pereyra 2003).

Although these are examples of important support activities, they are very much linked to particular campaigns. They do not advance us much on the role of transnational movement in forming anti-neoliberal master frames or overarching strategies, providing brokerage opportunities to link major domestic movement organizations, fostering enduring networks to maintain those links, and promoting popular sector collective power during the episodes of anti-neoliberal contention. Key examples would be uncovering a role for transnational movements in the formation and posture of the Estado Mayor del Pueblo in Bolivia,

---

[7] In fact, the whole phenomenon of the CMS, its origins, and development as a movement organization, remain seriously understudied because it is eclipsed by interest in CONAIE.

[8] Tarrow (2005) defined rooted cosmopolitans as individuals with substantial professional participation in transnational movements (such as organizing global direct action campaigns) but who have an organizational base in their country of origin and also act locally. They are links between the transnational and the domestic, as observed by Keck and Sikkink (1998) and Brysk (2000).

[9] A growing body of literature emphasizes researching reciprocal effects from the transnational to the national and the national to the transnational; see Della Porta and Tarrow (2004) and Desmarais (2007).

the Frente Patriótico in Ecuador, the development and adoption of the popular assembly as a fulcrum for rethinking citizen rights and participatory democracy, and other acts of diffusion in the strategy, tactics, and repertoire of contention. Teasing this out requires fertile research on two problems. The first one involves mapping the participation of key domestic movement organizations in major regional and world transnational movement organizations created during the 1990s and 2000s. These include the Hemispheric Social Alliance, the People's Global Action Network, the Latin American Coordinator of Rural Organizations, the Interamerican Regional Labor Organization, Vía Campesina, and, of course the World Social Forum.[10] What is the extent of membership overlap across transnational movement organizations? How many of the key movement organizations active in our cases participated in important transnational conventions, congresses, and workshops? The second, and related, research issue involves the role of major national urban and rural movements in the creation and expansion of *regional* transnational organizations.[11]

Moreover, we know next to nothing about equally pressing issues. What networks did these organizations build based on their involvement in transnational activism? How did participation in transnational organizations contribute to anti-neoliberal contentious politics back home? Are anti-neoliberal transnational movements building transnational collective power by linking indigenous, human rights, environment, and labor? If so, are they generating shared master frames and support for overarching strategies of contentious action applied at the national level?[12]

My hypothesis would be that most anti-neoliberal transnational movements were too much in their formative stages to significantly influence our episodes of contention, with the possible exception of Bolivia in October 2003 and, perhaps, the struggle to oust the disappointing Gutiérrez in Ecuador in the mid-2000s. But to the extent they are expanding now, they may be of relevance to the struggles of the next decade and beyond.[13] In any case, research should not only consider the

---

[10] Early efforts include Desmarais (2007), Seoane and Taddei (2001), Anner and Evans (2004), Bülow (2007), Munck (2007).

[11] Only spotty evidence exists for these questions. For example, the Peoples Global Action Network organized an international convention in Cochabamba in September 2001, capitalizing on the imagery and energy of the 2000 Water War. The Argentine Polo Obrero piquetero organization, the CMS, and the CSUTCB participated; see PGA Third International Conference (www.agp.org, accessed 7/7/2008). There is some information on the formation of other key transnational movements (Albro 2005; Brysk 2000; Edelman 2005; Legler 2000; Saguier 2007; Seoane and Teddei 2002; Tarrow 2005). More information exists in these organizations' websites. Deeper knowledge would involve researching their archives, campaigns, conference proceedings, and, especially, in-depth interviews of major participants.

[12] Anner and Evans (2004) move us in this direction in an examination of alliances between U.S. and Latin American labor and NGOs.

[13] Again, to the extent that these movements and their repertoire of contention are replacing the central role of unions and the general strike of the 19th and 20th centuries, the study of transnational movements and their domestic effects parallels interest in international political parties and transnational labor movement organization support for domestic labor movements in the past.

formation of transnational movement coalitions and their global campaigns: It should also focus on the effect of such participation on major national movements and the diffusion and coordination of strategies, tactics, frames, and repertoire of contention.

On Alternatives to Neoliberalism

For analytic purposes I used the election of governments more committed to planning and socialization to demarcate the end of episodes of contention that challenged neoliberalism in South America. This decision raises a critical question. To what extent have those governments developed policies conducive to the construction of alternatives to neoliberalism? In other words, what might the legacy of massive anti-neoliberal mobilization be for state formation and a more just society?

Although one's answer depends on the scale of expected change, it is clear that efforts to apply planning and socialization to reform neoliberal capitalism vary greatly.[14] Venezuela occupies one end of the spectrum. Chávez, who has been in office nearly 10 years, strengthened the executive by concentrating power in it, thus permitting greater state intervention in the economy (including nationalization of private companies) and capacity to negotiate with international firms. He has also reorganized the delivery of expanded social services to poor neighborhoods and begun a new agrarian reform program. The "Bolivarian Revolution" carried those principles into its foreign policy by confronting U.S.-sponsored free trade agreements, promoting economic linkages among South American countries, and providing economic aid to them. Resources for these efforts flow principally from oil revenues, which were plentiful given the high price of hydrocarbon-based energy until the end of 2008. Bolivia's Morales follows Venezuela on the spectrum, although he has been in power a far shorter time than Chávez. He has confronted international firms in the oil and gas sectors, partially nationalized them, and attempted more redistributive social policies. It is still too early to tell what Correa may accomplish in Ecuador.

Then there is Argentina under Kirchner. His administration confronted the IMF, and with Venezuelan aid paid off its debt to that institution to raise revenue for domestic programs. His macroeconomic program is perhaps closer to that of contemporary Chile as are his governments' social programs, which are also targeted to vulnerable populations. However, up to now, the Argentine state (again like Chile) is not much involved in planning by, for example, industrial policy or nationalization. Peronists under Cristina Fernández de Kirchner, who succeeded her husband in 2007, have followed much the same line, although she attempted to extract more taxes from agribusiness to expand social services.

---

[14] For works assessing the leftward trend, see Arditi (2008); Castañeda and Morales (2007); Roberts (2007).

Understandably, skepticism over these developments and their future abounds. None of these political movements has developed a cohesive, comprehensive model for an alternative national project to neoliberalism. No country seems to have a well-thought-out industrial policy or coherent plan for the redistribution of the national wealth. Even Venezuela apparently lacks a socioeconomic development policy beyond using oil revenues to promote its pan-American foreign policy and to fund a proliferating patchwork of social programs, along with hastily conceived agrarian reform and a hodgepodge of nationalizations. What would happen with a change in the fortunes of oil? What can countries that do not have the blessing (or curse) of oil bounty hope to achieve without more thorough political and economic change? All that can be observed, for the most part, are more or less partial, gradual, halting, timid, and possibly contradictory reforms to neoliberal capitalism. Some would argue the small adjustments Argentina and Chile made are virtually indistinguishable from it (Martínez and Díaz 1996; Petras and Veltmeyer 2005).

In my view, such perspectives ask too much of these fledgling social and political movements at such an early stage of an unfolding historical process. There seems little reason to dismiss the effects of anti-neoliberal episodes of contention because they did not immediately usher in a new, fully formed development model and the sociopolitical power to sustain it. Historical precedent supports approaching problems from a more modest midrange theoretical position.[15]

The current era bears significant similarities to the birth of national populism in the first half of the 1900s, which was a Polanyian countermovement to the original global spread of liberal capitalism in Latin America. Rather than excoriate or dismiss "national populism" because of its shortcomings, from a comparative historical perspective it is more fruitful to think of it as an early 20th-century effort to include large swaths of excluded populations during a period of intense economic and political change.[16] It was the region's first foray into building more politically and socioeconomically inclusive societies in the modern era; a Latin American version of developed country welfare states mixed with a dose of industrial policy and neomercantilism.

Then, as now, its political leaders used incendiary rhetoric against the rich, the well-born, and powerful (the oligarchy) and extolled the virtues of the popular sectors. Then as now, they were *reformists:* economic nationalists who used state planning to gain some control over international capital but never sought to overturn capitalism. They tried to include the popular sectors not only politically (as voters) but also socioeconomically with labor codes, social services, and agrarian reform. They deflected class conflict and channeled popular sector discontent within capitalism (Conniff 1999, 1982; Drake 1978: 6–11).

---

[15] I am indebted to Paul Drake for this historical insight; see Drake (1996, 1978).
[16] Then, those changes involved transformations from agrarian societies and patrimonial upper-class states.

Conclusion

But "model" national populism did not spring forth fully formed. It developed over at least a 20-year period. In its origins from the 1920s to the early 1940s, national-populist leaders and the political movements that sustained them introduced a hodgepodge of piecemeal, partial, gradual, sometimes tepid, sometimes more radical, contradictory, and fluctuating reformist measures. Those policies fomented the mixed economy and included some of the popular sectors in the policy-making process and in the fruits of the economy they were building. The hodgepodge of policies emerged as a coherent "model" only in the late 1940s and early 1950s (Silva 2007). Why should our era be different? Moreover, then as now, reformist national populists faced opposition in difficult international and domestic political–institutional contexts. It was far from certain that their supporting social and political movements would consolidate under those pressures (often they did not). Insofar as they were reformist and sought to reequilibrate polities in crisis, revolutionaries and more radical reformers excoriated them. Last but not least, there was tremendous variety in the pace, depth, and timing of national-populist reforms in Latin America (Conniff 1982; Drake 1978). We observe the same today and, in time, a "model" (or "models") may emerge.

This all-too-brief foray into historical comparison takes nothing away from the vital importance of the difficult challenges contemporary leadership faces. How does one reestablish a measure of planning and socialization in the interest of socioeconomic and political inclusion and justice that avoids the worst pitfalls of the past and thus is capable of generating reasonable political stability with adequate economic growth? Debates will rage, but one issue, hopefully, has been settled. Attempts to revive market society, to reshape entire societies and the guiding principles of social order at the service of market efficiency to the exclusion of other values are not the path. They did not even, on average, deliver sustained high growth rates or contribute to greater social equity, quite the contrary (Weaver 2000). Instead, just as more moderate analysts feared, they generated escalating contention and political instability, either reformist or revolutionary (Haggard and Kaufman 1995).

Clearly, then, our episodes of anti-neoliberal contestation support Mahoney's (2001) broader theses. The imposition of either radical liberal reforms (Argentina and Bolivia) or aborted liberal reforms (Ecuador and Venezuela) mobilized the popular sector. Moreover, the current situation in Argentina and Chile confirm Mahoney's expectation (derived from the Costa Rican case) that mild inclusion makes free-market-oriented economic reforms compatible with broader political stability. A reformist liberal path to necessary structural socioeconomic adjustment, rather than the imposition of *market society*, offers the best chance to avert massive politically destabilizing popular sector mobilization and insurrection.[17]

---

[17] This being Latin America, a "normal" amount of contentious politics in the form of demonstrations, marches, strikes, and, now, roadblocks is to be expected, but falling far short of nationwide upheavals forcing sitting presidents out of office.

But what of the staying power of reformist political and socioeconomic forces that support socialization and planning? Centeno (2002) offers a pessimistic outlook. As we saw in Chapter 1, he argued that Latin American states are too weak to impose development models, lack autonomy from dominant classes to sustain models that emphasize socioeconomic equity, and are too weak to enforce order. Hence, under conditions of high inequality, perpetual popular mobilization and political instability are the norm. Stable state formation with greater socioeconomic inclusion of the popular sectors depends on raising tax revenues, not debt, but, unfortunately, insufficient state autonomy from dominant classes does not permit that.

Indeed, a number of countries appear to be living up to Centeno's bleak expectations. In some, such as Ecuador, Bolivia, and Venezuela, constant mobilization has become politics as usual. By the same token, it is difficult to extract higher taxes from upper-income groups and large-scale business in Argentina, Bolivia, and elsewhere.

Centeno underscored some hard truths about Latin American politics and society. Nevertheless, his insights may mislead us if we are not careful. They tempt analysts to dismiss recent episodes of anti-neoliberal contention as irrelevant and the emphasis too quickly shifts to the imperative of state modernization, which can take authoritarian turns. Following Mann (1986), I would argue that success in policy reform and manageable levels of contentious politics are not just a function of state strength and autonomy from social groups – measures that can quickly turn tautological. States and social actors are immersed in other networks of power.[18] For example, the Venezuelan state has a large income based on revenue from nationalized oil. It is relatively autonomous from domestic dominant classes. Yet it faces significant mobilization because opponents have support from political parties, private domestic economic power, civil society associations, and international diplomatic and political sources (mainly the United States). By contrast, the Chilean state has little autonomy from dominant classes but its steadfast implementation of piecemeal reforms to neoliberal social policies over 18 years limits contentious politics.

My point is that, even if countries in the region have a tendency to contentious action as part of "normal" politics, understanding the dynamics of anti-neoliberal contention contributes to the analysis of contemporary state formation in Latin America. For example, it is important to comprehend the motivation for protest. Otherwise political decisions and public policy are likely to inflame tempers and exacerbate mass mobilization and countermobilization. It makes a difference if people demand socioeconomic equality, democratization, good governance,

---

[18] Thus state strength and relative autonomy probably depend on the articulation of these power centers to the state instead of viewing them as the state's capacity to impose its will unilaterally. Peter Evans' (1995) concept of embedded autonomy may be a good starting point for such an exercise. It offers a means to examine the institutionalization in the policy process of social coalitions that support regimes.

cultural survival, or ethnic autonomy. Treating protestors as undifferentiated mobs encourages their exclusion and the perpetuation of injustices behind mobilization. Thus, whether states are weak or strong, relatively autonomous or not, political leaders ignore contentious politics at their peril. Finding a way to include the concerns of the popular sectors in normal politics goes a long way to maintaining order.[19]

The episodes of anti-neoliberal contention analyzed in this book contribute to the analysis of key elements in contemporary state formation, especially with respect to the rearticulation of the popular sectors to the state. These include a shift in the logic of movement organization from the point of production to the territorial, the characteristics of major new social movement organizations, their demands, the basis for their concatenation, and new connections to political (and perhaps transnational) power.

Still, whatever the path to greater popular sector inclusion, experience shows countries should heed one of Centeno's (2002) major conclusions. Stable state formation with greater socioeconomic inclusion for the popular sectors depends on raising tax revenue not debt. Despite the difficulties in some cases, many governments seeking to reform neoliberalism appear to take this policy prescription to heart. These include Chile, Argentina, and Brazil, and possibly Bolivia, Ecuador, and Venezuela. In any case, the experience of the first three suggests that moderate revenue increases and modest projects for social inclusion may suffice to keep political and social stability.

In conclusion, because the effort to reform neoliberalism is taking place in the context of democratic politics, we cannot, on average, expect sweeping changes because opposition to planning and socialization has the potential for fatal destabilizing polarization. This would hold true regardless of the relative autonomy states may have from dominant classes. We should remain alert to innovations in planning and socialization policy, as well as to the development of institutions that reincorporate the popular sectors in politics and into the benefits of the economy.[20] In the process, we cannot lose sight of how changes in popular

---

[19] Of course, as many, including Centeno, have pointed out, inflexible socioeconomic elites can be great impediments. However, that is where, especially in democracy, the art of compromise comes in. Similarly, some countries may very well have higher levels of "normal" mobilization than others, especially if institutional channels enforce exclusion. But, to the extent that some effort is being made by the authorities, mobilization does not necessarily have to escalate culminating in explosions bent on bringing down governments.

[20] Under these circumstances, opportunity and the "art of the possible" play a larger role than comprehensive planning. New reformist administrations understand they operate in a globalizing international political economy. Rescuing the concept of the mixed economy, greater regulation of international capital, and more spending on social services cannot be at the expense of sharp declines in economic growth and loss of macroeconomic discipline. Reckless pursuit of comprehensive reform at all costs is a path to polarization and conflict that would, at the very least, destroy their electoral viability and, at worst, the democratic polity that nurtured them. Reactionary, repressive military dictatorship would be the likely outcome, not leftist authoritarian rule. Again, oil revenues, in no small measure, have permitted Chávez to pursue more far-reaching

sector social movement organization, and its articulation to the state and political parties, affect reform of neoliberalism. Similarly, the impact of transnational movements remains to be determined. Over time, a model will suggest itself and generate a lively debate over its causes, variation within it, and which arrangements contribute most to longer-term socioeconomic and political stability.

reforms and endure greater degrees of conflict, although even there the mixed economy prevails and he has pursued policy objectives piecemeal over a decade. The other countries do not possess that cushion and have had presidents in office a much shorter time. Each prioritizes reform measures based on calculations over what the traffic might bear. How this process unfolds and what drives it will be worthy subjects of research to complement heated debates over its impact for democracy and economic development.

References

Abel, Christopher and Colin M. Lewis, eds. 2002. *Exclusion and Engagement: Social Policy in Latin America*. London: Institute of Latin American Studies.

Acuña, Carlos H. 1994. "Politics and Economics in the Argentina of the Nineties (Or, Why the Future No Longer Is What It Used to Be)." In *Democracy, Markets, and Structural Reform in Latin America: Argentina, Bolivia, Brazil, Chile, and Mexico*, edited by W. C. Smith, C. H. Acūna, and E. A. Gamarra. New Brunswick, NJ: Transaction Publishers.

Airriess, Maggie. 2008. "Critics Contend that Argentine Farmers' Grain and Meat Export Strike Wrongfully Blamed by President for Government's Irresponsible Mismanagement of Economic Policy." Council on Hemispheric Affairs (June 11). Available from http://www.coha.org.

Albó, Xavier. 2004. "Ethnic Identity and Politics in the Central Andes: The Cases of Bolivia, Ecuador, and Peru." In *Politics in the Andes: Identity, Conflict, Reform*, edited by J.-M. Burt and P. Mauceri. Pittsburgh: University of Pittsburgh Press.

_____. 2002. *Pueblos indios en la política*. La Paz: Plural Editores.

_____. 1999. "Etnias y pueblos originarios: Diversidad étnica, cultural y lingüística." In *Bolivia en el siglo XX: La formación de la Bolivia contemporánea*, edited by F. Campero. La Paz: Harvard Club de Bolivia.

Albro, Robert. 2005. "The Indigenous in the Plural in Bolivian Oppositional Politics." *Bulletin of Latin American Research* 24(4):433–453.

Alderete, Juan Carlos and Arnoldo Gómez. 1999. *La desocupación en el infierno menemista*. Buenos Aires: Editorial Agora.

Almeida, Paul D. 2007. "Defensive Mobilization: Popular Movements Against Economic Adjustment Policies in Latin America." *Latin American Perspectives* 34(3):123–139.

Almeida, Paul D. and Hank Johnston. 2006. "Neoliberal Globalization and Popular Movements in Latin America." In *Latin American Social Movements: Globalization, Democratization, and Transnational Networks*, edited by H. Johnston and P. D. Almeida. Lanham, MD: Rowman and Littlefield.

Altamira, Jorge. 2003. "La estrategia política a la luz de la rebellion del pueblo boliviano." *En Defensa del Marxismo* 32 [cited 9/10/06]. Available from www.po.org.ar.

_____. 2002. *El argentinazo: el presente como historia*. Buenos Aires: Ediciones Rumbos.

Alvarez, Angel E. 2003. "State Reform Before and After Chávez's Election." In *Venezuelan Politics in the Chávez Era: Class, Polarization and Conflict*, edited by S. Ellner and D. Hellinger. Boulder, CO: Lynne Rienner.

Andolina, Robert James. 2003. "The Sovereign and Its Shadow: Constituent Assembly and Indigenous Movement in Ecuador." *Journal of Latin American Studies* 35:721–750.

_____. 1999. "Colonial Legacies and Plurinational Imaginaries: Indigenous Movement Politics in Ecuador and Bolivia." Ph.D. Dissertation, University of Minnesota.

Andrenacci, Luciano, María Rosa Neufeld, and Liliana Raggio. 2001. "Elementos para un análisis de programas sociales desde la perspectiva de los receptores." *Serie Informes de Investigación 11*. Universidad Nacional de General, Sarmiento.

Angell, Alan. 2007. *Democracy After Pinochet: Politics, Parties and Elections in Chile*. London: University of London.

_____. 1991. "Unions and Workers in Chile During the 1980s." In *The Struggle for Democracy in Chile, 1982–1990*, edited by P. W. Drake and I. Jaksic. Lincoln: University of Nebraska Press.

Angell, Alan and Benny Pollack, eds. 1993. *The Legacy of Dictatorship: Political, Economic, and Social Change in Pinochet's Chile*. Liverpool: The University of Liverpool.

Anglade, Cristián and Carlos Fortín, eds. 1985. *The State and Capital Accumulation in Latin America*. Pittsburgh: Pittsburgh University Press.

Anner, Mark and Peter Evans. 2004. "Building Bridges Across a Double Divide: Alliances Between US and Latin American Labour and NGOs." *Development in Practice* 14(1–2): 34–47.

Arce, Moisés. 2008. "The Repoliticization of Collective Action After Neoliberalism in Peru." *Latin American Politics and Society* 50(3):37–62.

_____. 2006. "The Societal Consequences of Market Reform in Peru." *Latin American Politics and Society* 48(1):27–54.

Arceneaux, Craig and David Pion-Berlin. 2005. *Transforming Latin America: The International and Domestic Origins of Change*. Pittsburgh: University of Pittsburgh Press.

Arditi, Benjamin. 2008. "Arguments About the Left Turns in Latin America: A Post-Liberal Politics?" *Latin American Research Review* 43(3):59–81.

Armony, Ariel C. and Victor Armony. 2005. "Indictments, Myths, and Citizen Mobilization in Argentina: A Discourse Analysis." *Latin American Politics and Society* 47(4): 27–54.

Arrighi, Giovanni and Beverley Silver. 1999. *Chaos and Governance in the Modern World System*. Minneapolis: University of Minnesota Press.

Assies, Willem. 2004. "Bolivia: A Gasified Economy." *European Review of Latin American and Caribbean Studies* 76(April):25–43.

_____. 2003. "David versus Goliath in Cochabamba: Water Rights, Neoliberalism, and the Revival of Social Protest in Bolivia." *Latin American Perspectives* 30(3): 14–36.

Assies, Willem and Ton Salman. 2005. "Ethnicity and Politics in Bolivia." *Ethnopolitics* 4: 269–297.

_____. 2003. *Crisis in Bolivia: The Elections of 2002 and Their Aftermath*. London: Institute for Latin American Studies.

Auyero, Javier. 2007. *Routine Politics and Violence in Argentina: The Gray Zone of State Power*. Cambridge: Cambridge University Press.

_____. 2006. "The Political Makings of the 2001 Lootings in Argentina." *Journal of Latin American Studies* 38:241–266.

_____. 2005. "Protest and Politics in Contemporary Argentina." In *Argentine Democracy: The Politics of Institutional Weakness*, edited by S. Levitsky and M. V. Murillo. University Park: Pennsylvania State University Press.

_____. 2004. "What are they Shouting About? The Means and Meanings of Popular Protest in Contemporary Argentina." In *The Argentine Crisis at the Turn of the Millennium: Causes, Consequences and Explanations*, edited by F. Fiorucci and M. Klein. Amsterdam: Aksant.

References

———. 2003. *Contentious Lives: Two Women, Two Protests, and the Quest for Recognition.* Durham, NC: Duke University Press.

———. 2002. "Fuego, carpas y barricadas. Retratos de la beligerancia popular en la Argentina democrática." *Nueva Sociead* 179 (May-June): 144–162.

Ayres, Jeffrey M. 2004. "Framing Collective Action Against Neoliberalism: The Case of the 'Anti-Globalization' Movement." *Journal of World Systems Research* 10(1):11–34.

Bachrach, Peter and Morton S. Baratz. 1962. "The Two Faces of Power." *American Political Science Review* 56:947–952.

Balladares, Carina. et al. 2005. "El desempleo y la reconstrucción de lazos solidarios: La experiencia del MTD (1996)." In *De la culpa a la autogestión: Un recorrido del Movimiento de Trabajadores Desocupados de La Matanza,* edited by Toty Flores. Buenos Aires: Ediciones Continente.

Balbi, Carmen Rosa. 1997. "Politics and Trade Unions in Peru." In *The Peruvian Labyrinth: Polity, Society, Economy,* edited by M. Cameron and P. Mauceri. University Park: The Pennsylvania State University Press.

Baldez, Lisa. 1999. "La política partidista y los límites del feminismo de estado en Chile." In *El modelo chileno: Democracia y desarrollo en los noventa,* edited by P. W. Drake and I. Jaksic. Santiago: LOM Ediciones.

Ballvé, Teo. 2006. "Bolivia de pie." In *Dispatches from Latin America: On the Frontlines Against Neoliberalism,* edited by V. Prashad and T. Ballvé. Cambridge, MA: South End Press.

Barbetta, Pablo and Pablo Lapegna. 2001. "Cuando la protesta toma forma: los cortes de ruta en el norte salteño." In *La protesta social en la Argentina: Transformaciones económicas y crisis social en el interior del país,* edited by Norma Giarraca. Buenos Aires: Alianza Editorial.

Barral, Carlos. 2005. *Hablan las organizaciones sociales: MTD Aníbal Verón* [cited 2/18 2005]. Available from http://www.segundoenfoque.com.ar.

Barrera, Manuel and J. Samuel Valenzuela. 1986. "The Development of Labor Movement Opposition to the Military Regime." In *Military Rule in Chile: Dictatorship and Oppositons,* edited by A. Valenzuela and J. S. Valenzuela. Baltimore: Johns Hopkins University Press.

Bates, Robert H. and Anne O. Krueger, eds. 1993. *Political and Economic Interactions in Economic Policy Reform.* Oxford: Blackwell.

Bebbington, Anthony. 1992. "Grassroots Perspectives on 'Indigenous' Agricultural Development: Indian Organizations and NGOs in the Central Andes of Ecuador." *European Journal of Development Research* 4(2):132–167.

Belaúnde, Javier de. 1998. "Justice, Legality and Judicial Reform." In *Fujimori's Peru: The Political Economy,* edited by J. Crabtree and J. Thomas. London: University of London.

Benavides, O. Hugo. 2004. *Making Ecuadorian Histories: Four Centuries of Defining Power.* Austin: University of Texas Press.

Berger, Suzanne D., ed. 1981. *Organizing Interests in Western Europe: Pluralism, Corporatism, and the Transformation of Politics.* Cambridge: Cambridge University Press.

Blanco, Daniel. 2001. "Los dos alzamientos que conmovieron a Bolivia." *En Defensa del Marxismo* 29 [cited 10/3/07]. Available from www.po.org.ar.

Blank, David Eugene. 1984. *Venezuela: Politics in a Petroleum Republic.* New York: Praeger.

Block, Fred. 2003. "Karl Polanyi and the Writing of the Great Transformation." *Theory and Society* 32:275–306.

Block, Fred and Margaret R. Somers. 1984. "Beyond the Economistic Fallacy: The Holistic Social Science of Karl Polanyi." In *Vision and Method in Historical Sociology,* edited by T. Skocpol. Cambridge: Cambridge University Press.

Bolton, Maggie. 2007. "Counting Llamas and Accounting for People: Livestock, Land and Citizens in Southern Bolivia." *The Sociological Review* 55(1): 5–21.

Bonasso, Miguel. 2002. *El palacio y la calle: Crónicas de insurgentes y conspiradores*. Buenos Aires: Planeta.

Bond, Robert D. 1977. *Contemporary Venezuela and its Role in International Affairs, A Council on Foreign Relations Book*. New York: New York University Press.

Borzutzky, Silvia. 2002. *Vital Connections: Politics, Social Security, and Inequality in Chile*. Notre Dame, IN: University of Notre Dame Press.

Borzutzky, Silvia and Lois Hecht Oppenheim, eds. 2006. *After Pinochet: The Chilean Road to Democracy and the Market*. Gainesville: University Press of Florida.

Bretón, Víctor. 2003. "Desarrollo rural y etnicidad en las tierras altas de Ecuador." In *Estado, etnicidad y movimientos sociales en América Latina: Ecuador en crisis*, edited by V. Bretón and F. García. Barcelona: Icaria.

Briceño, Gustavo Tarre. 1993. "Opposition in Times of Change." In *Venezuela in the Wake of Radical Reform*, edited by J. S. Tulchin and G. Bland. Boulder, CO: Lynne Rienner.

Bryant, Jessica and Chris Sweeney. 2008. "Bolivia in Crisis." Available at http://www.coha.org.

Brysk, Alison. 2000. *From Tribal Village to Global Village: Indian Rights and International Relations in Latin America*. Stanford, CA: Stanford University Press.

Bulmer-Thomas, Victor. 2003. *The Economic History of Latin America Since Independence*. Cambridge: Cambridge University Press.

Bülow, Marisa von. 2007. "Networks of Trade Protests in the Americas: The Roles of Labor and Its Allies." Paper presented at the Latin American Studies Association, Montreal, Canada, September 5–8. 2007.

Burgess, Katrina. 2004. *Parties and Unions in the New Global Economy*. Pittsburgh, PA: University of Pittsburgh Press.

Burggraaff, Winfield J. and Richard L. Millett. 1995. "More Than Failed Coups: The Crisis in Venezuelan Civil-Military Relations." In *Lessons of the Venezuelan Experience*, edited by L. Goodman, J. M. Forman, M. Naím, J. S. Tulchin, and G. Bland. Baltimore: Johns Hopkins University Press.

Burt, Jo-Marie. 1997. "Political Violence and the Grassroots in Lima, Peru." In *The New Politics of Inequality in Latin America: Rethinking Participation and Representation*, edited by D. A. Chalmers, C. M. Vilas, K. Hite, S. B. Martin, K. Piester, and M. Segarra. New York: Oxford University Press.

Burt, Jo-Marie and Philip Mauceri, eds. 2004. *Politics in the Andes: Identity, Conflict, Reform*. Pittsburgh, PA: University of Pittsburgh Press.

Buxton, Julia. 2003. "Economic Policy and the Rise of Hugo Chávez. In *Venezuelan Politics in the Chávez Era: Class, Polarization, and Conflict*, edited by S. Ellner and D. Hellinger. Boulder, CO: Lynne Rienner.

———. 2001. *The Failure of Political Reform in Venezuela*. Aldershot, UK: Ashgate Publishing.

Camarasa, Jorge. 2002. *Dias de Furia*. Buenos Aires: Sudamericana.

Cameron, Maxwell. 1997. "Political and Economic Origins of Regime Change in Peru: The Eighteenth Brumaire of Alberto Fujimori." In *The Peruvian Labyrinth: Polity, Society, Economy*, edited by M. Cameron and P. Mauceri. University Park: Pennsylvania State University Press.

Cameron, Maxwell A. and Philip Mauceri, eds. 1997. *The Peruvian Labyrinth: Politics, Society, Economy*. University Park: Pennsylvania State University Press.

Campbell, Hartford. 2006. *Argentina's Néstor Kirchner: Peronism Without the Tears*. Council on Hemispheric Affairs (Jan 27) [cited 9/28 2007]. Available from http://www.coha.org.

References

Campbell, John L. 2005. "Where Do We Stand? Common Mechanisms in Organizations and Social Movements Research." In *Social Movements and Organization Theory*, edited by G. F. Davis, D. McAdam, W. R. Scott, and M. N. Zald. Cambridge: Cambridge University Press.

Campero, Guillermo and Jose A. Valenzuela. 1984. *El movimiento sindical en el régimen militar chileno*, 1973–1981. Santiago: Instituto Latinoamericano de Estudios Transnacionales.

Caram, Oscar, ed. 2002. *Que se vayan todos: Asambleas, horizontes y resistencias (un cruce de voces en el movimiento popular)*. Buenos Aires: N.P.

Cardoso, Fernando Henrique and Enzo Faletto. 1979. *Dependency and Development in Latin America*. Berkeley: University of California Press.

Carey, John M. and Matthew Soberg Shugart, eds. 1998. *Executive Decree Authority*. Cambridge: Cambridge University Press.

Carrera, Nicolas Iñigo and María Celia Cotarelo. 2003. "Social Struggles in Present Day Argentina." *Bulletin of Latin American Research* 22:201–213.

Castañeda, Jorge G. 1993. *Utopia Unarmed*. New York: Vintage Books.

Castañeda, Jorge G. and Marco A. Morales. 2007. "The Left Turn Continues." *Brown Journal of World Affairs* 13:201–209.

Cavallo, Ascanio, Manuel Salazar, and Oscar Sepúlveda, eds. 1988. *La historia oculta del régimen militar*. Santiago: La Epoca.

CEPAL, (Comisión Económica para América Latina y el Caribe). 2000. Anuario Estadísitico de América Latina y el Caribe. Santiago: United Nations.

Centeno, Miguel Angel. 2002. *Blood and Debt: War and the Nation-State in Latin America*. University Park: The Pennsylvania State University Press.

Centeno, Miguel Angel and Fernando López-Alves, eds. 2001. *The Other Mirror: Grand Theory Through the Lens of Latin America*. Princeton, NJ: Princeton University Press.

Chan, Steve and James R. Scarritt, eds. 2002. *Coping with Globalization: Cross National Patterns in Domestic Governance and Policy Performance*. London: Frank Cass.

Cohen, Robin and Shirin M. Rai, eds. 2000. *Global Social Movements*. London: Athlone.

Collier, David ed. 1979. *The New Authoritarianism in Latin America*. Princeton, NJ: Princeton University Press.

Collier, Ruth Berins. 1999. *Paths Toward Democracy: The Working Class and Elites in Western Europe and South America*. New York: Cambridge University Press.

Collier, Ruth Berins and David Collier. 1991. *Shaping the Political Arena: Critical Junctures, the Labor Movement, and Regime Dynamics in Latin America*. Princeton, NJ: Princeton University Press.

Collins, Jennifer N. 2006. "A Sense of Possibility: Ecuador's Indigenous Movement Takes Centre Stage." In *Dispatches From Latin America: On the Frontlines Against Neoliberalism*, edited by V. Prashad and T. Ballve. Cambridge, MA: South End Press.

———. 2004. "Linking Movement and Electoral Politics: Ecuador's Indigenous Movement and the Rise of the Pachakutik." In *Politics in the Andes: Identity, Conflict, Reform*, edited by J.-M. Burt and P. Mauceri. Pittsburgh, PA: University of Pittsburgh Press.

Colloredo-Mansfeld, Rudi. 2002. "Don't be Lazy, Don't Steal: Community Justice in the Neoliberal Andes." *American Ethnologist* 29: 637–662.

Conaghan, Catherine M. 2008. "Ecuador: Correa's Plebiscitary Presidency," *Journal of Democracy* 19(2):46–60.

———. 2005. *Fujimori's Peru: Deception in the Public Sphere*. Pittsburgh, PA: University of Pittsburgh Press.

———. 1988. *Restructuring Domination: Industrialists and the State in Ecuador*. Pittsburgh, PA: University of Pittsburgh Press.

References

Conaghan, Catherine M. and James M. Malloy. 1994. *Unsettling Statecraft: Democracy and Neoliberalism in the Central Andes*. Pittsburgh, PA: University of Pittsburgh Press.

CONAIE. 1994. "Mandato de la Movilización por la Vida," Asamblea Extraordinaria de la CONAIE, Riobamba, 7–8 June [cited 6/27/08]. Available from http://abyayala.nativeweb.org/ecuador.

Conniff, Michael L. 1999. "Introduction." In *Populism in Latin America*, edited by M. L. Conniff. Tuscaloosa: The University of Alabama Press.

———. 1982. "Introduction." In *Latin American Populism in Comparative Perspective*. Albuquerque: University of New Mexico, Press.

Contreras, Manuel. 2003. "A Comparative Perspective on Education Reforms in Bolivia, 1950–2000." In *Proclaiming Revolution: Bolivia in Comparative Perspective*, edited by M. S. Grindle and P. Domingo. London/Cambridge: ILAS and David Rockefeller Center.

Cook, Maria Lorena. 2007. *The Politics of Labor Reform in Latin America: Between Flexibility and Rights*. University Park: Pennsylvania State University Press.

Coppedge, Michael. 1996. "Venezuela: The Rise and Fall of Partyarchy." In *Constructing Democratic Governance: South America in the 1990s*, edited by J.I. Domínguez and A. Lowenthal. Baltimore, MD: Johns Hopkins University Press.

———. 1994. *Strong Parties and Lame Ducks: Presidential Partyarchy and Factionalism in Venezuela*. Stanford, CA: Stanford University Press.

Coronil, Fernando and Julie Skurski. 1991. "Dismembering and Remembering the Nation: The Semantics of Political Violence in Venezuela." *Comparative Studies in Society and History* 33:288–335.

Corradi, Juan E. 1985. *The Fitful Republic: Economy, Society, and Politics in Argentina*. Boulder, CO: Westview Press.

Corrales, Javier. 2002. *Presidents Without Parties: The Politics of Economic Reform in Argentina and Venezuela in the 1990s*. University Park: Pennsylvania State University Press.

Cotler, Julio. 2005. "Bolivia, Ecuador and Peru, 2003–04: A Storm in the Andes." Real Instituto Elcano.

Crabtree, John. 2005. *Patterns of Protest: Politics and Social Transformation In Bolivia*. London: Latin American Bureau.

Crabtree, John and Jim Thomas, eds. 1998. *Fujimori's Peru: The Political Economy*. London: University of London Press.

Crespo, Carlos F. 2000. "Continuidad y ruptura: la 'Guerra del Agua' y los nuevos movimientos sociales en Bolivia." *Revista OSAL* 2 (September):21–28.

Crisp, Brian. 2000. *Democratic Institutional Design: The Powers and Incentives of Venezuelan Politicians and Interest Groups*. Stanford, CA: Stanford University Press.

———. 1998. "Lessons from Economic Reform in the Venezuelan Democracy." *Latin American Research Review* 33(1):7–41.

Crisp, Brian F. and Daniel H. Levine. 1998. "Democratizing the Democracy? Crisis and Reform in Venezuela." *Journal of Interamerican Studies and World Affairs* 40(2):27–61.

Crozier, Michael, Samuel P. Huntington, and Jojo Watganuki, eds. 1975. *The Crisis of Democracy: Report on the Governability of Democracies to the Trilateral Commission*. New York: New York University Press.

Dahl, Robert. 1968. "Power." In *International Encyclopedia of the Social Sciences*, edited by D. L. Shills. New York: Macmillan.

de Brito, Alexandra Barahona. 1998. *Human Rights and Democratization in Latin America: Uruguay and Chile*. Oxford: Oxford University Press.

de Janvry, Alain 1981. *The Agrarian Question and Reformism in Latin America*. Baltimore: Johns Hopkins University Press.

References

Degregori, Carlos Ivan. 1994. "The Origins and Logic of the Shining Path: Two Views." In *The Shining Path of Peru*, edited by D. S. Palmer. New York: St. Martin's Press.

Deheza, Grace Ivana. 2007. "Bolivia 2006: Reforma estatal y construcción del poder" *Revista de Ciencia Política* (volumen especial):43–57.

Delamaza, Gonzalo. 2005. *Tan lejos tan cerca: Políticas públicas y sociedad civil en Chile*. Santiago: Lom Ediciones.

Della Porta, Donatella and Sidney Tarrow, eds. 2005. *Transnational Protest and Global Activism: People, Passions, and Power*. Oxford: Rowan and Littlefield.

Desmarais, Annette Aurelie. 2007. *La Via Campesina: Globalization and the Power of Peasants*. Halifax, Nova Scotia: Fernwood Publishing.

Di Marco, Graciela and Héctor Palomino. 2003. *Movimientos sociales en la Argentina. Asambleas: La politización de la sociedad civil*. Buenos Aires: Jorge Bandino Ediciones.

Di Palma, Giuseppe. 1990. *To Craft Democracies: An Essay on Democratic Transitions*. Berkeley: University of California Press.

Diamond, Larry. 1999. *Developing Democracy: Towards Consolidation*. Baltimore: Johns Hopkins University Press.

Diamond, Larry, Jonathan Hartlyn, Juan J. Linz, and Seymour Martin Lipset, eds. 1999. *Democracy in Developing Countries: Latin America*. 2nd ed. Boulder, CO: Lynne Rienner.

Diamond, Larry and Marc Plattner, eds. 1995. *Economic Reform and Democracy*. Baltimore: Johns Hopkins University Press.

Diani, Mario. 2003. "'Leaders' or Brokers? Positions and Influence in Social Movement Networks." In *Social Movements and Networks: Relational Approaches to Collective Action*, edited by Mario Diani and Doug McAdam. Oxford: Oxford University Press.

Diani, Mario and Doug McAdam, eds. 2003. *Social Movements and Networks: Relational Approaches to Collective Action*. Oxford: Oxford University Press.

Dietz, Henry A. and David J. Myers. 2007. "From Thaw to Deluge: Party System Collapse in Venezuela and Peru." *Latin American Politics and Society* 49(2):59–86.

Dinerstein, Ana C. 2003a. "Que se Vayan Todos! Popular Insurrection and the *Asambleas Barriales* in Argentina." *Bulletin of Latin American Research* 22:187–200.

_____. 2003b. "A Silent Revolution: The Unemployed Workers' Movement in Argentina and the New Internationalism." *Labour, Capital and Society* 34:166–183.

_____. 2001. "Roadblocks in Argentina: Against the Violence of Stability." *Capital and Class* 74:1–7.

Domingo, Pilar. 2005. "Democracy and New Social Forces in Bolivia." *Social Forces* 83:1727–1744.

Domínguez, Jorge I. and Abraham F. Lowenthal, eds. 1996. *Constructing Democratic Governance: South America in the* 1990s. Baltimore: Johns Hopkins University Press.

Dornbusch, R. and S. Edwards. 1991. "The Macroeconomics of Populism." In *The Macroeconomics of Populism in Latin America*. Chicago: University of Chicago Press.

Drake, Paul W. 1996. *Labor Movements and Dictatorships: The Southern Cone in Comparative Perspective*. Baltimore: Johns Hopkins University Press.

_____. 1978. *Socialism and Populism in Chile, 1932–52*. Urbana: University of Illinois Press.

Drake, Paul W. and Eric Hershberg, eds. 2006. "The Crisis of State-Society Relations in the Post-1980s Andes." In *State and Society in Conflict: Comparative Perspective on Andean Crises*. Pittsburgh, PA: University of Pittsburgh Press.

Dunkerley, James. 2007. "Evo Morales, the 'Two Bolivias' and the Third Bolivian Revolution." *Journal of Latin American Studies* 39:133–166.

———. 1993. "The Crisis of Bolivian Radicalism." In *The Latin-American Left: From the Fall of Allende to Perestroika*, edited by B. Carr and S. Ellner. Boulder, CO: Westview Press.

Dunn, Emily. 2008. "An Embattled Cristina Fernández de Kirchner: Can She Restore Her Popularity and Aid in Argentina's Recovery?" Council on Hemispheric Affairs [cited 7/30/2008]. Available at http://www.coha.org.

Eaton, Kent. 2007. "Backlash in Bolivia: Regional Autonomy as a Reaction Against Indigenous Mobilization." *Politics and Society* 35:71–102.

———. 2005. "Menem and the Governors: Intergovernmental Relations in the 1990s." In *Argentine Democracy: The Politics of Institutional Weakness*, edited by S. Levitsky and M. V. Murillo. University Park: Pennsylvania State University Press.

Eckstein, Susan, ed. 1989. *Power and Popular Protest in Latin America: Latin American Social Movements*. Berkeley: University of California Press.

Eckstein, Susan Eva and Timothy P. Wickham-Crowley, eds. 2003. *Struggles for Social Rights in Latin America*. New York: Routledge.

Economist Intelligence Unit, "Country, Report. 2000:Venezuela." London: Economist Intelligence Unit.

Ecuador. 2007. In *Europa World Yearbook* 2007. London.

Edelman, Marc. 2005. "Bringing the Moral Economy back into the Study of 21st-Century Transnational Peasant Movements." *American Anthropologist* 107: 331–345.

Edwards, Sebastian. 1995. *Crisis and Reform in Latin America: From Despair to Hope*. Oxford: Oxford University Press.

Edwards, Sebastian and Alejandra Cox Edwards. 1987. *Monetarism and Liberalization: The Chilean Experiment*. Cambridge, MA: Ballinger Publishing.

Ellner, Stéve. 2007. "The Movimiento Quinta República (MVR) and the Chavista Rank and File." Paper presented at the Latin American Studies Association, Montreal, Canada. September 5–8.

———. 2005. "The Emergence of a New Trade Unionism in Venezuela with Vestiges of the Past." *Latin American Perspectives* 32(2): 51–71.

———. 2003. "Introduction: The Search for Explanations." In *Venezuelan Politics in the Chávez Era*, edited by S. Ellner and D. Hellinger. Boulder, CO: Lynne Rienner.

———. 1999. "The Impact of Privatization on Labor in Venezuela: Radical Reorganization or Moderate Adjustment?" In *Political Power and Social Theory*, edited by D. E. Davis. Stamford, CN: Jai Press.

———. 1995. *El sindicalismo en Venezuela en el contexto democratico (1958–1994)*. Caracas: Universidad de Oriente.

———. 1993. *Organized Labor in Venezuela, 1958–1991: Behaivor and Concerns in a Democratic Setting*. Wilmington, DE: Scholarly Resources. Inc.

Ellner, Steve and Miguel Tinker Salas. 2007. *Venezuela: Hugo Chávez and the Decline of an "Exceptional Democracy."* Lanham, MD: Rowan and Littlefied.

Epstein, Edward C. 1992. "Labor Conflict in the New Argentine Democracy: Parties, Union Factions and Power Maximizing." In *The New Argentine Democracy: The Successful Formula*, edited by E. C. Epstein. Westport: Praeger.

Erro, David G. 1993. *Resolving the Argentine Paradox: Politics and Development, 1966–1992*. Boulder, CO: Lynne Rienner.

Escobar, Arturo and Sonia E. Alvarez. 1992. *The Making of Social Movements in Latin America: Identity, Strategy, and Democracy*. Boulder, CO: Westview Press.

Esping-Andersen, Gosta. 1990. *The Three Worlds of Welfare Capitalism*. Princeton, NJ: Princeton University Press.

References

Espinosa González, Gabriel. 2004. "Welcome to Washington, Mr. Peruvian President." Council on Hemispheric Affairs [cited 9/28 2007]. Available from http://www.coha.org.

Espinosa González, Gabriel and Matthew B. Riley. 2004. "Argentina's President Kirchner Continues His Daring Departure from Past Practices." Council on Hemispheric Affairs (Oct. 20) [cited 9/28 2007]. Available from http://www.coha.org.

Europa World, Online. *Argentina*. Routledge [cited 10/17/2007]. Available from http://www.europaworld.com/pub/entry/ar.dir.

Evans, Peter B. 1995. *Embedded Autonomy: States and Industrial Transformation*. Princeton, NJ: Princeton University Press.

Evans, Peter B., Dietrich Rueschemeyer and Theda Skocpol. 1985. *Bringing the State Back In*. Cambridge: Cambridge University Press.

Fanelli, Jose María and Roberto Frenkel. 1999. "The Argentine Experience with Stabilization and Structural Reform." In *After Neoliberalism: What Next for Latin America?* edited by L. Taylor. Ann Arbor: University of Michigan Press.

Fernández Anderson, Cora. 2006. "Constructive Riots. Ruptures and Continuities in the December 2001 Uprising in Argentina." Paper presented at the Latin American Studies Association, San Juan, Puerto Rico. March 15–18.

Ferrara, Francisco. 2003. *Más allá del corte de rutas: La lucha por una nueva subjetividad*. Buenos Aires: La Rosa Blindada.

Fernández-Kelly, Patricia and Jon Shefner, eds. 2006. *Out of the Shadows: Political Action and the Informal Economy in Latin America*. University Park: The Pennsylvania State University Press.

Ffrench-Davis, Ricardo. 1999. *Entre el neoliberalismo y el crecimiento con equidad: Tres décadas de política económica en Chile*. Santiago: Dolmen Ediciones.

Figueroa, Adolfo. 1998. "Income Distribution and Poverty in Peru." In *Fujimori's Peru: The Political Economy*, edited by J. Crabtree and J. Thomas. London: University of London Press.

Flores, Toty. 2005. *De la culpa a la autogestión: Un recorrido del movimiento de trabajadores desocupados de La Matanza*. Buenos Aires: Ediciones Continente.

Fontaine, Arturo. 1988. *Los economistas y el Presidente Pinochet*. Santiago: Editora Zig-Zag.

Foran, John. 2005. *Taking Power: On the Origins of Third World Revolutions*. Cambridge: Cambridge University Press.

Foweraker, Joe. 2005. "Towards a Political Sociology of Social Mobilization in Latin America." In *Rethinking Development in Latin America*, edited by C. H. Wood and B. R. Roberts. University Park: The Pennsylvania State University Press.

————. 1995. *Theorizing Social Movements*. London: Pluto Press.

Foxley, Alejandro 2004. "Successes and Failures in Poverty Eradication: Chile." In *Reducing Poverty, Sustaining Growth – What Works, What Doesn't and Why*. Washington, DC: World Bank.

————. 1983. *Latin American Experiments in Neo-Conservative Economics*. Berkeley: University of California Press.

Frank, Volker. 2002. "The Elusive Goal in Democratic Chile: Reforming the Pinochet Labor Legislation." *Latin American Politics and Society* 44(1):35–68.

Frías, Patricio. 1989. *El movimiento sindical chileno en la transición a la democracia*. Santiago: Programa Economía y Trabajo.

Frieden, Jeffrey. 1991. *Debt, Development and Democracy*. Princeton, NJ: Princeton University Press.

Fukuyama, Francis. 1992. *The End of History and the Last Man*. New York: Free Press.

Furtado, Celso. 1976. *Economic Development of Latin America: Historical Background and Contemporary Problems*. 2nd ed. New York: Cambridge University Press.

Gamarra, Eduardo, A. 2003. "Political Parties Since 1964: The Construction of Bolivia's Multiparty System." In *Proclaiming Revolution: Bolivia in Comparative Perspective*, edited by M.E. Grindle and P. Domingo. London/Cambridge, MA: ILAS and David Rockefeller Center.

———. 1994. "Crafting Political Support for Stabilization: Political Pacts and the New Economic Policy in Bolivia." In *Democracy, Markets, and Structural Reform in Latin America: Argentina, Bolivia, Brazil, Chile, and Mexico*, edited by W. C. Smith, C. H. Acuña, and E. A. Gamarra. New Brunswick, NJ: Transaction Publishers.

García, Francisco. 2003. "De la 'década perdida' a otra 'década perdida'? El impacto del ajuste estructural en Ecuador y en América Latina, 1980–2002." In *Estado, etnicidad y movimientos sociales en América Latina: Ecuador en crisis*, edited by V. Bretón and F. García. Barcelona: Icaria.

García-Guadilla, María Pilar. 2003. "Civil Society: Institutionalization, Fragmentation, Autonomy." In *Venezuelan Politics in the Chávez Era: Class, Polarization and Conflict*, edited by S. Ellner and D. Hellinger. Boulder, CO: Lynne Rienner.

García Linera, Alvaro. 2005. "The Indigenous Movements in Bolivia." *Diplomacy, Strategy & Politics* 1:12–30.

———. 2004. *Sociología de los movimientos sociales en Bolivia: Estructuras de movilización, repertorios culturales y acción política*. La Paz: Plural Editores.

García Linera, Alvaro, Raquel Gutiérrez, Raul Prada, and Luís Tapia. 2000. *El retorno de la Bolivia plebeya*. La Paz: Muela del Diablo Editores.

García-Serrano, Fernando. 2003. "Politica, Estado y diversidad cultural: A propósito del movimiento indígena ecuatoriano." In *Estado, etnicidad y movimiento sociales en América Latina*, edited by V. Bretón and F. García. Barcelona: Icaria.

Garretón, Manuel Antonio. 1993. "The Political Dimension of Processes of Transformation in Chile." In *Democracy, Markets, and Structural Reform in Latin America: Argentina, Bolivia, Brazil, Chile, and Mexico*, edited by W. C. Smith, C. H. Acuña and E. A. Gamarra. New Brunswick, NJ: Transaction Publishers.

———. 1991. "The Political Opposition and the Party System Under the Military Regime." In *The Struggle for Democracy in Chile, 1982–1990*, edited by P. W. Drake and I. Jaksic. Lincoln: University of Nebraska Press.

———. 1989. *The Chilean Political Process*. Boston: Unwin Hyman.

———. 1983. *El proceso político chileno*. Santiago: FLACSO.

Garretón, Manuel Antonio et al., eds. 2003. *Latin America in the 21st Century: Toward a New Sociopolitical Matrix*. Miami, FL: North-South Center Press, University of Miami.

Garrido, Luciana. 2005. *Hablan las organizaciones sociales: Movimiento Teresa Rodríguez* [cited 2/18 2007]. Available from http://www.segundoenfoque.com.ar.

Gereffi, Gary. 1994. "Rethinking Development Theory: Insights from East Asia and Latin America." In *Comparative National Development: Society and Economy in the New Global Order*, edited by A. D. Kincaid and A. Portes. Chapel Hill: University of North Carolina Press.

Gerlach, Alan. 2003. *Indians, Oil, and Politics: A Recent History of Ecuador*. Wilmington, DE: Scholarly Resources Inc.

Gerstenfeld, Pascual. 2002. "Social Policy Delivery: The New Economic Model and the Reform of the State." In *Exclusion and Engagement: Social Policy in Latin America*, edited by C. Abel and C. M. Lewis. London: Institute of Latin American Studies.

Giarracca, Norma. 2001. *La protesta social en la Argentina: Transformaciones económicas y crisis social en el interior del país*. Buenos Aires: Alianza Editorial.

References

Giarracca, Norma and Juan Wahren. 2006. "Recuperación de estado, ¿qué estado? Mosconi, Argentina después de ocho años de lucha." Paper presented at LASA International Congress, San Juan, Puerto Rico. March 15–18.

Gibson, Edward L. 1997. "The Populist Road to Market Reform: Policy and Electoral Coalitions in Mexico and Argentina." *World Politics* 49:339–370.

Giddens, Anthony. 1994. *Beyond Left and Right: The Future of Radical Politics*. Stanford, CA: Stanford University Press.

Gilly, Adolfo. 2005. "Bolivia: A 21st-Century Revolution." *Socialism and Democracy* 19(3):41–54.

Glatzer, Miguel and Dietrich Rueschemeyer, eds. 2005. *Globalization and the Future of the Welfare State*. Pittsburgh: University of Pittsburgh Press.

Goldstein, Judith. 1986. "The Political Economy of Trade: Institutions of Protection." *American Political Science Review* 80(1): 161–184.

Goldstone, Jack A. and Charles Tilly. 2001. "Threat and (Opportunity): Popular Action and State Response in the Dynamics of Contentious Action." In *Silence and Voice in the Study of Contentious Politics*, edited by R. R. Aminzade, J. A. Goldstone, D. McAdam, E. J. Perry, W. H. S. Jr., S. Tarrow and C. Tilly. Cambridge: Cambridge University Press.

Gómez, Luis. 2004. *El Alto de pie: Una insurrección aymara en Bolivia*. La Paz: HdP, Comuna, and Indymedia.

Gómez-Calcaño Luis. 1998. "Redefining the State's Social Policies: The Case of Venezuela." In *The Changing Role of the State in Latin America*, edited by M. Vellinga. Boulder, CO: Westview Press.

Goodwin, Jeff. 2001. *No Other Way Out: States and Revolutionary Movements, 1945–1991*. Cambridge: Cambridge University Press.

Gott, Richard. 2000. *In the Shadow of the Liberator: Hugo Chávez and the Transformation of Venezuela*. London: Verso.

Gourevitch, Peter Alexis. 1986. *Politics in Hard Times: Comparative Responses to International Economic Crises*. Ithaca, NY: Cornell University Press.

Graham, Carol. 2000. "From Safety Nets to Social Sector Reform: Lessons from the Developing Countries for the Transition Economies." In *Social Development in Latin America: The Politics of Reform*, edited by J. S. Tulchin and A. M. Garland. Boulder, CO: Lynne Rienner.

Greaves, Edward. 2007. "Institutional Innovation and Urban Poor People's Movements in Chile: Social Welfare, Poverty Alleviation and the *Movimiento Poblacional*." Paper presented at the Latin American Studies Association, Montreal, Canada. September 5–8.

Grindle, Merilee S. 2003. "Shadowing the Past? Policy Reform in Bolivia, 1985–2002." In *Proclaiming Revolution: Bolivia in Comparative Perspective*, edited by M. S. Grindle and P. Domingo. London/Cambridge, MA: ILAS and David Rockefeller Center.

———. 2000. *Audacious Reforms: Institutional Invention and Democracy in Latin America*. Baltimore: Johns Hopkins University Press.

Grindle, Merilee S. and Pilar Domingo, eds. 2003. *Proclaiming Revolution: Bolivia in Comparative Perspective*. London/Cambridge: ILAS and David Rockefeller Center.

Guerrero, Andrés. 1993. "De sujetos indios a ciudadanos-étnicos: de la manifestación de 1961 al levantamiento indígena de 1990." In *Democracia, etnicidad y violencia política en los países andinos*, edited by A. Adrianzén et al. Lima, Peru: IEP Ediciones and Instituto Francés de Estudios Andinos.

Haagh, Louise 2002. *Citizenship, Labour Markets and Democratisation: Chile and the Modern Sequence*. Basingstoke, UK: Palgrave Macmillan.

Haber, Stephen. 2006. "The Political Economy of Industrialization." In *The Cambridge Economic History of Latin America*, edited by V. Bulmer-Thomas, J. Coatsworth, and R. C. Conde. Cambridge: Cambridge University Press.

Haggard, Stephan. 1990. *Pathways from the Periphery: The Politics of Growth in the Newly Industrializing Countries*. Ithaca, NY: Cornell University Press.

Haggard, Stephan and Robert R. Kaufman. 1995. *The Political Economy of Democratic Transitions*. Princeton, NJ: Princeton University Press.

Haggard, Stephan and Steven B. Webb, eds. 1994. *Voting for Reform: Democracy, Political Liberalization, and Economic Adjustment*. Oxford: Oxford University Press.

Hagopian, Frances and Scott Mainwaring, eds. 2005. *The Third Wave of Democratization in Latin America: Advances and Setbacks*. Cambridge: Cambridge University Press.

Haworth, Nigel. 1993. "Radicalization and the Left in Peru, 1976–1991." In *The Latin American Left: From the Fall of Allende to Perestroika*, edited by B. Carr and S. Ellner. Boulder, CO: Westview Press.

Hayek, Friedrich. 1994. *The Road to Serfdom*. Chicago: University of Chicago Press.

Healy, Kevin. 1991. "Political Ascent of Bolivia's Peasant Coca Leaf Producers." *Journal of Interamerican Studies and World Affairs* 33(1):87–121.

———. 1988. "Coca, the State, and the Peasantry in Bolivia, 1982–1988." *Journal of Interamerican Studies and World Affairs* 30(2/3 Special Issue: Assessing the Americas' War on Drugs):105–126.

Healy, Kevin and Susan Paulson. 2000. "Political Economies of Identity in Bolivia, 1952–1998." *The Journal of Latin American Anthropology* 5(2):2–29.

Hellinger, Daniel. 2009. "Venezuela." In *Politics of Latin America: The Power Game*, edited by H. Vanden and G. Prevost. Oxford: Oxford University Press, 3rd edition.

———. 2006. "Venezuela." In *Politics of Latin America: The Power Game*, edited by H. E. Vanden and G. Prevost. New York: Oxford University Press.

———. 2003. "Political Overview: The Breakdown of *Puntofijismo* and the Rise of *Chavismo*." In *Venezuelan Politics in the Chávez Era*, edited by S. Ellner and D. Hellinger. Boulder, CO: Lynne Rienner.

———. 1996. "The Causa R and the *Nuevo Sindicalismo* in Venezuela." *Latin American Perspectives* 23(3):110–131.

———. 1991. *Venezuela: Tarnished Democracy*. Boulder, CO: Westview Press.

Hillman, Richard S. 1994. *Democracy for the Privileged: Crisis and Transition in Venezuela*. Boulder, CO: Lynne Rienner.

Hirschman, Albert O. 1971. *A Bias for Hope: Essays on Development and Latin America*. New Haven, CN: Yale University Press.

Hite, Katherine. 2007. "'The Eye That Cries: The Politics of Representing Victims in Contemporary Peru." *A Contra Corriente* 5(1):108–134.

Hodges, Donald C. 1993. "The Argentine Left Since Perón." In *The Latin American Left: From the Fall of Allende to Perestroika*, edited by B. Carr and S. Ellner. Boulder, CO: Westview Press.

Howard, Alan. 2002. "The Future of Global Unions: Is Solidarity Still Forever?" *Dissent* Fall:62–70.

Huber, Evelyne. 2005. "Globalization and Social Policy Developments in Latin America." In *Globalization and the Future of the Welfare State*, edited by M. Glatzer and D. Rueschemeyer. Pittsburgh, PA: University of Pittsburgh Press.

———, ed. 2002. *Models of Capitalism: Lessons for Latin America*. University Park: Pennsylvania State University Press.

———. 1983. "The Peruvian Military Government, Labor Mobilization, and the Political Strength of the Left." *Latin American Research Review* 18:57–93.

References

Huber, Evelyn and Fred Solt. 2004. "Successes and Failures of Neoliberalism." *Latin American Research Review* 39:150–164.

Hunefeldt, Christine. 1997. "The Rural Landscape and Changing Political Awareness: Enterprises, Agrarian Producers, and Peasant Communities, 1969–1994." In *The Peruvian Labyrinth: Polity, Society, Economy*, edited by M. Cameron and P. Mauceri. University Park: Pennsylvania State University Press.

Huntington, Samuel P. 1968. *Political Order in Changing Societies*. New Haven, CT: Yale University Press.

Hurtado, Osvaldo. 1980. *Political Power in Ecuador*. Translated by N. D. Mills. Albuquerque: University of New Mexico Press.

Hylton, Forest. 2008. "Reactionary Rampage: The Paramilitary Massacre in Bolivia." Available at http://www.nacla.org.

Hylton, Forest and Sinclair Thomson. 2006. "The Roots of the Rebellion: Insurgent Bolivia." In *Dispatches from Latin America: On the Frontlines Against Neoliberalism*, edited by V. Prashad and T. Ballvé. Cambridge, MA: South End Press.

Ibáñez Rojo, Enrique. 2000. "The UDP Government and the Crisis of the Bolivian Left (1982–1985)." *Journal of Latin American Studies* 32(1):175–205.

International Labor Organization (ILO). 1998. "Labor Overview: Latin America and the Carribean." Lima: International Labor Organization.

Isaacs, Anita. 1993. *Military Rule and Transition in Ecuador, 1972–92*. Pittsburgh: University of Pittsburgh Press.

Jadresic, Esteban. 1986. "Evolución del empleo y desempleo en Chile, 1970–85. Series anuales y trimestrales." *Colección Estudios Cieplan* 20:147–193.

Jasper, Miranda Louise and Clare Ribando Seelke. 2008. "Peru: Political Situation, Economic and Conditions and U.S. Relations." *CRS Report for Congress* RS22715: 1–6.

Jelin, Elizabeth and Eric Hershberg, eds. 1996. *Constructing Democracy: Human Rights, Citizenship, and Society in Latin America*. Boulder, CO: Westview Press.

Jenkins, Rhys. 1997. "Trade Liberalisation in Latin America: The Bolivian Case." *Bulletin of Latin American Research* 16:307–325.

Joseph, Anita. 2006. "Direct Intervention: A Call for Bush and Bolivia's Morales to Take a Leap of Faith and Change Presidential Issues into Personal Ones." Council on Hemispheric Affairs (June 8) [cited 7/2/07]. Available from http://www.coha.org.

Katzenstein, Peter J. 1985. *Small States in World Markets: Industrial Policy in Europe*. Ithaca, NY: Cornell University Press.

Kay, Cristóbal. 2004. "Rural Livelihoods and Peasant Futures." In *Latin America Transformed: Globalization and Modernity*, edited by R. N. Gwynne and C. Kay. London: Arnold, 2nd edition.

———. 1999. "Rural Development from Agrarian Reform to Neoliberalism and Beyond." In *Latin America Transformed: Globalization and Modernity*, edited by R. N. Gwynne and C. Kay. London: Arnold.

Kay, Cristóbal and Patricio Silva. 1992. *Development and Social Change in the Chilean Countryside: from the Pre-land Reform Period to the Democratic Transition*. Amsterdam, Netherlands: Centre for Latin American Research and Documentation.

Keck, Margaret E. and Kathryn Sikkink. 1998. *Activists Beyond Borders: Advocacy Networks in International Politics*. Ithaca, NY: Cornell University Press.

Kelly, Janet and Pedro A. Palma. 2004. "The Syndrome of Economic Decline and the Quest for Change." In *The Unravelling of Representative Democracy in Venezuela*, edited by J. L. McCoy and D. J. Myers. Baltimore: Johns Hopkins University Press.

Kelsey, Sarah and Steven Levitsky. 1994. "Captivating Alliances: Unions, Labor Backed Parties and the Politics of Economic Liberalism in Argentina and Mexico." Paper presented at the XVIII International Congress of the Latin American Studies Association, Atlanta, Georgia. March 10–12.

Kenney, Charles. 1996. "¿Por qué el autogolpe? Fujimori 1990–1992." In *Los enigmas del poder: Fujimori 1990–1996*, edited by F. T. Soldevilla. Lima: Fundación Friedrich Ebert.

Kingstone, Peter R. 1999. *Crafting Coalitions for Reform: Business Preferences, Political Institutions, and Neoliberal Reform in Brazil*. University Park: Pennsylvania State University Press.

Klein, Herbert S. 2003. *A Concise History of Bolivia*. Cambridge: Cambridge University Press.

———. 1992. *Bolivia: The Evolution of a Multi-Ethnic Society*. Oxford: Oxford University Press.

Kohan, Aníbal. 2002. *A las calles: Una historia de los movimientos piqueteros y caceroleros de los '90 al 2002*. Buenos Aires: Colihue.

Kohl, Benjamin and Linda Farthing. 2006. *Impasse in Bolivia: Neoliberal Hegemony and Popular Resistance*. London: Zed Books.

Kornblith, Miriam. 1998. *Venezuela en los noventa. Las crisis de la democracia*. Caracas: Ediciones IESA.

Korovkin, Tanya. 1998. "Commodity Production and Ethnic Culture: Otavalo, Northern Ecuador." *Economic Development and Cultural Change* 47: 125–154.

———. 1997. "Modernization of Agriculture: Chimborazo, 1964–1991." *Latin American Perspectives* 24(3) 25–49.

Krasner, Stephen. 1978. *Defending the National Interest: Raw Material Investments and Foreign Policy*. Princeton, NJ: Princeton University Press.

Krueger, Anne O. 1974. "The Political Economy of the Rent-Seeking Society." *American Economic Review* 64(3):291–303.

Kuczynski, Pedro-Pablo and John Williamson, eds. 2003. *After the Washington Consensus: Restarting Growth and Reform in Latin America*. Washington, DC: Institute for International Economics.

Kurtz, Marcus J. 2004. "The Dilemmas of Democracy in the Open Economy: Lessons from Latin America." *World Politics* 56:262–302.

Lander, Edgardo. 2005. "Venezuelan Social Conflict in a Global Context." *Latin American Perspectives* 32(2):20–38.

———. 1996. "The Impact of Neoliberal Adjustment in Venezuela." *Latin American Perspectives* 23(3):50–73.

Larraín, Felipe. 1991. "The Economic Challenges of Democratic Development." In *The Struggle for Democracy in Chile, 1982–1990*, edited by P. W. Drake and I. Jaksic. Lincoln: University of Nebraska Press.

Laserna, Roberto. 2001. "Conflictos sociales y movimientos políticos: El año 2000 en Bolivia." Documentos de Trabajo, Centro de Estudios de la Realidad Económica y Social.

———. 1985. *Democracia y conflicto social*. Cochabamba: CERES.

Laufer, Rubén and Claudio Spiguel. 1999. "Las 'pueblladas' argentinas a partir del 'santiagueñazo' del 1993. Tradición histórica y nuevas formas de lucha." In *Lucha popular, democracia, y neoliberalismo: Protesta popular en América Latina en los años del ajuste*, edited by M. López Maya. Caracas: Editorial Nueva Sociedad.

Lazar, Sian. 2008. *El Alto, Rebel City: Self and Citizenship in Andean Bolivia*. Durham, NC: Duke University Press.

References

———. 2006. "El Alto, Ciudad Rebelde: Organisational Bases for Revolt." *Bulletin of Latin American Research* 25:183–199.

———. 2004. "Personalist Politics, Clientelism and Citizenship: Local Elections in El Alto, Bolivia." *Bulletin of Latin American Research* 23:228–243.

Lazarte, Jorge. 1989. *Movimiento obrero y procesos políticos en Bolivia: Historia de la C.O.B., 1952–1987*. La Paz: Taller Grafico de Editorial Offse Boliviana.

Lebowitz, Michael A. 2007. "Venezuela: A Good Example of the Bad Left of Latin America." *Monthly Review* 59(3):1–14.

Ledebur, Kathryn and Coletta A. Youngers. 2008. "Balancing Act: Bolivia's Drug Control Advances and Challenges." *Andean Information Network*. Available from http://www.ain-bolivia.org/AINWOLABalancingAct52308.pdf.

Legler, Thomas. 2000. "Transnational Coalition-Building in the Americas: The Case of the Hemispheric Social Alliance." Paper presented at the Summer Institute on "Building the New Agenda: Hemispheric Integration and Social Cohesion," Robards Centre for Canadian Studies, York University, Toronto. July 10–20.

Lettieri, Michael. 2006. "Morales Does the Unthinkable–He Carries out his Campaign Pledge." Council on Hemispheric Affairs (May 4) [cited 5/4/06]. Available from http://www.coha.org.

Levitsky, Steven. 2005. "Crisis and Renovation: Institutional Weakness and the Transformation of Argentine Peronism, 1983–2003." In *Argentine Democracy: The Politics of Institutional Weakness*, edited by S. Levitsky and M. V. Murillo. University Park: Pennsylvania State University Press.

———. 2003. "From Labor Politics to Machine Politics: The Transformation of Party-Union Linkages in Argentine Peronism, 1983–1999."*Latin American Research Review* 38:3–36.

Levitsky, Steven and María Victoria Murillo. 2008. "Argentina: From Kirchner to Kirchner" *Journal of Democracy* 19:16–30.

———, Eds. 2005. *Argentine Democracy: The Politics of Institutional Weakness*. University Park: Pennsylvania State University Press.

Lind, Amy. 2004. "Engendering Andean Politics: The Paradoxes of Women's Movements in Neoliberal Ecuador and Bolivia." In *Politics in the Andes: Identity, Conflict, Reform*, edited by J.-M. Burt and P. Mauceri. Pittsburgh: University of Pittsburgh Press.

Lindblom, Charles. 1977. *Politics and Markets*. New York: Basic Books.

Linz, Juan J. 1978. *The Breakdown of Democratic Regimes: Crisis, Breakdown, and Reequilibration*. Baltimore: Johns Hopkins University Press.

Linz, Juan J. and Alfred Stepan. 1996. *Problems of Democratic Transition and Consolidation: Southern Europe, South America, and Post Communist Europe*. Baltimore: Johns Hopkins University Press.

Lira, Elizabeth. 2006. "Human Rights in Chile: The Long Road to Truth, Justice, and Reparations." In *After Pinochet: The Chilean Road to Democracy and the Market*, edited by S. Borzutzky and L. H. Oppenheim. Gainesville: University Press of Florida.

Llanos, Mariana and Ana Margheritis. 2006. "Why Do Presidents Fail? Political Leadership and the Argentine Crisis (1999–2001)." *Studies in Comparative International Development* 40(4):77–103.

Long, Norman and Bryan R. Roberts. 1994. "The Agrarian Structures of Latin America, 1930–1990." In *The Cambridge History of Latin America*, edited by L. Bethell. Cambridge: Cambridge University Press.

López-Levy, Marcela. 2004. *We Are Millions: Neo-Liberalism and New Forms of Political Action in Argentina*. London: Latin American Bureau.

López Maya, Margarita and Edgardo Lander. 2005. "Popular Protest in Venezuela: Novelties and Continuities." *Latin American Perspectives* 32(2): 92–108.

López Maya, Margarita. 2003. "Hugo Chávez Frías: His Movement and His Presidency." In *Venezuelan Politics in the Chávez Era*, edited by S. Ellner and D. Hellinger. Boulder, CO: Lynne Rienner.

———. 1999a. "La protesta popular venezolana entre 1989 y 1993 (en el Umbral del neoliberalismo)." In *Lucha popular, democracia, neoliberalismo: Protesta popular en América Latina en los años de ajuste*, edited by M. Lopez Maya. Caracas: Nueva Sociedad.

———. 1999b. "Venezuela; La rebellión popular del 27 de febrero de 1989." *Revista Venezolana de Economia y Ciencias Sociales* 5(2–3):177–200.

———. ed. 1999c. *Lucha popular, democracia, neoliberalismo: Protesta popular en América Latina en los años del ajuste*. Caracas: Nueva Sociedad.

———. 1997. "The Rise of Causa R in Venezuela." In *The New Politics of Inequality in Latin America: Rethinking Participation and Representation*, edited by D. A. Chalmers, C. M. Vilas, K. Hite, S. B. Martin, K. Piester, and M. Segarra. New York: Oxford University Press.

Loveman, Brian. 1993. "The Political Left in Chile." In *The Latin American Left: From the Fall of Allende to Perestroika*, edited by B. Carr and S. Ellner. Boulder, CO: Westview Press.

Lowenthal, Abraham F. and Gregory F. Treverton, eds. 1994. *Latin America in a New World*. Boulder, CO: Westview Press.

Lukes, Steven, ed. 1986. *Power*. Oxford: Blackwell.

Lustig, Nora. 1998. *Mexico, the Remaking of an Economy*. 2nd ed. Washington, DC: Brookings Institution Press.

Lvovich, Daniel. 2000. "Colgados de la soga. La experiencia del tránsito desde la clase media a la nueva pobreza en la ciudad de Buenos Aires." In *Desde abajo: La transformación de las indentidades sociales*, edited by Maristella Svampa. Buenos Aires: Editorial Biblos.

Macbeth, Hampden. 2005. "Peru: A Broken Democracy." Council on Hemispheric Affairs [cited 9/28/07]. Available from http://www.coha.org.

Machado Puertas, Juan Carlos. 2008. "Ecuador . . . Hasta que se fueron todos." *Revista de Ciencia Política* 28(1):189–215.

Madrid, Raúl L. 2003. *Retiring the State: The Politics of Pension Privatization in Latin America and Beyond*. Stanford, CA: Stanford University Press.

Mahoney, James. 2001. *The Legacies of Liberalism: Path Dependence and Political Regimes in Central America*. Baltimore: Johns Hopkins University Press.

Mainwaring, Scott and Aníbal Pérez-Liñán. 2005. "Latin American Democratization Since 1978: Democratic Transitions, Breakdowns, and Erosions." In *The Third Wave of Democratization in Latin America: Advances and Setbacks*, edited by F. Hagopian and S. Mainwaring. Cambridge: Cambridge University Press.

Mainwaring, Scott, Guillermo A. O'Donnell, and Arturo Valenzuela, eds. 1992. *Issues in Democratic Consolidation: The New South American Democracies in Comparative Perspective*. Notre Dame, IN: University of Notre Dame Press.

Mainwaring, Scott P. and Eduardo Viola. 1984. "New Social Movements, Political Culture, and Democracy: Brazil and Argentina in the 1980's." *Telos* 61(Fall):17–53.

Mann, Michael. 1993. *The Sources of Social Power, Vol. 2*. Cambridge: Cambridge University Press.

———. 1986. *The Sources of Social Power, Vol. 1*. Cambridge: Cambridge University Press.

Manzetti, Luigi. 1999. *Privatization South American Style*. Oxford: Oxford University Press.

References

Marcel, Mario and Patricio Meller. 1986. "Empalme de las cuentas nacionales de Chile 1960–1985: Métodos alternativos y resultados" *Colección Estudios CIEPLAN* 20(Diciembre): 121–146.

Martínez, Javier and Alvaro Díaz. 1996. *Chile, the Great Transformation*. Washington, DC: Brookings Institution.

Martz, John D. 1966. *Acción Democrática: Evolution of a Modern Political Party in Venezuela*, Princeton, NJ: Princeton University Press.

Martz, John D. and David J. Myers, eds. 1977. *Venezuela: The Democratic Experience*. New York: Praeger.

Marx, Karl and Friedrich Engels. 1992. "Marx and Engels." In *Socialist Thought: A Documentary History*, edited by A. Fried and R. Sanders. NewYork, NY: Columbia University Press.

Mauceri, Philip. 2006. "An Authoritarian Presidency: How and Why Did Presidential Power Run Amok in Fujimori's Peru?" In *The Fujimori Legacy: The Rise of Electoral Authoritarianism in Peru*, edited by J. Carrion. University Park: Pennsylvania State University Press.

———. 1997. "The Transition to 'Democracy' and the Failures of Institution Building." In *The Peruvian Labyrinth: Polity, Society, Economy*, edited by M. Cameron and P. Mauceri. University Park: Pennsylvania State University Press.

———. 1995. "State Reform, Coalitions, and Neoliberal Autogolpe in Peru." *Latin American Research Review* 30(1): 7–37.

Maxfield, Sylvia. 1989. "National Business, Debt-Led Growth and Political Transition in Latin America." *In Debt and Democracy in Latin America*, edited by B. Stallings and R. Kaufman. Boulder, CO: Westview Press.

Mayorga, Fernando. 2006. "El gobierno de Evo Morales: entre nacionalismo e indigenismo" *Nueva Sociedad* 206:4–13.

Mayorga, René Antonio. 2005. "Bolivia's Democracy at the Crossroads." In *The Third Wave of Democratization in Latin America: Advances and Setbacks*, edited by F. Hagopian and S. Mainwaring. Cambridge: Cambridge University Press.

McAdam, Doug, Sidney Tarrow, and Charles, Tilly. 2001. *Dynamics of Contention*. Cambridge: Cambridge University Press.

McCaughan, Michael. 2004. *The Battle of Venezuela*. New York: Seven Stories Press.

McClintock, Cynthia. 1996. "La voluntad política presidencial y la ruptura constitucional de 1992 en el Perú." In *Los enigmas del poder: Fujimori 1990–1996*, edited by F. T. Soldevilla. Lima: Fundación Friedrich Ebert.

———. 1989. "Peru's Sendero Luminoso Rebellion: Origins and Trajectory." In *Power and Popular Protest: Latin American Social Movements*, edited by S. Eckstein. Berkeley: University of California Press.

———. 1981. *Peasant Cooperatives and Political Change in Peru*. Princeton, NJ: Princeton University Press.

McClintock, Cynthia and Fabian Vallas. 2003. *The United States and Peru in the 1990s: A Handshake for a Peruvian Caudillo*. New York: Routledge Press.

McCoy, Jennifer, Andrés Serbín, William C. Smith, and Andrés Stambouli, eds. 1995. *Venezuelan Democracy Under Stress*. New Brunswick, NJ: Transaction Publisher.

McCoy, Jennifer and William C. Smith. 1995. "From Deconsolidation to Reequilibration? Prospects for Democratic Renewal in Venezuela." In *Venezuelan Democracy Under Stress*, edited by J. McCoy, A. Serbín, W. C. Smith, and A. Stambouli. New Brunswick, NJ: Transaction Publishers.

McGuire, James W. 1997. *Peronism Without Peron: Unions, Parties and Democracy in Argentina*. Stanford, CA: Stanford University Press.

_____. 1996. "Strikes in Argentina: Data Sources and Recent Trends." *Latin American Research Review* 31(3):127–150.

McNeish, John-Andrew. 2006. "Stones on the Road: The Politics of Participation and the Generation of Crisis in Bolivia." *Bulletin of Latin American Research* 25:220–240.

Mesa-Lago, Carmelo. 1978. *Social Security in Latin America: Pressure Groups, Stratification, and Inequality*. Pittsburgh, PA: University of Pittsburgh Press.

Middleton, Alan. 1982. "Division and Cohesion in the Working Class: Artisans and Wage Labourers in Ecuador." *Journal of Latin American Studies* 14(1):171–194.

Miliband, Ralph. 1983. *Class Power and State Power*. London: Verso.

Migdal, Joel S. 1998. *Strong Societies and Weak States: State-Society Relations and State Capabilities in the Third World*. Princeton, NJ: Princeton University Press.

Ministry of Economy and Finance, Republic of Peru. 2005. Bulletin of Macrosocial Transparency, edited by DGAES.

Mokhtari, Nicki. 2007. "No Smooth Sailing for Bolivia's Morales." Council on Hemispheric Affairs (Feb. 23) [cited 2/23/07]. Available from http://www.coha.org.

Montero, Alfred P. 2001. "Making and Remaking 'Good Government' in Brazil: Subnational Industrial Policy in Minas Gerais." *Latin American Politics and Society* 43(2): 49–80.

Munck, Ronaldo. 2007. *Globalization and Contestation: The New Great Counter-Movement*. London: Routledge.

_____. 2002. "Globalization and Democracy: A New 'Great Transformation'?" *The Annals of the American Academy of Political and Social Science* 58:10–21.

Muñoz, Heraldo. 1994. "A New *OAS* for the New Times." In *Latin America in a New World*, edited by A. F. Lowenthal and G. F. Treverton. Boulder, CO: Westview Press.

Murillo, María Victoria. 2001. *Labor Unions, Partisan Coalitions and Market Reforms in Latin America*. Cambridge: Cambridge University Press.

_____. 2000. "From Populism to Neoliberalism: Labor Unions and Market Reforms in Latin America." *World Politics* 52(2):135–174.

_____. 1997. "Union Politics, Market-Oriented Reforms and the Reshaping of Argentine Corporatism." In *The New Politics of Inequality in Latin America: Rethinking Participation and Representation*, edited by D. A. Chalmers, S. B. Martin, and K. Piester. Oxford: Oxford University Press.

Murillo, María Victoria and Lucas Ronconi. 2004. "Teachers' Strikes in Argentina: Partisan Alignments and Public Sector Labor Relations." *Studies in Comparative International Development* 39(1):77–98.

Naím, Moises. 1993. *Paper Tigers and Minotaurs*. Washington, DC: Carnegie Endowment for International Peace.

Nash, June C. 1992. *I Spent My Life in the Mines: The Story of Juan Rojas, Bolivian Tin Miner*. New York: Columbia University Press.

Norden, Deborah L. 2003. "Democracy in Uniform: Chávez and the Venezuelan Armed Forces." In *Venezuelan Politics in the Chávez Era*, edited by S. Ellner and D. Hellinger. Boulder, CO: Lynne Rienner.

_____. 1998. "Democracy and Military Control in Venezuela: From Subordination to Insurrection." *Latin American Research Review* 33(2):143–165.

North, Liisa L. 2004. "State Building, State Dismantling, and Financial Crises in Ecuador." In *Politics in the Andes: Identity, Conflict, Reform*, edited by J.-M. Burt and P. Mauceri. Pittsburgh, PA: University of Pittsburgh Press.

Nurse, Charles. 1989. "Ecuador." In *The State, Industrial Relations and the Labour Movement in Latin America*, edited by J. Carriere, N. Haworth, and J. Roddick. New York: St. Martins.

References

Obando, Enrique. 1998. "Fujimori and the Military." In *Fujimori's Peru: The Political Economy*, edited by J. Crabtree and J. Thomas. London: University of London Press.

O'Conner, Erin. 2003. "Indians and National Salvation: Placing Ecuador's Indigenous Coup of January 2000 in Historical Perspective." In *Contemporary Indigenous Movements in Latin America*, edited by E. D. Langer and E. Muñoz. Wilmington, DE: Scholarly Resources.

O'Donnell, Guillermo A. 1996. *Delegative Democracy*, edited by L. Diamond and M. Plattner. Baltimore: Johns Hopkins University Press.

———. 1978. "State and Alliances in Argentina, 1956–1976." *Journal of Development Studies* 15(1):3–33.

———. 1973. *Modernization and Bureaucratic-Authoritarianism: Studies in South American Politics*. Politics of Modernization Series, no. 9. Berkeley: Institute of International Studies, University of California.

O'Donnell, Guillermo A. and Philippe C. Schmitter. 1986. *Transitions From Authoritarian Rule: Tentative Conclusions About Uncertain Democracies*. Baltimore: Johns Hopkins University Press.

O'Donnell, Guillermo A., Philippe C. Schmitter, and Laurence Whitehead, eds. 1986. *Transitions From Authoritarian Rule: Comparative Perspectives*. Baltimore: Johns Hopkins University Press.

Ohmae, Kenichi. 2005. *The Next Global Stage: Challenges and Opportunities in Our Borderless World*. Upper Saddle River, NJ: Wharton School Publishing.

———. 1995. *The End of the Nation State: The Rise of Regional Economies*. New York: Free Press.

Olivera, Oscar and Tom Lewis. 2004. *Cochabamba: Water War in Bolivia*. Cambridge, MA: Southend Press.

Oppenheim, Lois Hecht. 2007. *Politics in Chile: Socialism, Authoritarianism, and Market Democracy*. Boulder, CO: Westview Press.

Oviedo, Luis. 2002. "Una historia del movimiento piquetero." *Razón y Revolución* 9: 1–8

———. 2001. *Una historia del movimiento piquetero*. Buenos Aires: Ediciones Rumbos.

Oxhorn, Philip D. 1998. "Is the Century of Corporatism Over? Neoliberalism and the Rise of Neopluralism." In *What Kind of Democracy? What Kind of Market? Latin America in the Age of Neoliberalism*, edited by P. D. Oxhorn and G. Ducatenzeiler. University Park: Pennsylvania State University Press.

———. 1995. *Organizing Civil Society: The Popular Sectors and the Struggle for Democracy in Chile*. University Park: Pennsylvania State University Press.

———. 1994. "Where did all of the Protesters Go? Popular Mobilization, Transition to Democracy, and the New Democratic Regime in Chile." *Latin American Perspectives* 21(3):49–68.

Paley, Julia. 2001. *Marketing Democracy: Power and Social Movements in Post-Dictatorship Chile*. Berkeley: University of California Press.

Pallares, Amalia. 2002. *From Peasant Struggles to Indian Resistance: The Ecuadorian Andes in the Late Twentieth Century*. Norman: University of Oklahoma Press.

Palmer, David Scott, ed. 1994. *The Shining Path of Peru*. New York: St. Martin's Press.

Parker, Dick. 2005. "Chávez and the Search for an Alternative to Neoliberalism." *Latin American Perspectives* 32(2):39–50.

Parsa, Misagh. 2000. *States, Ideologies, and Social Revolutions: A Comparative Analysis of Iran, Nicaragua and the Philippines*. Cambridge: Cambridge University Press.

Parsons, Talcott. 1960. *Structure and Process in Modern Societies*. New York: Free Press.

Patzi-Paco, Félix. 1999. *Insurgencia y sumisión: Movimientos indígeno-campesinos, 1983–1998*. La Paz: Muela del Diablo Editorees.

Penfold-Becerra, Michael. 2007. "Clientelism and Social Funds: Evidence from Chávez's Misiones." *Latin American Politics and Society* 49(4): 63–84.

Pereira, Luiz Carlos Bresser, Jose Maria Maravall, and Adam Przeworski, eds. 1993. *Economic Reforms in New Democracies: A Social-Democratic Approach*. Cambridge: Cambridge University Press.

Pérez, German J., Martín Armelino, and Federico M. Rossi. 2003. "Autogobierno o representación? La experiencia de las asambleas en la Argentina." *Revista de Ciencias Sociales* 14: 175–205.

Pérez Sáins, Juan Pablo. 2005. "Exclusion and Employability: The New Labor Dynamics in Latin America." In *Rethinking Development in Latin America*, edited by C. H. Wood and B. R. Roberts. University Park: The Pennsylvania University Press.

Perreault, Thomas. 2006. "From the Guerra Del Agua to the Guerra Del Gas: Resource Governance, Neoliberalism and Popular Protest in Bolivia." *Antipode* 38(1):150–172.

Peruzzotti, Enrique. 2005. "Demanding Accountable Government: Citizens, Politicians, and the Perils of Representative Democracy in Argentina." In *Argentine Democracy: The Politics of Institutional Weakness*, edited by S. Levitsky and M. V. Murillo. University Park: Pennsylvania State University Press.

Petras, James and Henry Veltmeyer. 2005. *Social Movements and State Power: Argentina, Brazil, Bolivia, Ecuador*. London: Pluto Press.

Pinto Ocampo, María Teresa. 2004. "Entre la represión y la concertación: Los cocaleros en el Chapare y en el Putumayo." In *Informe final del concurso: Movimientos sociales y nuevos conflictos en América Latina y el Caribe*. Programa Regional de Becas CLASCO.

Polanyi, Karl. 2001. *The Great Transformation*. Boston: Beacon Press.

Posner, Paul W. 2007. "Development and Collective Action in Chile's Neoliberal Democracy." In *Political Power and Social Theory*, edited by D. E. Davis. Amsterdam: JAI.

Postero, Nancy Grey. 2007. *Now We Are Citizens: Indigenous Politics in Postmulticultural Bolivia*. Stanford, CA: Stanford University Press.

Prashad, Vijay and Teo Ballvé, eds. 2006. *Dispatches From Latin America: On the Frontlines Against Neoliberalism*. Cambridge, MA: South End Press.

Prebisch, Raul. 1970. *Change and Development: Latin America's Great Task*. New York: Praeger.

Przeworski, Adam. 1995. *Sustainable Democracy*. Cambridge: Cambridge University Press.

———. 1991. *Democracy and the Market: Political and Economic Reforms in Eastern Europe and Latin America*. Cambridge: Cambridge University Press.

———. 1986. "Some Problems in the Study of the Transition to Democracy." In *Transitions from Authoritarian Rule: Comparative Perspectives*, edited by G. A. O'Donnell, P. C. Schmitter, and L. Whitehead. Baltimore: Johns Hopkins University Press.

Przeworski, Adam and Michael Wallerstein. 1988. "Structural Dependence of the State on Capital." *American Political Science Review* 82(1):11–29.

Puryear, Jeffrey M. 1994. *Thinking Politics: Intellectuals and Democracy in Chile, 1973–1988*. Baltimore: Johns Hopkins University Press.

Raczynski, Dagmar. 2000. "Overcoming Poverty in Chile." In *Social Development in Latin America: The Politics of Reform*, edited by J. S. Tulchin and A. M. Garland. Boulder, CO: Lynne Rienner.

———. 1998. "The Crisis of Old Models of Social Protection in Latin America: New Alternatives for Dealing With Poverty." In *Poverty and Inequality in Latin America: Issues and New Challenges*, edited by V. E. Tokman and G. A. O'Donnell. Notre Dame, IN: University of Notre Dame Press.

———. 1983. "Reformas al sector salud: Diálogos y debates." *Colección Estudios Cieplan* (10): 5–44.

References

Ramírez, Cristóbal Valencia. 2007. "Venezuela's Bolivarian Revolution: Who are the Chavistas?" In *Venezuela: Hugo Chávez and the Decline of an "Exceptional Democracy,"* edited by S. Ellner and M. Tinker Salas. Lanham, MD: Rowan and Littlefield.

República de Venezuela. 1995. *Venezuela ante la cumbre mundial sobre desarrollo social.* Caracas. Republica de Venezula.

Ribando Seelke, Clare. 2008. "Ecuador: Political Situation, Economic and Conditions and U.S. Relations." *CRS Report for Congress* RS21687:1–6.

Rinne, Jeffrey. 2003. "The Politics of Administrative Reform in Menem's Argentina: The Illusion of Isolation." In *Reinventing Leviathan: The Politics of Administrative Reform in Developing Countries,* edited by B. R. Schneider and B. Heredia. Miami: North-South Center Press, University of Miami.

Rivera-Cusicanqui, Silvia. 2006. "The Roots of the Rebellion: Reclaiming the Nation." In *Dispatches from Latin America: On the Frontlines Against Neoliberalism,* edited by V. Prashad and T. Ballve. Cambridge, MA: South End Press.

_____. 1991. "Aymara Past, Aymara Future." *Report on the Americas* 25(3):18–24.

Roberts, Bryan R. 2005. "Citizenship, Rights and Social Policy." In *Rethinking Development in Latin America,* edited by C. H. Wood and B. R. Roberts. University Park: Pennsylvania State University Press.

Roberts, Kenneth M. 2007. "Latin America's Populist Revival." *SAIS Review* 27(1): 3–15.

_____. 2006. "Do Parties Matter? Lessons from the Fujimori Experience." In *The Fujimori Legacy: The Rise of Electoral Authoritarianism in Peru,* edited by J. Carrion. University Park: Pennsylvania State University Press.

_____. 2003a. "Social Polarization and Populist Resurgence in Venezuela." In *Venezuelan Politics in the Chávez Era,* edited by S. Ellner and D. Hellinger. Boulder, CO: Lynne Rienner.

_____. 2003b. "Social Correlates of Party System Demise and Populist Resurgence in Venezuela." *Latin American Politics and Society* 45(3):35–57.

_____. 2003c. "Party System Collapse Amidst Restructuring." In *Post-Stabilization Politics in Latin America: Competition, Transition, Collapse,* edited by Carol Wise and Riordan Roett. Washington, DC: Brookings Institution Press.

_____. 1998. *Deepening Democracy? The Modern Left and Social Movements in Chile and Peru.* Stanford, CA: Stanford University Press.

Roberts, Kenneth and Mark Peceny. 1997. "Human Rights and United States Policy Toward Peru." In *Peruvian Labyrinth: Polity, Society, Economy,* edited by M. Cameron and P. Mauceri. University Park: Pennsylvania State University Press.

Rock, David. 2002. "Racking Argentina." *New Left Review* 17(September/October): 55–86.

Rodríguez, Francisco. 2008. "An Empty Revolution: The Unfulfilled Promises of Hugo Chávez." *Foreign Affairs* 87(2):49–62.

Romero, Aníbal. 1997. "Rearranging the Deck Chairs on the Titanic: The Agony of Democracy in Venezuela." *Latin American Research Review* 32(1):7–36.

Routledge, Paul. 2004. "Convergence of Commons: Process Geographies of People's Global Action." *The Commoner* 8: 1–20.

Roxborough, Ian. 1994. "The Urban Working Class and the Labour Movement in Latin America Since 1930." In *The Cambridge History of Latin America, Volume VI, Latin America Since 1930: Economy, Society, and Politics,* edited by L. Bethell. Cambridge: Cambridge University Press.

Rueschemeyer, Dietrich, Evelyn Huber Stephens, and John D. Stephens. 1992. *Capitalist Development and Democracy.* Chicago: University of Chicago Press.

References

Ruíz-Tagle, Jamie. 1985. *El sindicalismo chileno dspués del plan laboral.* Santiago: Academia de Humanismo Cristiano.
Saguier, Marcelo I. 2007. "Expanding the Boundaries of Public Debate on Trade Politics: the Hemispheric Social Alliance and the Free Trade of the Americas Process." Paper presented at the International Studies Association Annual Convention, Chicago. USA. February/March.
Salamanca, Luis. 1999. "Protestas venezolanas en el segundo gobierno de Rafael Caldera: 1994–1997." In *Lucha popular, democracia, neoliberalismo: Protesta popular en América Latina en los años de ajuste,* edited by M. López Maya. Caracas: Nueva Sociedad.
Salman, Ton. 2006. "The Jammed Democracy: Bolivia's Troubled Political Learning Process." *Bulletin of Latin American Research* 25(2):163–182.
———. 1994. "The Diffident Movement: Generation and Gender in the Vicissitudes of the Chilean Shantytown Organizations, 1973–1990." *Latin American Perspectives* 21(3):8–31.
Saltos Galarza, Napoleón. 2001. "Movimiento indígena y movimientos sociales: Encuentros y desencuentros." *Publicación mensual del Instituto Científico de Culturas Indígenas* 3(27):n.a.
Sanabria, Harry. 2000. "Resistance and the Arts of Domination: Miners and the Bolivian State." *Latin American Perspectives* 27(1):56–81.
———. 1999. "Consolidating States, Restructuring Economies, and Confronting Workers and Peasants: The Antinomies of Bolivian Neoliberalism." *Comparative Studies in Society and History* 41:535–562.
Sánchez, Alex. 2006. *The Next Domino? Ollanta Humala, Presente!* Council on Hemispheric Affairs [cited 9/28/07]. Available from http://www.coha.org.
Sandoval, Godofredo and M. Fernanda Sostres. 1989. *La ciudad prometida: Pobladores y organizaciones sociales en El Alto.* La Paz: ILDIS.
Sautu, Ruth. 2001. *La gente sabe: Interpretaciones de la clase media acerca de la libertad, la igualdad, el éxito y la justicia.* Buenos Aires: Ediciones Lumiere.
Sautu, Ruth and Ignacio Perugorria. 2004. "Credibility and Trust in Economic and Political Actors and Institutions. Their Effects for the Argentine Democracy." Paper presented at Latin American Studies Association, Las Vegas, Nevada. October 7–9.
Sawyer, Suzana. 2002. "Bobbittizing Texaco: Dis-Membering Corporate Capital and Re-Membering the Nation in Ecuador." *Cultural Anthropology* 17(2): 150–180.
Schmidt, Gregory D. 2007. "Back to the Future? The 2006 Peruvian General Election." *Electoral Studies* 26:813–819.
Schneider, Ben Ross and Blanca Heredia, eds. 2003. *Reinventing Leviathan: The Politics of Administrative Reform in Developing Countries.* Miami, FL: North-South Center Press of the University of Miami.
Schodt, David W. 1987. *Ecuador: An Andean Enigma.* Boulder, CO: Westview Press.
Schvarzer, Jorge. 2003. "La crisis en Argentina: el fracaso histórico de un sistema perverso." *Revista Europea de Estudios Latinoamericanos y del Caribe* 74(April):85–92.
———. 1998. Economic Reform in Argentina: Which Social Forces for What Aims? In *What Kind of Democracy? What Kind of Market? Latin America in the Age of Neoliberalism,* edited by P. D. Oxhorn and G. Ducatenzeiler. University Park, Pennsylvania: Pennsylvania State University Press.
Schwartzman, Stephan. 1991. "Deforestation and Popular Resistance in Acre: From Local Social Movement to Global Network." *The Centennial Review* 35:397–422.
Scribano, Adrián. 1999. "Argentina 'Cortada': Cortes de ruta y visibilidad social en el contexto del ajuste." In *Lucha popular, democracia, neoliberalismo: Protesta popular en América Latina en los años del ajuste,* edited by M. López Maya. Caracas: Editorial Nueva Sociedad.

References

Scott, James C. 1976. *The Moral Economy of the Peasant: Rebellion and Subsistence in Southeast Asia*. New Haven, CT: Yale University Press.

Sehnbruch, Kirsten. 2006. *The Chilean Labor Market: A Key to Understanding Latin American Labor Markets*. New York: Palgrave Macmillan.

Selverston-Scher, Melina. 2001. *Ethnopolitics in Ecuador: Indigenous Rights and the Strengthening of Democracy*. Coral Gables, FL: North-South Center Press.

Seoane, José. 2002. *Crisis de régimen y protesta social en Argentina*. OSAL [cited 2/17/07]. Available from http://www.observatorio.org.ar.

Seoane, José and Emilio Taddei. 2002. "From Seattle to Porto Alegre: The Anti-Neoliberal Globalization Movement." *Current Sociology* 50(1):99–122.

———. eds. 2001. *Resistencias Mundiales: De Seattle a Porto Alegre*. Buenos Aires: CLASCO.

Seoane, José, Emilio Taddei, and Clara Algranati. 2005. "The New Configurations of Popular Movements in Latin America." *Politics and Social Movements in an Hegemonic World: Lessons from Africa, Asia and Latin America*, edited by Atilio A. Borón and Gladys Lechini. CLASCO, Cosejo Latinoamericano de Ciencias Sociales, Ciudad Autónoma de Buenos Aires, Argentina.

Serrano, Helga N. and G. Eduardo Tamayo. 2008. "Change Triumphs in Ecuador's Constitutional Referendum." *America's Policy Program*. Available from http://www.americaspolicy.org

Shah, Monica. 2008. "Bolivia Struggles with its Proposed New Constitution." Council on Hemispheric Affairs (April 18) [cited 9/30/08]. Available from http://www.coha.org.

———. 2006. "Redirection of Peruvian Economic Strategy in the 1990s: Gains, Losses, and Clues for the Future." In *The Fujimori Legacy: The Rise of Electoral Authoritarianism in Peru*, edited by J. Carrion. University Park: Pennsylvania State University Press.

Sheahan, John. 1999. *Searching for a Better Society: The Peruvian Economy from 1950*. University Park: Pennsylvania State University Press.

Sigmund, Paul E. 1980. *Multinationals in Latin America: The Politics of Nationalization*. Madison, WI: University of Wisconsin Press.

Silva, Eduardo. 2007. "The Import-Substitution Model: Chile in Comparative Perspective." *Latin American Perspectives* 34(3):67–90.

———. 2006. "Chile." In *Politics of Latin America: The Power Game*, edited by H. Vanden and G. Prevost. Oxford: Oxford University Press, 2nd edition.

———. 2002. "Capital and the Lagos Presidency: Business as Usual? *Bulletin of Latin American Research* 21: 339–357.

———. 1997. "Business Elites, the State, and Economic Change in Chile." In *Business and the State in Developing Countries*, edited by S. Maxfield and B. R. Schneider. Ithaca, NY: Cornell University Press.

———. 1996. *The State and Capital in Chile: Business Elites, Technocrats, and Market Economics*. Boulder, CO: Westview Press.

Silver, Beverley. 2003. *Forces of Labor: Worker's Movements and Globalization Since 1870*. Cambridge: Cambridge University Press.

Sklair, Leslie. 2002. *Globalization: Capitalism and Its Alternatives*. Oxford: Oxford University Press.

Skocpol, Theda. 1979. *States and Social Revolutions: A Comparative Analysis of France, Russia, and China*. New York: Cambridge University Press.

Skog, Alissa. 2007. "Pending the Birth of a Constitution: Bolivia's Contentious Presidential Future." Council on Hemispheric Affairs (July 2) [cited 7/2/07]. Available from http://www.coha.org.

Slater, David. 1994. "Power and Social Movements in the Other Occident: Latin America in an International Context." *Latin American Perspectives* 21(2):11–37.

_____. 1985. "Social Movements and a Recasting of the Political." In *New Social Movements and the State in Latin America*, edited by D. Slater. Amsterdam: CEDLA.

Smith, William C. 1989. *Authoritarianism and the Crisis of the Argentine Political Economy.* Stanford, CA: Stanford University Press.

Solimano, Andrés, Eduardo Aninat, and Nancy Birdsall, eds. 2000. *Distributive Justice and Economic Development: The Case of Chile and Developing Countries.* Ann Arbor: University of Michigan Press.

Soros, George. 1998. *The Crisis of Global Capitalism: Open Society Endangered.* New York: Public Affairs.

Spronk, Susan. 2006. "Roots of Resistance to Urban Water Privatization in Bolivia: The 'New Working Class,' the Crisis of Neoliberalism, and Public Services." Paper presented at the annual meeting of the Canadian Political Science Association. York University, Toronto.

Stallings, Barbara. 1978. *Class Conflict and Economic Development in Chile, 1958–1973.* Stanford, CA: Stanford University Press.

Stallings, Barbara and William Peres. 2000. *Growth, Employment, and Equity: The Impact of the Economic Reforms in Latin America and the Caribbean.* Washington, DC: Brookings Institution Press.

Stallings, Barbara and Robert Kaufman, eds. 1989. *Debt and Democracy in Latin America.* Boulder, CO: Westview.

Starr, Laura. 2007. *Boliva's "Agrarian Revolution" Hanging In.* Council on Hemispheric Affairs [cited 11/19/07]. Available from http://www.coha.org.

Starr, Pamela. 2003. "Argentina: Anatomy of a Crisis Foretold." *Current History* 102(661):65–71.

Stepan, Alfred. 1978. *The State and Society: Peru in Comparative Perspective.* Princeton, NJ: Princeton University Press.

Stiglitz, Joseph E. 2002. *Globalization and Its Discontents.* New York: Norton.

_____. 2001. "Foreword." In *The Great Transformation: The Political and Economic Origins of Our Time*, by Karl Polanyi. Boston: Beacon Press.

Stokes, Susan. 1996. "Peru: The Rupture of Democratic Rule." In *Constructing Democratic Governance*, edited by J. I. Dominguez and A. F. Lowenthal. Baltimore: Johns Hopkins University Press.

_____. 1995. *Cultures in Conflict; Social Movements and the State in Peru.* Berkeley: University of California Press.

Sunkel, Osvaldo. 1994. "La crisis social de América Latina: Una perspectiva neoestructuralista." In *Pobreza y Modelos de Desarrollo en América Latina*, edited by E. S. Bustelo, F. Bombarolo, and H. E. Caride. Buenos Aires: Programa de Fortalecimiento Institucional y Capacitación de Organizaciones no Gubernamentales.

Svampa, Maristella and Sebastian Pereyra. 2003. *Entre la ruta y el barrio: La experiencia de la organizaciones piqueteras.* Buenos Aires: Editorial, Biblos.

Sweeney, Chris. 2008. "Bolivia: Between Popular Reform and Illegal Resistance." Council on Hemispheric Affairs. (June 24) [cited 9/30/08]. Available from http://www.coha.org.

Tanaka, Martin. 1998. "From Movimientismo to Media Politics: The Changing Boundaries Between Society and Politics in Fujimori's Peru." In *Fujimori's Peru: The Political Economy*, edited by J. Crabtree and J. Thomas. London: University of London Press.

Tapia, Luis. 2000. "La crisis política de abril." *Revista OSAL* (September): 3–6.

Tarrow, Sidney. 2005. *The New Transnational Activism.* Cambridge: Cambridge University Press.

_____. 1998. *Power in Movement: Social Movements and Contentious Politics.* 2nd ed. Cambridge: Cambridge University Press.

References

———. 1996. "States and Opportunities: The Political Structuring of Social Movements." In *Comparative Perspectives on Social Movements: Political Opportunities, Mobilizing Structures, and Cultural Framings*, edited by D. McAdam, J. D. McCarthy, and M. N. Zald. Cambridge: Cambridge University Press.

Taylor, Lance, ed. 1999. *After Neoliberalism: What Next for Latin America?* In *Development and Inequality in the Market Economy*, edited by A. Solimano. Ann Arbor: University of Michigan Press.

Tedesco, Laura and Jonathan R. Barton. 2004. *The State of Democracy in Latin America: Post-Transitional Conflicts in Argentina and Chile.* New York: Routledge.

Teichman, Judith A. 2004. "The World Bank and Policy Reform in Mexico and Argentina." *Latin American Politics and Society* 46(1):39–74.

———. 2001. *The Politics of Freeing Markets in Latin America: Chile, Argentina, and Mexico.* Chapel Hill: University of North Carolina Press.

Thomas, Jim. 1998. "The Labour Market and Employment." In *Fujimori's Peru: The Political Economy*, edited by J. Crabtree and J. Thomas. London: University of London.

Thorp, Rosemary. 1998. *Progress, Poverty and Exclusion: An Economic History of Latin America in the 20th Century.* Washington, DC: Inter-American Development Bank.

———, Ed. 1979. *Inflation and Stabilisation in Latin America.* New York: Holmes and Meier.

Thorp, Rosemary and Francisco Durand. 1997. "A Historical View of Business-State Relations: Colombia, Peru, and Venezuela Compared." In *Business and the State in Developing Countries*, edited by S. Maxfield and B. R. Schneider. Ithaca, NY: Cornell University Press.

Ticona, Esteban. 2000. *Organización y liderazgo aymara, 1979–1996.* La Paz: Universidad de la Cordillera, AGRUCO.

Ticona, Esteban, Gonzalo Rojas, and Xavier Albó. 1995. *Votos y whipalas: Campesinos y pueblos originarios en democracia.* La Paz: Fundación Milenio.

Tilly, Charles. 2004. *Contention and Democracy in Europe: 1650–2000.* Cambridge: Cambridge University Press.

———. 1978. *From Mobilization to Revolution.* New York: Random House.

Tinker Salas, Miguel. 2005. "Staying the Course: United States Oil Companies in Venezuela, 1945–1958." *Latin American Perspectives* 32(2): 147–170.

Tokman, Víctor E. and Guillermo A. O'Donnell, eds. 1998. *Poverty and Inequality in Latin America: Issues and New Challenges.* Notre Dame, IN: University of Notre Dame Press.

Topik, Steven. 2001. "Karl Polanyi and the Creation of 'Market Society'." In *The Other Mirror: Grand Theory Through the Lens of Latin America*, edited by M. A. Centeno and F. López-Alves. Princeton, NJ: Princeton University Press.

———. 1999. "The Construction of Market Society in Latin America: Natural Process or Social Engineering?" *Latin American Perspectives* 26(1):7–36.

Torre, Juan Carlos. 2005. "Citizens Versus Political Class: The Crisis of Partisan Representation." In *Argentine Democracy: The Politics of Institutional Weakness*, edited by S. Levitsky and M. V. Murillo. University Park: Pennsylvania State University Press.

Urquijo-García, José Ignacio. 2000. *El movimiento obrero de Venezuela.* Caracas: OIT-UCAB-INAESIN.

Vacs, Aldo. 2006. "Argentina." In *Politics of Latin America: The Power Game*, edited by H. Vanden and G. Prevost. Oxford: Oxford University Press, 2nd edition.

Valenzuela, Arturo. 1991. "The Military in Power: The Consolidation of One Man Rule in Chile." In *The Struggle for Democracy in Chile, 1982–1990*, edited by P. W. Drake and I. Jaksic. Lincoln: University of Nebraska Press.

Valenzuela, Arturo and J. Samuel Valenzuela. 1976. *Chile: Politics and Society.* New Brunswick, NJ: Transaction Books.

_____, eds. 1986. *Military Rule in Chile: Dictatorship and Oppositions.* Baltimore: The Johns Hopkins University Press.

Van Cott, Donna Lee. 2005. *From Movements to Parties in Latin America: The Evolution of Ethnic Politics.* Cambridge: Cambridge University Press.

_____. 2003. "From Exclusion to Inclusion: Bolivia's 2002 Elections." *Journal of Latin American Studies* 35:751–775.

_____. 2000. *The Friendly Liquidation of the Past: The Politics of Diversity in Latin America.* Pittsburgh: University of Pittsburgh Press.

Varas, Augusto. 1991. "The Crisis of Legitimacy of Military Rule in the 1980s." In *The Struggle for Democracy in Chile, 1982–1990,* edited by P. W. Drake and I. Jaksic. Lincoln: University of Nebraska Press.

Vargas, Humberto and Thomas Kruse. September 2000. "Las victorias de abril: Una historia que aún no concluye." *Revista OSAL* (2):7–14.

Venezuela. 2004. In *Europa World Yearbook 2004.* London: Europa.

_____. 2000. In *Europa World Yearbook 2000.* London: Europa.

Verdugo, Patricia. 2001. *Chile, Pinochet, and the Caravan of Death.* Translated by M. Montecino. Miami, FL: University of Miami North-South Center Press.

Vergara, Pilar. 1985. *Auge y caída del neoliberalismo en Chile.* Santiago: Flacso.

Villegas, Mauricio Antezana. 1993. *El Alto desde El Alto II.* La Paz: Palabra de Nación.

Walker, Thomas W. and Ariel C. Armony, eds. 2000. *Repression, Resistance, and Democratic Transition in Central America.* Wilmington, DE: Scholarly Resources.

Weaver, Frederick Stirton. 2000. *Latin America in the World Economy: Mercantile Colonialism to Global Capitalism.* Boulder, CO: Westview Press.

Weber, Max. 1978. *Economy and Society.* Berkeley: University of California Press.

Weyland, Kurt. 2006. "The Rise and Decline of Fujimori's Neopopulist Leadership." In *The Fujimori Legacy: The Rise of Electoral Authoritarianism in Peru,* edited by J. Carrion. University Park: The Pennsylvania State University Press.

_____. 2002. *The Politics of Market Reform in Fragile Democracies: Argentina, Brazil, Peru, and Venezuela.* Princeton, NJ: Princeton University Press.

Wheeler, Katherine. 2007. "COHA Report: What is Happening with Morales and his Vision for Bolivia?" Council on Hemispheric Affairs (April 30) [cited 4/30/07]. Available from http://www.coha.org.

White, Judy, ed. 1974. *Chile's Days of Terror: Eyewitness Accounts of the Military Coup.* New York: Pathfinder Press.

Whitehead, Laurence, ed. 2002. *Emerging Market Democracies: East Asia and Latin America.* Baltimore: Johns Hopkins University Press.

Whitten, Norman, Jr., Dorothea Scott Whitten, and Alfonso Chango. 2003. "Return of the Yumbo: The *Caminata* from Amazonia to Andean Quito." In *Millennial Ecuador: Critical Essays on Cultural transformations and Social Dynamics,* edited by N. E. Whitten, Jr. Iowa City, IA: University of Iowa Press.

Williamson, John. 1993. "Democracy and the 'Washington Consensus'." *World Development* 21:1329–336.

_____, ed. 1990. *Latin American Adjustment: How Much Has Happened?* Washington DC: Institute for International Economics.

Williamson, John and Pedro-Pablo Kuczynski, eds. 2003. *After the Washington Consensus: Restarting Growth and Reform in Latin America.* Washington DC: Institute for International Economics.

References

Winn, Peter. 2004. *Victims of the Chilean Miracle: Workers and Neoliberalism In the Pinochet Era, 1973–2002.* Durham, NC: Duke University Press.

Wise, Carol. 2006. "Against the Odds: The Paradoxes of Peru's Economic Recovery in the 1990s." In *The Fujimori Legacy: The Rise of Electoral Authoritarianism*, edited by J. Carrion. University Park: Pennsylvania State University Press.

———. 1997. "State Policy and Social Conflict in Peru." In *The Peruvian Labyrinth: Polity, Society, Economy*, edited by M. Cameron and P. Mauceri. University Park: Pennsylvania State University Press.

Wise, Carol and Riordan Roett, eds. 2003. *Post-Stabilization Politics in Latin America: Competition, Transition, Collapse.* Washington DC: Brookings Institution Press.

Wolf, Eric R. 1999. *Peasant Wars of the Twentieth Century.* Norman: University of Oklahoma Press.

Wolff, Jonas. 2007. "(De)Mobilising the Marginalised: A Comparison of the Argentine *Piqueteros* and Ecuador's Indigenous Movement." *Journal of Latin American Studies* 39(1):1–29.

Wood, Charles H. and Bryan R. Roberts, eds. 2005. *Rethinking Development in Latin America.* University Park: University of Pennsylvania Press.

Woy-Hazelton, Sandra and William A. Hazelton. 1994. "Shining Path and the Marxist Left." In *The Shining Path of Peru*, edited by D. S. Palmer. New York: St. Martin's Press.

Yashar, Deborah J. 2005. *Contesting Citizenship in Latin America: The Rise of Indigenous Movements and the Postliberal Challenge.* Cambridge: Cambridge University Press.

———. 1999. "Democracy, Indigenous Movements and the Postliberal Challenge in Latin America." *World Politics* 52(1):76–104.

Youngers, Colleta A. and Eileen Rosin, eds. 2005. *Drugs and Democracy in Latin America.* Boulder, CO: Lynne Rienner.

Zamosc, León. 2007. "The Indian Movement and Political Democracy in Ecuador." *Latin American Politcs and Society* 49(3):1–34.

———. 2004. "The Indian Movement in Ecuador: From Politics of Influence to Politics of Power." In *The Struggle for Indigenous Rights in Latin America*, edited by N. G. Postero and L. Zamosc. Brighton, UK: Sussex Academic Press.

———. 2003. "Agrarian Protest and the Indian Movement in the Ecuadorian Highlands." In *Contemporary Indigenous Movements in Latin America*, edited by E. D. Langer and E. Muñoz. Wilmington, DE: Jaguar Books.

———. 1994. "Agrarian Protest and the Indian Movement in the Ecuadorian Highlands." *Latin American Research Review* 29(3):37–68.

Zúquete, José Pedro. 2008. "The Missionary Politics of Hugo Chávez." *Latin American Politics and Society* 50(1):91–121.

Zurita, C. 1999. "Estratificacion social y trabajo: Imágenes y Magnitudes en Santiago del Estero." *Trabajo y Sociedad* 1:1–22.

Index

Index

economic crisis
  and neoliberal power, 31, 54, 57, 70, 87, 97,
    108, 123, 133, 176–177, 180–181, 184,
    200, 219, 221, 224
  and countermovement power, 3–4, 37, 39,
    41, 50, 52, 134, 175, 188, 196, 199, 231,
    234–235, 237–238, 241, 243, 247, 251–253
economic exclusion
  general, 26, 47, 49
  in Argentina, 61, 70–72, 87–88, 94
  in Bolivia, 109–110, 123, 125, 133, 139, 140
  in Ecuador, 157, 162, 170, 175–176, 181
  in Venezuela, 195–196, 201, 203, 217, 219,
    223
  in Peru and Chile, 241, 246, 247, 249–251,
    259
ECUARUNARI (Ecuador Runacunapac
  Riccarimui), 156, 158
El Alto (Bolivia), 134–137, 139–143
electoral volatility, 53, 132, 219–220, 224, 237,
  267
  and neoliberal power, 53, 132, 219–220, 237,
    267
  and countermovement power, 219–220, 224,
    237, 267
employment (also see unemployment)
  formal sector, 20–22, 24, 26–27, 38, 56, 62,
    66, 70, 74, 78, 88, 94, 104, 110, 112, 121,
    126, 133, 138, 152, 203, 218, 241, 243,
    253, 260
  informal sector, 7, 20, 27, 37–38, 49, 52,
    62–63, 70, 87, 99, 109–111, 126, 135–136,
    149, 154, 165, 181–182, 186, 199,
    202–203, 209, 217–218, 223, 226, 237,
    241–243, 247, 253, 260–261, 271–272
Employment Act of 1995 (Argentina), 70
encapuchados, 214
episodes of contention, 2, 4, 11, 14–19, 41, 50,
  76, 95, 154, 205, 219, 271, 273–274,
  278–280
exchange, 17, 36–37, 51, 60, 271–272, 274
exclusion (also see inclusion)
  general, 4, 11, 17, 19, 26–30, 32, 40–41,
    43–44, 46–47, 49–50, 53–54, 266, 281,
    283
  in Argentina, 56, 61–62, 64, 66, 70–74,
    87–88, 91, 94, 96–97, 100
  in Bolivia, 109–110, 117, 121, 123–125,
    127–28, 131, 133–135, 139–140, 142–143
  in Ecuador, 147–148, 155–157, 162–163,
    170, 175–178, 181, 183, 185–186
  in Venezuela, 195–196, 198, 200–201, 203,
    205, 207, 210, 214, 216–219, 223
  in Peru and Chile, 231–232, 234, 240–241,
    246–247, 249–251, 259

executive decree powers, 28, 44
  in Argentina, 59–60, 73, 101
  in Bolivia, 107–108, 110, 112, 121, 125, 133,
    143
  in Ecuador, 147–148, 151–152, 158, 161,
    164, 171, 175, 177, 192
  in Venezuela, 201, 203, 210, 213, 229
  in Peru, 236, 238, 245

Febres Cordero, León, 151–152, 154–155, 157,
  160, 162
Federación Departamental Cochabambina de
  Organizaciones de Regantes (FEDECOR)
  origins, 125
  demands, 126
Federación Departamental de Trabajadores
  Fabriles de Cochabamba (Fabriles)
  origins, 126
  demands, 127, 129
  collective power, 136
Federación Tierra y Vivienda (FTV)
  origins, 80, 86–87
  demands, 90, 92, 209, 270, 276–277
  and collective power, 86, 93, 268
Fejuve (Federación de Juntas Vecinales),
  135–136, 140
Fernández de Kirchner, Cristina, 99, 101,
  279
Flores, Toty, 85
framing
  defined, 3, 11, 40–41, 47
  general, 267, 273, 276–277
  and antineoliberal, 13, 50, 55
  in Argentina, 62, 71, 78–79
  in Bolivia, 104, 112, 115, 121–123, 127, 129,
    131, 137–138
  in Ecuador, 156–157, 161, 164–166, 169 [fn
    24], 170, 179–181, 188
  in Venezuela, 207, 213, 216
  in Peru and Chile, 230
Free Trade Association of the Americas
  (FTAA), 228
Frente Popular, 172, 179, 185–188, 239
Frente Gremial de Lucha (Argentina), 67
Frente Unitario de Trabajadores (FUT)
  origins, 149, 151
  demands, 154–155, 176
  and collective power, 156, 160, 162–164,
    166–168, 171–172, 177–178, 181,
    185–186, 189–190, 205, 208, 270
Frepaso (Frente por un País en Solidaridad)
  origins, 64–65
  demands, 88–89, 93
  and collective power, 68–69, 75, 79, 84–87,
    210, 270

Index